THE CHALET ENCYCLOPAEDIA
VOLUME IV

ALISON McCALLUM

edited by
RUTH JOLLY

Girls Gone By Publishers

Published by
Girls Gone By Publishers
The Vicarage, Church Street, Coleford, Radstock, Somerset, BA3 5NG, UK

First published 2016
Chalet School characters © Girls Gone By Publishers
Text © Alison McCallum 2016
Trips and Excursions © Charmian Bilger 2016
Half Terms at the Chalet School © Charmian Bilger 2016
A Little Brief Authority © Helen Barber 2016
Photographs pp 17, 18, 158 © Christine Woodall
Photographs pp 44, 55, 56, 59, 89, 105, 127, 129, 141, 188 © Adrianne Fitzpatrick
Photographs pp 57, 58 © K J Fitzpatrick
Design and Layout © Girls Gone By Publishers 2016
Cover illustration © Girls Gone By Publishers 2016
Author photograph © Eion Johnston

The moral right of Alison McCallum to be identified as the author of this book has been asserted by her in accordance with the Copyright, Designs and Patents Act 1988.

All rights reserved.
Without limiting the rights under copyright reserved above,
no part of this publication may be reproduced, stored in or introduced into a retrieval system, or transmitted, in any form or by any means (electronic, mechanical, photocopying, recording or otherwise), without the prior written permission of the above copyright owners and the above publisher of this book.

Neither Girls Gone By Publishers nor any of their authors or contributors have any responsibility for the continuing accuracy of URLs for external or third-party websites referred to in this book; nor do they guarantee that any content on such websites is, or will remain, accurate or appropriate.

Edited by Ruth Jolly
Cover design by Ken Websdale
Typeset in England by Books to Treasure
Printed and bound by Short Run Press, Exeter, EX2 7LW

ISBN 978-1-84745-217-7

CONTENTS

About the Author	7
Introduction	9
Acknowledgements	13
R	15
Trips and Excursions	54
S	60
Half Terms at the Chalet School	88
T	91
A Little Brief Authority	119
U	127
V	128
W	138
X	182
Y	182
Z	185
Chalet School Series by Location	186
Character Index by Christian Names	189

To
MY LATE HUSBAND SANDY
WHO ENCOURAGED ME
IN MY
CHALET SCHOOL RESEARCH

ABOUT THE AUTHOR

Alison McCallum was born in Edinburgh, Scotland, where she still lives. While at school she spent many hours voluntarily helping at a Church of Scotland children's home next door to her parents' home. On leaving school she worked in Edinburgh Central Library for a few years before leaving to train to be a Nursery Nurse. In 1969 she married Sandy and their two sons David and Colin were born in 1972 and 1974.

Alison has been involved with Guiding since she became a Brownie at the age of seven, and later a Guide and a Land Ranger. Alison and another girl represented Scotland at Expedition Hävlingen, a camp in Sweden, and she mentioned the camp in the New Chalet Club's supplement *Good Little Girls in Blue*. She also wrote a chapter in *True to the Trefoil*, published by GGBP, about her Guide Company, 4th Edinburgh, of which she was the Leader for many years. After organising her Guide Company's Centenary celebrations she relinquished her role in favour of younger and more active leaders but stayed on as a Leader with the Rainbow Unit that she helped to start in 1989. Alison has also been involved with St Serf's Players for many years although she spends more time now working on costume and watching plays than treading the boards. She is currently working in The Scottish Community Drama Association's National Library, which she recently helped to relocate to new premises.

Alison enjoys reading and owns a full set of hardback Chalet School books, although only one of the earlier books, *Jo of the Chalet School*, which belonged to her mother, has the wonderful illustrations inside by Nina K Brisley. Alison started working on *The Chalet School Encyclopaedia* in 1998 after her younger son left home to get married and left her a spare room to use as a study. Alison's disabled husband Sandy encouraged her in her Chalet School research, but without the help of her Chalet School friends, Ruth Jolly and Girls Gone By Publishers *The Chalet School Encyclopaedia* would not exist.

INTRODUCTION

It is with great pleasure that we present the fourth, and final, volume of *The Chalet School Encyclopaedia*, bringing us to the end of the alphabetic list of names and including information on many more well-loved characters as well as some who are less widely known.

The *Encyclopaedia* is the work of one remarkable woman, and all who have been involved in editing and checking it can only marvel at Alison's dedication and perseverance in assembling this comprehensive summary of the available information about every character in the Chalet School series—and also from Elinor Brent-Dyer's other connecting works such as the Chudleigh Hold and La Rochelle series. The result is an engrossing compilation of facts which will provide many hours of fascinated browsing.

Huge credit must also go to the dedicated band of volunteer checkers (see Acknowledgements on p13), each of whom read and documented one or more books from these series to provide a body of information against which to check Alison's findings. *The A–Z of Chalet School Characters* (New Chalet Club, 2000) has also proved a valuable resource in the checking process. Every entry in the *Encyclopaedia* has been verified by four or five people, to attain the highest possible level of accuracy. My especial thanks are due Helen Barber, for checking just about everything, and to Grace Tomlinson for much able assistance with the editing. Elinor would surely have been touched if she could have known of the time and devotion that has been expended on this project.

It has not, of course, been possible to note every mention of every character, nor would this have made for good reading. Joey's signature hairstyle of broad fringe plus plaits coiled into earphones/whorls/shells over her ears receives upwards of 30 mentions in the series, and to itemise these would have become tedious to say the least of it. Her golden voice is equally well documented. We have therefore striven to provide information which is as comprehensive as possible, rather than repeat the same detail many times. We have, however, tried to make sure that if a character is mentioned anywhere in a book, however minor the reference, that book has been included: and this has meant that some stories which became Chalet School legends (for example, Con's assertion that Daniel bit the lions) may in practice be mentioned more than once. References to quizzes and family trees in the *Chalet Club News Letters* have been omitted, as they add nothing to our knowledge.

We have as far as possible refrained from interpreting information, and have endeavoured to use Elinor's own words wherever we perceived ambiguity.

How to use this book

The characters are listed in alphabetical order, by surname and then by Christian name, and we have assigned generations and family positions to them by a system of letters and numbers in brackets after their names. Thus **RUSSELL, JOSEPHINE MARY (C) (3)** is the third child in the third generation of her family to be documented. In the case of twins where it is not known which is the elder, we have used 1/2 for each of them. For major families, the children are cross-referenced below their mother's entry, and a simple list is also included under their father's entry.

Where there are two characters with exactly the same name, they are differentiated as (i) and (ii). If a character's Christian name is not known, s/he is listed as eg Mr or Miss at the beginning of the entries for that surname.

Where characters have more than one surname (through marriage or inconsistency), they have been listed under the name by which they are best known, and a cross-reference is given from the other name(s). Thus Dick Bettany's wife Mollie, née either Avery or Fitzgerald, has her entry under Bettany, Mary Patricia (Mollie).

Matrons have for the most part been listed under M for Matron, but Matrons Graves, Henschell and Venables are to be found under their own surnames because we hear about them in other capacities also.

At the back of the book you will find an index by Christian name of all pupils and staff, listed under the school(s) to which they belong. We hope this will prove helpful in identifying those elusive members whose surname may not appear in every book. Where the character is generally known by a 'short' or nickname, the name under which they are listed in the *Encyclopaedia* is included in brackets after their surname: eg Tom Gay (Lucinda Muriel); Bride Bettany (Bridget).

Book titles and page references

A complete list of the books referenced in the *Encyclopaedia* is given below, together with the abbreviation used for each title. We have fitted the 'connectors' into the series as best we could. All page numbers are from Chambers hardback editions where these exist. We have used the pagination from the combined Armada *Mystery/Rosalie* for these two titles, the Bettany Press edition for *The School by the River* and the Lutterworth Press edition for *Monica Turns up Trumps*. Short story page numbers are from the *Chalet Books for Girls*, and those from the *Chalet Club News Letters* are from the Girls Gone By edition.

The Armada paperback editions of the Chalet series had a slightly different numbering, as some books were split into two volumes (and some titles were also changed). For the sake of those who have Armadas in their collections, we have included the approximate series numbers in the listing.

Number (Chambers/GGBP)	Book/story title	Number (Armada)	Abbreviation
1	The School at the Chalet	1	School at
2	Jo of the Chalet School	2	Jo of
3	The Princess of the Chalet School	3	Princess
1st CBG	'Joey Shoves her Oar In'	–	'Joey Oar'
2nd CBG	'Joey's Convict'	–	'Joey's Convict'
1st CBG	'The Rescue of Woolly Bear'	–	'Woolly Bear'
4	The Head Girl of the Chalet School	4	Head Girl
5	The Rivals of the Chalet School	5	Rivals
6	Eustacia Goes to the Chalet School	6	Eustacia
7	The Chalet School and Jo	7	And Jo
8	The Chalet Girls in Camp	8	Camp
9	The Exploits of the Chalet Girls	9	Exploits
10	The Chalet School and the Lintons	10/11	Lintons
11	The New House at the Chalet School	12	New House
3rd CBG	'Woollen Measles'	–	'Woollen Measles'
11a	The Chalet Girls' Cook Book	–	Cook Book
12	Jo Returns to the Chalet School	13	Jo Returns
13	The New Chalet School	14/15	New CS
14	The Chalet School in Exile	16	Exile
15	The Chalet School Goes to It	17	Goes to It
1st CBG	'The Triumvirate Went Ski-ing'	–	'Triumvirate'
16	The Highland Twins at the Chalet School	18	Highland Twins
17	Lavender Laughs in the Chalet School	19	Lavender
18	Gay from China at the Chalet School	20	Gay

INTRODUCTION

3rd CBG	'A New Flavouring for Pies'	–	'New Flavouring'
19	*Jo to the Rescue*	21	*Rescue*
2nd CBG	'Beth's Diary'	–	'Beth's Diary'
19a	*The Mystery at the Chalet School*	23	*Mystery*
2nd CBG	'The Midnight that Didn't Come Off'	–	'Midnight'
19b	*Tom Tackles the Chalet School*	22	*Tom*
2nd CBG	'Smells of Soot'	–	'Smells of Soot'
19c	*The Chalet School and Rosalie*	23	*Rosalie*
20	*Three Go to the Chalet School*	24	*Three Go*
21	*The Chalet School and the Island*	25	*Island*
22	*Peggy of the Chalet School*	26	*Peggy*
23	*Carola Storms the Chalet School*	27	*Carola*
24	*The Wrong Chalet School*	28	*Wrong*
25	*Shocks for the Chalet School*	29	*Shocks*
26	*The Chalet School in the Oberland*	30	*CS Oberland*
27	*Bride Leads the Chalet School*	31	*Bride*
28	*Changes for the Chalet School*	32	*Changes*
29	*Joey Goes to the Oberland*	33	*Joey Goes*
30	*The Chalet School and Barbara*	34	*Barbara*
31	*see* 19b	-	
32	*The Chalet School Does It Again*	35	*Does It Again*
33	*A Chalet Girl from Kenya*	36	*Kenya*
34	*Mary-Lou of the Chalet School*	37	*Mary-Lou*
35	*A Genius at the Chalet School*	38/39	*Genius*
36	*A Problem for the Chalet School*	40	*Problem*
37	*The New Mistress at the Chalet School*	41	*New Mistress*
38	*Excitements at the Chalet School*	42	*Excitements*
39	*The Coming of Age of the Chalet School*	43	*Coming of Age*
40	*The Chalet School and Richenda*	44	*Richenda*
41	*Trials for the Chalet School*	45	*Trials*
42	*Theodora and the Chalet School*	46	*Theodora*
43	*Joey and Co. in Tirol*	47	*Joey and Co.*
44	*Ruey Richardson—Chaletian*	48	*Ruey*
45	*A Leader in the Chalet School*	49	*Leader*
46	*The Chalet School Wins the Trick*	50	*Trick*
47	*A Future Chalet School Girl*	51	*Future*
48	*The Feud in the Chalet School*	52	*Feud*
49	*The Chalet School Triplets*	53	*Triplets*
50	*The Chalet School Reunion*	54	*Reunion*
51	*Jane and the Chalet School*	55	*Jane*
52	*Redheads at the Chalet School*	56	*Redheads*
53	*Adrienne and the Chalet School*	57	*Adrienne*
54	*Summer Term at the Chalet School*	58	*Summer Term*
55	*Challenge for the Chalet School*	59	*Challenge*
56	*Two Sams at the Chalet School*	60	*Two Sams*
57	*Althea Joins the Chalet School*	61	*Althea*
58	*Prefects of the Chalet School*	62	*Prefects*
N18	'Joey Goes on Television'	–	'Television'
-	*Chalet Club News Letters*	–	*N1–20*

It's hard to fit the La Rochelle books into the rest of the series with any accuracy, though we can say that they all take place before *Exile*, where many of the characters meet the Chalet School. *Gerry* was the first book EBD ever wrote. The eponymous heroine turns up briefly in *Rivals*, where she is a friend of Grizel's at the Conservatoire. So *Gerry* is probably set about the same time as *School At*.

Monica takes place not long before Monica joins the School in *Goes to It*, and *Lost Staircase* not long before Jesanne and Lois join the School in *Lavender*. *Chudleigh Hold* takes place sometime before *Gay from China*, in which its story is mentioned.

A	*Gerry Goes to School*	Gerry
B	*A Head Girl's Difficulties*	HG Difficulties
C	*The Maids of La Rochelle*	Maids
D	*Seven Scamps*	Scamps
E	*Heather Leaves School*	Heather
F	*Janie of La Rochelle*	Janie of
G	*Janie Steps In*	Steps In
H	*Chudleigh Hold*	Chudleigh Hold
I	*Monica Turns Up Trumps*	Monica
J	*The Lost Staircase*	Lost Staircase
K	*The School by the River*	School by the River

We hope you will enjoy your voyage of discovery among the characters of the Chalet School. In addition to the character listings, we have included articles of general interest on the subject of school trips, excursions and half terms, and on the characteristics of a good head girl. Long live the Chalet School!

Ruth Jolly

ACKNOWLEDGEMENTS
VOLUNTEERS WHO CHECKED A BOOK (OR BOOKS) FOR THE *ENCYCLOPAEDIA*

Vicky Aldred
Beverley Allen
Jenni Ambridge
Helen Anderson
Jennifer Annison
Hilary Bailey
Helen Barber
Rosemary Barber
Dawn Beck
Janice Benson
Margaret Bird
Gil Bomber
Lucy Bradley
Cherrill Braithwaite
Eleanor Brennan
Kerri Brennan
Janice Brown
Emily Bruce
Katherine Bruce
Nicola Cameron
Ellen Campbell Beare
Dallas Carter
Katharine Childs
Georgia Corrick
Michelle Creasy
Angela Cummings
Moya Dean
Lyn Dodd
Heather Edmonds

Rona Falconer
Barbara Farn
Adrianne Fitzpatrick
Caroline German
Deborah Guest
Kerry Hale
Belinda Haley
Avril Hannah-Jones
Rosemary Hargrave
Jane Harris
Melanie Haydon
Betty Hayes
Mel Heale
Janet Henderson
Di Henley
Alison Hicks
Jennifer Hill
Margaret Hill
Robin Hollands
Clare Hollowell
Rosie Hopkins
Mo Horne
Zihua Hua Su
Judith Humphrey
Catherine Inchmore
Fiona Jackman
Siv Jansson
Karen Jenkins
Julie Kedward
Jennie Kelly
Linda Keown
Sharon Khan
Caroline Lessiter
Catrin Littlejohn
Hannah Lloyd
Ann Longfield
Kirsten Lowson
Anna Ludlow
Celia Lythgoe
Rowena Magdan
Sarah Makin
Amanda McDonald
Victoria McDonald
Joshua Mallabar
Ruth Mallabar
Kirsty Merchant
Karen Miller

Jane Morgan
Adeline Moston
Gemma Muncy
Camery Newman
Jo Ord
Rebecca Osorio
Tanya Oxlade
Rachel Parker
Jane Parslow
Susan Petrie
Louise Plewes
Samantha Rowan
Susan Royall
Penny Sainsbury
Kathleen Shaw
Jacky Simmons
Catherine Slavin
Alison Smith
Caroline Spearing
Julie Stewart
Layla Stock
Sue Surman
Jean Tait
Kathryn Taylor
Helen Thornton
Mary Timmis
Jane Twitty
Susan Vass
Cath Vaughan-Pow
Nicky Wade
Alison Wagstaff
Angela Wansborough
Naomi Ward
Elaine Wells
Madeline Westbury
Joanna Whale
Karen White
Wendy Whymant
Veronica Whymant
Sian Williams
Clare Wills
Julia Wills
Felicity Wilson
Louise Wilson
Joyce Wong
Cat Wright

RABY, KATHLEEN: Kathleen is in IIIA at St Peter's School in *Gerry* (p185).

RAMBEAU, COMTESSE: The Comtesse Rambeau is going to open the Chalet School Sale in *Jane*. Unfortunately she is prevented from doing this because her face is swollen with toothache, and Joey steps in. The Comtesse has a niece at the Chalet School named Marie (p199).

(RAMBEAU), MARIE: Marie has an aunt, the Comtesse Rambeau, who is going to open the Chalet School Sale in *Jane*. She is unfortunately prevented from doing this because of toothache and Joey steps in (p199). Marie's surname is not given.

RAMBEAU, THÉRÈSE: Thérèse is at a cookery lesson with VB in *Ruey* (p117; p114 for form). She later plays in a friendly lacrosse match with joint teams from the Chalet School and St Mildred's (p163). Thérèse is French and takes Solange de Chaumontel round the Chalet School Sale in *Trick* (p188). Thérèse is in VA when they put on a play, *The Little Germaine*, written by Eloïse Dafflon and Priscilla Dawbarn, for their entertainment in *Jane* (p59). Thérèse and Odette Mercier organise a group of girls to make 'Barques des légumes' for the Seniors' sheets and pillowcase party at the Maynards' house in *Adrienne* (p106). Thérèse lives in the Haute Savoie, not far from the town of Anneçy on Lake Anneçy (p137). She is a prefect in *Summer Term* and surveys the ruined cricket pitch with Miss Wilmot and some of the other girls (p178/179).

RAMSEY, JACK: Jack is one of Elma Conroy's male friends when she is a pupil at Welsen in *CS Oberland*. Elma considers Jack to be too young for her to want to marry him (p110).

RANDOLPH, HELEN (née MORDAUNT): Nell Randolph's mother Helen is known to Miss Annersley in *Peggy*. Mrs Randolph goes to look after her elderly aunt Emily who has been ill (p45/241). In *CS Oberland* we learn that Nell is the daughter of a cousin of Miss Annersley's. Mrs Randolph is a widow, and thankfully accepts Miss Annersley's offer to pay her young cousin's school fees (p8/21/22). In *New Mistress* we learn that Nell took a post at the South Wales branch of the Chalet School at Carnbach to be near her mother, who is delicate. Nell lives at home in their small house in Carnbach and goes into school daily (p15). Josette Russell informs the other prefects in *Trick* that Nell's mother, who was Miss Annersley's favourite cousin, has died (p103).

RANDOLPH, NELL: Tall, brown-eyed Nell meets Peggy and Bride Bettany and the Wintertons on a train in *Peggy* when she is returning to Branscombe Park School outside Ludlow. The Chalet girls are on the wrong train and Nell, who is meeting her young cousin at Gloucester, offers to ask her uncle to help them (p38). Nell informs the girls that her school does not play lacrosse but she saw one or two big club matches in London when she stayed with her Granny and Auntie Muriel and thought it looked a wizard game. She is a month or two younger than Peggy (p39/40). Nell introduces the girls to her cousin Althea and her uncle, Flight Commander Edgar Mordaunt, who turns out to be Hilda Annersley's distant cousin, with whom she had lost touch when he was training in Canada (p42/68). Nell appears unexpectedly at the Chalet School with her uncle when Branscombe Park is in quarantine for measles and the prefects ask her to explain to the younger girls why Peggy was on the wrong train (p240/241). Miss Annersley asks after her during a phone conversation in *Wrong* (p125). Nell and her Branscombe Park School friend Lucy Holmes start at the Welsen Branch in the Oberland when it opens in *CS Oberland*. We are informed that Nell is friendly with Peggy Bettany and is the daughter of a cousin of Miss Annersley's (p7/8). Nell is nearly eighteen and is described as long-legged, brown-eyed and brown-haired, with a sprinkling of freckles across the bridge of her short, straight nose. Her long plaits are swung round her head but she still looks a mere schoolgirl. As money is short at home, Miss Annersley is paying her school fees and Nell's widowed mother has gratefully accepted this (p18/21/22). On a walk, a group of girls including Nell have a problem with ants after some girls sit down on a log inhabited by an ant colony (p58). We learn that Nell can walk on skis a little as she learned when she was living near Buxton and there was heavy snow, and she has already learnt not to cross her toes. She has the makings of a good ski-er (p94/174). The girls perform a pantomime, *The Sleeping Beauty*, for the staff, and long-legged Nell is picked for the Prince (p183). Nell is still at Welsen in *Does It Again* and is in Peggy Bettany's first circle of friends. She plays the part of Chang in the *Willow Pattern* pantomime (p172/191). Nell takes part in the end-of-term sports in *Kenya* (p198). In *New Mistress* we learn that Kathie Ferrars was friendly with Nell at Oxford. Nell has taken a post at the South Wales branch of the Chalet School at Carnbach to be near her delicate mother and she lives at home in their small house in Carnbach and goes in to school daily. Nell is Miss Annersley's cousin and we are told that she only had a term at Welsen, the finishing branch (p15/16). Josette Russell tells the other prefects in *Trick* that Nell could not attend Peggy Bettany's wedding because her mother was ill. Mrs Randolph has since died. Nell is still teaching at St Agnes', the English branch of the Chalet School (p103).

RAOUL: Raoul is a taxi driver who drives Allegra Atherton out to see Janie Lucy at La Rochelle in *Janie of* (p189).

RAPHAEL, DUC di MIROLANI: see HELSTON, RAPHAEL

RAPHAEL, MAJOR CHARLES: Major Raphael and his wife Clare are dissatisfied with the behaviour of their eldest daughter in *Heather* (p9). They have three daughters, Heather, Hazel and Honey, and we learn that their youngest daughter was born during the last year of the First World War when her father was in France (p10/11). Major Raphael has black hair, clear green eyes and pale olive skin. The family name was originally Di Rafaello but has been anglicised. After the war Major Raphael was sent to West Africa and has only been in England some six months. He retired from the army and may join an exploring expedition to the Amazon next year (p13/15). Charles Raphael and his family live at the Towers at Shottery, eighty miles from Ripley where Heather is at school (p21/40/41). The Raphaels visit Guernsey during the summer holidays and Heather meets Janie Temple and Pauline Ozanne on the boat. Major Raphael had known Janie's father, Captain Michael Temple, very well seven years previously (p48/49/52). Héloïse de Garis works for the Raphaels in their summer cottage in Guernsey (p66). Major Raphael has been presented with the Victoria Cross. We are told that he is not a patient man (p80/94). The Raphaels have a staff of Jakes the stableman, Miss Christopher the governess, Barnes the old butler, Nurse, Cook, Dora the schoolroom maid, Simmonds, Louie, Alice, Nancy, Sally and Tom at the Towers. Major Raphael is Alured Saxon's godfather (p125/136/138/140/181). The Raphaels are invited to Janie and Julian Lucy's wedding in Guernsey in *Janie of* (p29). Major Raphael is a magistrate and Janie and Julian visit the Towers when they go over to England for Rosamund and Nigel Willoughby's wedding (p106/115). Mrs la Touche mentions that Major Raphael discovered wonderful Aztec ruins in Central America two years previously (p188).

RAPHAEL, CLARE: Major Raphael and his wife Clare live at the Towers at Shottery in *Heather* (p9/40) with their three daughters, Heather, Hazel and Honey. We learn that Honey was a delicate baby, who was born during the last year of the First World War, when her father was in France. Mrs Raphael had been unwell and her friend Miss Garland organised the baby's baptism and mistakenly gave her the name of Honeysuckle. We are informed that Clare has blue eyes (p11/12). The Raphaels visit Guernsey during the summer holidays and although Clare Raphael has a nervous fear of water she allows Julian Lucy to teach her three daughters to swim. The Raphaels' governess Miss Christopher describes Mrs Raphael as charming and polite (p92/125). Mrs Raphael is very keen on English folk dancing and has had the villagers properly taught so they all dance well. She plays the violin for the country dancing in the barn at the Towers. Mrs Raphael is the daughter and granddaughter of soldiers (p199/200/238). The Raphaels visit Guernsey for Janie and Julian Lucy's wedding in *Janie of* (p29).

RAPHAEL, DOROTHEA: Lady Dorothea is mentioned in *Heather* as an ancestress of the Raphael family (p142/143).

RAPHAEL, GEORGE: George Raphael is mentioned in *Heather* as an ancestor of the Raphael family, who married Lady Dorothea, a Duke's daughter (p143).

RAPHAEL, HAZEL (2): Hazel and Honey Raphael are Heather's young sisters who are being schooled at home in *Heather*. Hazel is a jolly little person with blue eyes and curly brown hair (p10/12). Hazel visits Guernsey with her family during the summer and is taught to swim by Julian Lucy (p46/92). On their return home Hazel and her sisters, and Cressida, Hero, Portia and Cleopatra Shakespeare, start to have lessons together and they have a governess named Miss Christopher. Hazel is not so robust as the other children (p104/119). Later, she is described as delicate but merry, with heaps of go in her (p126). Hero races round to the Towers to tell Miss Christopher where they will be when Hazel and Honey are missing in the Monk's Passage (p141/142). Miss Christopher starts a Guide Company in the village and the Raphael and Shakespeare girls join. Hazel is eighteen months younger than Heather and is nearly thirteen (p162/167/183). We are told that Hazel is to have another year at home before going to school in Paris (p244). The Raphaels visit Guernsey for Janie and Julian Lucy's wedding in *Janie of*. Fifteen-year-old Hazel is a slim, pretty girl who, after the summer, is going to a Convent school in France with Honey, Hero, Portia and Pat (p29/30).

RAPHAEL, HEATHER (1): Heather is at Ripley Collegiate at the beginning of *Heather*. The school's atmosphere has influenced her badly and during the recent Easter holidays, her slangy, rude and boisterous behaviour set a bad example to her young sisters, Hazel and Honey. Her father has therefore decided to remove her from school at the end of the summer term. Heather's father employs a governess, Miss Christopher, for his three daughters and the four Shakespeare girls (p9/10/14). Fourteen-year-old Heather has black hair, clear green eyes and pale-olive skin and has been at Ripley since she was eleven years old. Heather's friends the Townsend twins, Millicent Edwards, Doreen and Mollie Fitzgerald and the four Colwyn sisters are also removed from Ripley by their parents (p13/16). Heather is angry to learn she will not return to Ripley as she would have been in the House hockey team next term and was a certainty for her Third Eleven jersey. She has always longed to be a Guide but there are

Dom Hue Island

no Guides at Shottery, the village where she lives (p21/26). The Raphaels visit Guernsey during the summer holidays and Heather meets Janie Temple and Pauline Ozanne on the boat. The Ozannes live in Peterport but have taken a cottage at Petit Bôt for the summer, next door to the Raphaels' summer cottage (p48/50/55). Heather is rude to her father one morning, but apologises to him after a talk with Janie (p62/68/72). Janie, Pauline and the Raphael girls have a picnic at Pleinmont and Raoul le Pelley and the Lemercier boys steal their shoes (p73/81/86). Heather is taught to swim by Julian Lucy and it is mentioned that she has always longed to learn to swim. Heather and Julian are the only ones who enjoy the rough sea passage from Guernsey to Southampton when they return home at the end of the summer holidays (p92/98). Miss Christopher starts at the Towers and we learn that Heather has been taught to play the piano on the Matthay system and is a very good pianist for her years. Miss Christopher describes Heather as a bright, clever child who picked up undesirable language at her previous school (p104/111/126). Heather helps Miss Christopher to search for Hazel and Honey when they are missing in the Monk's Passage (p134/140/142). The Raphael and Shakespeare girls join a Guide Company that Miss Christopher starts in the village (p162). Janie and Pauline visit the Raphaels at Christmas (p174/180) and Janie helps Heather and Cressida Shakespeare when thieves break into the Towers (p220/228/232). Heather strikes her head, has severe concussion for several days and is ill for several weeks (p234/235/239). Janie is engaged to Julian when she and Pauline visit the Raphaels in June and we learn that Heather and Cressida will be going to school in Paris after the summer holidays (p244). Heather is in Paris at a French Convent School with Pauline in *Janie of* (p12/31). She expects to return home to Shottery to be with her mother when her sisters start school in France. Sir Alured Saxon, an old family friend, leaves his estate of Saxonhurst to Heather, who intends taking up Guides again and is seventeen (p12/13/55).

Fort Grey at Rocquaine

The Raphaels visit Guernsey for Janie and Julian Lucy's wedding and tall, graceful Heather is one of the bridesmaids (p30/33). It is mentioned that Heather is beginning to take hold at Saxonhurst and see that the tenants are all right. She sees herself as Alured's steward and wants things done as he would have had them (p106/107). Heather is a bridesmaid when Rosamund Atherton marries Nigel Willoughby. Going to the Sacré Coeur in Paris has made a different girl of Heather although she had changed a good deal before she ever went there (p115/175).

RAPHAEL, HONEYSUCKLE (HONEY) (3): Honey Raphael has two older sisters, Heather and Hazel, in *Heather*. Honey was born during the last year of the First World War, when her father was in France, and was a delicate baby. Mrs Raphael had been unwell and Miss Garland, a friend, had organised the baby's baptism and mistakenly given her the name of Honeysuckle. It is normally abbreviated to Honey. She is a sunshiny little person with honey-coloured hair, blue eyes and a rosy face (p10/11/12). Eleven-year-old Honey and her family visit Guernsey during the summer and Mr Raphael shows Honey the engines on the boat as she has a passion for anything mechanical (p20/47/48). Honey and her sisters are taught to swim by Julian Lucy (p92). When they return home they start to share their new governess, Miss Christopher, with the four Shakespeare girls. Honey is just beginning to play the violin (p106/124). Hero Shakespeare races round to the Towers to tell Miss Christopher where Hazel and Honey will be when the girls are missing in the Monk's Passage (p141/142). Miss Christopher starts a Guide Company in the village and the Raphael and Shakespeare girls join. Heather mentions that Hero and Hazel will have another year at home before going to school in Paris (p162/245). Honey is about to start at a Convent school in France with her sister Hazel and also Hero, Portia and Pat Shakespeare in *Janie of* (p12/30). The Raphael family visits Guernsey for Janie and Julian Lucy's wedding. Honey is one of the group who visit a beach on Sark during Janie and Julian's honeymoon, thus unwittingly forcing the newlyweds to hide in a cave (p29/58). Honey is described as 'painfully truthful'. Honey and Hazel play jokes on Janie and Julian when they visit the Raphaels by putting brushes in Julian's bed and sewing up Janie's pyjamas (p112/113/114).

RAPHAEL, COLONEL MILES: Heather Raphael's ancestor Miles's portrait is the first one that thieves start cutting from its frame when they break into the Towers in *Heather* (p232).

RAPHAEL, NICHOLAS: We are told in *Heather* that Heather Raphael's ancestor Nicholas lived at the Towers and knew about the Monk's Passage. Nicholas lost his life in the 1745 Jacobite rising (p148).

RAPHAEL, SIR WALTER: Sir Walter was an ancestor of Heather Raphael's and in *Heather* we are told that he was given the Towers when his house was burnt down in the reign of Elizabeth I. It has a secret passage known as the Monk's Passage because part of it had formerly been a monastery (p159).

RAYMOND: Raymond is one of Nan Blakeney's cousins mentioned in *Steps In*, who sometimes wears a seraphic expression when he is thinking of a piece of mischief (p42).

RAYMOND, AMABEL (AMY) (née LUCAS): Amabel and her husband Oliver have been looking after their fourteen-year-old niece Mélanie Lucas for two years in *Future* (p9/11). Mélanie's parents, Mrs Raymond's twin brother and his Breton wife, are in Mañaos in the heart of Brazil (p9/8/11). They move to a furnished flat in Geneva as soon as Mélanie has recovered from chickenpox (p20). Oliver sometimes calls his wife Amy (p24).

RAYMOND, LEONARD: Leonard is mentioned in *Future* as an older cousin of Oliver Raymond (p31).

RAYMOND, LEONARD OLIVER, 'SUNNY': Oliver Raymond and his wife Amabel are looking after their fourteen-year-old niece Mélanie Lucas when they go out to Geneva in Switzerland to live in *Future* (p7/9/20). Mr Raymond's new boss is the Maynards' friend Martin Embury, and we learn that the men were at prep school together. Mr Embury calls Oliver 'Sunny'. Mr Oliver's real name is Leonard but he used his middle name, Oliver, at his public school as his cousin Leonard, who was a year older, had been at prep school a year before him (p27/30/31).

RAYNOR, STUART: We are told in *CS Oberland* that Elma Conroy, a pupil at Welsen, became friendly with Stuart Raynor during the holidays. He is lazy and plays cards for money (p111). Elma's parents disapprove and when Stuart writes to her at school, she gets into serious trouble (p136/139). Peggy Bettany helps to resolve the matter (p152/153).

REAVELEY, IDA: Ida is in the Fifth form at St Scholastika's in *Lintons* and is dressed as a Turkish man in the Fairy Tale Bazaar (p291). She transfers to the Chalet School in *New CS* with her friends Hilary Burn and Nancy Wilmot, and becomes Head of the Yellow dormitory at Ste Thérèse (p25/68/69). Ida, Hilary, Nancy and Irene Silksworth become Chalet School prefects. Ida is devoted to animals and is asked to be the Pets Prefect (p80/102/103). Ida discovers that the Middles are getting out on to the St Clare's roof garden at night and the prefects and Joey Bettany investigate (p190/207/208). They realise that the younger girls have organised a dramatic society, led by Elizabeth Arnett and Betty Wynne-Davies, and also find a packet of cigarettes. Ida is to leave school at the end of the Christmas term (p217/226/318). Ida is in the WRNS with Anne Seymour, Nancy, Elsie Carr and Irene in *Goes to It* (p104).

REAY, JOANNA: Brown-eyed Joanna starts at the Chalet School in *Rosalie* and lives near Gay Lambert. She is not troubled by shyness and up to now has been at a small preparatory school. Joanna is ten years old (p104/105/106).

REDFIELD (REDMOND), LEONARD: Leonard, Louise Redfield's brother, is at the Sanatorium in *New CS*. We are informed that Louise spent the holidays at the Sonnalpe with her little brother Leonard, who unfortunately will never be able to live away from the mountains (p65/141). We learn in *Exile* that Louise and her family have left Austria and are now in America, in a house in the Rockies that suits Leonard (p173). In *Wrong* the Redmonds are living on Vancouver Island, where they settled after Leonard's death (p97).

REDFIELD (REDMOND), LOUISE V (BUREN, LOUISE van): American Louise is new to the Chalet School in *Eustacia* and is in the Fifth form (p160). Louise visits Fulpmes at the foot of the Stubai glacier at half term with Miss Wilson and Miss Stewart in charge (p169/170) and is a Catholic. It is mentioned that her hair is shingled and so won't get in the way when she is climbing. She temporarily becomes Louise Redmond (p189/196/263). Louise's surname is Redfield when she teams up with Margia Stevens at tennis to make a formidable pair of champions

in *And Jo* (p147). Louise is at Guide Camp at the Baumersee in *Camp* with her great friend Anne Seymour and is taking the Boatswain's badge (p69/182). Louise and Anne are both in the Sixth form in *Exploits*. Louise and Thora Helgersen, the two biggest girls in the Sixth, are strong and used to hiking and they help Thekla von Stift on an excursion (p48/115). Louise plays the part of the Beast at the Fairy Tale Bazaar in *Lintons* (p290). She is a prefect in *New House* and it is arranged that she will help Eva with the pets (p100). Charming Louise becomes Head Girl in *Jo Returns* and we are told that she is from one of the southern states of America (p7). She plays the part of the Madonna in the Christmas Play (p299). Louise is still Head Girl in *New CS*. She spent the holidays at the Sonnalpe where her little brother Leonard is ill again (p65/141). Louise is described as a handsome, dark-eyed girl from New Orleans. She drives Miss Annersley and baby Sybil Russell to St Scholastika's in the school car (p72/176). Ida Reaveley discovers that the Middles are getting out on to St Clare's roof garden at night and the prefects, led by Louise and Joey, who unexpectedly appears, investigate (p190/207/217). Louise puts up a notice asking some of the girls to report to her and signs it Louise V. Redfield (p239). The girls visit Salzburg at half term and Louise is among those who have to spend the night in a bus that gets stuck in a rising flood on the return journey (p264). There is a fire in Hall when Anne leaves the iron on during preparations for the end-of-term entertainment and Louise rushes in to rescue a copy of Joey's first book, *Cecily Holds the Fort*, which has just arrived from the publisher. Hilary Burn goes in to rescue her and fortunately the fire is put out before too much damage is done (p314/316). This is Louise's last term (p318). Louise is living at the Sonnalpe in *Exile* and will be asked to join the Peace League. She returns to America to a house in the Rockies that suits Leonard, and later meets Marie von Wertheim in Toronto (p58/173). Elizabeth Arnett recalls in *Goes to It* that Louise was on the trip when the bus was caught in floods in the Tyrol (p200). Louise is married in *Wrong* and has a two-month-old daughter, Louette. Her maiden name is given as Redmond. She lives on Vancouver Island where her family settled after her brother Leonard's death and where Louise met her husband, Mr van Buren (p97). Joey is hoping to visit Lulu on Vancouver Island in *Shocks* (p192). A comment of hers about the sinful propensities of Middles is recalled in *Trials* (p155). Marjorie Durrant, now Mrs Redmond, is unable to come to Joey's gathering in *Reunion* as she is in Jamaica and is going to spend Easter with Louise van Buren, formerly Redmond, in the Bahamas. Louise is taking her three children, and her husband Pieter will join them later on (p17).

CHILDREN:
1) LOUETTE: see BUREN, LOUETTE van
2) & 3) Two UNNAMED CHILDREN

REDFORD, REVD MR: Jocelyn's father is the Rector at Little Berkeley, a small village outside Medbury, in *Monica*. Mr Redford coaches a girls' hockey team and we learn that he played for his college when he was at Cambridge (p39/65).

REDFORD, JOCELYN: Jocelyn, a reddish-haired girl with a pleasant face, is a pupil at Braemar House in *Monica*. Her father is the Rector at Little Berkeley, a small village outside Medbury (p32/39). Jocelyn and some of the girls play hockey on the glebe behind the Rectory. Jocelyn wants to take up secretarial work when she leaves school (p64/66). She is a new girl at the Chalet School in *Goes to It* and joins the Fifth form with Monica Marilliar and Myfanwy Tudor from Braemar House, a Medbury school that has recently closed down. Jocelyn and Monica both want to be gym mistresses (p108/109). Jocelyn is a sturdy, jolly-looking girl of seventeen with short, thick curls that show reddish glints in the sunlight in *Highland Twins*. She has a pleasant, good-tempered face that is attractive without being in the least pretty. Jocelyn is a prefect and hopes to be a gardener. She is in the Sixth form (p64/65/265). She is present when Jesanne and Lois tell their friends about Lavender Leigh's new hairstyle in *Lavender* (p284). Jocelyn is in charge of the School library in 'New Flavouring' in *3rd* (p128). Jocelyn is studying for a piano exam in *Gay*. She dances a Morris jig at the end-of-term concert with Monica (p90/238). Jocelyn is the Games Prefect in *Mystery* and is a pleasant-looking girl with thick reddish hair drawn back in a long pigtail (p17). She is mentioned in *Wrong* as having once lent Daisy Venables a tennis frock after a nervous Junior spilled a plate of soup over Daisy (p169).

REDMOND, MR: Mr Redmond's wife, formerly Miss Durrant, returns to the Chalet School in *Gay* after four mistresses are involved in a bus accident, leaving them short of staff. Mr Redmond is with his ship at sea, and their home near Portsmouth has been bombed, and their little daughter Elizabeth killed, in a raid. Marjorie Redmond has had no word from her husband for weeks (p54/55/108). We are told in *Three Go* that Marjorie has lost her husband and little daughter (p81/82).

REDMOND, ALLEGRA: see ATHERTON, ALLEGRA

REDMOND, ELIZABETH: Elizabeth's mother, Marjorie Redmond (née Durrant), a former mistress, returns to the Chalet School in *Gay* to take Miss Annersley's English classes after a bus accident. She lost her daughter Elizabeth in a raid that also destroyed her home near Portsmouth. Marjorie wears a miniature of her daughter, in which she looks a sweet soul with a jolly smile and eyes like Marjorie's (p54/109).

REDMOND, HUGH: Hugh is the juvenile in a good touring stage company that Allegra Atherton is with and they become engaged in *Janie of*. Hugh is very nice and has a little money of his own but they will both have to continue to work. He is very clever, is the eldest of a large family and his father is a bank manager (p110/127/128). Allegra visits Janie Lucy at La Rochelle after breaking off her engagement to Hugh out of jealousy (p189/190/192). Fortunately he follows her to the Lucys' home and they are married the following July. Pauline Ozanne sends her play to Hugh, who passes it on to someone he knows to produce (p194/196/215). Allegra and Hugh have twins in *Steps In* (p13).

REDMOND TWINS (C): Allegra and Hugh Redmond have twins in *Steps In* (p13).

REDMOND, LOUISE: see REDFIELD, LOUISE

REDMOND, MARJORIE: see DURRANT, MARJORIE

REDMOND, SIR MICHAEL: Sir Michael Redmond, a friend of Bob Maynard's, allows Mollie Maynard, Joey Bettany and Robin Humphries to use his island in 'Woolly Bear' in *1st*. Whilst there, Miss Maynard helps some girls from Kingscote School with their sick dog (p107).

REDMOND, MOIRA: Moira is a pupil at the Chalet School in 'Midnight' in *2nd*. Irish Moira is gifted with a vivid imagination and is ten or eleven years old (p150/151/152).

REES: Rees appears to be an employee of Sir Ambrose in *Lost Staircase* (p169).

REEVES, HELEN: Barbara Chester mentions in a letter that Helen is in Lower IVA and is one of the younger pupils in *Barbara* (p104).

REID, MR AND MRS: Mr and Mrs Reid are hosts at a party in *Monica* (p167/177).

REID, PEGGY: Peggy is a jolly-looking girl of fourteen at Braemar House School in *Monica* (p32). Monica and Alixe go to a party at her home on the other side of Medbury (p166/167/177).

REISINGER, HERR and FRAU: Herr Reisinger is a mountaineer and he and his son Franz rescue some girls in a snowstorm in *Barbara*. Frau Reisinger, a small, dumpy woman who speaks broad Low German, gives the girls hot drinks and food (p146/147).

REISINGER, FRANZ: Herr Reisinger's son Franz helps to rescue some girls in a snowstorm in *Barbara* (p146/147).

RÉNAULT, MADAME: Mme Rénault runs the Pension Caramie in *Trick* (p77).

RENNISON, MR: The money left to Peter Chester by his godfather was embezzled by Mr Rennison, a lawyer in the north of England, causing Peter to lose his private income two years before the events of *Steps In*. Mr Rennison was caught in Paris and given twelve years in prison (p100/101/102).

REVILLIER, MR: Mr Revillier is Winnie Embury's surgeon when she has appendicitis in *Problem* (p143).

RHODA: Rhoda, a bright, pretty maid, is evacuated with the Chalet School from Guernsey along with Michelle, Annette, Olivette and Dulcie, and we learn in *Lavender* that they are all in the services and Rhoda is in the WAAF (p21).

RICCI, SIGNOR di (i): Vanna di Ricci's uncle, Signor di Ricci, lives in Verona and helps Joey, Juliet and Robin change trains on their journey to Belsornia in *Princess*. Juliet later mentions that Signor di Ricci is nice, but dull (p293/294).

RICCI, SIGNOR di (ii): Giulia di Ricci's father, Signor di Ricci, is a banker in *Ruey* (p59).

RICCI, SIGNORA di: Vanna di Ricci's mother is mentioned in *School at* as a charming Italian lady who comes to make inquiries about her daughter's education (p101). Vanna is an only child and will return home at the end of term in *New House* to help her invalid mother (p250).

RICCI, GIULIA di: Giulia, the niece of an Old Girl, is elected to be the Bank Prefect in *Ruey* as her father is a banker. Giulia places flowers before the statue of St Clare in the new School Chapel, *Our Lady of the Snows*, in memory of her Zia Luigia who was a Poor Clare. Luigia died in a concentration camp during the war and Giulia never knew her (p59/76). Giulia, a quiet Italian girl, is at the outdoor prefects' meeting in *Trick* which is interrupted by Val Gardiner and Celia Everett throwing a stink bomb. Giulia is still Bank Prefect (p50/53).

RICCI, VANNA di: Vanna is Italian and is first mentioned in *School at* when her mother arrives to make inquiries about her education (p101). Vanna starts at the Chalet School in *Jo of*. Highly-strung and excitable, she becomes completely hysterical and loses control during the flood (p13/41/300). Her uncle lives in Verona and he helps Joey, Juliet and Robin change trains on their journey to Belsornia in *Princess* (p293). Vanna is a sub-prefect in *Head Girl* and is a great favourite with everybody. She is the Music Prefect as she learns music with Herr Anserl (p80/87). Vanna, who is from South Italy, partners Mary Burnett on a walk in *Rivals*. She is given the part of the peasant mother in the Christmas Play. Vanna's long hair is plaited (p38/65/75). Vanna is still a prefect in *And Jo* and prefers not to be the Music Monitress as she lives in mortal dread of Herr Anserl and would have driven him mad with her meticulous neatness and order. She volunteers to be Break duty Prefect (p42/44). Vanna is a graceful Italian girl of Joey's age in *Camp*. She has had her thick hair cut off (p47). She goes to Guide Camp at Lake Baumersee and rushes into camp to tell the others that Joey has disappeared when she falls down the pit. Vanna is one of the four Patrol Leaders (p106/152). She is the oldest of the eight prefects in *Exploits* and has a motherly way that endears her to all the young children in Le Petit Chalet. She is the Junior Library Prefect and like the other prefects is in the Sixth form (p12/42/48). We learn that Vanna has put her hair up and is rather addicted to giggling (p156/204). Vanna has the part of the Sleeping Beauty at the Sale in *Lintons* (p291). She is the Hobbies Prefect in *New House*. Vanna is an only child and will return home at the end of term to help her invalid mother (p100/250). We learn in *Rescue* that Vanna is a soprano soloist and has performed at concerts (p19).

RICH, PROFESSOR: We learn in *Highland Twins* that Jeanne le Cadoulec has the offer of a good post under Professor Rich at Cambridge (p168/169).

RICHARDS, NURSE: Nurse Richards accompanies Mrs Linton and her daughters Gillian and Joyce on their journey to the Sonnalpe Sanatorium in *Lintons* (p20/29/30).

RICHARDS, JANICE: Fifteen-year-old Janice is at the Chalet School in *Changes*, having come from the Tanswick Chalet School the previous term. It is mentioned that she was promising at tennis the previous year but lacks stamina (p102).

RICHARDSON, EVELYN (née THOMPSON): Evelyn was Ruey, Roger and Roddy Richardson's mother and was Scottish (p39/95). Daisy and Laurie Rosomon visit the Maynards in *Joey and Co.* and discover that they are related to the family through Evelyn. Her maiden name was Thompson. She worked in a bank as a secretary to the manager, eloped with George and was married by special licence in London (p203/205/206). In *Future* we are told that Mrs Richardson died when Ruey was twelve (p146).

RICHARDSON, EVELYN RUHANNAH (RUEY) (2): The Maynard triplets are out for an early morning walk in *Joey and Co.* and bump into the three Richardsons on the lake path near Briesau. Ruey is looking after her two brothers and her father in a small chalet along the Tiern Pass. She tells the triplets that she gets her name Evelyn from her mother and Ruhannah from her father's American mother (p22/25/39). Fourteen-year-old Ruey is taken down to Innsbruck by Joey to buy her some decent clothes and get her hair styled. Her rats-tails are beautifully cut to the nape of her neck, with a fringe that reduces the length of her thin face (p55/62). Ruey shares a pretty bedroom with Len when the three Richardsons move in with the Maynards. We learn that her mother was Scottish and that Ruey has hazel eyes (p63/95/110). Joey and Jack Maynard take on the legal guardianship of the three Richardsons before their father disappears into space. When Daisy and Laurie Rosomon visit the Maynards, the Richardsons discover that they are related to Laurie through their mother, Evelyn (p113/203). Ruey is living at Freudesheim with the Maynards and starts at the

Chalet School in *Ruey*. She is in the same form as Margot and is in the Gentian dormitory, where Len Maynard is Head. The triplets and Ruey are all in Ste Thérèse (p9/11/12). Ruey is placed in VB and meets Francie Wilford, who is unfriendly. Ruey will be fifteen on 11th December and, thanks to the Maynards, manages to understand a little French and German (p18/30/32/33). We learn that Ruey played lacrosse for a private club in England and that while she is only averagely clever, she is very artistic. Lacrosse is revived in the Chalet School through a suggestion originally from Ruey (p43/58/66). Ruey is not mathematically inclined and manages to hurt one of her fingers badly during a maths lesson (p80/81). She is a guest at Peggy Bettany's wedding and travels to England with the Swiss party. To her surprise and delight, Roger and Roddy also attend the wedding (p171/176). Later on, Ruey and Francie have an unexpected bath in a wet ditch when they are out for a walk (p184/188). Ruey receives a letter from Roger mentioning that their father is going off to explore space in December. Ruey and Francie resolve their differences at the Staff Evening (p207/208/218). Red-haired Ruey has heard nothing about her Dad in *Leader* (p20/87). She is among the top four girls in VB. Mary-Lou hears from her stepfather that Professor Richardson has taken off into space again (p99/140). We are told in *Trick* that there has been no further news of him and his companion (p34/123). Len, Con, Margot and Ruey spend half term at Freudesheim and decorate two rooms for the use of Mrs Carey, Mary-Lou's mother (p124). Ruey, Margot and Francie form a trio in VB. Ruey is dreading the (GCE) General Literature paper (p150/198). Ruey and her brothers arrive at the Tiernsee for a few weeks with the Maynards after visiting cousins in *Future* and red-headed Ruey is a slim slip of a girl with friendly hazel eyes. Unfortunately Mélanie, a visiting schoolgirl, initially takes a violent dislike to Ruey (p100/142). Ruey tackles her and explains her circumstances, and the two girls are reconciled (p155/159). Ruey is Captain of lacrosse in *Feud* (p38). She is in the Fifth form in *Triplets* and is to sit her GCE exams in July (p181). Ruey is in VA in *Jane* and is stage manager when they put on a play, *The Little Germaine*, for their form entertainment (p58). Roger, Ruey and Roddy are visiting relations in England in *Redheads* (p54).

Ruey replaces Len as dormitory prefect in Jack Lambert's dormitory and we learn that she is in the Upper Fifth (p88/204). Ruey, a ward of the Maynards, is in VIB in *Adrienne* (p162/163). She and Tina Harms have the job of cleaning the corridor after Emilie Laurent and Thérèse Parrais bump into Frau Mieders, who is carrying a bucket of buttermilk, in *Summer Term* (p134). Ruey is sub-prefect for lacrosse in *Challenge* (p141). She is probably in VIB and is Audrey Everett's friend and ally in *Two Sams* (p150). Joey mentions to Hilda Annersley in *Althea* that Ruey has decided to go in for PT training. Ruey is a prefect when they are arranging a Sale of Work with the theme of the seasons, and she practises lifesaving at Lake Thun with her two great chums Margot Maynard and Mélanie Lucas (p22/67/86). Ruey is one of twelve Sixth-form girls who go on an art expedition when Len trips and falls on her oil painting (p133/138). Ruey is described as a brown-eyed girl with trim brown hair framing a thin, freckled face in *Prefects*. Len mentions that at least fifteen members of VIB will be going on to St Mildred's the following term but Ruey will be going to Bedford to begin her PT training (p14/53/54).

RICHARDSON, FRANCESCA (FRANKIE): Frankie is a Junior Middle in the Poppy dormitory and is in Lower IVB in *Does It Again* (p14/16).

RICHARDSON, PROFESSOR GEORGE THEOPHILUS ARCHIBALD BAYNARD: We first meet Professor Richardson, a widower, in *Joey and Co.*, where we learn he is an astronomer with three children, Roger, Ruey and Roddy. His daughter Ruey is named after his American mother Ruhannah (p30/39). We are told that after his wife's death, the Professor moved from Ruey's birthplace to near Croydon, where they had a housekeeper, Miss Wotherspoon (p50). The family have been living in a small chalet at the Tiernsee since June. Professor Richardson likes to climb mountains to observe the sky more clearly with his telescope (p35). Every so often he descends from the mountains to check up on his children and leave some money but his greatest interest is space travel (p54). His children become friendly with the Maynards and while out on the lake one day they see the Professor, who informs them that he is going away immediately, possibly for a year or two, and has entered the boys as boarders at their school. He has written to Ruey's school asking

him and his companion (p34/123). There is still no news in *Future* of the Professor and Mr Johnston on their attempt to reach the moon and we learn that the radio telescope at Jodrell Bank was unable to pick up any trace of them after the first day or two. Ruey thinks that her father didn't like children (p146/157). Professor Richardson's appointment of Joey and Jack as guardians is referred to in *Summer Term* (p152). EBD tells a reader in *N16* that the Professor has vanished into space (p68).

RICHARDSON, RODERICK (RODDY) (3): Roddy, with his siblings Roger and Ruey, meets the Maynard triplets on an early morning walk at the Tiernsee in *Joey and Co.* (p22). After Roger's accident it is mentioned that Roddy is not an imaginative youth (p47). Their father leaves Austria, entering Roddy and Roger as boarders at their school, St Paul's, before he goes (p110/115). The three Richardsons are left in the legal guardianship of Jack and Joey Maynard for as long as their father is away. Roddy lives one day at a time and does not worry about the future. He is nearly thirteen years old (p113/115/118). Len addresses him as 'Roderick' on an occasion when she is annoyed with him (p141). Roddy and Roger are invited to Peggy Bettany's wedding at half term in *Ruey*, to the surprise and delight of Ruey (p176). Roddy is mentioned in *Leader* as being just a kid who won't grasp the inwardness of it all when their father takes off into space and the Richardsons are left parentless (p149). Thirteen-year-old Roddy has red hair and is freckled like a plover's egg and brimful of mischief in *Future*. He announces that he is going in for sheep farming in New Zealand (p100/175). Roger and Roddy do not 'count' as potential boy-friends for Len in *Reunion* (p185). Roger, Ruey and Roddy are visiting relations in England in *Redheads* (p54). The three Richardsons are frequently at home at Freudesheim during school holidays in *Adrienne* (p20). Roddy is still at school in *Althea* (p28).

them to arrange somewhere for her to stay as he is going to give up the Croydon house. Instead Ruey is entered as a boarder at the Chalet School and Jack and Joey Maynard become their legal guardians (p108/110/113). Professor Richardson is last seen in Innsbruck with Jack signing the guardianship papers before he leaves to go up in a space rocket (p116). Roger mentions that his father's name is George Theophilus Archibald Baynard Richardson (p120). When Daisy and Laurie Rosomon arrive in the Tirol, they are able to tell the three Richardsons that they are Laurie's second cousins through their mother. The Professor met his wife Evelyn when he was at Liverpool University (p204/205). There has been no news of Professor Richardson for five weeks in *Ruey* and later Ruey is informed that her father has taken off into space (p185/230). We learn in *Leader* that Professor Richardson and a young man have gone into space again, having escaped death by nothing less than a miracle the previous time. Professor Richardson and Mr Johnston, his young companion, had a narrow shave from drowning. No signals are received after twelve hours on this latest mission (p140/148). We are told in *Trick* that there has been no further news of

RICHARDSON, ROGER (1): Roger is out for an early morning walk on the lake path near Briesau in *Joey and Co.* with his sister Ruey and brother Roddy when they meet the Maynard triplets. Roger trips and cuts his leg badly and the Maynards help him. Roger, Roddy and Ruey are staying in a small chalet along the Tiern Pass with their father, Professor Richardson (p22/25). Sixteen-year-old Roger refuses a cigarette as he informs

Joey that he is a Rugger man (p55/71). Professor Richardson enters Roger and Roddy as boarders at St Paul's School before leaving his children with the Maynard family in Austria (p110/115). He has made them wards of the Maynards. Roger is six feet tall and lanky, with dark red hair (p113/115/116). Money is left for the Richardsons' education and we learn that Roger wants to study for a BSc in Civil Engineering (p118). Roger and Roddy are invited to Peggy Bettany's wedding at half term in *Ruey*, to the surprise and delight of Ruey. Roger writes to Ruey with news of their father (p176/208). It is mentioned in *Leader* when his father disappears into space that seventeen-year-old Roger has plenty of sense (p148/149). Red-headed, brown-faced Roger is a big, powerfully built fellow of well over seventeen when he visits the Maynards in *Future*. The Richardsons are now parentless and are wards of the Maynards. Roger is in his last year at school. It is later mentioned that Roger is due to start at the University in October (p100/101/215). Roger and Roddy do not 'count' as potential boy-friends for Len in *Reunion* (p185). Roger, Ruey and Roddy are visiting relations in England in *Redheads* (p54). The three Richardsons are frequently at home at Freudesheim during school holidays in *Adrienne* (p20). Twenty-one-year-old Roger is at the University in *Althea* (p28).

RICHARDSON, RUEY: see **RICHARDSON, EVELYN RUHANNAH**

RICHARDSON, RUHANNAH (née BAYNARD): We learn in *Joey and Co.* that Ruey was named after Professor Richardson's American mother Ruhannah, who died shortly before Ruey was born, and that her maiden name was Baynard (p39/120).

RICHET, ANNELISE: Annelise is a new French-speaking girl who is making very heavy weather of speaking German in *Challenge* (p135).

RICHET, FRANÇOISE: Françoise is French and is in Inter V when they put on tableaux for their Saturday evening entertainment in *Adrienne* (p159/160).

RICKARDS, NELLIE: Nellie Rickards, Margot Venables's nursing friend in Australia, is mentioned in *New House*. Nurse Rickards looked after Margot, Daisy and Primula Mary when they returned to Brisbane but she later died of pneumonia, leaving everything to Margot (p52/57/72).

RICKY: Ricky and his Uncle Dick are passengers in a lift at the Trümmelbach Falls in *Reunion* (p91).

RIDER, GERTRUDE: see **MATRON RIDER, GERTRUDE**

RIDLEY, SARAH: Sarah and Jeanne Dubois are the only girls in Upper IVa who are fifteen years old in *Ruey* (p102).

RINCINI, HERR and FRAU: Bette Rincini's parents, Frau Rincini and her husband, have a house at Buchau in *School at*. Bette's cousins, Anita and Giovanna Rincini have come up from Innsbruck to visit their uncle and aunt for the summer months. During Joey's illness, Frau Rincini takes charge of Suzanne and Yvette Mercier (p66/302). Joey mentions in *Eustacia* that she met Bette and her mother and a young man in a café on Christmas Eve (p27). Bette has a wire in *Lintons* to say that her father is very ill and she must go at once (p159).

RINCINI, ANITA: Anita and her sister Giovanna start at the Chalet School in *School at*. They are Bette Rincini's cousins and have come up from Innsbruck to live at Buchau with their uncle and aunt for the summer. Anita is one of the girls involved in the cinema fiasco and we learn that her father is a great friend of Herr Mensch (p66/117/123). Anita and Giovanna are day girls and live at Torteswald, a little village beyond Seespitz, in *Jo of*, in a chalet named Wald Villa (p61/62/87). The Rincinis travel from a distance and will arrive late in the day for the new term in *Head Girl* (p247). The Middles play tricks on the Seniors in the dormitories in *Rivals* (p187) and Joey and her friends retaliate by powdering Cornelia, Evadne, Yvette and Anita's hair white with cornflour. Unfortunately Anita's black hair shows the cornflour badly even though she tries to brush it out (p195/203). It is mentioned in *Eustacia* that Anita and Sophie are Maria Marani's little cousins. They have not been brought up as strictly as the Marani children. Anita is in the Fifth form with Giovanna Donati (p42/98/99). Anita is in the team of girls practising for a boat race against St Scholastika's in *And Jo* (p220). She is at Guide Camp at the Baumersee in *Camp* and tires easily (p121). Anita and Giovanna are to be Bette's bridesmaids in *Exploits* (p45). They visit their cousin Bette Rincini, now Signora di Bersetti, at the end of term in *Lintons* (p307). Anita and Giovanna form a coterie with Gianetta di Patelli and Jeanne le Cadoulec in *New CS*. Anita is in the Yellow dormitory at Ste Thérèse with Giovanna and Joyce Linton and she is second in command (p68/69/70). The Rincinis have to leave the School because of the political situation in *Exile* (p115). Joey tells Madge that Anita is teaching in one of the public schools in Innsbruck and will be coming for the celebration weekend in *Coming of Age*. Anita arrives for the celebrations and stays with her old school friend Hilary Graves. Anita, a pretty Tirolean in her early thirties, wins Sybil Russell's embroidered afternoon teacloth at the School Sale and intends to give it to Hilary to mark the occasion of the birth of her second daughter that morning. Hilary names the new baby Lois Anita (p81/111/112).

RINCINI, BETTE (BERSETTI, BETTE di): Slight and graceful Bette starts at the Chalet School on its first day in *School at*. Bette has wavy brown hair, brown eyes and warm brown skin and is about fourteen and a half (p56/57). Catholic Bette's cousins Giovanna and Anita Rincini also join the Chalet School (p58/66). Bette becomes a sub-prefect and we learn that she is very quick at learning English, including slang (p77/92). She accompanies Joey, Grizel, Gisela and Herr Marani to Innsbruck to purchase a birthday present for Madge Bettany and they have their first encounter with Frau Berlin (p140/143). Herr Marani is Bette's uncle and we learn that Bette is half Italian (p148/242). Bette writes a story about the adventures of an old trunk for the first *Chaletian* magazine in *Jo of*. She is a keen geologist and her hobby is collecting rocks (p144/150). Bette is a prefect in *Princess* and it is mentioned that she is a very pretty Tyrolean. She is one of the original pupils of the School and has learned to speak English almost perfectly with an excellent use of English slang (p151). It is mentioned in *Head Girl* that Bette, who is only just eighteen, has left school and is at home. She was Head Girl during the previous term and showed leadership qualities even though it was only for one term (p10/77). Seventeen-and-a-half-year-old Bette comes back to visit the School with Bernhilda and Gisela (p287/294). Bette is likely to be betrothed soon in *Eustacia* (p27). Pretty Bette is betrothed in *And Jo* and will be married in the spring (p274). We learn in *Exploits* that Bette will be married at Christmas and Anita and Giovanna will be her bridesmaids (p45). We are informed in *Lintons* that Bette was married to Dr di Bersetti the previous summer and they live up at the Sonnalpe. Her father has been very ill (p38/159). Bette is too busy to join them on the birthday expedition to the Zillerthal in *New House* (p106). In *New CS* we learn that Bette's young husband and Captain Humphries were killed in a climbing accident the previous January when a rope broke. She was left with her little son and expecting a baby the following April. Bette gives her new daughter Robin Humphries's real name, Cecilia Marya, and calls on Robin to help her (p45/46/47). Bette's grey eyes are filled with sadness except when they dwell on her babies, little Giovanni and baby Cecilia. Her quiet courage influences Maria Balbini to face her own grief pluckily (p188). Bette is living at the Sonnalpe in *Exile* and leaves Austria with Gisela. Bette travels to Canada with her children, Giovanni and Marya, and has a job as housekeeper to a farmer out on the prairies. She has lost her husband Giovanni, her home and all her money (p42/58/288). In *Shocks* it is mentioned that Bette is living on a prairie farm in Canada with her two children, Giovanni and Cecilia, and that she donated the clock in the prefects' room in the Chalet School's early days (p194). Her gift of the clock is remembered again in *Changes* (p57). Joey is waiting for a reply to her invitation to Bette

in *Reunion*. They are obviously still in touch and Bette appears not to have remarried, as her surname is still di Bersetti (p16). EBD informs a reader in *N18* that Bette was Head Girl after Juliet for one term only (p76).

CHILDREN:
1) GIOVANNI: see BERSETTI, GIOVANNI DI
2) CECILIA MARYA: see BERSETTI, CECILIA MARYA DI

RINCINI, GIOVANNA: Giovanna and her sister Anita start at the Chalet School in *School at*. They are Bette's cousins and have come from Innsbruck to live at Buchau with their uncle and aunt for the summer (p66). Giovanna and Anita are day girls at the beginning of *Jo of* and are now living at Wald Villa in Torteswald, a little village beyond Seespitz (p61/62/87). The Rincinis travel from a distance and will arrive late in the day for the new term in *Head Girl* (p247). Giovanna is on the unexpected trek, due to the disintegration of the path, in *Rivals* and we are informed that she is apt to lag behind on all occasions (p102). A surnameless Giovanna listed with various people from the Fourth in *Eustacia* may well be Giovanna Rincini (p109). Anita and Giovanna are to be Bette's bridesmaids in *Exploits* (p45). Giovanna is in the Fifth form when she and her friends 'repair' the clock by boiling the parts, as Hilda Bhaer observed one of her sailor uncles doing this (p139). They go to stay with their cousin Bette Rincini, now Signora di Bersetti, at the end of term in *Lintons* (p307). Giovanna and Anita from Innsbruck are part of a coterie with Gianetta di Patelli and Jeanne le Cadoulec and they are all in the Yellow dormitory at Ste Thérèse with Joyce Linton in *New CS* (p68/69). Giovanna is on a train with other prefects in *Exile*. She is described as fair-haired and German looking and their anti-Nazi conversation is overheard (p37/38/39). Giovanna is one of the girls who form the Peace League but, fearing Nazi interrogation, she refuses to be involved in the hiding of the League document (p55/61). Giovanna is just over seventeen years old and the political situation prevents her return to school after Easter (p65/115). When the Chalet School opens in Guernsey, we are informed that Giovanna's cousin, Sigrid Björnesson, is at the School, but Giovanna is now in a Woman's Labour Corps, as are all unmarried women between the ages of seventeen and twenty-five on the orders of the Nazis, and is miserably unhappy (p204). Hilary Graves is expecting Giovanna to stay with her in *Coming of Age* and mentions that she is an old friend whom she has not seen since they were in the Tyrol. Later on that term Joey informs Madge that Giovanna is married and living in Vienna and it is doubtful if she will manage to come for the celebration weekend. It is Giovanna's sister Anita who arrives for the celebrations and stays with Hilary (p9/81/111).

RINCINI, SOPHIE: Herr Marani describes Sophie and Anita Rincini as Maria Marani's little cousins in *Eustacia*. It is possible that EBD intended to refer to Giovanna and Anita Rincini, though there are no other indications of a relationship between them and the Maranis in the series (p42).

RINCINI, ZITA: Zita is in Inter V and the Pansy dormitory in *Trials* and is Italian (p60/61; p182 for form). Zita is in Inter V in *Theodora* and her form mistress, Miss Moore, says she is not much better behaved than the young demons Prudence Dawbarn and Elizabeth Kemp (p37).

RINTELN, FRAU: Frau Rinteln is the proprietor of a *pension* in Zermatt in *Theodora* (p177). She

provides a lavish packed lunch for the girls (p178).

RIPLEY, DORA: Dora is a serious Senior Middle in *Barbara* who has to visit Matron, as she has earache. She normally partners Dorothy Ruthven on walks (p107/120; p58 for school division). Pretty Dora is very friendly with Dorothy Ruthven and is in Upper IVB in *Does It Again* (p24/25/26). Dora is a finalist in the blindfold race in *Coming of Age* (p215).

RITTER, HERR: The Chalet School buys Herr Ritter's Gasthaus on the Görnetz Platz for the finishing school in *Mary-Lou*. It is between the school and the Elstobs' place (p21).

RIVERS, MISS: It is mentioned in *Peggy* that Polly Winterton's mother had a bad experience as a child when she attended a school headed by Miss Rivers, a friend of her mother (p24/25).

ROBERTS, ENID: Enid wins the swimming race for the under-twelves in *Changes* and has a pretty style when she tries (p191). Enid moves with the Chalet School to the Görnetz Platz in Switzerland in *Barbara*. Enid and Emerence Hope normally liven up prep (p76).

ROBERTSON, MR and MRS: Jean Mackenzie's mother is a distant connection of the McDonalds at Erisay in *Highland Twins*. Mrs Robertson (for name see page 21) and her husband have lived in a flat since Jean's marriage and although they are able to put Jean and her son up during the war, they are unable to provide accommodation for the McDonalds (p9/10/12). Shiena, Flora and Fiona McDonald stay with the Robertsons in Edinburgh for a couple of days on their way to Joey's home. Mrs Robertson must know Joey Maynard because she assures the McDonalds that Joey is delightful. The girls travel in full Highland dress although Mrs Robertson advised them to buy more suitable clothes (p21/24).

ROBERTSON, KATHIE (KATHY), 'MOPS': Kathie starts in the Third form (p166/169) with Daisy Venables and Beth Chester when she joins the Chalet School at Plas Howell in *Goes to It*. Monica Marilliar describes her as a mop-headed kid from Edinburgh (p169). Kathie moves with the School to St Briavel's in *Island* and is now a Senior, whose untidy head of hair has earned for her the nickname of 'Mops'. She plays the violin and has an in-built natural sense of direction, which is attributed to the fact that she is Scottish (p26/28/30). During a science lesson she tries to help Ursula Nicholls with her bunsen burner and manages to singe her hair on her own burner (p107). Kathie is in St Agnes' when the boats are handed over (p148). Eighteen-year-old Kathie hopes to win the Thérèse Lepâttre scholarship. She does not want to teach as she would not have the patience, but intends to read Modern Languages and get a job as an interpreter. She wins the Senior pair-oars at the Regatta (p157/158/230). It is mentioned in *Peggy* that Kathie has left school (p59). Carola Johnstone mentions in *Carola* that she knew Kathie Robertson when she attended Monan House Kindergarten in Edinburgh, six years earlier. Kathie was a prefect at the Chalet School, but left in the summer to go to Edinburgh University (p92). Kathie's cousin Elspeth Henderson teaches at Moray House and Elspeth's sister Jean Henderson, plus Valerie Herriot and Edna Purdon, who were pupils there, all arrive at Welsen in *CS Oberland* (p81). Kathie is described in *Joey and Co.* as a big, jolly girl with an untidy mop of curly brown hair. Her nickname used to be Mops but her hair is now well groomed. Kathie will become the new Kindergarten Head the following term (p220). Kathy is in charge of the new Kindergarten at the Görnetz Platz in *Ruey* (p49). Kathie is at St Nicholas' where there are twenty-seven pupils in a space designed to accommodate twenty youngsters in *Trick*. Eleven more pupils are booked in next term and Kathie will have more help and room to provide for sixty pupils, to give a bit of leeway (p62). Len is excited in *Future* that the opening of the new St Nicholas' House means that Mops Robertson will once again be at the School proper (p193). Miss Robertson is still the Swiss Chalet School Kindergarten Head in *Althea* (p70).

ROBERTSON, LILIAS: Lilias is a very quiet, retiring girl who is promoted from Upper VA to the Lower Sixth in *Bride* (p87).

ROBINET, AIMÉE: Aimée is French and is first mentioned in *Ruey*. She becomes the Art Prefect and is thankful that she will be helping Miss Yolland and not Herr Laubach, who has just retired. Aimée and Monica Caird organise a game of rounders for the Juniors when the rest of the School are playing netball, hockey and lacrosse (p59/60/212). Aimée, described as a sparkling little Parisian, is quite good at tennis and practised the game with her father during the Easter holidays in *Trick*. She is chosen for the Tennis Six. Aimée and

Marie lose their set by two games to the Pension Daubeny (p48/88). Aimée accompanies the Lower Fourth forms on a walk in *Feud*. She is still Art Prefect and is described as a black-eyed, black-headed Valaisian who is reputed to be highly gifted in design (p63/64). Maeve Bettany mentions in *Triplets* that Aimée is going to the École des Beaux Arts (p130). Prefect Aimée is usually amiable but is in a rage in *Jane* because Jack Lambert has been rude to her (p39). Her mother wins Frau Mieders's cake at the Sale and presents it to the School (p208).

ROBINET, AMANDINE: Amandine Robinet and Lorraine Varley, who are Seniors, visit The Hague in Holland with Mr and Mrs Varley for half term in *Trials*. The girls are both very musical and are going to two big concerts during the weekend (p76/77). Amandine is at St Mildred's in *Ruey* and she plays in a friendly lacrosse match with joint teams from the School and St Mildred's. Miss Nalder suggests to Peggy Burnett that Amandine, the French girl, needs to work up her speed at lacrosse (p161/164).

ROBINS, MR: Mr Robins, Sir Ambrose's lawyer in *Lost Staircase*, is a tall, soldierly looking man in his sixties who has a grown-up family of seven (p53/55).

ROBINSON: The Robinsons visit Monica Marilliar in *Monica* (p48).

ROBINSON, MISS: Miss Robinson is a comparative newcomer to the Chalet School in *Highland Twins* and is one of the Guiders when Emmie and Joanna Linders tell the story of their adventurous escape (p112).

ROBINSON, YVONNE: Yvonne, who is English despite her name, is probably a Chalet School pupil in *Future* (p42).

ROBSON, DORA: Dora Robson and Bride Bettany are in the Lower Third and have a French lesson with Mlle Berné in *Lavender* (p81/83). Dora is in charge of hobbies supplies when they have Hobbies Club in *Peggy* and is in the Fifth form (p157/164). We learn in *Carola* that Dora is responsible for the Hobbies cupboard and Sybil Russell will ask her to show Carola all the things the girls have made for the Sale (p110/111). Dora plays netball with Carola Johnstone and Freda Lund in *Shocks* (p102). Dora is in the Sixth form and is a friend of Valerie Arnott in *Bride*. She takes over the netball when Julie Lucy has peritonitis,

and Tom Gay suggests she should take over Julie's other duties as well (p52/155/158). We learn that eighteen-year-old Dora is leaving at the end of term as she is going to Bartholomew's Hospital to start training to be a nurse (p161). Dora becomes a sub-prefect (p169). It is mentioned that she is a quiet girl, full of sterling good sense and with an unexpected gift for humour. She takes on all of Julie's duties (p174/185). Dora and Lesley Pitt are chosen to be Mr Arithmetic and Mr Mathematics at the end-of-term Sale based on *The Crown of Success* as they are the only mathematical geniuses of their year. Later, however, Dora has the part of Adjective (p232/281).

ROBSON, WENDY: Wendy is a new Junior in *Gay* who is given tennis coaching by Monica Marilliar. She is invited to Joey's party for new girls (p67/79). Wendy is the cox for Ste Thérèse at the Regatta in *Island* (p232). She is a member of the Lower Fourth in *Peggy* and is good natured (p53).

ROCHE, MONSIEUR and MADAME de la: We learn in *Summer Term* that M and Mme de la Roche, a middle-aged couple, are ghastly snobs of the French aristocracy. They visit Joey Maynard to explain who the orphaned baby Claire really is and what happened to her family, and we learn that Mme de la Roche is Marie-Claire de Mabillon's

(Claire's) paternal aunt (p145/146/147). Mme de la Roche and her husband come to meet their niece, Marie-Claire. They want to send Claire to a convent school but leave the little girl with the Maynards in the meantime. Joey hopes that in the end they may relinquish their claim (p149/150/151).

ROGER (RODGER): Roger is about to be married to Bridget Fitzgerald's daughter Patricia in *Bride* and they will live in Africa as Roger works on a coffee plantation in Kenya. Rodger wants to get back there as soon as possible as he has it with a syndicate of three others, and another of them wants to come home for *his* marriage (p15/19/20).

ROLLAND, MONSIEUR and MADAME: We learn in *Summer Term* that Babette and Cécile Rolland attended the Chalet School when their mother, Mme Rolland, was threatened with illness, but that when she recovered the girls left the Chalet School as their father had gained a transfer with his bank from Arras to the Riviera (p36).

ROLLAND, BABETTE and CÉCILE: Babette and Cécile are mentioned in *Summer Term* as former pupils of the convent school where Joey Maynard and Erica Standish are taken after the French train crash. They were at one time pupils of the Chalet School, because Mme Rolland was threatened with illness, but when she recovered they left, as their father had gained a transfer with his bank from Arras to the Riviera (p36).

ROLLEN, HERR: Herr Rollen is a patient at the Swiss Sanatorium in *Triplets* (p196).

ROMANDE, HORTENSE: Hortense is a nervy child who gets upset when some Juniors are locked into their common room after stuffing the latch with pencil shavings in *Two Sams* (p142/146).

ROMANDE, JEANNE: Jeanne is a very nervous new girl in Upper IVA who bursts into tears in *Challenge* when Kathy Ferrars collapses with appendicitis while trying to sort out their missing possessions (p100).

ROMUALD, FATHER: Father Romuald is a local priest mentioned in *Kenya* (p104).

RONSCHLAR, GERTRUD von: see STEINBRÜCKE, GERTRUD

RONSCHLAR, DOCTOR von: Gertrud Steinbrücke's fiancé, Dr von Ronschlar, is a new doctor in the X-Ray room at the Sonnalpe Sanatorium in *New House* (p113). We learn in *Rescue* that Gertrud and her husband have a daughter named Gretel (p175).

RONSCHLAR, GRETEL von: Simone mentions Gertrud Steinbrücke in *Rescue* and we learn that Gertrud's daughter Gretel is four years younger than little Natalie Mensch (p175).

ROOSJE: Roosje's mother Arda was formerly at the Chalet School and is mentioned in *New Mistress* (p32). Miss Andrews and Miss Burnett have been staying with Marie Drooglever (p20) and met Arda there (p32). Arda has three children and hopes to send Roosje to the School when a younger class is started. It is tempting to identify Arda as Arda van der Windt, in which case Roosje would be a very much younger sibling of her daughters Lysbet and Grietje who started at the Chalet School in *Shocks* (p75), but there is no way of knowing if this is what Elinor Brent-Dyer intended.

ROSA: see PFEIFFEN, ROSA

ROSALIND: Rosalind and Viola are the Shakespeares' cousins and they play netball at their school in *Heather* (p118).

ROSE, MISS: Miss Rose and Miss Mitchell are teachers at St Peter's Kindergarten in *Gerry* (p154). Miss Rose is Head of the Kindergarten at St Peter's in *HG Difficulties* (p138).

ROSE, JUDY: Judy is in the Upper Third and manages to hurt Lavender Leigh's ankle when they are playing hockey in *Lavender* (p115). Judy is in the same dormitory as Barbara Smith and Leslie Pitt in *Tom* and she and Bride are Third Form Prefects (p146/187). As Bride and Tom are in the Upper Third (p26/38) we may deduce that Judy is Lower Third Form Prefect. Advice given by Miss Burn to Judy about picking teams is quoted by Bride in *Rosalie* (p120). Pretty Judy is in the Sixth form in *Peggy* (p50). She becomes a sub-prefect and is made responsible for the staff (p58/85). Judy can manage French but has difficulties with German in *Carola* (p139). She is still at the School in *Wrong* (p52). Judy goes to the Welsen Branch in Switzerland when it opens in *CS Oberland* and shares a room with Nita Eltringham, Barbara Smith, Josephine Bellenger and Valerie Herriot (p39).

ROSELLI (ROSSELLI), ZITA: Zita Roselli is in VA in *Jane* when they decide to put on a play, *The Little Germaine*, written by Eloïse Dafflon and Priscilla Dawbarn, for their form's entertainment. Zita composes the incidental music for the play because her great passion is her violin (p57). Zita Rosselli helps Betty Landon, Eve Hurrell and Tina Harms concoct two enormous cakes for the Seniors' sheets and pillowcase party at the Maynards' house in *Adrienne* (p106). Zita Roselli is in VIB in *Prefects* and is the first person to notice that Reg Entwistle might be paying special attention to Len Maynard (p66).

ROSIER, GENEVIÈVE: Geneviève is in the Gentian dormitory where Len Maynard is Head in *Ruey*. She is a new girl from Fribourg (p12/13). Geneviève plays in a friendly lacrosse match with joint teams from the Chalet School and St Mildred's. She is a delightful girl in Inter V who came to school speaking nothing but her native French (p162/183). Geneviève is a Senior in *Adrienne* and dresses as a ghost at Joey's sheets and pillowcase party (p120).

RÖSLI ('THE COADJUTOR'): Rösli is the younger sister of a maid at Welsen and Nell Wilson persuades her to become a Coadjutor for Anna in the Maynard household when the family moves to Switzerland in *Joey Goes*. She is about sixteen or seventeen (p151). She is responsible for the Maynard children in *Kenya* and is described as a pleasant-looking Swiss girl of about seventeen (p16/17). Joey Maynard is grateful to have Anna and the Coadjutor to help with her family in *Problem* (p33). Rösli 'The Coadjutor' is heavy footed and has been with the Maynards for nearly three years in *Excitements*. She is less shy than she was (p43). The Coadjutor supervises the Maynard children making toffee and fudge in *Trials* (p14). Jack has to take the Coadjutor to Interlaken to have a tooth removed in *Theodora*, or she would not have gone (p14). Rösli and Anna are going to the Tiernsee with the Maynards in *Joey and Co.* (p9). Len fetches Rösli, known in the family as 'the Coadjutor', to help put the babies to bed in *Leader* (p88). Rösli can safely be trusted with the little children in *Trick* (p204). While she is looking after Win Everett, Rösli rushes to help Anna, who has spilt boiling jam on her hand, and Win subsequently goes missing (p207). Rösli and Anna attend the Nativity Play in *Feud* (p197). Joey goes to help Mary-Lou Trelawney in England in *Triplets* and leaves the triplets and Anna in charge of the babies because Rösli is away at her sister's wedding. Rösli returns with a great slice of bride-cake for the family (p174/191). Cecil vanishes while Rösli is looking after the children (p201). Joey tells Grizel in *Reunion* that she, Hilary and Biddy more or less share the Coadjutor, though she is actually part of the Maynard establishment, as help is hard to find on the Platz (p29). Geoff throws his mug at Rösli in a fit of naughtiness in *Jane* (p175). Rösli generally looks after Joey's babies in *Redheads* (p113). She looks after Joey's younger children in *Adrienne* (p134). She takes the small children for their walk in *Summer Term* (p138). Rösli is present when Samaris tries her flute in *Two Sams*, and jumps when the girl blows into the instrument (p184/185). Len views Anna and the Coadjutor as family in *Althea* (p167). Anna and the Coadjutor take charge of the children while Joey entertains four of the staff to tea in *Prefects* (p43).

ROSOMON: Anne Chester returns home from Devon in *Steps In* to find that apples have been ordered for her family from several places. Elizabeth Ozanne has ordered apples from the Rosomons' orchard and there are over twelve hundredweight of apples in total (p122/125/126).

ROSOMON, MRS (née THOMPSON): Laurie Rosomon's mother was Miss Thompson before her marriage and she is mentioned in *Joey and Co.* as being a pet (p204/207).

ROSOMON, DAISY: see VENABLES, MARGARET CECILIA

ROSOMON, DR LAURENCE (LAURIE): Daisy Venables is engaged to a young doctor at her hospital in *Carola* and she intends to have her sister Primula and the Maynard triplets to be her bridesmaids (p234/250). We are informed in *CS Oberland* that Daisy is postponing her wedding until Joey and Madge and their families return from Canada and plans to have it in the first week of June. Daisy's fiancé Dr Rosomon is now partner to a doctor in Devonshire (p12/14). Daisy marries Dr Laurence Rosomon at the beginning of *Joey Goes* and her bridesmaids are Robin, Primula and the triplets (p46). Laurence and Daisy visit Freudesheim on the way home from their honeymoon (p192). Joey informs everyone that she is now a Great Aunt when Daisy produces a baby son named Richard Anthony in *New Mistress*. Richard is after Dr Rosomon's father (p167/169). Len refers to the baby as Tony in *Excitements* (p68). Daisy and Laurie are bringing Tony and going to stay with Jo at Plas Gwyn when she goes to clear the house in *Coming of Age* (p172). Laurie and Daisy visit the Tirol in *Joey and Co.* and bring four of Joey's younger children who have been staying with the Russells (p172). Twenty-eight-year-old Daisy has a two- or three-month-old son called Peter (p172/200/201). She informs Ruey Richardson that Laurie is the Richardsons' second cousin through their mother's side (p204). Ruey is grateful for the relationship when she hears her father has taken off into space in *Ruey* (p230). Laurie will go and see the Richardson boys to tell them about their father in *Leader* (p149). He refuses in *Future* to have his daughter named Helena Constance Margaret, saying that she will be Mary Margaret, to be known by her first name. The three Richardsons will stay in Devonshire with Daisy and Laurie at Christmas. Joey tells her family that Laurie will be coming out to work at the Swiss Sanatorium next summer (p192/204/205). Daisy and Laurie have settled into their new house at Ste Cecilie in *Reunion* (p191). Daisy appears to be staying temporarily with Joey in *Jane* and has come from England (p81/88/97). Laurie is joining the Sanatorium staff and will take Dr Tyndall's place and the family will live at a chalet at Ste Cecilie (p101). The Rosomons are settled near St Hilda's School at Ste Cecilie in *Redheads* and have two boys and a girl (p50/51). They have found a house on the Görnetz Platz in *Adrienne* and Joey will look after the three children for a few days when they move (p143). Laurie looks after Erica Standish at the Sanatorium after an accident in *Summer Term* (p107). Laurie lives on the Görnetz Platz in *Althea* and is a cousin of the Richardsons (p28).

ROSOMON, MARY MARGARET (3): Joey receives news in *Future* that Mary Margaret was born during the summer (p192). There are two boys and a girl in *Redheads* and one-year-old Mary was born in Devonshire and has black hair and blue eyes (p50/51).

ROSOMON, PETER (2): Peter is two or three months old when Daisy and Laurie visit Joey in the Tirol in *Joey and Co.* (p202/172). Peter is starting to walk the following summer in *Future* and he is fourteen months old (p101/102). It is mentioned in *Redheads* that Peter and Tony are like their mother (p51).

ROSOMON, RICHARD: We are told in *Joey and Co.* that Mr Rosomon, Laurie's father, is a pet (p207). Laurie and Daisy name their baby son Richard after Laurie's father in *New Mistress* (p169).

ROSOMON, RICHARD ANTHONY (TONY) (1): Joey informs everyone that she is now a Great Aunt when Daisy produces a baby son named Richard Anthony in *New Mistress*. The baby is called Richard after Laurie's father, and Anthony is Daisy's favourite name and has not been used by Joey (p167/169). Len refers to the baby as Tony in *Excitements* (p68). Daisy and Laurie are bringing Tony and going to stay with Jo at Plas Gwyn when she goes to clear the house in *Coming of Age* (p172). The Rosomons visit Joey in the Tirol in *Joey and Co.* and Tony sleeps in the night nursery and shares a double pushchair with Cecil (p172/173/200). Tony is at the stage where he's into anything in *Future* (p102). Tony and Peter are like their mother whereas their sister Mary has black hair and blue eyes in *Redheads* (p51).

ROSS, MR: We learn in *Challenge* that Mr Ross died when Evelyn was a small child (p179).

ROSS, MRS: Widowed Mrs Ross is seriously ill with TB at the Sanatorium in *Challenge*, and Evelyn is her only child (p18). Evelyn slowly settles at school but is disturbed on a visit to her mother when she discovers that Mrs Ross is much worse than she had realised (p88/93). Mrs Ross

takes a bad turn and Evelyn is very upset, but Mary-Lou Trelawney appears unexpectedly and looks after her (p177/178/179). By the end of term, Mrs Ross is recovering slowly but will be frail for the rest of her life (p212/216).

ROSS, MISS: Miss Ross is Heather Raphael's Third form mistress at Ripley in *Heather* (p39).

ROSS, EVELYN: Sixteen-year-old Evelyn is much older than the other new girls at the Chalet School but her mother is very ill in the Sanatorium in *Challenge* and Evelyn is her only child, so she wants her close at hand. Evelyn is a tall, fair girl with light brown hair which she wears in a straight shoulder-length bob with a deep fringe, and she has grey-green eyes. She has been staying at the Pension Mallarmé (p18/19/20). Her previous school, Morven House, had only about eighty pupils and she would have preferred to stay on there and live with her Aunt Joan. We learn that Evelyn sat the 11-plus examination at the appropriate age with the idea of passing into the big county school in the nearby town, but did not reach the required standard. Evelyn meets Biddy Courvoisier, Hilary Graves and their families at the Görnetz Platz (p21/26). Evelyn is in VA and settles down slowly at school. She is in St Hild's House, in the Buttercup dormitory (p31/46/47). Evelyn attends the Protestant service. She is partnered by Jane Carew on a Fifth form walk, and we learn that she is not lacking in self-esteem (p53/56). Evelyn was in the hockey XI at Morven House, but is neither keen nor anxious to play well. She is apt to be lazy over physical exercise. She also has a habit of holding a grudge and is a very proud girl (p63/67/72). Evelyn is disturbed by a visit to her mother when she discovers that she is much worse than she had realised (p88/93). Evelyn is very friendly with Lesley Anderson, which is good as she is in need of a steady friend (p135). Whilst taking a Fifth form hockey practice, Margot Maynard loses her temper and this results in an accident when Evelyn hits the ball at Lesley, chipping her elbow (p142/143/144). Nancy Wilmot sends for Evelyn when her mother takes a bad turn, and Mary-Lou Trelawney appears unexpectedly and looks after the younger girl (p177/178). By the end of term Mrs Ross is recovering slowly but will be frail for the rest of her life. Evelyn plays the part of the rich merchant's wife in the School Nativity Play. After the play she realises that the Christmas story did truly happen and she has to live up to it (p212/216/222). EBD says in *N15* that Evelyn learns to put other people's needs and wishes before her own during the first half term (p66).

ROSS, JEAN: Jean Ross, Gerry Challoner, Dorothy Ellis and Maidie Penrose are pupils in IIIA at St Peter's School in *Gerry* (p73). They get a remove to IVB at Christmas (p201/240). Jean is in VA and taking the Oxford exam in *HG Difficulties*. Jean obtains first class honours and transfers to the Sixth form (p43/144/148). She is mathematically minded and is in the School tennis team when they play against The Grange (p152/295/302). Jean plays the part of Malvolio in the end-of-term Senior school play, *Twelfth Night* (p313).

ROSSELLI, ZITA: see ROSELLI, ZITA

ROSSER, MR and MRS: Mr and Mrs Rosser have a farm near the School and take in evacuee children in *Goes to It* (p127).

ROSSITER, MOLLIE: Mollie is in Lower IIIA with Jack Lambert in *Leader* and is missing being friendly with Barbara Hewlett when there has been a rift in the class (p180/181/200). Mollie, Jack and Gillie Garstin are in Len Maynard's dormitory in *Feud* (p25). Miss Charlesworth considers Mollie and Barbara to be the most responsible pair in her form (p44). Mollie is in IVA in *Redheads* and she goes on a dental visit to see Herr von Francius (p29/79). Mollie visits Lake Lucerne and Stans with Inter V in *Two Sams* (p112/113).

ROTH, WANDA: One of the Swiss girls in VB who are on a walk in *Theodora* is called Wanda, and this may be Wanda Roth (p107; p106 for form). Wanda Roth partners Margot at country dancing in *Ruey* (p136).

ROTHAUS, EDELGARDE von: Edelgarde is a new girl in the Second form in *Exploits* (p19).

ROTHEIM, LUISE von: Luise is in the Lower Fifth in *Lintons* and is one of the girls involved in a midnight feast. Luise goes to Miss Annersley to confess after Joyce Linton has been very sick. Joey points out that Luise and Hilda Bhaer have been at the Chalet School longer than any of the others (p89/106/110). Luise is Austrian (p112). She helps Joey erect a cottage for the Fairy Tale Sale of Work and dresses up as the wicked stepmother (p272/290). Luise is one of the girls who revive the SSM, led by Margia Stevens, to reform Matron Besly in *New House* (p161). Luise is in the Sixth form in *Exile* and is one of Miss Wilson's star science pupils (p44/45).

ROTHENFELS, GRÄFIN von: Paula and Irma's mother, Gräfin von Rothenfels, asks if Paula and Marie von Eschenau may join Miss Denny's Italian classes in *Jo of* (p233).

ROTHENFELS, FRANZ von: Franz is the husband of Irma von Rothenfels. Joey meets Irma (née Ancokzky) at the Tiernsee in *Future* and learns that she is married to the manager and chief engineer of the waterworks. They have been living for five months in the former Chalet School building at Briesau and before that lived in Bavaria. They have been married for seven years and have three sons, one of whom is named after his father, and a daughter (p93/95). Franz is later consulted about an abandoned chalet (p210/211).

CHILDREN: Leopold, Gottlieb, Fränzchen, Maria

ROTHENFELS, FRANZ (FRÄNZCHEN) von (3): Fränzchen is Irma and Franz's youngest son in *Future* and is named after his father Franz (p95).

ROTHENFELS, GOTTLIEB von (2): Gottlieb is Irma and Franz's middle son in *Future* (p95).

ROTHENFELS, IRMA von (i): Irma was to have played the part of a child in the cancelled Nativity Play in *Rivals* (p65). She is indignant that Eustacia has told tales in *Eustacia* (p75). Irma goes up to the Sonnalpe in *And Jo* to visit Robin Humphries because she is one of Robin's special friends. She has long, dark pigtails and is carried part of the way (p71/72/73). Irma is not strong and she is one of the pupils at the new Chalet School Annexe when it opens at the Sonnalpe in *Exploits* (p53/54). It is mentioned in *New House* that Irma is more musical than her sister Paula. She is still at the annexe but hopes to come back to the Chalet School proper in another year (p97/98). Joey and Robin accompany Irma and her sister Paula when they visit Salzburg at half term in *New CS* and stay with Wanda von Glück, to whom they are related. Irma and Robin return to school by train with Friedel von Glück and miss the flood that the other girls experience (p246/264).

ROTHENFELS, IRMA von (ii): see ANCOKZKY, IRMA

ROTHENFELS, LEOPOLD (LEO) von (1): Five-year-old Leopold is Irma and Franz's eldest son in *Future* (p95).

ROTHENFELS, MARIA ELISABETTA (LIESERL) von (4): Irma and Franz's baby daughter is just a year old in *Future* and is named Maria Elisabetta, but they call her Lieserl (p95).

ROTHENFELS, PAULA von: Paula starts at the

Chalet School with her cousins Wanda and Marie von Eschenau in *Jo of*. She is described as dark and very ordinary (p13/41/49). Her mother, the Gräfin von Rothenfels, asks if Paula and Marie may join Miss Denny's Italian classes. Paula is an excellent skater for her age and is with Joey when they go to the Ice Carnival (p233/242). Paula is the oldest girl to join the SSM, organised by Margia Stevens in *Princess*, but is not famed for originality (p62/83). It is mentioned in *Head Girl* that Paula and Marie will be bridesmaids at Wanda's wedding (p179). Paula is a prefect in *Rivals* and was to have played the part of the Innkeeper in the cancelled Nativity Play (p46/65). Paula appears still to be a prefect in *Eustacia* (p55/81) and is in the Fifth form. She is fully involved in a trick on the Fourth form (p263/265). Paula is not mentioned at the prefects' meeting at the beginning of term but is in the team of girls practising for a boat race against St Scholastika's in *And Jo* (p220). She attends Guide Camp at the Baumersee in *Camp* and is in the same patrol as Marie von Eschenau. We are told that Paula lives in Hungary (p100/177). Elisaveta, Paula and Cyrilla arrive back at camp dripping wet and covered in green weed, and Ilonka has the brilliant idea of doing some laundry when she discovers that the girls are wearing their last change of clothes (p205–216). Paula is in the Sixth form in *Exploits* (p48). Paula's younger sister Irma is at the Annexe and Paula stays there at half term, making a trip across to Die Rosen for an evening of tableaux (p53/153/191). We are told in *New House* that Paula's father, Siegmund von Rothenfels, has insisted that she has music lessons with Herr Anserl although she is not naturally musical. Paula is now a prefect and is a dark, somewhat ordinary-looking girl of sixteen (p96/97). Hungarian Paula is still a prefect in *Jo Returns* when Louise Redfield becomes Head Girl (p8). Ida Reaveley discovers that the Middles are getting out on to St Clare's roof garden at night in *New CS* and Paula is among the prefects who investigate (p190/199/207). Joey and Robin accompany Paula and Irma when they visit Salzburg with the School at half term and stay with their cousin Wanda von Glück. Paula is among the girls who spend the night in a bus that is stuck in a rising flood on the return journey. We are informed that Paula will be leaving at the end of the term (p246/264/318).

ROTHENFELS, GRAF SIEGMUND von: Paula's father, Graf von Rothenfels, gives his niece Wanda von Eschenau a string of pearls in *Head Girl* (p180). We are told in *New House* that Paula and Irma's father, Siegmund von Rothenfels, has organised music lessons for Paula with Herr Anserl although she is not naturally musical (p96).

ROUSSELLE, ADRIENNE: Adrienne is dressed as Father Christmas at the Chalet School Sale on a hot day in *Prefects*, and finds her robes very warm (p147).

ROVERIE, ANGÈLE: Janice Chester mentions in *Adrienne* that in a previous term Angèle burst into tears on hearing a rather morbid hymn (p124).

ROXALANNE, QUEEN of MIRANIA: see MIRANIA, ROXALANNE, QUEEN of

ROYALL, DR: Dr Marilliar leaves Dr Royall in charge when he goes to meet his nieces Vicky and Alixe McNab at Dover in *Monica* (p78).

RUFFELL, DAPHNE: Daphne appears to be Nina's sister in *HG Difficulties* (p320).

RUFFELL, MADELEINE: Madeleine is in the Remove at St Peter's School in *HG Difficulties* and she helps Miss Lawrence carry dictionaries into IIIA's formroom (p261).

RUFFELL, NINA: Nina is in the Remove at St Peter's School in *Gerry* and she plays the part of the gardener's boy in the end-of-term play (p234). Nina is the Second Prefect when Rosamund Atherton is Head Girl in *HG Difficulties* (p24). Nina and Rosamund play the parts of Naoise and Deirdre in the end-of-term Seniors' school play (p311). The Ruffells visit Cromer, and Nina and her sister Daphne hope to play tennis with their cousins Jim and Frank. Nina is going to be the next Head Girl (p320).

RUFUS: Joey Bettany's first dog, Rufus, is owned by a poor family and was born too late in the season to be sold to tourists as had been hoped. Joey and Eigen Pfeiffen rescue the puppy from a watery grave in *Jo of*. During the winter months the Chalet School give a home to his mother Zita, a magnificent St Bernard (p90/93). We learn in *Princess* that Rufus will live at the Sonnalpe with Madge when she is married (p159/160). Joey takes Rufus with her when she goes in search of Elisaveta, who has been kidnapped by Cosimo (p228). Rufus helps Grizel and Joey rescue Robin in *Head Girl* after she has been taken away from the School by a madman (p204/213). The Piensch family have better luck with their puppies in

Rivals, but are still glad for the School to keep Zita for the winter (p26). Rufus is Jo's best-loved possession (p181). Rufus goes to Guide Camp at the Baumersee in *Camp* and during the first night he causes a commotion, chasing away a strange dog (p73/95/97). Rufus considers himself the chosen guardian of the small folk at Die Rosen in *Exploits* (p157). He tracks the Balbini twins after they have kidnapped Sybil Russell in *New CS* (p168). Jockel, one of the Chalet School handymen, rescues Rufus after the School evacuates from Austria in *Exile* and they wander through Western Europe until they eventually arrive in Bordeaux, where Cornelia Flower's father finds them, exhausted and bedraggled. Mr Flower engages Jockel as a servant and sends Rufus to England. After six months in quarantine Rufus is flown over to Guernsey with Frieda, Bruno von Ahlen and Friedel von Glück to be reunited with Joey soon after her triplets are born (p320/325). Robin is dreaming about Rufus when the air-raid warning sounds in *Goes to It* (p185). Rufus will be ten years old in October in *Highland Twins* and was in such poor shape when he arrived in England that he was in danger being put down (p77/78). Joey and Jack will visit Pretty Maids in the Easter holidays following *Lavender* and take ten-year-old Rufus with them. Monica Marilliar suggests that Joey should write a book about his adventures (p284/285). Joey discovers a lump of raw meat that has been doctored and put in the garden for Rufus to find in *Rescue* (p119/122). The dog helps to repel burglars who want to steal Phoebe Wychcote's 'cello (p132/133). Rufus is given a part in the Christmas Play in *Mystery* (p92). One of Jo's books, *The Fugitive of the Salt Caves*, features a St Bernard called Rufino in *Tom* (p53). Seventeen-year-old Rufus is still around in *Island* and frets if he is separated from Jo for any length of time (p285). He is very old in *Peggy* and Peggy, Bride and Sybil greet him enthusiastically when they visit Joey's new house in Carnbach (p114/115). Rufus is nearly eighteen years old when Biddy O'Ryan visits Joey in *Carola* (p21). EBD mentions in *N11* that Rufus died shortly before Joey went to Canada (p49). In *Does It Again* it is two years since Rufus died and Joey is presented with a St Bernard puppy. She is delighted, but declines to call him Rufus II because there could only be one Rufus (p181/182). Margot mentions in *Kenya* that her mother couldn't bear to have another dog for a while although she wanted one. Jo Scott adores dogs, and Len shows her snaps of Rufus after she has met Bruno (p56). Len describes Rufus's death to Rosamund Lilley in *Problem*, saying: 'He died three years ago of old age, Papa said. He was just seventeen and Mamma got him when she was only thirteen. It was dreadful losing him, but he wasn't ill, thank goodness. We came down one morning and found him lying dead in the drawing-room on the bearskin rug where he slept. We missed him horribly, but it was just before we went to Canada or it would have been worse. I never remember a time till he died when Rufus wasn't there.' (p45) Sybil recalls Rufus's rescue of her from the Balbini twins in *Coming of Age* (p144). Rosalie Dene comments in *Richenda* that Bruno is not nearly as well trained as dear Rufus was (p133). In *Reunion*, Grizel remembers Rufus dying when Jo was living at Cartref (p32).

RUSSELL, MR (i) (A): We learn in *New House* that Jem and Margot Russell's parents objected to their daughter Margot's marriage (p51). Mr Russell was killed in a motoring accident seven years before Jem and Margot's reunion, and their mother, Margaret Russell, only survived him by three months (p76).

RUSSELL, MR (ii): Daphne's father is in the Navy in *CS Oberland* (p188).

RUSSELL, ALINE ELIZABETH (AILIE) (C) (4): Madge and Jem Russell's fourth child Aline is born in September near the end of Joey's holiday in *Rescue*. The eight-pound baby is a bonny little soul with long black lashes and a mop of dark curls (p34/221/227). Her godparents are Phoebe Wychcote, Dr Frank Peters and Elizabeth Ozanne (p236). Baby Ailie slumbers peacefully through the Christmas Play in *Mystery* (p87). Sybil is longing to see how much Ailie has grown in *Tom* (p75). Ailie is just four in *Three Go* when Mary-Lou Trelawney and the Maynard triplets carry Ailie and small Charles Maynard off to be white 'papooses' when they are playing at Red Indians. Madge mentions that Ailie shows signs of being a bigger imp than Sybil or Josette (p70/118/119). Josette and Ailie accompany their parents to Canada in *Island* (p16). Ailie is growing well in the Canadian climate in *Peggy* (p117). Ailie is not as pretty as her two sisters but is described as having a dear little face of her own in *Carola* (p27). She is at a kindergarten with Stephen and Charles in Canada in *Wrong* (p95). The entire Russell family is in Canada in *CS Oberland* (p12). Ailie is at St Agnes' in *Changes*. She is described as 'leggy' when she is in the under-tens swimming race (p66/190). It is mentioned in *Joey Goes* that Ailie will remain in England when the Chalet School opens in Switzerland (p66). Ailie transfers to the Chalet School at the Görnetz Platz in Switzerland in *Kenya* and is in the Third form with her great friend Janice Chester (p28). Ailie is one of the Juniors who will require help to make a costume for the sheets and pillowcase party in *Mary-Lou* (p84). Ten-year-old Ailie wins the prize for drawing the best pig with her eyes shut in *Genius* (p201). She is in IIA in *Problem* (p41). Ailie has a mass of fair curls in *New Mistress* (p54). She asks in *Excitements* if her mother will attend the coming-of-age celebrations (p65). Ten-year-old Ailie is a cheerful featherhead in *Coming of Age* (p62/63). She is a fleet-footed young person and wins five races at the School Sports Day. She may only keep three prizes and gives the others to Odette Bertoni and Janice Chester (p211). Ailie plays the part of a ragged child in the Nativity Play in *Richenda*, overacting at one point (p221). She and Janice are referred to as young demons who never bother to think, and they are in Lower IVA in *Trials*. Ailie, Janice and Judy are among the culprits collecting 'lost' property (p150/164). Ailie is a tow-headed irresponsible who scrambles through lessons as easily as she can manage in *Theodora* (p108). She is in Lower IVA (p144) or Lower IVB (p221). It is mentioned in *Joey and Co.* that Peggy Bettany wants her cousin Ailie to be one of her bridesmaids in October (p15). Ailie will fly for part of the journey to Peggy's wedding with the Maynards' party in *Ruey*. She is prone to train-sickness on occasion (p171). She is in Upper IVB in *Leader* (p22). Ailie remains behind in Joey's care when her family depart for Australia in *Trick*, as at her age it's important that she should not be uprooted (p102). She is described in *Future* as a nice mixture of young demon and tomboy (p203). Ailie is a Senior Middle in *Jane*, and with her friends Janice Chester and Judy Willoughby leads the other girls in more ways than one. Fifteen-year-old Ailie has a small, pointed face framed in a halo of fair curls. She is small and slight like her mother and looks younger than her age (p94/191). Joey mentions in *Redheads* that Ailie's birthday is in early September and that she is fourteen (p100/101). Curly-headed fifteen-year-old Ailie has an impish face and is in Inter V in *Adrienne* when she meets Robin Humphries and Adrienne Desmoines at the station in Paris. Ailie, Judy, Janice and Tessa de Bersac are put in charge of Adrienne. Ailie's grey-green eyes are alight with mischief (p35/36). Ailie is frankly lazy over anything that needs brainwork but is good at games and gymnastics. She is told that she will have to dig in at anatomy, science and other subjects if she wants to take PT (p50). Ailie flies out to Australia for Sybil's wedding (p136). She is in Inter V and the Jonquil dormitory in *Summer Term* and is nearly fifteen years old (p158/168/171). The Lost Property episode is recalled and emulated in *Challenge* (p110/126). The Russells are due home from Australia in the spring in *Two Sams*. Ailie is in VB with Janice Chester and has grey eyes and a small, attractive face (p46/47). She makes papier-mâché trays and bowls at the Hobbies Club and Judy and Janice help her to paint them (p170). Ailie and some other girls help Jack Lambert search for a burglar who she thinks is in the School one night in *Prefects*. When Ailie is the May Queen in the Sale Pageant she trips and nearly falls but is saved by Reg Entwistle (p124/144). EBD tells a reader in *N13* that Ailie and Co will be too young to take over as prefects when Len and her year leave (p57).

RUSSELL, DAPHNE (DAPH): Daphne is an outspoken child of twelve in the Upper Third in *Lavender*. She is not related to the Russell family but is a friend of Peggy Bettany (p163). Daphne goes on a winter walk to the Round House in *Tom* (p74). She and Peggy team up for a tub race at the Chalet School Regatta in *Island* (p235). Daphne is the youngest girl in the Sixth form, a sub-prefect and responsible for the School Magazine, *The Chaletian*, in *Peggy* (p51/58/85). She says in *Carola* that she will not be eighteen until December. She will have a year in the Special Sixth and go in thoroughly for languages (p141). Daphne is a Guide Cadet at the overnight Guide Camp at Kittiwake Cove in *Wrong*. She takes part in a swimming race with Katharine Gordon, Peggy Bettany, Dickie Christie and Nita Eltringham (p131/139). At half term Daphne and Nita are going with Peggy to North Devon to visit the Bettanys. Daphne is in the Chalet School Tennis Six when they play a match against Campden House (p144/145). She goes to the Welsen Branch in Switzerland when it opens in *CS Oberland* and shares a room with Dickie Christy in the Annexe (p40/41). When Daphne is getting ready for the first expedition, we are informed that her hair is normally in a long pigtail (p86). We are told that Daphne joined the Chalet School in Guernsey with Peggy and Nita Eltringham and they are five years younger than Gillian Culver, the new Welsen secretary. Peggy is sent for when Mollie Bettany becomes seriously ill and Miss Wilson explains the illness to Daphne and Dickie Christie. Daphne and Peggy have been friends since they were in the Kindergarten at the age of six (p113/118). Daphne feels the cold in Switzerland keenly, as she suffers from poor circulation (p157). Daphne is cast as the silly Queen in the pantomime *The Sleeping Beauty* which the girls put on for the staff (p183). The girls discuss the feast of St Nicholas and Daphne mentions that he is the patron saint of sailors. We learn that her father is in the Navy (p188). Daphne is still at Welsen in *Does It Again*. She is small and dark and plays the part of Li-Chi in the *Willow Pattern* pantomime (p191). Daphne lives in Charles Eltringham's new parish and we learn that she was delighted when she bumped into Nita in the High Street in *Coming of Age*. Daph gives Nita some photos and notes to add to the collection for the celebrations (p24). Daphne is part of the group who see Miss Bubb on their steamer on the lake (p90).

RUSSELL, DAVID JAMES (C) (1): David is the first child of the Russell family and he is born in May in *Head Girl* on the day that Marie Pfeiffen marries Andreas (p269). David, who is named after Madge's father and has James as his second name after his own father, has heaps of soft, black hair and is very like his mother. David is christened on his mother's birthday (p286/329/330). Madge and

Pertisau

David arrive at the Chalet School for the last three weeks of term in *Rivals* and he is a big bonny boy, very like his mother with her dark curls and big dark eyes (p174/184). David is nine months old at the start of *Eustacia* (p35). He celebrates his first birthday in *And Jo* and the entire School joins to buy a magnificent Hornby train set for his birthday, for him to play with when he is older. They also knit him balls and furry animals to play with now. He has solemn dark eyes, his mother's curly crop and his father's firm mouth and chin. Madge and David stay at the School while the staff and pupils visit Oberammergau (p150). David is a delightful person of fifteen months in *Camp* (p24). Rosa, his little nurse, looks after him in *Exploits*. David, like his mother, is friendly with everyone and he is nearly eighteen months old (p151/152/157). David has a new baby sister in *Lintons* and will be two in May (p155/158). He and his cousin Primula Mary are inseparable in *New House* (p246). David gets measles in *Jo Returns*, further delaying Jo's return to the Sonnalpe (p91). Gill Linton suggests that he could be hauled about the lake in a chair when it freezes in *New CS* (p319). Madge is able to do some teaching in *Exile* as Peggy, Rix, Bride and David go to school every morning (p50). There is a lapse of about a year before the Chalet School opens in Guernsey. David is a sturdy boy of seven and probably in the First form as he ages with Nancy Chester and Julie Lucy (p170/176/204). Seven-year-old David is probably still at the Chalet School when it opens at Plas Howell in *Goes to It* but will be going to a cathedral boys' school with his cousin Rix Bettany the following term (p214/215). David does his best to keep Sybil in her place in *Highland Twins* (p73). In *Lavender* it is mentioned that Bride Bettany is a few months older than David. David is like his father, a jolly, straightforward boy with an excellent brain and a passion for cricket and most other outdoor sports (p35/36). Thirteen-year-old David is at the Cathedral School in Armiford in *Gay* and falls out of a tree, breaking his collarbone, shortly before Josette's accident (p17/74). He is twelve-and-a-half years old in *Rescue* and visits a school chum during the summer holiday (p35/36). Bride is newly eleven and David is thirteen in *Tom* (p10/22). Mary-Lou is told about him in *Three Go* (p54/61/62). David is left in the care of the Maynards when the Russells go to Canada in *Island* (p17). He is in his school rugby team and debating society in *Peggy*. He is working jolly hard and wants to be a doctor. He is very sensible and placid and is at Winchester (p116/126/127). In *Carola* it is mentioned that David will be sixteen in May (p27). David is at Winchester in *Wrong* and is going to visit his parents in Canada in the summer holidays (p96). Kester Russell is the image of David in *CS Oberland* (p146). It is recalled in *Joey Goes* that David and Sybil were left in Jo's care when Madge went to Canada (p65). We are reminded in *Does It Again* that Madge had to give up teaching at the time of David's birth (p176). David is eighteen in *Kenya* (p28). It is mentioned in *Mary-Lou* that the brains of his family have gone to David and Josette (p75). Small Felix Maynard's dismissive behaviour towards Kathie Ferrars reminds Jo of David at the same age in *New Mistress* (p108). We are told in *Richenda* that Daphne Bettany resembles her Auntie Madge more than any of Madge's own children apart from David (p64). David wasn't at home in *Joey and Co.* when Kevin and Kester contracted measles, and his mother rang him up to tell him to stay away (p167). After Peggy Bettany's wedding in *Ruey*, his cousin Rix Bettany mentions that David will not be getting married for some time as doctors don't marry early as a rule and Jem would not be pleased if David produced a blushing bride at this stage (p177). Jem and Madge Russell visit the Tiernsee before going to Australia in *Future*, but most of their children, including David, do not join them on the trip. David is tied up with his hospital work and makes his own plans these days (p202). David is twenty-five in *Redheads* and too keen on his job to bother about girls (p101).

RUSSELL, JAMES GILBERT (FRANCIS, WILLIAM) FRCS (JEM) (SIR JAMES) (B): Madge and Joey Bettany, Juliet Carrick and Grizel Cochrane are involved in a train accident in *School at* and a big, fair man, who introduces himself as James Russell, helps to rescue them (p331/334). Joey and five friends go to the Ice Carnival without permission in *Jo of* and Joey falls in front of a speeding skater who turns out to be Dr James Russell. Jem later calls on the patient and introduces Joey to the 'Elsie' books (p242/244/249). Jem is opening a sanatorium for TB patients on the Sonnenscheinspitze in the little village on the Sonnalpe at the other side of the Tiernsee from the Chalet School. Jem has a chalet built above the village and becomes engaged to be married to

Madge Bettany. Captain Humphries is leaving Russia and will become Jem's secretary (p334/335). Jem sets the questions for the Guides' health test in *Princess* (p155). His marriage to Madge Bettany is to take place three days after the end of term, on 27th July. Joey, Juliet and Robin are bridesmaids at the wedding. Jem and Madge later join Joey in Belsornia (p159/288/295). Madge visits Vienna with Jem for a conference during the Christmas holidays in *Head Girl* (p16). Jem and Madge's first child is born during the following term and they call him David James (p269/286). Jem breaks the news of Jo's serious condition to Dick after her accident on the ice in *Rivals* and says how fond he is of her (p167/168). He declares in *Eustacia* that Joey's health problems are partly caused by the fact that for years she has rebelled against restrictions placed upon her. He believes in bringing his son David up to be obedient to his parents (p41). It is mentioned in *And Jo* that Dr Russell owns a pleasant baritone (p105). Dr Jem is one of the visitors at Guide Camp in *Camp* (p156). Jem is described in *Exploits* as a tall, fair man with a keen, clever face, blue eyes that twinkle and long, slender hands (p75). We are told in *Lintons* that owing to the generosity of Dr Russell and his wife the new Domestic Economy department at the Chalet School is possible (p64). At their new daughter's naming party we learn that Jem's mother was named Margaret, that his sister Margot lives in Australia and that Jem's middle name is William. Jem has had golf links laid out on the alm above the Sonnalpe (p169/178/208). Joey and Frieda meet Jem's sister Margot Venables with her two daughters, Daisy and Primula Mary, in Innsbruck in *New House*. We learn that Jem was not involved in the quarrel with Margot but she was not allowed to write to him (p47/51/52). Primula Mary is very like Jem in appearance as she is fair with blue eyes and the same nose and mouth. Margot is three years older than Jem, who must be thirty-five (p53/64). Jem had been very fond of his sister and her elopement had been a great shock to him. A letter that he had written to his sister after she was married had been returned and he had to give up. When Jo informs him of Margot's return he is in a hurry to see her again. Jem promises to provide for Margot. He mentions that their father was killed in a motoring accident seven years earlier and their mother only survived him by three months (p69/76). Joey has been practising typing on Jem's machine without his knowing in *Jo Returns* (p172). He comes down to the School when Mademoiselle is ill and explains to the girls how serious it is, asking them to pray for her (p262). The Russells move down to their new summer home at the lake in *New CS* and it is mentioned that Jem will be the guardian of Robin Humphries until she is twenty-five (p38/42/45). Mario Balbini fires pellets at Jem's head one day when he is on his way to the School (p109). When Jem catches him he administers a whipping, but uses moderation, as he would never be cruel. This is later approved of by the boy's father, Prince Balbini, as payment of a debt of honour (p111/114/115). Jem instigates a search for the Balbini twins when their mother is dying at the Sanatorium and is horrified when he learns that they have kidnapped baby Sybil. He takes charge and announces that he is returning home immediately and is sure that the children will be found soon. Jem meets the train in which Herr Anserl is travelling, bringing back Sybil and her kidnappers (p152/164/174). Jem decides to send Madge and the children out of Austria after the Peace Treaty picnic and the Gestapo visit in *Exile* (p110). Cornelia Flower's American millionaire father buys the old Chalet buildings and grounds from Jem Russell and the men speak Afrikaans on the telephone to confuse any spies who may be listening in (p116). Jem is detained at the Sonnalpe dealing with compensation for the Sanatorium and signs a letter 'James Gilbert Russell' (p161). They evacuate to Guernsey and Jem's sister, Margot Venables, dies soon afterwards. A new little Russell (Josette) has been born, two months after Joey's marriage to Jack Maynard, and the Russells live at Bonne Maison, an old farmhouse at Torteval (p170/174/177). The situation in Guernsey becomes worse in *Goes to It* and Jem insists that Madge take their nursery of children to England as soon as possible. Madge moves into an old Georgian hunting lodge not far from Howell village (p10/21). Jem is Head of the Guernsey Sanatorium and remains behind while the Islands are being evacuated. Jem arrives at his new English home via Ireland just before the first air raid and plans to open a sanatorium (p168/213/214). In *Highland Twins* we learn that Jem has been awarded a baronetcy in the Birthday Honours for his work with TB and has opened a new sanatorium in the Welsh mountains (p52/89). Dr Marilliar has asked Jem to ask Bride Bettany to befriend Lavender Leigh in *Lavender* (p33). We learn in *Gay* that Jem and Madge are expecting another baby in September (p33). Josette has a serious accident when she is scalded by boiling water from a kettle held by her sister Sybil. Jem is furious with Sybil over the accident although he is usually the mild one, but we are informed that he finally forgives Sybil, and talks very sweetly to her, after she has fretted herself into a fever (p94/95/119). Jem's servant, André Monier, and his wife Marie (née Pfeiffen) are still with the Russell family with their children, Greta, Jacques, José and baby André (p181). Jem is forty-eight in *Rescue* but looks a good ten years less when he becomes involved in a night raid by two burly men (p130/131). Jem and Madge have another daughter and name her Aline Elizabeth (p221/232). Lady Russell and her husband Sir James Russell attend the Nativity Play in *Mystery* (p87). Jem rescues Daisy, Elfie and Tom when they get lost in the snow in *Tom* (p95). He has restricted Elfie Woodward's sport due to an ankle injury in *Rosalie* (p124). We learn in *Three Go* that he is prone to holes in the toes of his socks (p119). We are told in *Island* that Jem is going to attend a TB conference in Canada. He will take Madge and their two younger daughters, Josette and Ailie, to Canada for six months in April. Fiona and Flora McDonald will travel with them, to be reunited with their sister Shiena who is now married and settled in Quebec. Margot Maynard also goes with them for her health (p16/17/19). Jem is anxious to join a group who are experimenting with a new drug that they hope will help with TB in bones in *Peggy*. He is invited to stay at the James M Mather Sanatorium, where they hope to try out the new drug in the autumn, and the Russells decide to stay longer in Canada (p109/124). Madge produces twin baby boys, Kevin and Kester. The older children are at La Sagesse Convent School in Toronto (p196/198). We are told in *Carola* that Jem saw Biddy on to the boat for Australia when she accompanied a university friend with TB, and he did not expect the friend to live as long as the fifteen months she actually managed (p28). Jem pays a flying visit to the Chalet School during a visit to the Welsh Sanatorium in *Wrong* (p243). He attends a conference in California in *Shocks* (p30). Jack carries on for him in Canada while Jem comes to England with Madge when Mollie is ill (p185). We learn in *CS Oberland* that a new sanatorium is to be built on a shelf farther up the mountain from the Swiss branch at Welsen. Jem and Madge fly over from Canada to be with the Bettany family when Mollie has her operation (p50/121). It is mentioned in *Bride* that Jem and Jack Maynard are responsible for the new small branch of the Sanatorium that has been opened in the Oberland (p84). We are told in *Changes* that Jem has flown across from Canada to inspect a derelict hotel at the Görnetz Platz, with the result that there are already men working on the interior and getting it ready for patients. Jem is seeing to the financial arrangements for the Swiss branch of the School. The Russells return home from Canada and Jem will remain with the Welsh Sanatorium where he wants to develop a new idea, whilst Jack Maynard takes charge in Switzerland (p11/12/68). Jem misses Daisy's wedding in *Joey Goes* because he is occupied in performing a lung resection (p45). Sir Jem has given Julie Lucy a complete overhaul and declared her as fit as a fiddle in *Does It Again* (p88). We are told in *Kenya* that Jem chipped in to

help buy Joey a big radio for Christmas. He contacts a man he was at school with who works in the Nairobi Government to find out what he can about the Scotts when they are missing (p148/155). Jem always flies if he is coming to the Swiss Sanatorium for a consultation, and he escorts Mary-Lou back to school in *Mary-Lou*. The Russells leave the Round House and move nearer the Sanatorium in the mountains (p5/150). Jem is still at the English Sanatorium and is always in demand for big international conferences in *Genius*. The Russells have a lovely house in the Welsh hills near the Sanatorium (p128). Dr Jem's opening of the Sonnalpe Sanatorium is recalled in *Problem* (p220). Sir James Russell is one of the big men on TB in *New Mistress* (p12). Madge, Jem, Dick and Mollie are all agreed in *Excitements* that school chapels are the best idea of the lot for the coming-of-age celebrations, and all plan to contribute (p148). It is mentioned in *Coming of Age* that Sir James and Lady Russell will donate the altar in the Protestant chapel (p34). Jem Russell and Jack Maynard are to attend a conference reviewing the rules governing sanatoriums in *Richenda*, and need to plan ahead to have their ideas clearly set out (p190). Mary-Lou is aware in *Trials* that a successful operation can be followed by severe shock, as she has heard Jack and Jem talking (p220). Jem is concerned about Joey's health after her faint in *Joey and Co.* (p8/10). The Chalet School chapels are dedicated in *Ruey* and the Russells present the altar at St Mary's (p74). We learn in *Trick* that Jem is going to a conference in Australia. He plans to take his wife and Sybil, Josette and the twins and they will live in a flat lent to them by Emerence Hope's people. After the conference Jem will visit sanatoriums all over Australia and then go on to New Zealand (p102). Jem and Madge visit the Tiernsee for a fortnight before going to Australia in *Future* with Sybil and Josette, leaving Ailie in Joey's care and the twins at the Bettanys'. David is training to be a doctor and is tied up with his hospital work. The Russells plan to visit Con Stewart in Sydney (p202). Jem intends to visit Tasmania and New Zealand but Madge plans to stay in Sydney with Sybil and Josette in *Triplets* (p17/27). Jem is in Sydney in *Jane* and is able to get information about the condition of Jane's mother when she is in a Sydney hospital following a car accident. He phones from Sydney to confirm that Lady Carew has come through her operation (p161/170). In *Redheads* Sybil is almost engaged to someone in the Australian Navy who is the son of a Sydney doctor, and Madge and Jem expect to return home in April (p100/101). Joey remarks in *Adrienne* that it is possible that Jem and Madge might have been told more than she was about Robin's mother (p180). Joey recalls in *Summer Term* how Jem and Madge, as her guardians, packed her off to India after leaving school to escape the attentions of a persistent young doctor (p13). Sir James is at Freudesheim when Reg goes missing during floods in *Prefects* and hopes that Reg's accident will settle things between the young doctor and Len (p160/164). EBD's family tree in *N8* gives Jem's names as James Francis Russell (p33).

CHILDREN: David, Sybil, Josette, Ailie, Kevin, Kester

WARDS: Juliet Carrick, Robin Humphries, Daisy and Primula Mary Venables

RUSSELL, JOSEPHINE MARY (JOSEPHINE MARGOT) (JOSETTE) (C) (3): Madge and Jem Russell's third child Josette is born fairly soon after Madge reaches Guernsey in *Exile* and two months after Joey's wedding. Joey's goddaughter Josette is a delicious little person, black-haired, blue-eyed and pink-cheeked and is ten months old when the School reopens (p174/178/192). Madge brings Josette with her when she joins the sewing party for Simone's wedding dress in *Goes to It* (p244). Josette is slightly older than the triplets and is newly four in *Highland Twins* (p92). Josette is nearly four in *Lavender* and shows signs of being domesticated (p35/36). She is five years younger than her sister Sybil, and will not be four until the summer (p52/225). Josette is nearly five years old in *Gay* and her name is given as Josephine Margot (p17/49). She has a nasty accident on Miss Bubb's first day at the Chalet School when she is scalded by boiling water from a kettle held by Sybil. Josette is very ill and the shock causes heart trouble (p73/94/182). Joey tells Phoebe Wychcote in *Rescue* that Josette is named Josephine Mary and that she was scalded in April. Josette is thrilled to have a baby sister and she will meet Aline at the same time as Sybil. Josette is much better by the end of the summer holidays and the heart trouble has cleared up, but it is decided to let her have another year before she starts school (p36/227/234).

The building that housed the Margaret Roper School

Miss Edwards takes the seven Kindergarten children left at school over half term to play with Josette at the Round House in *Mystery*. Josette attends the Chalet School Christmas Play with her parents and is due to start as a pupil after the summer (p40/87). Madge buys her some dolls' hats at the Sale in *Tom* (p183). Josette, a wild scamp, is a little younger than ten-year-old Mary-Lou Trelawney but she is clever and is in Upper IIA with the older girl in *Three Go*. Josette's ninth birthday is first said to fall in December in *Three Go* (p61/70), though a second reference suggests she will be ten on 23rd November. She is still thought to be delicate because of the scalding accident (p150/151). Josette and Ailie accompany their parents to Canada in *Island* (p16). Josette is in Canada in *Peggy* and her health has improved so that she is now sturdy (p71/117/125). It is mentioned in *Carola* that Josette was nearly five years old when her sister Ailie was born (p28). Josette is no longer fragile in *Wrong* and is speaking fluent French thanks to her time at La Sagesse, a French convent school in Canada (p95/97). She is still in Canada with her family in *Bride* (p113). Emerence Hope is the first girl to meet Josette and the Maynard triplets when they return to school in *Changes*. Josette is very pretty, with silky black curls rioting over her head, eyes of periwinkle blue, and a pink-and-white face. She is put into Upper IVA with her old friends. She wins the swimming race for the under-fourteens at the School Regatta (p74/78/191). Josette is just twelve years old in *Joey Goes* (p66). She is invited to tea with Joey Maynard, together with Barbara Chester, Vi Lucy and Maeve Bettany, in *Barbara* (p125). She is in the Middle School and is a member of Mary-Lou's Gang (p145/162). She plays the part of a Child Crusader in the Christmas Play (p206). Josette is in one of the Fourth forms in *Does It Again* (p68/69). She is put in charge of Jo Scott in *Kenya* and is described as pretty, with her black hair, blue eyes and pink-and-white colouring. Josette will be fifteen in October and is in Upper IVA. She is the youngest in her form (p21/28/29). She is in the Bluebell dormitory and it is mentioned that Tom Gay once caught her and some other girls having a midnight feast. Josette and Jo Scott become firm friends and we learn that the former has never had a real chum before. Josette goes on the near-fatal moss picking expedition (p35/46/88/175). She is in the Fifth form with Mary-Lou and her friends in *Mary-Lou* (p19). She is in VA in *Genius* and falls over her books during an English lesson (p147/148). It is mentioned in *Problem* that Josette, who is in the Upper Fifth, is one of six children, three girls and three boys (p41). Sybil says in *New Mistress* that Josette has never been half as much bother as Ailie (p218). Josette is VA's Form Prefect in *Excitements*. She is sixteen years old and is a strong, healthy girl (p160/188). She is VA's Sale committee representative in *Coming of Age* and is only a little older than her cousins, the Maynard triplets. She is brilliantly clever, the only one of the three Russell girls to be so. Josette proposes a Shakespeare Sale, saves her form's reputation and has the part of Oberon in the Sale. She has long legs and can look over her mother's head (p62/66/98). Josette is a prefect in *Richenda* when Mary-Lou is the Head Girl (p59). She is in VIB in *Trials*. Josette is the Library Prefect. She likes maths and carried on with the subject once she reached the specialising stage (p10/140). Josette is a tall, very pretty girl with wavy black hair and blue eyes in *Theodora*. She is exceedingly clever, by far the cleverest of the Russell girls, and is a great friend of Clare Kennedy (p108/149). It is mentioned in *Joey and Co.* that Josette will be a bridesmaid at her cousin Peggy's wedding to Giles Winterton in October. She is nearly two years older than the Maynard triplets (p15/105). Slightly built Josette is the Head Girl in *Ruey* although she is the youngest prefect, only having celebrated her seventeenth birthday the previous August. She is proving herself a born leader. Josette expects to go on to St Mildred's but Miss Annersley tells her during a meeting that she and Sybil will be leaving school at the end of the next Easter term. This is being told off the record and not to be repeated and Josette remains silent for the remainder of the time, too stunned by this shock to have anything to say (p31/53/151). Josette mentions that she will stay at the Quadrant for Peggy's wedding at half term. She wins VIA's prize for her costume of a Georgian court lady at the staff evening (p170/216/220). Josette is still the Head Girl in *Leader* and is marvellous at ski-ing (p22). Her last term at the Chalet School is in *Trick* and she is still Head Girl. We learn that she played tennis with Clare Kennedy on the town courts when she visited her during the Easter holidays (p46/47). Josette will soon be seventeen, but later we are told that she will be eighteen in September. She is wearing her hair up in plaits wreathed round her head for coolness (p53/56). Josette announces to the prefects that she will not be going on to St Mildred's next year because her parents want her to go to Australia with them, Sybil and the twins, Kevin and Kester. Jem Russell is going to Adelaide for a big world conference and is then going to inspect some Australian and New Zealand sanatoriums. Josette is going to study radiology but there will not be a vacancy in the hospital until the following summer. It seems she subsequently changes her mind, as she tells the triplets that she must face the Advanced Level exams in French if she means to go to the London School of Economics (p101/102/194). Jem and Madge Russell visit the Tiernsee for a fortnight before going to Australia with Sybil and Josette in *Future*. Josette intends to have a week at Elinor Pennell's home and then join Sybil at the Trelawneys' before they sail (p202). Josette and Sybil have promised accounts of the voyage and their adventures in Australia for *The Chaletian* in *Feud* (p34). Sybil and Josette are to remain with Madge in Sydney while Jem visits Tasmania and New Zealand in *Triplets* (p17). Joey tells Hilda Annersley in *Redheads* that eighteen-year-old Josette is engaged to the elder brother of a friend of hers at Sydney University. He is nine years older and is a flourishing young lawyer in partnership with his father. She is fourteen months older than the triplets and was born in September (p100). EBD gives a brief biography of Josette in *N15*, saying that she is nineteen and engaged to be married (p64). Jem Russell mentions in *Prefects* that Sybil and Josette are both married (p166).

RUSSELL, KESTER RICHARD (C): (5/6) Madge and Jem's twins Kevin and Kester are born in Canada in November in *Peggy*. Madge's father was named Richard, hence the middle name, and Kester is an old English form of Christopher. Kester is as dark as his fifteen-year-old brother David and is Madge's image. We are told that the twins were not expected until January (p196/197/202). Biddy O'Ryan looks at photographs of the twins in *Carola* (p27). Kester is like David, including his black Bubbles crop, according to Joey when she and her party arrive in Canada in *Wrong* (p94). The twins are crawling and Kester is trying to stand in *Shocks*. They both have Jem's features although Kester is fair and Kevin is dark (p33/190). Kester is the image of David in *CS Oberland* (p146). Madge brings the twins to show them off to the School in *Changes* (p156). Kevin and Kester are nearly three years old in *Kenya* (p28) and *Mary-Lou* (p75). Madge remembers in *Coming of Age* that when they were small, Kevin and Kester viewed paper as simply something to tear up (p102). We learn in *Joey and Co.* that Kester and Kevin have had measles (p167). The Russell twins start at the new Swiss Kindergarten when it opens in *Ruey* (p56). We learn in *Trick* that Madge and Jem plan to take the twins when they visit Australia (p102). Jem and Madge Russell visit the Tiernsee for a fortnight before going to Australia with Sybil and Josette in *Future*. They leave Ailie with Joey, and Kevin and Kester with Dick and Mollie Bettany (p202). Kester Richard is mentioned in EBD's Family Tree in *N8* (p33).

RUSSELL, KEVIN JOHN (C): (5/6) Madge and Jem's twins Kevin and Kester Russell are born in Canada in November in *Peggy* and we learn that Kevin has Jack Maynard's name for a middle name (p196/197). The twins were not expected until January. Kevin resembles Jem (p202/204). Biddy O'Ryan looks at photographs of the twins in *Carola* (p27). Kevin is described as the image of Jem when Joey's party arrive in Canada in *Wrong* (p94). The twins are crawling in *Shocks*. They both have Jem's features although Kevin is dark and Kester is fair (p33/190). Kevin looks like Jem in *CS Oberland* (p146). Madge brings the twins to show them off to the School in *Changes* (p156). The twins are nearly three years old in *Kenya* (p28) and *Mary-Lou* (p75). Madge remembers in *Coming of Age* that when they were small, Kevin and Kester viewed paper as simply something to tear up (p102). We learn in *Joey and Co.* that Kevin and Kester have had measles (p167). The Russell twins start at the new Kindergarten when it opens in *Ruey* (p56). It is mentioned in *Trick* that Madge and Jem will take Kevin and Kester with them when they visit Australia (p102). Jem and Madge Russell intend to stay at the Tiernsee for a fortnight before going to Australia with Sybil and Josette in *Future*. They are leaving Ailie with Joey and the twins with Dick and Mollie Bettany (p202). Kevin John is mentioned in EBD's Family Tree in *N8* (p33).

RUSSELL, MADGE: see BETTANY, MARGARET
RUSSELL, MARGARET (A): Joey mentions in

Lintons that Jem's mother's Christian name was Margaret (p169). We learn in *New House* that Jem and Margot's parents objected to their daughter Margot's marriage. Mrs Russell only survived for three months after her husband's motor accident (p51/76).

RUSSELL, MARGOT: see VENABLES, MARGOT

RUSSELL, SYBIL MARGARET (C) (2): Madge and Jem's second child is born in March at half term in *Lintons* and is their first daughter (p155). The baby is nearly two years younger than her brother David and has hair described variously as carrots, Titian red, ginger, and as being in thick coppery curls. She has deep blue eyes (p158/166/168). She is named Sybil Margaret (p182). Joey comments in *New House* that Sybil has ginger hair but Jem says they are chestnut curls (p23/73). Madge visits the Chalet School with Sybil and the baby has thick, deep chestnut curls, deep sapphire eyes and her small face is coloured like a wild rose (p245/246). Jo is knitting a little coat for Sybil in *Cook Book* (p203). Sybil is eight months old in *Jo Returns*. She has cut her first tooth and is about to start crawling (p198). The Balbini twins kidnap baby Sybil in *New CS* with help from Mélanie Kerdec, another member of the 'Mystic M' (see p121/129). Herr Anserl recognises his goddaughter Sybil in Spärtz and returns her to Jem (p157/174). Sybil has chestnut curls, blue eyes and a hot temper in *Exile*. She frequently spars with her cousin Rix Bettany. She resents Peggy's mothering, having a great opinion of herself as the only daughter in the Russell household (p15/16). There is no mention that Sybil is at school in *Goes to It*, although her cousin and co-baby Jackie does appear to be (p214). Sybil appears to be living with Joey Maynard in *Highland Twins* (p17/34). She is in the Lower Second with Jackie Bettany. She is the beauty of the family and has a very high opinion of herself but Fiona and Flora McDonald do not like her very much (p71/72/73). Nearly-nine-year-old Sybil has chestnut curls, sapphire-blue eyes, rose-petal skin and her mother's delicately cut features in *Lavender*, and is very aware she is a 'picture' child (p36/37). Sybil is annoyed by the way in which Bride and Peggy act like elder sisters when they are at home with her (p50). It is reported that Miss Norman, head of the Junior English staff, had on one occasion to carry Sybil Russell to Miss Annersley for a well-deserved Head's interview

(p120). Sybil can be unbearably rude and needs to get over her vanity and jealousy. She hates her older cousins living with her family, and this is one reason why Daisy and Primula are not at the Round House. After Stephen Maynard's baptism, Madge recalls that when Sybil was first taken to church she threw her collection penny at the collector because she didn't like his beard (p224/225/254). Sybil and Jack Bettany are ten years old in *Gay* and Sybil is responsible for Josette having a horrific accident when the younger child is scalded with boiling water. Matey finally sends for Jem to forgive Sybil as she is fretting herself into a fever (p17/94/119). Sybil is about ten and has a mop of chestnut curls when she visits Garnham in Yorkshire with a large party of adults and children in *Rescue*. She is described as a picture-child (p9/10/22). She learns from Reg Entwistle how to make whistles from willow-stems by removing the pith and manages to fall off a fence into the horse-pond (p127/143). Sybil, with her peach-like complexion, is embarrassed by the praise of Mrs Hart, having lost a lot of her conceit after the severe lessons of the year (p163/164). She is thrilled when Aline is born and Joey mentions to Madge that

Sybil has been very helpful and is a changed being (p233/234). Sybil goes on a walk to the Round House with Daisy in charge in *Tom* (p74). She plays tennis with Tom Gay, Rosalie Way and Primrose Day in *Rosalie*. She is only eleven but is good for her age (p128/129). In *Three Go* Sybil is a little younger than Primula Venables, who is nearly fourteen (p61/59). Sybil is not in the least clever and enjoys sewing and art better than lessons. She hopes to go to the Art Needlework School at South Kensington for two years when she is seventeen (p70/71). Sybil and Bride are in charge when the Russell, Maynard and Bettany children and Mary-Lou dye themselves red with ochre. Sybil and Betsy become friends with Clem and are as wild as she is (p123/124/149). Sybil and David stay with the Maynards when the Russells go to Canada in *Island*. Sybil is in Ste Thérèse when the boats are handed over (p17/147/152). She is in the Upper Fourth in *Peggy* and Madge wants her to come out to Canada with Joey (p53/129). Eilunedd Vaughn tries to use Sybil against Peggy, and is successful in persuading her to eat an illicit bun during a tea for those in detention, but she does not really enjoy it (p169/170). Sybil is involved in the prank where the girls begin to use Regency English (p173/174). Blossom Willoughby is Sybil's particular friend. Sybil later becomes wise to Eilunedd and avoids her (p186/207). Sybil is a really lovely girl of nearly fourteen in *Carola* and is in the Fifth form with Clem Barrass and Carola Johnstone. Her real hobby is embroidery and she still intends to go to the South Kensington School of Needlework when she leaves school. She goes on an icy walk with some of the Fifth formers and Biddy O'Ryan (p109/111/121). We are told in *Wrong* that Sybil has gone to Canada with Joey and her family to join Madge, Jem and the others and she is looking forward to meeting her new twin brothers. Sybil was Form Prefect the previous term and she is now fifteen years old (p25/94). Sybil helps Joey with the children in Toronto while her parents are in England with Kester and Kevin during Mollie Bettany's illness and operation in *CS Oberland* (p122). Sybil is in Canada with her family in *Bride* (p76/112). She returns to the Chalet School in *Changes* and it is reported that she can gabble away in French like a native, having been at La Sagesse, a French convent school in Toronto. She is not behind in other work (p66/67). Sybil is not yet sixteen in *Joey Goes* (p66). She takes part in an indoor boat race at the staff evening in *Barbara*. She plays the part of Mary in the Christmas Play (p198/206). Sixteen-year-old Sybil is in the Lower Fifth in *Kenya* and when she finishes school will do a training course at the South Kensington School of Needlework (p28/30). She is friendly with Ruth Lamont and Elinor Pennell (p88). Later in the term we are told that seventeen-year-old Sybil, who is not yet a prefect, has only been a member of the Upper Fifth since the Easter term, but there is a tendency for many of the Sixth Form to treat her as one of themselves. She is older than her age and has a little imperious air and a great deal of natural dignity. Sybil always feels responsible for Josette following the accident when Josette was four, for which she knows herself to have been to blame. Since then she has kept a watchful eye on her younger sister, frequently without much gratitude from Josette, who sometimes says that Sybil is too grannyish for words (p96). Sybil is in VIB in *Mary-Lou* and is one of the prettiest girls the School has ever boasted, with her delicate features, sapphire blue eyes and perfect colouring. Her brother David and sister Josette are more intelligent (p74/75). She suggests to the prefects that a sheets and pillowcase party might be suitable when they entertain the School and St Mildred's (p76). She is asked to assist at the party and is also made a sub-prefect. She will be seventeen in March and intends having a year at St Mildred's (p78/90/91). Sybil is still a sub-prefect in *Genius* and she helps Freda Lund as Second Hobbies Prefect (p58/59/60). She arranges the Tilting at the Ring activity at the Sale with Blossom Willoughby (p186). In *Problem* she partners Vi at tennis (p70) and joins in progressive games organised by the Sixth to make the numbers up (p81). Sybil is able to explain to the other prefects why Mary-Lou seems friendly with Joan Baker (p153/154). Len is very pleased to hear the arrangements for the Basle trip, which include having Sybil as one of their prefects (p168). Sybil helps to organise the prefects' entertainment in *New Mistress* and is described as having violet eyes, copper curls and a perfect complexion. She has delicate features and a certain little air of dignity and grace that is quite unconscious. Sybil is on the trip to the glacier and the accident comes as a bad shock to her as she is highly strung (p139/167). She is a prefect in *Excitements* and is friendly with Blossom Willoughby. She has a long-standing feud with Virginia Adams. Miss Annersley mentions that Sybil is one of the School's best prefects and is a lovely and trustworthy girl (p9/12/188). Sybil is still a prefect in *Coming of Age* and is domesticated, with a passion for needlework. She goes on the prefects' trip to the Tiernsee and remembers the Mystic M kidnapping. The train leaving Spärtz is what jogs her memory (p54/62/143). Sybil is the princess in the St Mildred's pantomime, *Puss in Boots*, in *Trials* and she has a sweet, clear speaking voice (p209). She is still at St Mildred's in *Theodora* and is only averagely clever (p108). It is mentioned in *Joey and Co.* that Sybil is to be a bridesmaid at Peggy's wedding to Giles Winterton in October. Sybil is eighteen years old (p15/172). She is still at St Mildred's in *Ruey* but will leave at the end of the Easter term (p151). Her forthcoming trip to Australia is mentioned in *Trick* (p102). Sybil visits the Trelawneys in *Future* before going out to Australia with her parents and Josette (p202). Josette and Sybil have promised accounts of the voyage and their adventures in Australia for *The Chaletian* in *Feud* (p34). Margot Maynard is afraid in *Triplets* that twenty-year-old Sybil will be bossy and prefecty, but Len disagrees (p17). Sybil has made a teacloth for the Sale in *Jane* (p208). Twenty-three-year-old Sybil is almost engaged in *Redheads* to someone in the Australian navy who is the son of a Sydney doctor (p99/100). The date of Sybil's wedding in Australia is finally settled in *Adrienne* and it is reported that Ailie is flying there and is allowed to stay for the Easter vacation (p104/136). Sybil contributes a beautifully embroidered afternoon tea-cloth and set of napkins to the School Sale in *Summer Term* (p162). Jem comments in *Prefects* that Sybs and Josette are both now married (p166). EBD says in *N19* that she has not mentioned Sybil's married name anywhere (p81).

RUTH: Gay Lambert's twin daughters Ruth and Gillian are mentioned in *Leader* (p11).

RUTH, NAOMI, ESTHER, ADAM and LUKE: Miss Annersley used to know this family, the offspring of a country Rector who were all given Biblical names, and mentions them in *Trials*. Naomi and Ruth are twins and were at school with her (p14).

RUTHERFORD, MR: We are told in *Genius* that Nina's grandpapa, Mr Rutherford, would not let his son Alan follow music for his career and wanted him to work in his business (p12).

RUTHERFORD, ALAN: We learn in *Genius* that Nina's father Alan Rutherford wanted to go in for music but his father wouldn't let him. Alan left his work when he married Nina's mother and went in for music after all. After the death of Nina's mother Alan went off with his eighteen-month-old daughter and travelled round the world. He had an accident to his right hand and lost three fingers so he turned to composition and made a living from it (p12). Nina is orphaned when her widowed father, Alan Rutherford, is drowned in Lake Maggiore trying to save the life of a child. His wife's name was Dorothy Embury (p13/131).

RUTHERFORD, ALISON: We learn in *Genius* that Alison learns the piano and has fair, rosy colouring (p15/17). Sixteen-year-old Alison and her twin Anthea are Nina Rutherford's cousins and their home is Brettingham Park near Newcastle. Alison has thick red curls inherited from her father. The twins and their elder sister Alix go to

St Cecilia's Catholic School (p25/32/34). Alison and Anthea go out to the Görnetz Platz and stay with the Graves family when Alix is ill. We are told that the twins will start at the Chalet School after next term (p198/199). The Rutherfords are living at the Élisehütte in *Problem* and Alison and Anthea are due to start at the Chalet School next term (p151/166). The twins are at the Chalet School in *New Mistress* and are making progress at skiing (p209). Alison, Anthea and Nina become day girls in *Coming of Age* to ease congestion when the St Mildred's girls arrive for the term (p12/17). We learn in *Trials* that the twins will be leaving school soon as Alison and Anthea are joining their parents and Alix on a long sea voyage to finish her cure (p153). None of the Rutherford family will be present at the dedication of the chapels in *Ruey* because they are far away on a long sea voyage (p73).

RUTHERFORD, ALIX (ALIXE): We are told in *Genius* that Nina Rutherford's cousin Alix is the eldest of Sir Guy's daughters and she is considered to be very good at playing the piano (p15/16). Seventeen-year-old Alix and her twin sisters Alison and Anthea go to St Cecilia's Catholic

School (p25/32/34) where the older girl is the best pianist and considered to be really musical (p31/34). Unfortunately Alix catches cold and has pleurisy and pneumonia, which affects one of her lungs (p108/110). It is decided to bring her out to Switzerland to the Görnetz Platz Sanatorium (p111/112). Alix is very ill and may be at the Sanatorium for several years. Alison and Anthea accompany Alix and their parents to Switzerland and stay with the Graves at the Görnetz Platz (p197/198/199). Alix is in the Sanatorium in *Problem* and it is mentioned that she is a shade better and will be able to have visitors soon. Her family are living at the Élisehütte (p66/106/151). Miss Annersley informs the girls in *Coming of Age* that in time, Alixe will be completely cured. Her parents are presenting a bell for the new chapels, and Anthea explains that the bell is a thank offering for Alixe getting better (p34). Delicate-looking Alixe is present at the School Sports and we learn that she is recovering (p214). We are informed in *Trials* that Alix is going on a long sea voyage to complete her cure and her family will accompany her (p153). The chapel bell is housed in a slender wooden tower in *Ruey* but none of the Rutherfords are present at the dedication as they are away on a long sea voyage and Nina is in Vienna (p73). Alix is a passenger in a car driven by her mother when the car crashes in *Two Sams*. She has bad bruising and a sprained wrist (p41).

RUTHERFORD, ANTHEA: We learn in *Genius* that Sir Guy's daughter Anthea plays the piano but has been promoted to the violin at her own request. Sixteen-year-old Anthea, her twin Alison and their elder sister Alix are Nina Rutherford's cousins and their home is Brettingham Park near Newcastle (p15/16/25). The three sisters go to St Cecilia's Catholic School (p32/34) and Anthea is the prettiest of Sir Guy and Lady Rutherford's daughters (p31). Alison and Anthea accompany Alix and their parents out to the Görnetz Platz and stay with the Graves, and we learn that the twins will start at the Chalet School after next term (p199). The Rutherfords are living at the Élisehütte in *Problem* and Alison and Anthea are due to start at the Chalet School next term (p151/166). Anthea plays her violin in the Chalet School Christmas Play in *New Mistress*. She is quite a nice girl and plays moderately well (p194). The twins take part in winter sports and their mother admires their progress (p209). Anthea is in VA in *Excitements* (p115). Alison, Anthea and Nina become day girls in *Coming of Age* to ease congestion when the St Mildred's girls arrive for the term (p12/17). Anthea is a member of the Lower Sixth in *Trials* and we learn that the twins will be leaving school soon as Anthea and Alison are going to join Alix on a long sea voyage to finish her cure (p153). None of the Rutherford family will be present at the dedication of the chapels in *Ruey* because they are far away on a long sea voyage that will round off Alixe's cure (p73). Anthea is a passenger in a car driven by her mother when the car crashes in *Two Sams*. Anthea is the least badly injured, having just some cuts and bruises. Mrs Maynard takes charge of the girl and telephones Brettingham Park to tell Sir Guy Rutherford (p41).

RUTHERFORD, DOROTHY (née EMBURY): We learn in *Genius* that Nina Rutherford's mother was a concert singer when she met Alan Rutherford, but died when Nina was eighteen months old. Nina's mother had been Dorothy Embury, a cousin of Martin Embury, and the Emburys want to help Nina (p12/131).

RUTHERFORD, FRANCIS: Nina's cousin Francis is Alix, Alison and Anthea's brother and is in the Navy in *Genius* (p30).

RUTHERFORD, SIR GUY: Sir Guy wants his fifteen-year-old cousin Nina to cut back on her piano practice and get a proper education as he feels that she is too young to specialise in *Genius*. Sir Guy, who is given to plain speaking, has recently become Nina's guardian following the death of her father, having had no contact with his cousin Alan for nearly fifteen years (p11/12/13). Sir Guy escorts Alan's daughter Nina back from Italy to England to his home at Brettingham Park near Newcastle. Sir Guy and his wife Yvonne have three daughters: seventeen-year-old Alix, and sixteen-year-old twins, Alison and Anthea. They also have two sons, Roger who is in the Air Force and Francis in the Navy (p15/25/30). Alix becomes ill and Sir Guy and Lady Rutherford take her out to the Görnetz Platz Sanatorium in Switzerland (p112/197). They are living at the Élisehütte to be near Alix in *Problem*. Alison and Anthea are due to start at the Chalet School next term (p151/166). Sir Guy is described as a big, red-headed man and he and his wife are present at the pantomime in *Excitements* (p132). The Rutherfords are still living at the Görnetz Platz in *Coming of Age* and are donating a bell for the chapels as a thank offering for their daughter Alixe's recovery (p12/19/34). In *Trials* Sir Guy has informed Anthea that she and Alison are to accompany Alix on a long sea voyage to finish off her cure (p153). Sir Guy and his family are away on a long sea voyage in *Ruey* and none of them will be at the dedication of the chapels (p73). It is mentioned in *Trick* that the Rutherfords are away on a long sea voyage and they have let the Élisehütte to Mrs Everett (p180). Sir Guy is at home at Brettingham Park when Mrs Maynard rings him to tell him of the accident involving his family and young cousin in *Two Sams*. He makes plans to hurry to Switzerland immediately (p41).

RUTHERFORD, KATHERINE: Katherine arrives at the Chalet School in *Feud* after her own school, St Hilda's, has burned down. She sits next to Marian Hadaway, who is fifteen. She is temporarily placed in Inter V but after tests she is moved to VB with Phyllis Garstin, who is also from St Hilda's (p33/55).

RUTHERFORD, NINA: We learn in *Genius* that fifteen-year-old Nina Rutherford hopes to be a concert pianist and that her mother was a concert singer but died when Nina was eighteen months old. Nina has been orphaned by the death of her father Alan Rutherford, who died trying to save a drowning child in the waters of Lake Maggiore, where they proposed to winter. Nina has a white wedge of a face under heavy black hair, a broad brow and enormous dark eyes. She has beautiful, long-fingered hands (p11/12/13/14). It is mentioned that Nina has missed out on usual things such as the fun of school-life, having a great friend and playing games, although she played tennis with her father. She is far too old and serious for her age but is free from self-consciousness or conceit over her music (p14). Her father's cousin, Sir Guy Rutherford, escorts her to his home in England and on the journey she meets Hilary Bennett, Lesley Malcolm, Viola Lucy and Barbara Chester returning home for Christmas. They mention that Margia Stevens, a concert pianist, and Jacynth Hardy, a 'cellist, are former pupils of the Chalet School (p19/21). The Rutherfords' home, Brettingham Park, is near Newcastle and Sir Guy and Lady Rutherford's three daughters, Alix and the twins Anthea and Alison, are there to meet Nina (p25). Nina does not settle down well at the Rutherfords' home, where her musical requirements are not properly understood. Nina's cousin only allows her two hours' piano practice until she understands Nina's ability, and then extra heating is provided and she is allowed four hours a day (p26/27/33). Sir Guy decides to enrol Nina at the Chalet School and she starts the following term in VA with Mary-Lou, Vi Lucy, Hilary Bennett and Lesley Malcolm. Nina speaks French and German fluently and also Italian (p35/38/39). Maeve Bettany shows her the Cornflower dormitory and admires Nina's long plait of black hair (p40/43). Nina attends Catholic Prayers with Clare Kennedy (p46). It is arranged that she will have music lessons with Herr von Eberhardt, a German whose wife is in the Sanatorium. Nina is delighted as she learned from him for two terms three years earlier when she and her father were in America (p56). Nina is able to ski and her father taught her to skate (p75/76). During a gym lesson Hilda Jukes knocks Nina over when playing leapfrog, and she hurts her wrist. Nina blames Hilda for the accident and with flashing eyes swears that she will never forgive the other girl because she has stopped her practice. Dr Graves keeps Nina from playing the piano for a while (p80/81). Nina has tea with Joey and later apologises shame-facedly to Hilda. Nina plays the piano for the St Mildred's pantomime, *Beauty and the Beast* (p88/89). Alix is ill and Mary-Lou learns that Nina has never told the Rutherfords about the Sanatorium as her letters home are very stiff and stilted. On the advice of Mary-Lou, Nina writes and suggests that Alix is brought to the Görnetz Sanatorium (p109/110/111). Nancy Wilmot meets Winifred Embury, formerly Silksworth, on a boat on Lac Léman and discovers that Nina's mother was Dorothy Embury, a cousin of her husband Martin, and that the Emburys want to help Nina (p127/131). Nina is to stay with the Emburys at Montreux during the Easter holidays and meet the rest of their family. She is delighted that she is not alone any more (p152/153/154). Nina composes a welcome to baby Cecily Maynard. It is in six-eight time, and shows the influence of Debussy and Ravel in the harmonisation, with a melody that has something of the tunefulness and gaiety of Mozart. She has often composed for her own amusement and is fond of improvising (p167/168). Nina is in Ste Thérèse House and we learn that Mary-Lou has submitted for the magazine a short composition that Nina has written to words by Herrick. It is slight, but foreshadows everything that she will do in the future (p178/179/181). Nina is in VB in *Problem* and her Aunt Yvonne and Uncle Guy are renting a chalet, as her cousin Alix is ill at the Görnetz Platz Sanatorium (p66/106). Nina is the official accompanist to the orchestra for the Christmas Play in *New Mistress*. She is gifted with a spark of genius and is entrusted with odd rehearsals when none of the music staff can spare the time (p194). She is in VA in *Excitements* and steps in to conduct the orchestra for the St Mildred's pantomime, *Aladdin*, when Mr Denny becomes ill with a touch of pneumonia. She takes control when a fire breaks out and keeps the orchestra playing to help calm the audience (p115/125/138). Nina gives a piano recital at the School Sale in *Coming of Age*. Later she is Sybil Russell's driver in a wheelbarrow race and they win their race (p110/214). Nina has written the overture for the Nativity Play in *Richenda* and we are told that she left school at the end of the previous term to take up her music studies seriously at a world famous conservatoire (p217). Nina is cited as someone who is unlike other girls in *Theodora* (p140). She is in Vienna working hard at her music at the time of the dedication of the two chapels in *Ruey* (p73). At the beginning of *Feud*, Miss Annersley tells her pupils that Nina made her début at Easter and is setting out on a small tour of some of the English concert halls. At the Christmas Play the girls sing 'Gloria in excelsis Deo' to music composed by Nina. She is making her name as a concert pianist and will make an even greater name for herself as a composer as the years go on (p35/199). Nina is chief soloist at a concert in the Kursaal in Interlaken which the School attends in *Redheads*. She plays her own composition, *The Platz*, which gives a musical picture of the Görnetz Platz (p158). We learn in *Challenge* that Nina has written the music of the opening hymn at Prayers, to words written by Con Maynard. Nina sometimes composes music for the Chalet School carol concerts and plays. We are reminded that she left school at seventeen to go to Vienna to finish her musical training (p54/151/152). It is again mentioned in *Two Sams* that Nina left school at seventeen and has been away now for four years. She has started her career as a concert pianist and is going on a tour of Canada, Australia and New

Zealand. She wants to endow a scholarship for musical girls and also to have an essay competition (p33/34). She is involved in a bad car crash with her aunt, Lady Rutherford, and her cousins Alix and Anthea outside the School. Nina hits her head on a stone and it is feared her skull may be fractured. She is unconscious for a few days but rouses fully at last and the doctors all say she will be all right in time (p41/66). Unfortunately she has to cancel her tour but is invited to Montreux by her cousins Martin and Winifred Embury and will go when she is well enough (p44/121). The two Sams visit Nina at the Sanatorium in *Two Sams* and she suggests that Samaris learns to play the flute. Nina arranges for her to borrow one (p132/135/176). She is becoming well known as a pianist in *Althea* (p55). Nina is mentioned in a synopsis of *Two Sams* in *N16*, as Samaris's interest in playing the flute provides a diversion after her accident (p70).

RUTHERFORD, ROGER: Nina's cousin Roger, who is Alix, Alison and Anthea's brother, is in the Air Force in *Genius*. He has a brother, Francis, who is in the Navy (p30).

RUTHERFORD, YVONNE (LADY RUTHERFORD): Yvonne is the wife of Sir Guy Rutherford, whose cousin, Alan Rutherford, has recently died, and Alan's orphaned daughter Nina comes to live with them in England. Yvonne and Sir Guy have three daughters, seventeen-year-old Alix and sixteen-year-old twins Alison and Anthea, as well as two sons, in *Genius*. Roger is in the Air Force and Francis is in the Navy (p13/25/30). Yvonne is described as kindly and tall, and when Nina goes to the Chalet School feels it is her duty to write to her every week (p31/34/103). Alix becomes ill and Sir Guy and Lady Rutherford take her to Switzerland, to the Görnetz Platz Sanatorium (p112/197). They are living at the Élisehütte to be near Alix in *Problem* and it is mentioned that Alison and Anthea will go to the Chalet School next term (p66/151/166). Lady Rutherford admires the progress Alison and Anthea are making at winter sporting in *New Mistress* (p209). Slim, anxious-faced Lady Rutherford attends the pantomime in *Excitements* (p132). The Rutherfords are still living at the Élisehütte in *Coming of Age* and they donate a bell to the chapels as a thank offering for their daughter Alixe's recovery (p12/19/34). Lady Rutherford presents the prizes on Sports Day (p221). The Rutherfords and their three daughters are away in *Ruey* on a long sea voyage to round off Alixe's cure and none of them will be present at the dedication of the chapels (p73). Lady Rutherford is driving Alix, Anthea and Nina when they are involved in a car crash in *Two Sams*. Lady Rutherford is slightly burned and suffers from cuts and bruises (p41).

RUTHVEN, DOROTHY: Dorothy is a Senior Middle and an enthusiastic Guide in *Barbara* (p58/59/121). Dorothy is in Upper IVB and is bosom friends with Dora Ripley in *Does It Again* (p25/26). She is in Upper IVB in *Kenya* and has been at school for some years but still frequently trips up in French (p61). Dorothy is apparently in the Fifth form in *Coming of Age* (p22).

RYDER, GERTRUDE: see MATRON RIDER, GERTRUDE

TRIPS AND EXCURSIONS

Following in the footsteps of Chalet School characters

The aim of this article is to provide a reference for real places described in the Chalet School books, as an aid for fans wishing to visit Chalet School locations. It does not aspire to include a comprehensive list of all countries, regions, towns and villages mentioned. Although it is commonly known that many fictional locations, for example the Tiernsee, Briesau and Armiford, are based on real places, these are outside the scope of this article as EBD has used poetic licence to make them fit her world.

Spelling of the place names: where there are variations, either between books or because of such differences in German/English (ü/u etc), I have put the version by which the place is generally known nowadays first and alternative spellings from the series second. The chapter numbers refer to the Chambers hardback and GGBP editions.

AUSTRIA
References appear both in the early Tyrol books and in several of the Swiss ones.

Innsbruck/Innsbrück
As the nearest town to the fictional Briesau and Spärtz, Innsbruck is used for changing trains, shopping, visits to the dentist and hairdresser, flying into/out of,* business and charity (supporting the 'poor parish') etc, as well as being the home of several characters.

There are brief mentions without further descriptions in:

Exploits
Jo Returns
New CS
New Mistress
Coming of Age
Joey and Co.
Redheads
Two Sams
Althea

More detailed descriptions, sometimes long, sometimes in passing to support the plot, can be found in:

School at	Chapter IV
Jo of	Chapters XIV–XVI
Head Girl	Chapter V
Eustacia	Chapters IV, V and XV
New House	Chapters IV and V

* This rather surprising fact, so early in the series, is included in *The New Chalet School*. Hilda Annersley flies back from Rome when Mademoiselle is taken ill and the Russells fly from Innsbruck to see a dying Ted Humphries.

Other places visited and described:

Area/town	Book	Chapter
Fulpmes, Stubaital	*Eustacia*	XV–XIX
Hall	*Joey and Co.*	XVI
Kufstein	*Future*	XVII and XVIII
Mayrhofen/Zillert(h)al	*Princess*	XI and XII
	New House	XVI
	Future	XIII
Salzburg	*Head Girl*	XVII
	New CS	XVI

GERMANY

The only place to be described in Germany is Oberammergau, in Chapters XIII–XV of *And Jo*.

FRANCE

Paris is mentioned throughout the series. In particular it is a place people pass through, somewhere to meet friends, join the school party and their escorts at the Gare du Nord/Gare de l'Est or stop over for a day or two. It is also a place of study (the Sorbonne and the Conservatoire). A little of the atmosphere is given in *Summer Term* in Chapter II. However, the only detailed description of landmarks is found in *School at* in Chapter III.

Boulogne is the point of entry into France from England. The busy atmosphere of the customs is described in *School at* (beginning of Chapter III) and *Joey Goes* (Chapter VII).

Other places mentioned but not described are Arles (*Joey & Co, Adrienne, Summer Term*) and Strasbourg (*Mary-Lou*).

ITALY

There is a brief reference in Chapter XXV of *School at* to South Tyrol, a German-speaking region with a chequered history belonging at that time, as now, to Italy. There are also brief references, which are plot-led, in:

Place	Book
Rome	*New CS*
Lake Maggiore	*Genius*
Bordighera	*Trials*

GUERNSEY

There are references to several places in *Exile* but there are no detailed descriptions. The following are mentioned: Torteval (Russells' house), St Pierre du Bois (Jo and Jack's house), Jerbourg (location of School and San), Vazon Bay, Cobo Bay, Pleinmont, and Rocquaine Bay (plane crash).

Although the beginning of *Goes to It* is set on Guernsey, there are no place references.

Apart from *Gerry Goes to School* and *A Head Girl's Difficulties*, all the books in the La Rochelle series have many references, with descriptions, to St. Peter Port (Peterport), Pleinmont, Rocquaine Bay, Petit Bot and Lihou Island. The Guille-Allès Library in St. Peter Port is mentioned several times. Although not technically within the scope of this article, these descriptions contribute much to the atmosphere of the island setting. Both Sark and Alderney are mentioned in *Heather Leaves School* and Sark again in *Janie of La Rochelle*.

ENGLAND & WALES

After the Chalet School's move to the fictional location of Howells Village, there are fewer descriptions of real places. Plas Howell is described variously as 'on the borders of Wales' by Ernest Howell in Chapter I of *Goes to It* and, in Chapter V, as 'in Armishire, close to the borders of South Wales'. The fictional town of Armiford is however closely based on Hereford.

At the time that EBD was writing, most Acts of Parliament listed Monmouthshire as part of England. In the rare event that an Act of Parliament was restricted to Wales, Monmouthshire was usually included, in the format 'Wales and Monmouthshire'. Although EBD seems to have considered the school to be based in England, many of the Howell family have Welsh first names and Gwensi speaks Welsh. The second location, the fictional St. Briavel's, is definitely in Wales.

Understandably there are no descriptions of excursions while the school is at Plas Howell as most books are set during the war years when there was fuel rationing and the possibility of air raids. Only in *Mystery*, first published in 1947, is there a mention (but no description) of a trip to Malvern and in *Rosalie*, published in 1951, there are mentions of a planned trip to Tintern Abbey, cancelled because of rain, and of a visit to the Memorial Theatre in Stratford (-upon-Avon). There is also a retrospective mention in *Wrong* of an expedition to Oxford having taken place two years previously.

After the move to St Briavel's detailed descriptions can be found in:

Area/town	***Book***	**Chapter**
Bournville (Cadbury's)	*Changes*	XII
Pembroke, Bosherston Lily Ponds	*Carola*	XIII

Bosherston Lily Ponds

TRIPS AND EXCURSIONS

SWITZERLAND
After the school's return to the Alps, to the fictional locations of Welsen and the Görnetz Platz, there are four main areas which are used in the same way as Innsbruck was in the early books.

Interlaken, Lakes Brienz and Thun, other towns round the lakes
This area is used for shopping, swimming and boating, posting urgent letters, concerts, sorting out book orders, getting 'fresh supplies', days out including for those off-duty staff, the dentist, stopping off for breakfast on the way back from Berne, interviewing new parents, the hairdresser, ordering ice cream and even visiting the casino (one of the San doctors).

There are brief references without descriptions in:
CS Oberland
Barbara
Kenya
Mary-Lou
Problem
New Mistress
Coming of Age
Excitements
Richenda
Theodora
Trick
Feud
Triplets
Reunion
Redheads
Adrienne
Challenge
Two Sams
Althea

Mountains above Interlaken

More detailed descriptions can be found in:
Barbara	Chapter VIII (description)
Kenya	Chapter XII (plot-led)
Coming of Age	Chapter VIII (mostly plot-led)
Jane	Chapter VII (mostly plot-led)

Bern(e)
Despite being about 70 kms away, with a probable travelling time of about an hour and a half, Bern(e) is used almost as often as the Interlaken area as a town for visits to the dentist and oculist, shopping, ordering supplies, 'attending to business'—and it is even the place of residence of the violin teacher. It is also used as a refreshment stop on longer journeys.

There are brief references without descriptions in:
Kenya	*Trick*
Problem	*Feud*
New Mistress	*Reunion*
Excitements	*Jane*
Coming of Age	*Redheads*
Richenda	*Adrienne*
Ruey	*Summer Term*

More detailed descriptions can be found in:
Barbara   Chapter XIV (description)
Triplets   Chapter XVII (mostly plot-led)

Basel/Basle
Approximately 160 kms away, with a probable travelling time in the 1950s of over 2½ hours from the Görnetz Platz, Basel is mentioned for two main reasons. Firstly, it is the home of Frieda von Ahlen, who not only puts up Joey (and family), Hilda and Rosalie but who also offers hospitality to Beth and Barbara Chester as well as helping Nancy Wilmot with the runaway Joan Baker. Secondly, its geographical position means that it is referred to in many journeys, including some in the Tyrol years. Interestingly, Nancy Wilmot and Kathie Ferrars attend university lectures there.

There are brief references without descriptions in:

School at
Head Girl
Joey Goes
Barbara
Genius
Coming of Age
Richenda
Ruey
Feud
Triplets
Adrienne

A more detailed description can be found in *Problem* in Chapters XVI & XVII.

Lake Geneva/Lac Léman area
This area is one of the favoured ones for excursions and half terms. It is also the area where people meet up with friends and which they visit with other family members. In addition, Montreux is home to the Embury family and second home to many of the Maynards.

There are brief references without descriptions in:

Kenya
Genius
Problem
Richenda
Trials
Trick
Triplets
Reunion
Redheads
Adrienne
Challenge
Two Sams
Althea
Prefects

Lake Geneva

More detailed descriptions can be found in:
Genius   Chapter XI, XII and XIII (good description, plus this is where the reader meets Winnie Embury)
Future   Chapter III (letter from Mélanie Lucas)
Triplets   Chapter XI & XII (description and plot)

Other places visited and described:

Area/town	Book	Chapter
Fribourg	*Kenya*	VII (letter from Jo Scott)
Luzern/Lucerne	*Does It Again*	IX, X
Neuchâtel/Neuchatel	*Feud*	XI
St Moritz	*Trials*	IX (+X–XII plot-led)
Schaffhausen/Falls of Rhine	*Mary-Lou*	X
	Head Girl	IV (Significant to plot but not actually a school trip)
	Barbara	(Mentioned as a potential destination for a trip)
Solothurn	*Excitements*	XIII, XIV
Stansta(a)d, Stanserhorn	*Two Sams*	X
Valais (canton of)	*Richenda*	XV
Wengernalb/Trümmelbach Falls	*Oberland*	VII
Zermatt	*Theodora*	XVI (+XVII, XIII mostly plot-led)
Zug	*Althea*	XVII–XIX
Zürich/Zurich	*Mary-Lou*	IX

Other places mentioned, sometimes as half-term destinations, with no descriptions: Adelboden (*Two Sams*), Arosa (*Jane*), Davos (*Genius*), Grindelwald & the Tschuggen (*Barbara*, *Kenya*, *Two Sams*), Lake Constance (*Genius*), Lauterbrunnen (*Barbara*), Morat/Murten (*Kenya*, *Excitements*), Reidenbach (*Genius*), Sarnen (*Feud*, *Althea*), Ticino (*Richenda*) and Weissenstein Wall (*Excitements*).

Charmian Bilger

Signa's walkway

SACKETT, LYDIA: Lydia is in Upper IVB in *Changes* when the Maynard triplets return to the Chalet School and Len joins the same form. Lydia and Heather Clayton are young for the form as they will only be twelve in the middle of May (p78).

St AMANT, GHISELAINE: Ghiselaine is a new girl at the Chalet School from Brussels in *Shocks* (p75). She is in the Lower Fourth with Mary-Lou Trelawney. She is a shy, quiet little girl, with silky black hair worn in a thick tail down her back and she has enormous dark eyes that all too soon swim with tears, although her new friends are doing their best to train her out of 'being a wet sponge'. She has spent all her life in an *appartement* in Brussels and knows nothing about gardening. Ghiselaine is in the Lower Fourth's gardening class when Peggy Burnett disappears down a disused well (p123/130). Ghiselaine, a little Belgian girl, flies to France with the French girls and Mlle de Lachenais at half term (p171).

Ste BARBE, ANGÉLIQUE: Angélique is in the Lower Fourth in *Challenge* and is thrilled when Jocelyn Marvell has the idea of annoying Upper IVA by moving their possessions around (p120). Carlotta von Eschenau receives a food parcel from home in *Prefects* and decides to have a midnight feast with some of her friends, including Angélique and Jocelyn. Angélique is Swiss. She is in the Marguerite dormitory with Barbara Craven and Anna Engels, another Swiss girl (p80/82).

St DENIS, LÉONIE: Léonie is French and in Inter V in *Adrienne* when they put on tableaux for their Saturday evening entertainment (p160).

St GEORGES, GHISELAINE: Ghiselaine and her twin sister Lesceline start at the Welsen Branch in the Oberland when it opens in *CS Oberland*. They were previously at Notre Dame Convent in Paris with Gabrielle Fournet. Ghiselaine is named after her grandmother and they come from Lisieux (p36/37/38). The twins, who have taken ballet lessons, are a quiet, rather demure pair, very pretty in their dark Latin way and so exactly alike that the other girls are often at a loss to know them apart. They arrange a ballet for the end-of-term pantomime, *The Sleeping Beauty*. Ghiselaine and her twin have plenty of mischief hidden under their quiet exteriors (p181/182/186). Ghiselaine and Lesceline are still at Welsen in *Does It Again* and arrange the ballet for the *Willow Pattern Story* (p191).

St GEORGES, LESCELINE THÉRÈSE: Lesceline and her twin sister Ghiselaine go to the Welsen Branch of the Chalet School when it opens in *CS Oberland*. They were previously at Notre Dame Convent in Paris with Gabrielle Fournet. Lesceline is named after the Comtesse de Lesceline, cousin to William the Conqueror, and they come from Lisieux (p36/37/38). The twins are a quiet, rather demure pair, very pretty in their dark Latin way and so exactly alike that the other girls are often at a loss to know them apart. They have taken ballet lessons and arrange a ballet for the end-of-term pantomime, *The Sleeping Beauty*. Lesceline and her twin have plenty of mischief hidden under their quiet exteriors (p181/182/186). Lesceline and Ghiselaine are still at Welsen in *Does It Again* and arrange the ballet for the *Willow Pattern Story* (p191).

St LAURENT (LAURENT), EMILIE (EMELIE): Emilie is in Upper IVB with Erica Standish in *Summer Term*. Emilie Laurent and Barbara Holmes are described as shining lights where maths is concerned (p56/100; p51 for form). Emilie Laurent, who is French, and her cousin Thérèse Parrais bump into Frau Mieders when she is carrying a bucket of buttermilk, and Emilie has to change as her frock is covered in buttermilk. Emilie is going out on Saturday with her newly married sister Hélène and her husband Georges to visit a cousin staying in Montreux (p133/134/135/144). Miss Annersley later gives Emilie's surname as St Laurent (p143). Erica introduces Althea Glenyon to Emilie St Laurent in *Althea*. Emilie lives on the Görnetz Platz at present (p39). Emelie St Laurent is a Senior Middle in *Prefects* when she has an argument with Erica Standish (p140).

(St LAURENT), HÉLÈNE: Emilie is due to go out on Saturday with Hélène, her newly married elder sister, and her husband Georges to visit a cousin staying in Montreux in *Summer Term* (p134/135).

St MICHEL, AMANDINE: Amandine is a new girl in VA in *Richenda*. She is a slightly built girl with smooth black hair and sparkling black eyes (p63).

SALLY: Sally, Alice, Simmonds, Louie, Nancy and Tom are servants at the Raphaels' home, The Towers, in *Heather*. They help to search for Hazel and Honey Raphael when they are missing in the Monk's Passage (p140).

SALNIO, BARONESS: Baroness Salnio is a lady-in-waiting in *Princess* (p26).

SAMANTHA: We learn in *Two Sams* that Samantha van der Byl's great-grandmother Samantha was a quiet, biddable girl and had a younger twin sister named Samaris (p207).

SAMARIS: We learn in *Two Sams* that Samaris Davies's great-grandmother Samaris was the younger twin of Samantha van der Byl's great-grandmother Samantha. Samaris's elopement with a young Englishman at the age of seventeen led to her estrangement from her family (p207).

SAMBEAU, CORINNE: French Corinne is in Lower IIIA with Jack Lambert in *Leader* (p66; p16 for form). Corinne is in Lower IVB and in the Violet dormitory with Jack and Barbara Hewlett in *Jane* (p9).

SANCIA: Sancia appears to be a pupil in the Fourth form with Jane Carew and Jack Lambert in *Jane* (p207).

SANDERS, CAROLINE: Caroline is in Upper IVB in *Barbara* with Barbara Chester and Vi Lucy (109; p107 for form). When Caroline puts her library book in her shoe locker and it is found by Matron, she accuses Barbara Chester of sneaking (p119/128). Caroline is described as a pleasant girl, although not particularly clever, and she later admits that she has made a mistake about Barbara (p130/134). Caroline is in Upper IVB in *Does It Again* (p25). She is still in Upper IVB in *Kenya* and needs a lot of help with her French (p61). Caroline is one of the older pupils in Inter V in *Excitements*, being well over sixteen (p15).

SANDERSON, MISS: Miss Sanderson and Lady Carew are passengers in a car that is involved in an accident in *Jane*. Miss Sanderson breaks her collar bone and is badly shocked (p175).

SANDON, MR: Mr Sandon, the curate at the parish church in Howells village, and Father Antony, from the big Benedictine monastery nine miles away, visit the Chalet School in *Tom*. They are great friends as they were at Oxford together (p72/73).

SANDYS, JOAN: Joan is a short, plump girl in St Scholastika's House who knows nothing about rowing when the boats are handed over to the School in *Island* (p149). Joan is a plump, capable-looking girl in *Peggy* and games are her highlight. She is the best all-rounder the School has and is even good at rowing, having only started the previous term (p49). Joan was a Junior Prefect the previous year and she becomes Games Prefect (p54/58/73). Joan is Games Prefect in *Carola* but is unable to organise practices because of the bad weather (p131/132). It is mentioned in *Wrong* that Joan is going to the new branch of the Chalet School in Switzerland next term. She is not at Guide Camp at Kittiwake Cove because she is in the Second School Guide Company (p31/129/140). Joan is still the Games Prefect, prefers playing cricket to tennis and is in the First Eleven (p144/145/146). Joan has left school in *Shocks* (p52). Former Games Prefect Joan is a

plump, capable-looking person who has short, smooth brown hair in *CS Oberland* (p41/86). In *New Mistress* it is mentioned that Mollie Carew and Joan Sandys were in the year ahead of Kathie Ferrars and Nell Randolph at Oxford (p15).

SARAZIN, JEANNE: Jeanne is in Upper IVB in *Summer Term* when they set up a bookstall for the Kate Greenaway Sale of Work (p156; p154 for form). Jeanne is still at the Chalet School in *Challenge* and speaks in quick, idiomatic French (p31).

SARTORIUS, HERR: The Maynards go down to Innsbruck in 'Minnie' in *Future* so that Margot can visit Herr Sartorius, their dentist (p165).

SARTOU (SARTORI), ANGÈLE (ANGELA): Angèle Sartou comes from the South of France and is in Lower IIIA with Jack Lambert in *Leader* (p44; p16 for form). Her name is later given as Angela Sartori. She has fair, fluffy hair (p179/180). Angèle Sartou is in IVA in *Redheads* and visits Herr von Francius, the School dentist, in Berne (p78/79).

SATSON, CATRIONA: see WATSON, CATRIONA

SAUMAREZ, NICOLE de: Nicole is one of the Middles involved in a Dramatic Society on St Clare's roof at night led by Elizabeth Arnett and Betty Wynne-Davies in *New CS* (p218/219). The Chalet School opens at Sarres in Guernsey in *Exile* and Nicole is in the Fourth form. She takes part in Miss Everett's gardening lesson (p218). Nicole and Biddy O'Ryan join the Seniors on an excursion to Pleinmont and we learn that Nicole is from Jersey. The girls witness a German aeroplane crashing (p290/292/294). Nicole is in a dormitory with Beth Chester when the Chalet School moves to Plas Howell near Armiford in *Goes to It*. Nicole is in the Fourth form with Elizabeth Arnett and Betty and is the oldest pupil at newly fifteen (p97/163/167). Nicole has passed her public exams and has obtained a distinction in French in *Highland Twins* (p9). She comes from Guernsey, is the Second Prefect and is a leading member of the Sixth form. Her special friend is Mary Shand (p82/99/127). Nicole is still at school and a prefect in *Gay* and has been staying with Enid Sothern (p43). Nicole de Saumarez (maybe a different girl of the same name?) is about thirteen in *Rosalie* and in the Upper Third with Bride Bettany and her friends. She is described as slender and very dark (p117).

SAUNDERS: Saunders is a servant at Pretty Maids in 'Joey's Convict' in *2nd* (p74).

SAUNDERS, DOROTHY: Dorothy is a pupil at Braemar House in *Monica* and is good-natured, but very untidy. Dorothy's father is dead and she lives in a small house outside Medbury (p23/29).

SAUSSURE, YOLANDE de: Ten-year-old Yolande is in the Lower Third and involved in a treasure hunt which the Chalet School mistresses organise for the half-term holiday in *Adrienne* (p93).

SAXON, LADY: Lady Saxon of Saxonhold has been dead for two or three years in *Heather* (p187).

SAXON, ALURED (ALLY): Alured Saxon of Saxonhold meets Janie Temple and Pauline Ozanne on a train during the Christmas holidays in *Heather*. The train stops because of an accident and he gives the two girls a lift to meet up with Heather Raphael and her mother. He has been in Switzerland for his health and is returning home, as there is no cure for him. Alured is a tall, fair young man with gaunt cheeks and merry eyes and Mr Raphael is his godfather (p181/182). Heather calls him 'Ally' when she invites him to come over and see them (p183). Alured, Janie, Heather and Cressida Shakespeare help fight thieves who break into The Towers. Unfortunately Alured has a terrible coughing fit which results in a haemorrhage and he dies (p230/234/237). We learn in *Janie* of that Alured left his Saxonhurst estate to Heather Raphael (p13).

SAXON, ROSWITHA: Roswitha is first mentioned in *Gay*, but is apparently not a new girl since she is not mentioned as attending Joey's party (p79). Roswitha is in the Lower Fourth with Jacynth Hardy and has very fair colouring. She is not clever and hates Latin with all her heart (p114).

SCHEITZER, OTTO: After escaping through a tunnel from Spärtz in *Exile*, Joey takes little Daisy Venables to Otto, one of the mountain herdsmen, to escort home to Die Rosen (p129).

SCHENKE, HERR and FRAU: Herr Schenke owns a Gasthaus at Geisalm and is a little dark man, with bright, quick-glancing eyes, who speaks the broadest patois. Herr Schenke and his wife help the schoolgirls when the Chalet School Seniors and Middles and some of the Saints encounter a fault on the path in *Rivals*. The Schenkes provide them with food before the girls start the long trek home over the pass, escorted by Mlle Lepâttre and Miss Wilson (p97/99).

SCHIEDMANN, DR: Doctor Schiedmann of Wien comes to the Sonnalpe in *And Jo* to discuss a new treatment with the Sanatorium doctors. Whilst he is there he examines Robin Humphries and finds that though she is very delicate, she does not have TB (p88/135).

SCHMALTZ, BETTE: Bette is Head of one of the top forms of the Middle School in *Jo Returns* (p164).

SCHMIDT, FRAU: Frau Schmidt lives in Mechthau and gives the girls hot milk and slices of black bread thickly spread with sweet butter in *Exploits* (p112/113).

SCHMIDT, FRÄULEIN: Fräulein Schmidt, a pleasant middle-aged person who can speak English, works in the shop at the Post hotel in *Future* (p115).

SCHMIDT, HERR (i): Herr Schmidt is the Tyrolean proprietor of the Seehaus hotel in *New CS* (p54).

SCHMIDT, HERR (ii): Herr Schmidt is the driver of the ambulance that nearly runs over Ruey, Con, Margot and Francie when they are standing arguing in the middle of the road and do not hear the ambulance hooting as it approaches a corner in *Ruey* (p191).

SCHMIDT, ALOÏS: Aloïs plays the part of St Andrew in the Passion Play in *And Jo* (p172).

SCHMIDT, DOROTA ('CHUDLEIGH' DOROTA): 'Merrill Chudleigh's' mother Dorota, née Schmidt, is mentioned in *Chudleigh Hold* (p14). She may be an invention by 'Merrill'.

SCHMIDT, MARIE: Marie, the aunt of the impostor 'Merrill Chudleigh' and the sister of 'Merrill's' mother, is mentioned in *Chudleigh Hold* (p13). She may well have been invented by 'Merrill'.

SCHNEIDER, HERR: Herr Schneider is a carpenter who is asked to mend some broken chairs after Elsie Carr and Maria Marani's misadventure in *And Jo* (p142).

SCHULZ, HERR: Herr Schulz keeps pigs in Zermatt in *Theodora* (p185).

SCHULZ, HANSI: Hansi helps his father with the pigs in *Theodora* (p185).

SCHUMACHER, FRAU: A strange woman shows a peculiar interest in Cecil Maynard in *Triplets* and subsequently kidnaps her. Len, Con and Margot go the rescue (p187/200). Believing Cecil to be her own daughter, the lady attacks Len, but Dr Jack and Gaudenz arrive in time to restrain her (p212/214). Joey explains that the lady, Frau Schumacher, is a widow whose daughter Cecilie died of polio aged three (p217).

SCHUMACHER, CECILIE: We learn in *Triplets* that Cecilie died of polio when she was three years old and her mother kidnaps Cecil Maynard because she looks like her dead daughter (p212/217).

SCHWARZ, EITEL: Eitel is a simple, gangling lad of sixteen who does odd jobs at the Sanatorium and causes a fire in *Excitements* (p139).

SCOTT, DOLLY: Dolly is a St John's Ambulance worker 'from "canny Soo' Shields"' who is on the same train as the McDonald sisters in *Highland Twins* (p29).

SCOTT, JANET: Janet is in the Fifth form with Daisy, Beth and Gwensi in *Gay* and displays Scots common sense (p92 for form; p94/100). She is a quiet clever-looking girl from Edinburgh and is a prefect in *Three Go*. As her father is a doctor the girls ask her opinion on Mollie Avery's health (p102/109). Janet is one of the tallest girls when the Chalet School moves to St Briavel's Island in *Island* (p25). She is in the Sixth form (p110—she is present at a science lesson with Miss Wilson; p106 for form) and is in St Scholastika's house, representing them when the boats are handed over (p148/149). Eighteen-year-old Janet sits for the Thérèse Lepâttre scholarship and intends to take up teaching. We are told that before coming to the Chalet School she was at school near Glasgow (p157/158/165). Janet wins the Senior pair-oars and teams up with Ursula Nicholls for a tub race in the School Regatta (p230/234).

SCOTT, JOSEPHINE MARY (JO): Jo starts at the Chalet School in *Kenya*. Her mother, Maisie Gomme, was a pupil at St Scholastika's and named Jo after Joey Bettany, whom she considers to be her daughter's unofficial godmother. Jo's parents have

a coffee farm in Kenya and their finances fluctuate but they have inherited her grandfather's money, which will pay for her education (p13/15/20). She becomes friendly with Josette Russell. Jo was previously at a boarding school in Nairobi from the age of seven (p25). She has thick dark-red plaits and grey-green eyes and was fourteen on 15th April (p26/27/29). She enjoys making clothes and doing embroidery and is in the Bluebell dormitory with Josette, Vi Lucy and Barbara Chester (p29/35). Jo is a Protestant and is placed in Upper IVB. She is adopted into the Gang and becomes firm friends with Josette Russell (p41/54/88). It is Jo's personality which has drawn her into the Gang (p132). The Scotts live near Nyeri in Kenya. Jo's parents are attacked and Joey Maynard hears on the radio that they have disappeared. As Jo's only relation is her mother's brother, who is at sea, Joey feels very responsible for the girl (p139/150/151). She tells Jo of the Mau-Mau attack on her parents. Maisie is found badly injured and Jo's father is eventually found in a pit not too badly wounded (p157/161/162). Jo goes on a moss picking expedition and saves Emerence Hope from falling down a precipice (p175/178). She becomes a full member of Mary-Lou's Gang (p189/190). At the end of term she is awarded the Margot Venables Prize for her bravery and her readiness to help at all times (p200). Jo's parents have moved to Switzerland in *Mary-Lou* and are living near Thun on the Thunersee as the Rösleinalp is too high up for Mrs Scott, whose heart is weak. Mrs Scott has a bad heart attack (p98/125). The Scotts are living in a chalet in a small village on the shores of Lake Lucerne in *Genius* (p101). Fifteen-year-old Jo is in Upper IVA and so still a Middle in *Problem* (p34/139). Jo is described as a bright-faced girl of fifteen in *New Mistress*. She is Inter V's Form Prefect and Kathie Ferrars is their Form Mistress (p56). Jo, Len and Con Maynard, Rosamund Lilley, Eve Hurrell and Pamela Jackson are the six people who represent most of the common sense of Inter V in *Excitements* (p21). Jo is still Inter V's Form Prefect in *Coming of Age* (p49; p44 for form). She wins the Senior sack race and is a finalist in an end-of-term blindfold race (p212/215). We learn in *Richenda* that Jo and Len Maynard were bracketed second in last term's exams and are safe for a remove. Jo has a thick pigtail of reddish hair and is the Pansy dormitory prefect. She is promoted to

VB (p25/45/61). Jo is VB's Form Prefect in *Trials* (p40). Jo and Con Maynard are becoming friends in *Theodora*. She invites Primrose Trevoase and Eve Hurrell to go home with her at half term. The Scotts are leaving Switzerland to try fruit and vegetable farming in Jersey (p111/148). Jo is VA's Form Prefect in *Ruey*. She is keen on hockey and has a chance of her First XI colours this term (p70/130). Jo is VA's Form Prefect in *Leader* (p41). She is still Form Prefect and hopes to go to horticultural college to learn to grow flowers in a big way in *Trick*. Jo helps Sue Mason, Rikki Fry, Carmela Walther and the Maynard triplets to clear up the Abendessen which has been ruined with pepper after a tennis match (p36/39/90). We are informed in *Reunion* that Jo was an excellent prefect (p57).

SCOTT, MAISIE: see GOMME, MAISIE

SCOTT, PAUL: Jo Scott's father Paul and his wife Maisie have a coffee farm in Kenya in *Kenya*. Their finances fluctuate but they inherit Jo's grandfather's money, which pays for their daughter's education at the Chalet School (p13/20). Maisie and Paul, who live near Nyeri (p139), are attacked by the Mau-Mau (p157) and Joey Maynard hears on the radio that they have disappeared (p151). Maisie is found badly injured and Paul is eventually found in a pit, not too badly wounded (p155/161/162). Paul plans to bring Maisie to Switzerland to convalesce and they will be moving to a chalet at the Rösleinalp in September (p163/190). The Scotts leave Kenya because of Maisie's poor health and in *Mary-Lou* they are living in Switzerland near Thun on the Thunersee, because Maisie's weak heart meant the Rösleinalp was unsuitable (p98). They are living in a chalet in a small village on the shores of Lake Lucerne in *Genius* and come to the School Sale (p101/196). The Scotts are leaving Switzerland to go to Jersey to try fruit and vegetable farming in *Theodora* (p148). Jo Scott says in *Trick* that if she has to give up her career plans to care for her mother, her father has promised to make it up to her somehow (p39).

SCUDAMORE, TOM: Gay Lambert's Uncle Tom is mentioned in *Lavender* (p148). Gay mentions in *Gay* that she and her twin brother Mike were five years old when they went to live with their Uncle Tom Scudamore in China (p134).

SEFTON, MR and MRS: We are informed in *Mary-Lou* that Jessica Wayne's mother is a great friend of Lucia Gordon (p39). She was nineteen when Jessica was born and was widowed when her daughter was two years old. Two years before Jessica began at the Chalet School, Mrs Wayne married Mr Sefton, a bank manager who has an invalid daughter, Rosamund (p40/133). They are mentioned in *Coming of Age* (p25/26).

SEFTON, ROSAMUND: Rosamund, Jessica Wayne's invalid stepsister, is mentioned in *Mary-Lou* and we are informed that she is a little younger than Jessica. Rosamund has something wrong with her spine and cannot walk (p40). Jessica hated fourteen-year-old Rosamund at first as her mother paid her a lot of attention, but Mary-Lou helps her to sort out her resentment (p133/134/135). Jessica is very worried about Rosamund's poor health in *Coming of Age* (p25/26). Rosamund's health is failing and she asks Jessica to come home quickly. Mary-Lou accompanies Jessica to Basle airport when Rosamund is dying at home. Rosamund sends Jessica off for her supper, feels sleepy and dies in her sleep (p198/200/203).

SÉGUINÉ, MADEMOISELLE de: Mlle de Séguiné is one of Princess Elisaveta's governesses in *Princess* and teaches her pupil French, literature and astronomy. She escorts Princess Elisaveta to the Chalet School (p11/15/71).

SEMERLING, MARTA: Marta sits next to Jane Carew in Upper IVB in *Jane*, and offers to share her textbooks until Jane is issued with some. Marta's father and brothers make woodcarvings for the Sale (p29/207).

SEMMERING, HERR and FRAU: Herr Semmering and his wife have a farm at the Baumersee in *Camp* and he and his men fish up the 'body' that Juliet catches in the lake. Frau Semmering is all agog to discuss the matter (p132/135/136). Herr Semmering is described as a big, fair man with a good-natured, stupid face (p137).

SEMPLE, LAILA: Laila is mentioned (p124) among the girls who transfer from the Tanswick Chalet School, where free discipline was practised, in *Bride*, and cause a lot of trouble to the staff (p114). She is placed in Lower VA with Diana Skelton and Sylvia Peacock and it is thought she may be cheating (p124; p115 for form).

SETON, VERONICA: Veronica is in the Second form at St Peter's School in *Gerry* and is chosen to be a delegates in the fags' strike (p186).

SEVERN, MARY: Mary is a pupil at Kingscote School in 'Woolly Bear' in *1st* (p99).

SEYMOUR, MR and MRS: Anne Seymour's father is the proprietor of three big hotels in England in *Exploits* (p57). Anne's mother is up at the Sonnalpe with her sister Lucia who is very ill in *New CS*. Mrs Seymour manages to come down for the end-of-term entertainment (p311).

SEYMOUR, ANNE: Anne is a pretty girl of nearly sixteen in the Fifth form with Margia Stevens in *Eustacia* (p76/160). Anne goes on the expedition to Fulpmes at the foot of the Stubai glacier at half term with Miss Wilson and Miss Stewart in charge. She ties her hair back in one long plait with a big black bow when the girls are tidying themselves (p170/185). Anne is a Catholic (p189). She volunteers to look after Robin Humphries for one day of the holiday, and is in charge of her when the rest of the party are delayed overnight on the mountain (p188/210/235). Anne is in the Fifth form in *And Jo* but shares the Middles' accident-prone prep as an electric wire has fused in the Fifth's room. We are told that Anne is at the Chalet School because one of her family is in the Sanatorium (p60/77). The Chalet School goes to see the Passion Play at Oberammergau and on the day they arrive Elsie, Evadne, Cornelia, Maria and Ilonka decide to act out the story of Pocahontas and use Anne's oil paints to colour their faces. Anne wasn't using the paints that afternoon as she was sketching in pencil, producing the loveliest little things to show back at school (p184/185). Anne is in a team of girls practising for a boat race against St Scholastika's (p220). She goes to Guide Camp at the Baumersee in *Camp* and expects to be in the Sixth form next term (p48). Anne, whose great friend is Louise Redfield, is tall with dark eyes (p69/166/231). Anne and Louise are in the Sixth form in *Exploits* and we learn that Anne's father is the proprietor of three big hotels in England. Anne plays the piano and is clever at improvising (p48/57/194). She is described as a pretty English girl of seventeen who plays the accompaniment for dancing on the first evening of term in *Lintons* (p66). Anne is a pretty English girl of almost seventeen in *New House*. She is a sub-prefect and will probably be Games Prefect in the autumn term (p34). Anne considers that music is not her strong point, but drawing is. She is the sub-prefect of games and the Tennis Captain (p97/100). Anne offends Jo and is amazed when Jo is subsequently chilly towards her. Frieda suggests that Anne's behaviour was inappropriate from a sub-prefect to the Head Girl, but Anne is not prepared to apologise. The Seniors go up the

Bärenbad and Joey helps to rescue Anne when she falls down a slippery rock face (p249/256/257). In *Jo Returns* we are told that Anne ought to have succeeded Jo as Head Girl; however, she loses the post to Louise Redfield thanks to the escapade on the Bärenbad. Anne does leatherwork at Hobbies Club. She is a stern disciplinarian and rules with a rod of iron during working hours, though at other times she is pleasant enough and a popular person (p8/121/132). Seventeen-year-old Anne is described as slender and pretty in *New CS* (p30). She is ironing morse-flags for the end-of-term entertainment when her mother unexpectedly arrives from the Sonnalpe where her sister Lucia, Anne's youngest aunt, is very ill (p309/311). The hall catches fire because Anne leaves the iron on, but not too much damage is done (p312/316). This is her last term at the Chalet School (p318). The fire caused by her carelessness is recalled in *Exile* (p297). Anne is in the WRNS in *Goes to It* with Elsie Carr, Nancy Wilmot, Ida Reaveley and Irene Silksworth (p104). The plundering of her paintbox is recalled in *Lavender* (p207).

(SHAKESPEARE), GRANDMOTHER: The Shakespeares stay with their grandmother at Tynemouth during the summer holidays in *Heather* (p112).

SHAKESPEARE, MRS: We learn in *Heather* that Mrs Shakespeare died ten years ago when Pat was six months old. All four of her daughters are named after Shakespearean heroines (p102).

SHAKESPEARE, CLEOPATRA OPHELIA (PAT) (4): The Shakespeares' youngest daughter Pat and her sister Portia are friendly with Hazel and Honey Raphael and it is arranged in *Heather* that they will share a governess, Miss Christopher (p10). We learn that Mrs Shakespeare died ten years ago when Pat was six months old. Pat is a happy little ignoramus with short yellow curls, round blue eyes and a sweet nature. Miss Christopher starts a Guide Company in the village and the Raphaels and Shakespeares join (p102/104/162). We are told in *Janie of* that Pat attends the Sacré Coeur Convent School in France with Hazel, Honey, Hero and Portia (p30/175).

SHAKESPEARE, CRESSIDA IMOGEN (CRESSIE) (1): The Shakespeares' eldest daughter, fifteen-year-old Cressida, is described in *Heather* as a tall, pale girl with a thick brown pigtail that is always tidy and rather hard grey eyes. We learn that Mrs Shakespeare died ten years ago when Pat was six months old and Cressie nearly six and the older child is perilously near being a thorough little prig. The Shakespeare sisters share a governess with the Raphael girls (p102/103/104). Cressie is very domineering and tries to prevent Hero from telling the Raphaels where Hazel and Honey are when they are missing in the Monk's Passage (p142). Mr Shakespeare leaves his daughters with the Raphaels and goes to Switzerland after a bad attack of influenza. The Raphaels and Shakespeares join a Guide Company which Miss Christopher, their governess, starts in the village. Mrs Raphael's opinion of Cressie is that of a self-sufficient, domineering young person who needs discipline from a school and never owns she is wrong (p161/162/178). Janie Temple visits the Raphaels at Christmas and helps Cressida and Heather when thieves break into The Towers. Heather bangs her head and is unconscious for several days and Cressida breaks her collarbone (p228/234). We learn that Cressida and Heather will be going to school in Paris after the summer (p244/245). We are told in *Janie of* that Cressida, Heather and Pauline are leaving their convent school (p30).

SHAKESPEARE, HERO MIRANDA (2): Hero is the second Shakespeare daughter and she is a jolly tomboy in *Heather*. She has untidy curly red hair, round blue eyes and a rosy face (p102/103). Hero races round to The Towers to tell Miss Christopher where Hazel and Honey are when they go missing in the Monk's Passage (p141/142). Miss Christopher starts a Guide Company in the village and the Raphaels and Shakespeares join (p162). Hero goes to a French convent school with Hazel, Honey, Portia and Pat in *Janie of* (p30).

SHAKESPEARE, PAT: see SHAKESPEARE, CLEOPATRA

SHAKESPEARE, PORTIA VALERIA (3): Portia, the Shakespeares' third daughter, and her young sister Pat are friendly with Hazel and Honey Raphael in *Heather*. Portia Valeria and her sisters are going to share schooling with the Raphaels' governess, Miss Christopher (p10). Portia has thick, brown, wavy hair and hazel eyes. Although a delicate child, Portia has spirit and is the only daughter to have inherited their father's brains (p102/103/104). The Raphaels and Shakespeares join a Guide Company which Miss Christopher starts in the village (p162). Portia goes to a French convent school with Hazel, Honey, Hero and Pat in *Janie of* (p30).

SHAKESPEARE, REVD WILLIAM: Mr Shakespeare intends to find a new governess for his four daughters in *Heather* but Mrs Raphael suggests that Miss Christopher, her daughters' new governess, should instead teach them with the Raphael girls (p10). We learn that Mr Shakespeare had insisted on calling each of his four daughters after Shakespearean heroines and his late wife named their daughters Cressida, Hero, Portia and Cleopatra. Revd William Shakespeare is a dreamy local rector who leaves his elder daughter Cressida to look after her younger sisters (p102/103/152). After a bad attack of influenza his doctor orders him to Switzerland for the winter months, leaving his four daughters with the Raphaels. The Rector returns home in June, much stronger and with the fear of further trouble at an end (p161/162/244).

SHAND, MARY: Mary is an inmate of the Wheatfield dormitory when the ceiling comes down in *Jo Returns* but is not listed among the girls evacuated to Ste Thérèse for the night. She is described as a nervy child from Louisiana and squeaks with horror at prep one evening when Alixe von Elsen makes unearthly screeches with a balloon creature outside their window (p133/134/187). Mary looks after Dorothea Buck, a new English pupil, in 'Woollen Measles' in *3rd* (p147). She is in the Fourth form when the Chalet School opens in Guernsey in *Exile*. Mary is gardening when Elizabeth Arnett and Betty Wynne-Davies hide the tools. Some of the Fourth formers are involved in mixing black pepper with powdered charcoal in the science lab, causing a sneezing fit, and we learn that Mary did the deed but Elizabeth Arnett thought of it (p218/291). Mary is still in the Fourth form with Betty Wynne-Davies at Plas Howell near Armiford in *Goes to It*. Mary is now from South Carolina and has not been allowed to take the risk of crossing the Atlantic since the outbreak of war. Her elder sister teaches history in the High School at Union near their home (p160). Mary is Head Girl in *Highland Twins* and her best friend is Nicole de Saumarez (p127). She has fair hair that looks almost silver in the moonlight, and she and Robin Humphries chase after a school intruder, who ends up in the ornamental pool in the rose garden (p156/158/160). Mary is described in *Lavender* as a short, rather thick-set girl

with a short, wavy crop round a pleasant face. She appears now to be Head Librarian instead of Head Girl (p53).

SHAW, MARY: American Mary comes from Union, Massachusetts, and starts in the Third form at the Chalet School in *Exploits*. Mary is a brown-haired, brown-eyed elf with a demure air that they are to find is somewhat misleading (p17/18). Mary is the Third form ringleader in *Lintons* and is one of the girls involved in a midnight feast with Joyce Linton (p89). Mary, who is in the Green dormitory, is sick and complains of pain (p101/102). Mary is in the extra French classes given by Miss Norman when the girls misbehave. She and the other younger girls are twelve years old (p186/195/196). Cornelia rebukes Mary for using slang in *New House* (p114/117), and Mary, Kitty Burnett, Biddy O'Ryan, Emmie Linders, Enid Sothern, Irma Ancokzky and Alixe von Elsen consider this unreasonable and make a Baby Voodoo doll to dangle over Cornelia and Ilonka's window during the night, to frighten the two older girls (p125/128). Mary is in the Leafy dormitory when Biddy O'Ryan tells Irish Banshee stories which cause Alixe to walk in her sleep wailing (p189/198/199). Miss Denny asks Joey Bettany to take Mary, Joyce and Enid for German coaching in *Jo Returns*. Mary is famed for the fertility of her wits. She is at prep one evening when Alixe von Elsen makes unearthly screeches with a balloon creature outside the window (p105/186). She is mentioned in *New CS* as a 'bright star' for bad behaviour (p31). The girls visit Salzburg on a half-term trip and Mary is among the girls who have to spend a night in a bus which becomes marooned in a rising flood on the return journey (p285). Mary is in the Fourth form with Biddy O'Ryan when the Chalet School opens in Guernsey in *Exile*. Gardening lessons are introduced and Mary is in Miss Everett's gardening class when Fourth formers Elizabeth Arnett and Betty Wynne-Davies hide their tools. Mary knew a trick was to be played on Miss Everett but was not involved (p214/218/222). She moves to Plas Howell near Armiford in *Goes to It* and is still in the Fourth form (p123/124). Mary and Betty Wynne-Davies help to clear away the folding chairs in *Highland Twins* (p85). Slangy Mary is in the Lower Sixth in *Lavender* (p92). Mary is one of the examination people who become ill with German measles in *Gay* (p211).

SHEPPARD, GRIZEL: see COCHRANE, GRIZEL

SHEPPARD, DR NEIL ALBERT: Grizel Cochrane meets tall, dark Dr Neil Sheppard on a cargo boat on her way home from New Zealand in *Reunion* (p19/22). Dr Sheppard and his fellow traveller Ian Hamilton intend to pay a short visit to Dr Sheppard's sister Mrs Carrel and her two children at Cape Town before continuing their journey by air. They insist on taking Grizel around Cape Town and to meet Mrs Carrel (p23/26). Dr Sheppard is described as a tall, lean man in his early forties when he and Ian notice Grizel's sightseeing party on a train going up to Wahlstein. Neil, who has a thin, clever face, and Ian, his climbing companion, are fairly nearby and are able to assist with Grizel after an accident (p64/66/70/129). Neil is offered a post at the Swiss Sanatorium and we learn that his middle name is Albert (p143/155). We learn that Neil knew the youngest Macdonald brother, Kenneth, in New Zealand. Neil visits England and stays with Ian Hamilton in his rooms in Hampstead while he settles his affairs before returning to take up his position at the Görnetz Platz (p181/188). Neil returns to Switzerland and comes to Freudesheim to propose to Grizel. They are married from Carn Beg (p203/205). Grizel and Neil have a little boy in *Summer Term* and live in a flat in Neuchâtel. Neil helps to rescue Erica Standish when she falls into a crater (p173/174/195). Neil and Grizel have moved to Ste Cecilie in *Challenge* and are busy decorating as they have added some rooms to their new house. Young Nigel keeps Grizel busy (p115).

SHEPPARD, NIGEL: Grizel and Neil have a little boy and live in a flat in Neuchâtel in *Summer Term* (p173). Young Nigel keeps Grizel busy in *Challenge* (p115).

SIEBUR, JOHANNES: Johannes Siebur lives in Fulpmes and is the girls' rather reluctant mountain guide on an expedition in *Eustacia* (p187/210). He takes charge of arrangement in the mountain hut after Miss Wilson has met with an accident (p220/221). He is the father of three little daughters (p234).

SIGNA: see JOHANSEN, SIGNA

SILKSWORTH, IRENE: Irene and her sister Winnie are at St Scholastika's in *Rivals* (p118). Irene transfers to the Chalet School with Hilary Burn, Nancy Wilmot and Ida Reaveley in *New CS* and becomes the Staff Prefect (p80/103). Irene joins the Wrens in *Goes to It* along with Anne Seymour, Nancy Wilmot, Ida Reaveley and Elsie Carr (p104). Irene becomes a nurse and is the Matron at a big hospital in the north not far from Newcastle where Alix Rutherford is a patient in *Genius*. She is about four years older than her sister Winifred and appears to be about thirty-five. Nancy Wilmot mentions that Irene left school before she got there (p130/132). Irene visits Winnie at her home in Montreux in *Future*. Joey mentions that Irene is older than her and awfully keen on sports (p38/39).

SILKSWORTH, WINIFRED, 'WINNIE SILK' (EMBURY, WINNIE): Winifred and her sister Irene are pupils at St Scholastika's in *Rivals* (p118). Winnie is present at a friendly snow-fight in *Eustacia* (p153). She is St Scholastika's cox in the boat race in *And Jo* (p255). We may infer that Winifred transfers to the Chalet School in *New CS* when the rival school closes, since in *Exile*, where she is referred to as 'Winnie Silk', Enid is disappointed that she has not returned to the School (p201). Hilary Burn remembers Winnie Silk in *Island* as helping to win the Tennis Cup for St Scholastika's House. Unfortunately Hilary has lost touch with Winnie but remembers her as being a really nice girl, very pretty and charming but with no brains to speak of. We are informed that Winnie was a good enough tennis player to be professional (p203/204). Winifred is a large lady weighing approximately fourteen stone when she meets Nancy Wilmot on a boat going to Geneva in *Genius*. Nancy remembers that Winifred was a prefect when she herself was a Junior at St Scholastika's. Winifred and her husband have seven sons. The three eldest children, Rupert, Lionel and Maurice, are at school in England. Robin and Paul and the two youngest ones are at home in Montreux (p126/127/128). Winifred explains that Nina Rutherford's late mother was Dorothy Embury, a cousin of Winifred's husband Martin, and the Emburys want to help Nina, who has recently been orphaned. Winifred is about thirty-one or thirty-two years old, about the same age as Joey (p131/132). She has acute appendicitis in *Problem* and Joey stays at her home in Montreux to look after Winifred's younger children and also her own infants (p140). Michael Maynard is sent down to Montreux to stay with Winnie Embury as a weekly boarder in *New Mistress* and takes lessons with Robin and Paul's tutor (p33). Maria Marani, Joey's mother's help, becomes engaged to the Emburys' tutor, Walter McLaren, in *Coming of Age* and he intends to get a secretarial job in Switzerland when the youngest boys go to school in England. The Emburys find a small *appartement* in Montreux for Walter and Maria (p79/80). We are told in *Richenda* that Joey took over Winifred's house in Montreux for six weeks when the latter had appendicitis (p141). Matron instructs Hilda Annersley to visit Winifred at half term in *Trials* to have a thorough rest after the strain of the scarlet fever epidemic (p74). Winifred has Felix and Felicity to stay for a fortnight in *Theodora* to give Joey a break (p81). Stephen and Charles Maynard stay with the Emburys in *Joey and Co.* (p17). Mr and Mrs Embury attend the consecration of the School chapels in *Ruey* (p77). Mr Embury is the boss of Mélanie Lucas's Uncle Raymond in *Future*. The Emburys' seven sons are seventeen-year-old Rupert, sixteen-year-old Lionel, Maurice, Robin, Paul, Guy and seven-year-old Alan, who is now at school. Mélanie and her aunt cannot stay at the Emburys' home as Winnie's elder sister Irene, a Matron in a Newcastle hospital, is coming to stay (p27/28/38). Joey visits Winnie when she produces a baby daughter in *Feud* (p19). Con Maynard is sent to spend a quiet weekend with Winnie in *Triplets* to recover when she has been sleep-walking in reaction to the nervous strain of the blizzard (p66). Joey sends her four eldest boys, Stephen, Charles, Mike and Felix, along with Felicity and Cecil, to the Emburys' house when she has her house party in *Reunion*. Felicity's friend Lucy Peters goes to keep her company. We learn that the Embury baby's name is Angela (p38). The Maynard children delay their return home as they start chickenpox. Winnie now loathes being called 'Winnie' and insists on 'Winifred' (p144). The Emburys invite Nina Rutherford to stay with them in Montreux to convalesce in *Two Sams* (p121).

CHILDREN:
1) **RUPERT:** see EMBURY, RUPERT
2) **LIONEL:** see EMBURY, LIONEL
3) **MAURICE:** see EMBURY, MAURICE
4) **ROBIN:** see EMBURY, ROBIN
5) **PAUL:** see EMBURY, PAUL
6) **GUY:** see EMBURY, GUY
7) **ALAN:** see EMBURY, ALAN
8) **ANGELA:** see EMBURY, ANGELA

SIMMONDS: Simmonds is a parlour maid at the Raphaels' home, The Towers, in *Heather*. She helps to search for Hazel and Honey when the girls are missing in the Monk's Passage (p140/172).

SIMPSON, REVD and MRS: Mr Simpson was the locum at Polquenel when Mr Charteris, the vicar, was on a long, much-needed rest, before the start of *Three Go*. Mary-Lou Trelawney was invited to tea to play with his daughters Anne and Margaret and left the garden after a short time, refusing to return. Mrs Simpson scolded her daughters for patronising Mary-Lou and threatened them with a governess for the rest of the holiday (p19).

SIMPSON, MISS (i): Miss Simpson does a lot of church work at Shottery in *Janie of* (p112).

SIMPSON, MISS (ii): Miss Cundell's niece, Miss Simpson, teaches Junior mathematics and also some of the geography and botany at Braemar House in *Monica* (p28).

SIMPSON, ANNE: Thirteen-year-old Anne and her eight-year-old sister Margaret lived temporarily at the vicarage at Polquenel before the start of *Three Go*. Mary-Lou Trelawney was invited to tea to play with Anne and Margaret and left the garden after a short time, refusing to return, because the sisters were being gently patronising (p19).

SIMPSON, AUDREY: Audrey is in the Lower Third with Lavender Leigh during a French lesson with Mlle Berné in *Lavender* (p83; p81 for form). Audrey is a great friend of Barbara Smith (p174). Matey comes into the dormitory to rub Audrey's chest with camphor oil in *Tom* and skids on Barbara's toothpaste tube (p145). Audrey is in the Upper Third with Bride, Tom and Barbara and is 'a far from shining light' (p192/194). Audrey moves with the Chalet School to St Briavel's Island in *Island* and is one of St Scholastika's representatives when the boats are handed over. She strokes for St Scholastika's at the Regatta (p149/231). Audrey is in the Fifth form in *Peggy* and makes carpets for Tom Gay's dolls' house. She is a shy, quiet girl (p149/161/162). Audrey makes little carpets to sell separately at the Sale in *Carola*. She is a very quiet member of Lower VA (p110/210). Audrey is a sub-prefect and represents hockey on the games committee in *Shocks*. She also becomes the Stationery Prefect. Audrey plays centre-half in a practice hockey match (p73/84/102). Audrey is one of the prefects out for an early evening walk when Julie Lucy becomes stuck in mud due to the

old well being cleared (p155/159). Audrey attends Catholic Prayers, taken by Miss Derwent (p202). Audrey is still the Stationery Prefect in *Bride* (p47) and expects to have another year at school. She is a sub-prefect but is promoted to being a full prefect (p161/163/171). She is described as quiet and very reserved, and hates being the focus of all eyes when Diana Skelton apologises to her and Primrose Day publicly for rudeness (p206). Audrey has the part of Writing in the end-of-term Sale based on the *Crown of Success*, and is dressed as a nun (p282). Audrey and Beth Lane win the two life-saving classes at the Regatta in *Changes*. Audrey is easily the best in the School at life-saving and is complimented on her professional approach. Audrey manages to wet Miss Armitage when she falls into the sea during the greasy pole competition (p191/195).

SIMPSON, HILARY: Hilary is a Junior in IIA in *Two Sams* and plays the part of a rat in the St Mildred's pantomime *Dick Whittington* (p206).

SIMPSON, MARGARET: Eight-year-old Margaret and her thirteen-year-old sister Anne lived temporarily at the vicarage at Polquenel before the start of *Three Go*. Mary-Lou Trelawney was invited to tea to play with Anne and Margaret and left the garden after a short time, refusing to return, because the sisters were being gently patronising (p19).

SINCLAIR, DR: Dr Sinclair's daughter taught Gerry Challoner when she lived with her great aunts in *Gerry* (p41).

SINCLAIR, MISS: Dr Sinclair's daughter used to give Gerry daily lessons when she lived with her great aunts in *Gerry* (p41).

SINDON, MR: Mr Sindon is the business manager of a film crew filming *Life in the Austrian Tyrol* in *School at* (p115/116).

SKELTON DIANA: Diana has fairy-tale golden curls, big blue eyes and a pink-and-white face in *Bride* (p75/76). She has transferred from the Tanswick Chalet School. Her voice is rather high-pitched, with a distinctly cockney accent. She joins Betsy Lucy and Bride Bettany in Lower V<small>A</small> and does not attempt to work. Miss Slater mentions that Diana is so eaten up with vanity and self-conceit that she regards everyone else as being slightly less than the dust. Although her parents are hoping she will go on to the Welsen branch, there will not be a vacancy for Diana (p88/89/115). Her father is very rich and manufactures Skelton's glues. Diana appears to cheat with her French homework and is insolent in history lessons (p117/118). During tea one afternoon she is rude to Primrose Day and refuses to apologise. Sixteen-and-a-half-year-old Diana likes tennis and enjoys playing cards with Sarah Lomax, Sylvia Peacock and Pamela Morton. She is very keen on Bridge and Canasta (p166/178/189). She is also friendly with Iris Drew. She is made to apologise publicly to Primrose and Audrey Simpson for her rudeness (p193/197/205). Diana's boon companions are Iris and Sylvia (p203). Diana wrecks Bride Bettany's study and blackmails Marian Tovey into helping her (p246/260/262), but escapes expulsion and on the last night of term apologises to Bride (p272/296). We learn in *Changes* that during the Easter holidays Diana played cards for money and sold two of her mother's rings to pay the debt she owed. Her father decides that Diana will not be returning to school. We later learn that Diana loved tennis and had been a demon tennis player on her day (p27/28/100).

SKELTON, MR and MRS JOHN: Diana Skelton's father is very rich and manufactures Skelton's Glues in *Bride*. We are told that his father was foreman in a knacker's yard and John went into the business when he left school at thirteen. He was a hardworking, clever lad and when older attended nightschool, began to experiment and the result was Skelton's Glues. He is ambitious for his only child, whom his wife spoils, but he sometimes puts his foot down. Mr Skelton wants Diana to have the education he missed (p117/199). We learn in *Changes* that during the Easter holidays Diana played cards for money and sold two of her mother's rings to pay the debt she owed. Her father decides that Diana will not return to school (p27).

'SKINNY': 'Skinny' is mentioned in *Lintons*. She taught Joyce Linton at her High School (p24).

SLATER, MISS: Miss Slater is the Headmistress at Ripley Collegiate School for Girls where Heather Raphael is a pupil in *Heather*. Miss Slater alters things when she realises there are problems at the school, but too late to prevent Heather and her friends becoming slangy, rude and boisterous, with the result that their parents decide to remove them from Ripley (p10/16/17).

SLATER, PAM: We learn in *Highland Twins* that Miss Slater has taken Simone de Bersac's place as mathematics mistress at the Chalet School since baby Thérèse was born. Unfortunately Miss Slater breaks her leg in a bicycle accident, so Simone

fills in, taking baby Thérèse with her (p148). Miss Slater is back at school at the end of term to help at the Christmas Play but still uses a stick (p278). She returns to teaching in *Lavender* and is the Lower Third's Form Mistress. She has now been at the Chalet School for about two years (p69/81/218). Miss Slater is pleased because Lois Bennett should do well in her maths exams and because she herself has managed to write her reports without spoiling any (p274). Miss Slater is a maths mistress and acts as escort for girls coming from the north, including Gay and Jacynth, in *Gay* (p21/28). She doesn't like to be kept waiting. Miss Slater is about twenty-six when Miss Annersley, Miss Wilson, Mlle Lachenais and Miss Edwards are involved in a bus accident in Devon (p33). She is described as a tall young mistress with a smiling face (p41). Miss Slater temporarily becomes Head of the Junior School and Simone returns to teach Senior maths during the staff shortage. Miss Slater is the Lower Fourth's Form Mistress and is very nice and all the girls like her (p54/102/103). She is known for her tendency to hound the girls when she is on the warpath in *Mystery* (p66). Miss Slater takes the Upper Third for afternoon prep in *Tom* (p50; p113 for form). She meets some girls at Crewe station and takes them on a train to Armiford in *Rosalie*, knitting industriously in the corner of the compartment as she chats with the small girls (p111). She is the Senior maths mistress and Form Mistress for Upper IIIA in *Three Go* (p98/141). Miss Slater shares a car with Miss Linton and Miss Carey (p197). Later she appears to be replaced as Upper IIIA's form mistress by Miss Burnett (p203). Miss Slater has been with the Chalet School for around five years by the time they move to St Briavel's Island in *Island* (p42). She puts Polly and Lala Winterton through form tests in *Peggy* and is the Senior maths mistress (p52/121). Miss Slater, one of the mistresses meeting the girls from the train and putting them on coaches to school in *Carola*, tries to find Carola on a list of girls (p40). She is still teaching maths and speaks fluent French, but is not too happy when they have to speak in German, having learnt only enough to pass her exams (p132/133/135). She is not impressed with Biddy O'Ryan because she remembers her as a nuisance of a pupil (p136). Miss Slater is the Upper Fourth's Form Mistress in *Wrong* (p75/78). Miss Slater is the senior mistress at the station when they meet the girls in *Shocks* (p60). We are told in *Bride* that she is an excellent maths teacher but has a quick temper (p105). Miss Slater is the Upper Fourth's Form Mistress in *Changes* (p46/47). We learn her Christian name when Joey addresses her as Pam (p63). Miss Slater dislikes ten-and-a-half-year-old Margot Maynard, considering that she only works for her own ends. The mistress is one-track-minded and dislikes girls who show their distaste for her subject (p92). Miss Slater decides that she doesn't want to move to Switzerland and obtains a post as Head of the maths department at Selling Grammar School, not far from where she lives. Instead of being an assistant mistress she will be head of a department with six other mathematics staff. Miss Slater is thirty-five and has been with the Chalet School for ten years. After two or three years at Selling she plans to try for a headship (p122/124/125). The girls speculate about her successor in *Barbara*, and Maeve Bettany comments that Miss Slater hated anyone who was not wizard at maths. She was also very easily offended (p61/89/106/107). She is Head of the mathematical department of a very big day-school near London in *Excitements* (p189). Miss Slater, an old friend of Miss Derwent, is the Headmistress of a county high school in *Challenge* (p115).

SMITH (i): Smith is a crew member on board Nigel Willoughby's steam-yacht *Sea Dweller* when it sails to Bordeaux in a storm in *Scamps*. The yacht returns to Guernsey three days later and Sir Piers discovers that Nigel took Smith and Wilson with him, leaving Captain Polperran behind. Smith and Wilson are responsible for saving the ship (p169/170/172).

SMITH (ii): Smith owns horses at the 'Alfred's Jewel' in *Heather* (p180).

SMITH, MISS: Miss Smith comes out daily from Armiford to teach Junior mathematics in *Goes to It* while Mlle de Lachenais is in a nursing home recovering from a bad appendicitis operation and Simone Lecoutier has taken over some of her French classes (p223).

SMITH, BARBARA: Barbara is in the Lower Third with Bride Bettany in *Lavender* when Bride and Lavender have a fight. She is a great friend of Audrey Simpson (p75/174). Barbara is in the Upper Third in *Tom* and makes dolls' hats for the School Sale. She and Audrey are in the

same dormitory when Barbara drops her tube of toothpaste in the dormitory and Matey skids on it and sits down on the floor with a bang (p145; p144/113 for form). Thirteen-year-old Barbara is in the Upper Third with Bride, Tom and Elfie in *Rosalie* and is described as a solemn-faced person (p119). Barbara moves with the Chalet School to St Briavel's Island in *Island* and is in St Clare's House when the boats are handed over. She can row as she has lived by the sea all her life (p149). Barbara is good at games in *Peggy*, is in the Sixth form but not a prefect, and takes music (p49/85). Barbara goes to the Welsen Branch when it opens in *CS Oberland* and shares a room with Nita Eltringham, Judy Rose, Josephine Bellenger and Valerie Herriot (p39).

SMITH, CAROLINE: Caroline is probably in IIIA with Jack Lambert in *Leader* (p44/46).

SMITH, DEBORAH: Miss Smith is Upper IVB's Form Mistress in *Summer Term* (p53; p51 for form). She is a very pleasant person who has a fad for having her form sitting primly in their seats during register. She teaches Latin to IIIA and Nancy Wilmot refers to her as Deb at a staff meeting (p54/78/79). Kathy Ferrars addresses her as Deborah after Gretchen von Ahlen's yellow-wash accident (p131). Miss Smith is present at a staff meeting in *Challenge* (p115). She meets Samaris Davies at Interlaken in *Two Sams* and escorts her to the Chalet School for her first term there (p9).

SMITH, EILEEN: Eileen is a pretty, fair-haired child of eleven at Braemar House in *Monica* (p39).

SMITH, HILDA: Fifth-former Hilda forms a quartette with Jean Downes, Jane Thomas and Lorna Wills, and they make dolls' sheets for the School Sale in *Peggy* (p164).

SMITH, ROSEMARY: Rosemary is in the Wallflower dormitory when its occupants practise Jiu-jitsu after lights out in *Wrong*. Rosemary is the dormitory prefect (p102/112/114).

SMITHERS, VERA: Vera is at St Scholastika's School in *Rivals* and is friendly with Elaine Gilling, the Head Girl. Vera is an appalling snob and her people are wealthy, having made a fortune during the war (p118/137). Miss Browne finds a forbidden light novel in her desk and also some pieces of scrap paper on which Vera has been practising script so that she can write anonymous letters to Princess Elisaveta of Belsornia. Miss Browne expels her from St Scholastika's (p261/268).

SMITHSON, MISS: Polly Heriot's prim governess, Miss Smithson, is mentioned in *Jo Returns* (p97).

SMYTH, MR: Mr Smyth is a busy man of affairs who rarely troubles about his daughter Adelicia in *HG Difficulties*. He dismisses Adelicia's weak, silly governess and persuades Miss Phillips to take his daughter at St Peter's School (p166).

SMYTH, ADELICIA (BLOSSOM): Adelicia is a strange new girl in the Sixth form at St Peter's School in the spring term in *HG Difficulties*. She tells the other girls affectedly that she prefers to be known as Blossom. She is a tall, weedy girl with a quantity of mouse-coloured hair, elaborately waved and tied back with violent green ribbons. She has a thin, sallow face, light blue-grey eyes and a wide, ugly mouth (p146/147). Adelicia encourages the younger girls to be sentimental and influences the younger members of the school (p154/163/168). Although she is nearly eighteen she has never been to school before but has remained with her mother, a silly, affected woman who idolises her only child.

We learn that her father dismissed her weak, silly governess and persuaded Miss Phillips to take his daughter at St Peter's School (p166). The prefects seek to cure Adelicia and finally have the upper hand. Adelicia leaves at the end of the summer term as she is going to Paris to a finishing school (p242/252/320).

SMYTHE, MISS: Miss Smythe is Joyce Linton's Latin teacher at the High School in *Lintons* (p16).

SNEIDER, HERR: Herr Sneider delivers post at the Chalet School in *School at* (p267). He is the postman at the Tiernsee in *Princess* (p31). He delivers the post at the Sonnalpe twice a week in the winter in *Eustacia* (p21).

SNEIDER, OTTILLIE (OTILIE): Ottillie Sneider is in the Lower Fourth in *Challenge* and is thrilled when Jocelyn Marvell encourages her friends to annoy Upper IVA by moving their possessions around. Ottillie is a page in the house of the little rich girl in the Christmas Play. We learn that she is well meaning but never tactful (p120/191/196). Otillie passes on a garbled tale to her cousin Maria Uilseli about Len becoming covered in oil paint in *Althea* (p148). Carlotta von Eschenau and her friends, including among others Ottillie, Angélique Ste Barbe and Jocelyn Marvell, decide to have a midnight picnic when Carlotta receives a food parcel from home in *Prefects*. The girls are in different dormitories and Ottillie is in Edelweiss (p80/82).

SOAMES, MISS: Miss Soames teaches mathematics at St Scholastika's in *Rivals*. We are informed that she has been a Guide for years and would be delighted to start a Guide Company with Miss Elliott at the school but is unable to obtain permission from Miss Browne (p118/136). Miss Soames is present at a friendly snow-fight in *Eustacia* (p152). She helps to count the money at the end of the Fairy Tale Sale in *Lintons* (p302). She transfers to the Chalet School in *New CS* and replaces Miss Leslie, who left the previous term to get married (p19). Miss Soames is one of the senior mistresses present when Jem Russell informs the staff that the Chalet School will move up to the Sonnalpe for safety in *Exile* (p25).

SOAMES, CAROLINE (CAROL), 'CAR': Bride Bettany escorts her sister Maeve, Gay Spencer, Polly and Lala Winterton, and Polly's great friend Car Soames back to school in *Shocks*. Caroline has been staying with the Winterton girls (p38). Carol then seems to have become younger in *Changes* as she is friendly with the Dawbarn twins. She always does what the others want. She is not going to Switzerland, and Caroline's people have given no reason for declining to send her there (p169). Carol's father has a large farm and she is knowledgeable about the pigs in the orchard. Near the end of term Carol, Prudence and Priscilla Dawbarn, Primrose Trevoase and Peggy Harper decide to have a moonlight picnic in the Old Orchard where there are some pigs living temporarily. Unfortunately Prudence trips over one of the pigs and the girls are chased over the gate by the squealing animals (p171/175).

SOFIE, AUNT: Marie von Eschenau's Tante Sofie is mentioned in *Head Girl* (p178). She is also related to Paula von Rothenfels and may even be her mother, although this is not stated.

SOMERS, MARY: Mary is a great friend of Monica's at The Gables in *Monica* (p130).

SONNENSCHEIN, LINDA: Linda starts in the Second form at the Chalet School in *Exploits* with some other new girls, Edelgarde von Rothaus, Elsa Fischer and Joanna Linders (p19).

SOPHIE, SOEUR: Soeur Sophie is one of the nuns who help Joey and Erica Standish when their train crashes in *Summer Term* (p34).

SORABJI, MISS: Miss Sorabji is a speaker at a meeting in Malesford in *Monica* (p88).

SORCIÈRE BLANCHE, La: La Sorcière Blanche, or the White Witch, visits the de Garis family in *Maids* to cure their baby. She is a little old woman with a brown, wrinkled face and nutcracker jaws. Her hair is white as snow and so are her beetling eyebrows that overhang her eyes. Peter Chester is later asked by her granddaughter to visit the ninety-year-old professionally as she has sciatica (p83/223). La Sorcière Blanche starts a cliff fire which nearly engulfs the Athertons' holiday home (p271/277) and the old lady dies in the fire with Peter de Garis (p273/275). Janie refers to her adventure with the White Witch in *Scamps*, and is teased for believing in witches at her age (p156).

SOTHERN, MR: Grizel Cochrane's lawyer and trustee Mr Sothern is mentioned in *Carola* (p242/243).

SOTHERN, ENID: Enid, who is English, starts at the Chalet School in *Exploits*. Jolly-looking Enid is in the Fourth form with Violet Allison and Ruth Wynyard and is about the same age as twelve-year-old Alixe von Elsen. Joey informs her friends that Enid looks as full of mischief as a monkey and may be a handful (p16/20). On a scramble up a mountain, Enid and three other Middles venture over a fence in search of some juicy blackberries and Cornelia disappears down a crack into a cavern (p84/85). Enid is a pickle of about twelve years old and a devoted follower of new girl Joyce Linton when she is involved in a midnight feast in *Lintons*. She is in extra French classes given by Miss Norman (p88/186/195). After Cornelia has told Mary Shaw off for using slang in *New House*, Enid, Mary, Kitty Burnett, Biddy O'Ryan, Emmie Linders, Irma Ancokzky and Alixe von Elsen make a Baby Voodoo doll to dangle over Cornelia and Ilonka's window during the night to frighten them (p117/118/128). Miss Denny asks Joey to take Enid, Joyce Linton and Mary Shaw for German coaching in *Jo Returns* as she is already teaching Polly Heriot. Enid, an imp of twelve, is at prep one evening when Alixe von Elsen, supposed to be practising for her piano lesson, makes unearthly screeches with a balloon creature outside the window (p105/184). Fourteen-year-old Enid is in the Fifth form when the Chalet School opens in Guernsey in *Exile*. She has a tilted nose, curly hair and impish blue eyes and her boon companion is Dorothy Brentham (p198/200/206). Enid is much the youngest girl in the form at only just fourteen, but despite a harum-scarum personality, is exceedingly clever and even brilliant on occasion (p230). Enid is one of the Senior girls who visit Pleinmont and witness a German aeroplane crashing. The girls try to save the two men in it and Cornelia, Maria and Violet are the first on the scene, while Enid tries to put out the fire in the plane, in case there are papers that can be salvaged (p297). Enid is still in the Fifth form in *Goes to It*. She is fifteen, and has no need to work, since her father is well off, but wants to join the VAD when she is old enough (p108/110). Seventeen-year-old Enid is described as a merry-faced, blue-eyed person in *Highland Twins*. She has passed her public exams and is from Devon. Enid is a prefect and is friendly with Elizabeth Arnett (p62/65). She is also very friendly with Robin, Amy and Lorenz and is now stated to be from Cornwall (p187/265). Enid is a small, jolly-looking girl with twinkling blue eyes, peach-like face and a quick, decided manner in *Lavender* (p53/54). She is from Cornwall and is short and inclined to be plump (p96/97). Enid is friendly with Nicole de Saumarez in *Gay*. She is a prefect and her home is close to the Cornish border in Devonshire. Her game is really tennis and she is last man in the Cricket Eleven (p43/90).

SOULANGER, PÈRE: Père Soulanger is a French parish priest who helps Adrienne Desmoines after her father dies in *Adrienne* (p9/13).

SOUTHERN, ALTHEA: Althea is a Middle at St Peter's School when they rebel against the Upper School in *Gerry*. She is probably Philippa's youngest sister as she is in the Second form (p176). Althea, Allegra Atherton and Fiamma Vivalanti bring out a Middle and Junior School Gazette in *HG Difficulties*. Althea is in IIIA and Miss Lawrence is her form mistress (p74/256/259/260). In *Scamps* we learn that Althea has moved to outside Steyne Winting near the Willoughby family. Marjolaine has met her. Althea is now at a boarding school (p149).

SOUTHERN, PHILIPPA: Philippa is a prefect and the school librarian at St Peter's School in

Gerry. She is a tall, graceful girl of seventeen who comes from Dawley (p167). She learns that her family (ie her sisters Rosalie and Althea) are involved in a rebellion against the Upper School (p176).

SOUTHERN, ROSALIE: Rosalie and Althea are Philippa's younger sisters. Rosalie is a Middle at St Peter's School when they rebel against the Upper School in *Gerry* (p176). Rosalie is promoted from the Second form at the end of term (p240). Rosalie is mentioned in *HG Difficulties* when a prosaic note written by her is found amongst the other girls' sentimental letters (p226). Rosamund Atherton mentions in *Scamps* that Rosalie was chummy with her sister Allegra. The Southerns have moved to near Steyne Winting (p149).

SPENCE (SPENCER), CHARMIAN: Charmian Spence is a new girl in Inter V in *New Mistress* and her work is up to standard for this form (p80). She is friendly with Francie Wilford and Heather Clayton and is an imp of the first water and one of the naughtiest girls in the form in *Excitements*

(p20). Later in the term she turns the school lights off at the main switch to get out of sewing and causes chaos, particularly in Inter V (p104/105). Charmian Spencer is in VB, is not very strong and is caught in a storm when they are out on a ramble in *Richenda*. She is at the Chalet School because her eldest brother is at the Sanatorium for observation (p99; p97 for form; p118). Charmian Spencer goes on a ramble to Mahlhausen with Miss Ferrars in *Theodora*. On the half-term trip she suffers from mountain sickness at the Gornergrat and has to return to Zermatt (p48/179). EBD states in *N16* that Charmian Spence is now at St Mildred's (p68).

SPENCER, GAY: Gay is in the Wallflower dormitory with Maeve Bettany when its occupants practise Jiu-jitsu after lights out in *Wrong* (p111/112). Gay, who is Maeve's friend, has been visiting the Quadrant in *Shocks* because her younger brother John has had scarlet fever and infected her baby sister. She never managed to get home during the holidays as they were in quarantine for six weeks. It is implied that she is a lively girl, since Nancy Chester takes the trouble to pair her with someone who has 'more or less of a character' for the coach journey (p39/58).

SPENCER, JOHN: Gay Spencer's young brother John has scarlet fever in *Shocks* and then passes it on to their baby sister (p39).

SPENDER, MISS: Miss Spender is a French mistress at Audrey Everett's former school and is mentioned in *Trick* (p29).

SPIKE, MRS: Mrs Spike, Sir Ambrose's housekeeper, welcomes Jesanne Gellibrand to the Dragon House in *Lost Staircase*. She is described as a portly presence all in black with a friendly smile (p15/18).

STANDISH, DACIA-DENISE (née PARSON, DACIA-DENISE): We learn in *Summer Term* that Joey Bettany met Dacia-Denise Parson on her visit to India with Robin Humphries before the war. Dacia's father was District Commissioner for Coorg and she herself was the mother of Erica Standish. Dacia has recently died in Kashmir and left Erica to Jo's guardianship (p11/12/15).

STANDISH, ERIC: It is mentioned in *Summer Term* that Erica Standish's father Eric died in a flying accident when Erica was a baby (p10/13/15).

STANDISH, ERICA JANE: Joey Maynard meets Erica Standish in the middle of Oxford Street in London in *Summer Term*. Erica is a slender child of twelve or thirteen with big blue eyes. She has just arrived from Kashmir accompanied by her former governess, Miss Waller. We are told that her mother, Dacia-Denise Parson, was one of Joey's friends from her visit to India and she has recently died (p9/11). Joey learns that she is to be Erica's new guardian and that Miss Waller is getting married and returning to India with her new husband Mr Parker, a missionary (p12/14). Erica's father, Eric, died in a flying accident when Erica was a baby. Erica has straight waist-length fair hair held back from her face with an Alice-in-Wonderland band (p13/15). After Miss Waller's wedding Joey takes charge of Erica (p16/18). They are involved in a train accident on their journey from Paris to Switzerland and Erica finds a baby girl whose mother has been killed. She wants to adopt little Marie-Claire (p27/32/38). Erica is placed in Upper IVB and attends Catholic prayers (p43/48). She is in the Gentian dormitory and soon settles into school life. She makes friends with Astrid Anderssen, Agneta Gabrielli, Nita Tarengo, Clare Kynaston, Freda Kendal and Gretchen von Ahlen and her favourite lessons are literature, languages, art and history. She plays tennis and starts to weave a set of dinner mats for the new Mrs Parker. Erica enjoys needlework and, encouraged by Sara Carlyon, starts to dress a Breton fisher girl doll (p49/61/62). She does not get on well with Victoria Wood, resenting her airs of superiority (p84). Erica falls and breaks her ankle while out on a ramble and is sent to the accident ward in the Sanatorium as she is suffering from nerves after both her accidents (p103/105/106). When she recovers she is brought back to school and greeted by Joey and little Marie-Claire, who is now living at the Maynards' home (p113). Rita Quick receives a bottle of sweet pea scent, which is accidentally sprayed over Erica and she immediately becomes the target of a swarm of bees. Victoria Wood's father is an enthusiastic amateur beekeeper and Victoria holds Erica to keep her steady until Herr Antonelli arrives to remove the swarm, thus healing the rift between them (p120/121). After the School Sale has been abandoned because of a thunderbolt and landslide (p165/169), Erica and Victoria decide to toboggan down the main staircase on one of Karen's trays, resulting in Erica damaging her ankle once again (p175/181). The girls are sent off on expeditions

but Erica remains behind as she is supposed to be resting her ankle. She goes off to look at a crater in the cricket pitch and falls headlong into it, but fortunately is noticed by Joey (p186/187). Eugen Courvoisier, Reg Entwistle and Neil Sheppard rescue Erica just before the whole lot caves in (p192/195/196). Erica is in Upper IVA when Miss Ferrars collapses in their class with appendicitis while trying to sort out their missing possessions in *Challenge* (p96). Erica is in Upper IVA in *Two Sams* and has long fair hair like Alice in Wonderland (p49). She has had her fair hair cropped and cut with a deep fringe in *Althea*. She is nearly a year older than Althea Glenyon and is friendly with Clare Kynaston (p31/35/36). Erica visits Zurich and Zug on the half-term excursion (p156). The prefects meet in *Prefects* to discuss the end-of-term sports and also a Regatta that will be the first proper one since leaving St Briavel's Island. Erica, Jocelyn Marvell and Althea interrupt the meeting to propose that they have motor boat races at the Regatta (p15/16). A summary of *Summer Term* is given in *N13*. EBD mentions in *N16* that the Maynard wards comprise three Richardsons and one Standish, while Marie-Claire is legally adopted (p68). She says in *N20* that Joey and Jack Maynard include Erica, the Richardsons and Marie-Claire as their adoptees (p84).

STARKEN, LUISE von: Luise is a Middle in the Leafy dormitory in *New House*. Lieschen von Hoffman is the dormitory head and Luise is her second, although she is a harum-scarum and hand-in-glove with most of the wicked spirits (p129/189).

STEBBINGS, MR and MISS: Captain Temple's solicitor Mr Stebbings and his elderly spinster sister accompany Elizabeth Temple when she goes over to Guernsey to see Javotte about renting La Rochelle in *Maids* (p19/21/31).

STEELE, MR: The Chudleighs' family lawyer Mr Steele is mentioned in *Chudleigh Hold* (p15).

STEFAN, VATER: The Chalet School girls make gifts of toys and garments for the children of Vater Stefan's parish in Innsbruck in *Jo Returns* (p13). Joey Bettany receives £35 for the copyright when *Cecily Holds the Fort* is published and she decides to buy some presents and give the rest of the money to Vater Stefan to give to the poor children in Innsbruck (p285/287). Vater Stefan is a young man, dark and slight, with smooth black hair and a pair of magnificent grey eyes that glow as he thanks the girls for their gifts when he comes to their Christmas Play. He is a cultured Benedictine priest and highly educated (p290/291).

STEIDHAHL, GRETE: Herr Semmering's niece Grete ran away with a young French artist who dumped his lay figure into the lake. Joey Bettany, Juliet Carrick and Grizel Cochrane fish it up in *Camp* (p138/139/146).

STEIN, AUGUST: August Stein owns a horse and hay cart in *Rivals* and is able to take the weary girls home after their unexpected walk when the path breaks up (p99/113). He also comes to the rescue with his hay cart in *Exploits* (p116).

STEINACH, HERR: Herr Steinach is Len Maynard's violin teacher in *Richenda* (p54).

STEINBRÜCKE, HERR and FRAU: Gertrud's mother Frau Steinbrücke has long wanted to send her daughter to an English school in *School at*. She is a stout, cheery lady (p56/59). Gertrud's parents rent a chalet at the Tiernsee for the summer in *Princess* and are able to attend Madge and Jem's wedding (p284).

STEINBRÜCKE, unnamed BROTHER: Gertrud Steinbrücke has a brother who makes a set of bookshelves for the prefects' room in *School at* (p91).

STEINBRÜCKE, unnamed SISTER: Gertrud's unnamed little sister starts at the Chalet School in *Jo of* (p48).

STEINBRÜCKE, GERTRUD (RONSCHLAR, GERTRUD von): Gertrud, a Tyrolean, starts on the Chalet School's first day in *School at*. She is brown-haired, grey-eyed and very pretty and is about fourteen years old (p55/56/57). She is a Catholic and lives at Torteswald, a small village about twenty minutes' walk from Seespitz. Gertrud and her friend Bette Rincini are anxious to know all they can about English schools. They become sub-prefects (p58/62/77). Gertrud is the first prefect to realise that there is a problem with Juliet Carrick and Grizel Cochrane (p90). She produces a set of bookshelves that her brother has made for their new prefects' room (p91). She visits Spärtz weekly for her violin lesson (p247). Gertrud's unnamed little sister starts school in *Jo of* (p48). Gertrud contributes a word picture of the lake for the first *Chaletian* magazine (p145). She is one of the oldest members of the School in *Princess* and is in a dormitory with Grizel. Her parents rent a chalet at the Tiernsee for the summer and are able to be at Madge and Jem's wedding (p271/284). Gertrud goes for a walk with Grizel, Joey, Marie, Simone and Frieda, among others, in 'Joey Oar' in *1st* (p90). Gertrud becomes the Games Prefect when Grizel is promoted to Head Girl in *Head Girl* (p12/79). She is anxious to have things as English as possible and we are told that she passed her Guide First Class test during the previous term (p80/82). Gertrud leaves school after the summer term (p270). She is mentioned in *Eustacia* as a former pupil (p77). Robin Humphries' health gives cause for concern in *And Jo* and it is decided to open an annexe up at the Sonnalpe for the more delicate children. Juliet Carrick, Grizel Cochrane and Gertrud will be on the staff. Gertrud lives up at the Sonnalpe and looks very pretty and shy, as a young doctor who has recently come to join the Sanatorium spends a good deal of his spare time with her (p135/136/274). Joey mentions that Bette Rincini and Gertrud are too busy to join them on Madame's birthday expedition to the Zillerthal in *New House*. We learn that Gertrud is to be married in June to Dr von Ronschlar, the new doctor in the

X-ray room at the Sanatorium (p106/113). Her name is included in a list of former Head Girls in *Jo Returns* (p14). She is still living at the Sonnalpe in *Exile* (p42). Simone mentions in *Rescue* that Gertrud's daughter Gretel is four years younger than little Natalie Mensch and it is six years since any of them last saw Gertrud (p175). Gertrud lives in Salzburg in *Coming of Age* and Wanda has been in touch. Joey is looking forward to meeting Gertrud at their reunion, as they haven't met since the evacuation from the Sonnalpe (p81).
CHILDREN:
GRETEL: see RONSCHLAR, GRETEL von
STEINDAHL, FRAU and GREDEL: German Frau Steindahl and her eighteen-year-old niece Gredel are passengers in a lift at the Trümmelbach Falls in *Reunion*. Gredel is frightened and becomes hysterical when the lift stops part way and the lights go out, and Margot Maynard slaps her to stop the hysteria (p89/90/92).
STEINDAL, HERR and FRAU: Herr Steindal, a woodman, lives in a fairy-tale cottage near the Chalet School with his wife and two children in *Eustacia* (p112/113).
STEINDAL, GREDEL: Gredel is suffering from consumption and lives with her family in a house up the valley in *Eustacia* (p112/113/115).
STEINES, FRAU: We are told in *Jane* that Frau Steines used to have the chalet at Ste Cecilie where the Rosomon family are going to live (p101).
STEINMACH, FRAU: Len Maynard and Maeve Bettany deliver a knitted patchwork blanket to Frau Steinmach, a pensioner at the Görnetz Platz, in *Triplets* (p70/72).
STEINMANN, HERR: Herr Steinmann is a house agent in the firm of Steinmann Brüder in Innsbruck in *Future* (p211/212).
STEINMANN, FRAU: Frau Steinmann's brother in Canada became her heir when she died, and Mary-Lou Trelawney and Jocelyn Marvell shelter in her empty chalet in *Challenge* (p209).
STÉPHANIE: Sixteen-year-old Stéphanie starts at the Chalet School as a day boarder after Christmas in *Jo of*. She is a Senior and lives up the valley in a huge chalet just beyond the fencing. We learn that she has been at school in Vienna but her mother has been ill so Stéphanie returned home and is coming to the Chalet School for a year (p219). Stéphanie, Gisela, Bernhilda and Bette are invited to come over to the School when Wanda and Friedel come on a visit from Vienna in *Head Girl* (p288). Stéphanie and Carla live in the Tiern valley at the start of *Exile* (p58).
STEPHENS, IRIS: Iris is a new girl in the Sixth form at the Chalet School in *Goes to It*. She has probably been at Braemar House with Vicky McNab and Gwladys Evans (p127).
STEPHENS (STEVENS), IVY, 'STEVE': Miss Stephens is described in *Highland Twins* as 'another old friend', meaning she is among those who were already at the Chalet School in its Austrian days. She is Tawny Owl for the School's Brownie Pack when Emmie and Joanna Linders tell the School of their adventurous escape (p113). Her surname is Stevens in *Lavender*. She takes all Junior geography and is teaching physical geography to the Lower Third (p88). Miss Edwards and Miss Stevens—known to the girls as 'Steve' and normally sweet-tempered—are in charge of the Third forms on a winter's walk. They have difficulty rescuing Lavender Leigh when Joy Bird pushes her into a snowdrift (p174/175/179). Miss Stevens teaches geography to Jacynth Hardy's form (Lower Fourth, p102) in *Gay* (p180). Miss Stevens and Miss Phipps are the Heads of the Kindergarten in *Tom* (p199). Miss Stephens seems to be responsible for the Juniors and also teaches geography to the Sixth form in *Peggy* (p121/135). She takes dictation with the Fourth forms and punishes Sybil for calling Peggy names, condemning her to 'Miss Stephens' walks' (very prim and formal) instead of games. She also teaches the Fourths geography (p167/225). Miss Stephens is one of the mistresses who accompany the Junior Middles on a winter walk in *Carola* and she is Con Maynard's Form Mistress (p122/176). Miss Alton helps her to umpire an inter-school tennis match in *Wrong*, during which Blossom

Willoughby manages to get locked into the Art Annexe (p174). Miss Stephens is on escort duty in *Shocks* and still teaches geography (p60). Joey Maynard greets Ivy Stevens as an old friend in *Changes* when she returns from Canada. Jo seems to imply that Ivy has been absent from the Chalet School for some time (p66). Miss Stevens is at the English branch in *Kenya* (p77). Nancy Wilmot mentions a Miss Stevens in *Challenge* who apparently taught mathematics to Joey Bettany when she was at school (p114). (She probably means Kath Leslie, who became Mrs Stephenson!)

STEPHENSON, MISS: Miss Stephenson is the resident art mistress in *Bride* (p64).

STEPHENSON (STEVENS), MRS: see LESLIE, KATHERINE

STEPHENSON, MICHAEL: Mr Stephenson is married to Miss Leslie, a former Chalet School mistress in *Goes to It*, and they have twin sons (p104). We learn in *Three Go* that Doris Hill's Uncle Michael is married to Kath Leslie, a former Chalet School mistress (p235). Kit Leslie and her husband have five boys and are settled outside Sydney in *Island* (p42).

STEVENS, MISS: see STEPHENS (STEVENS), IVY and LESLIE, KATHERINE

STEVENS, AMY: Eight-year-old Amy and her older sister Margia start at the Chalet School in *School at*. Their father is Foreign Correspondent for a great London daily paper and is going to Bergen. Amy is dainty, fairylike and delicate. Her mother does not want to send the girls to a convent school (p65/66). Amy writes four lines entitled *A Rime* for the first *Châletian* magazine in *Jo of*. It is considered to be very good for an eight-year-old and Miss Maynard predicts that Amy will become a poetess (p145/146). Margia and Amy's father accompanies Grizel to London. Margia and Amy spend Christmas in Salzburg, where they have a magnificent time (p170/218). Amy, Robin Humphries and Simone Lecoutier fall into a muddy ditch during a walk after a flood (p312). Amy is ten years old in *Princess* (p103). It is mentioned in *Head Girl* that Amy is one of Robin's greatest friends (p45). She has resolved to be a writer and her bent is for verse. She has written some very pretty things already and we are told that she is a great favourite (p174/175). Amy is a Middle in *Rivals*, having become one the previous term. She is on an unexpected trek when the path breaks up (p47/102). She is in the Third form in *Eustacia* (p251). Amy is a small, fair girl who is friendly with Robin Humphries in *And Jo*. We are informed that she once stunned herself whilst tilting her chair and, since then, tilting is strictly forbidden (p31/57). She is going to the new Annexe when it opens the following term and Amy, Robin and Signa (probably Signa Johansen, although this is not explicitly stated) will be prefects there (p135/280). Amy is too young to go to Guide Camp in *Camp* (p47). She and her friends go down to the Chalet School for the last two weeks of term to participate in the Christmas Pageant in *Exploits* (p283). Amy is an old witch in Rapunzel's cottage at the Fairy Tale Bazaar in *Lintons* (p278/290). In *New House* it is hoped that Amy will return to the Chalet School proper in September (p98). Amy returns to the main School in *Jo Returns* and is in the Fifth form with Polly Heriot (p104; p93/113 for form). Fourteen-year-old Amy stays at school at half term and is dressed as a white butterfly at the sheets and pillowcase party (p229/233). She is mentioned in *New CS* as having once had a bad fall through tilting her chair (p135). Amy is back at the Annexe with Robin Humphries and Laurenz Maïco when the main School moves up to the Sonnalpe in *Exile*. We learn that Amy returned to the Annexe when she had a cold the previous winter (p44). Amy shares a small dormitory with Polly Heriot, Lorenz Maïco and Kitty Burnett when the Chalet School opens in Guernsey (p196). Amy is in the Fifth form with her friends Robin, Lorenz and Kitty and is fifteen (p207/208/209). Some of the Seniors visit Pleinmont and witness a German aeroplane crashing. They try to save the two men in it and Amy, Lorenz and Enid Sothern scoop up sand with their hands to fling on the flames (p297). Amy moves with the Chalet School to Plas Howell in *Goes to It* and is in the Fifth form. She is a year older than her form, having been held back due to continued attacks of cold. She mentions that she wants to teach (p108/109). She spends the first part of term off school with a cold in *Highland Twins*. She is still friendly with Robin, Lorenz and Enid Sothern and they are a most united quartette (p188). Amy is eighteen, nearly nineteen and described as a slender, delicate girl in *Lavender*. Her parents are living in a farmhouse near Armiford and she went home for Christmas although her father is now in Egypt. She is entered for Oxford in the coming October and hopes to teach when she finishes her degree (p93/94). Amy plays in a string trio with Myfanwy Tudor and Ernestine Benedict at the end-of-term concert in *Gay* (p238). We learn in *Coming of Age* that Amy has two daughters, Margaret and Celia (p105). The episode where she fell in the muddy ditch is recalled in *Reunion* (p98). She is mentioned in *N17* in a list of Old Girls who are now married (p71).

STEVENS, MR and MRS CHARLES: Mr Stevens is Foreign Correspondent to a great London daily paper and he and his wife are going to Bergen in *School at*. They have two daughters, Margia and Amy, who is delicate. They don't want to send them to a convent school and enrol the girls in the Chalet School (p65/66). Mr Stevens accompanies Grizel to London in *Jo of* (p170). We are reminded in *Princess* that Mr Stevens is Foreign Correspondent to one of the big London dailies, and travels a great deal in Europe (p103), and we learn in *Head Girl* that the family have spent more than one winter in Salzburg (p230). It is mentioned in *Rivals* that Charles Stevens is the author of *Glorious Prague* (p138). Mr and Mrs Stevens are present at the Christmas Pageant in *Exploits* (p289). Charles Stevens is again mentioned in *Lintons* as the author of *Glorious Prague* (p11). The Stevens family live in a farmhouse near Armiford in *Lavender*. Mr Stevens is now in Egypt (p93).

STEVENS, KATH: Joan Baker's pretty and empty-headed friend Kath Stevens is mentioned in *Problem* (p10/11).

STEVENS (STEVENSON), MARGIA: Eleven-year-old Margia starts at the Chalet School with her young sister Amy in *School at* as their parents are going to Bergen. Their father is Foreign Correspondent to a great London daily paper. Margia is described as a motherly person who adores her little sister Amy. She is intensely musical and means to be a pianist (p65/189). Margia plays a piano solo at the Nativity Play in *Jo of* and will some day surprise the world with her music (p163). Margia and Amy's father accompanies Grizel to London and the sisters spend Christmas in Salzburg, where Margia claims they had 'the *magnificentest*' time (p170/218). Margia is with Joey and her friends when they go to the Ice Carnival and is an excellent skater (p242). Margia is the ringleader of the Middles in *Princess* and combines musical ability and original sin in a remarkable manner (p62). Elisaveta recognises Margia, who is masked, by her thick, curly mop of hair when she is being introduced to the SSM. Margia has music lessons with Herr Anserl as she shows enough promise to merit lessons from him (p65/66/86). Margia has a particularly soft, pretty speaking voice and has to remember to shout when the SSM decide to imitate Matron Webb's voice (p92). She is very musical and Herr Anserl wants

her to concentrate more on her music but Madge Bettany refuses to let her drop her other lessons. Thirteen-year-old Margia sets words written by Jo Bettany to music to create a song to commemorate Miss Bettany's birthday (p103/118/131/132). Margia composes a little dance and shows it to Madge Russell in *Head Girl*. She is expected to do great things in later years (p129). Margia is Head of the Middles in *Rivals* and is in the Fourth form. She leads the girls in a campaign against the Saints (p47/48). Her father is mentioned as the author of *Glorious Prague* (p138). The Middles play tricks on their Seniors in the dormitories so Joey and her friends retaliate by powdering their hair white and also tying Margia and Suzanne Mercier's bedclothes together (p187/195). Simone Lecoutier asks fourteen-year-old Margia and Evadne Lannis to look after Eustacia Benson in *Eustacia* (p60). Margia is Protestant. Her bosom friend is Elsie Carr and she is in the Fourth form (p63/69/70). Margia is in the Fifth form later that term and has trouble with her form when she is ink monitor because the Fourth formers have emptied their inkwells. As Margia is still fourteen she ranks as a Middle at present (p159/263/269). Stacie Benson sends her love to everyone by Joey in *And Jo* and particularly to Margia (p31). Margia is described as the leader of the Middles. She is late for prep after lingering talking to Elsie Carr by the lockers, and gets into trouble with Miss Wilson for her untidy locker (p49/51/52). Margia is late for a music lesson one day, trips over some stationery lying in the middle of the corridor and falls, clutching at a stepladder that Frieda Mensch is on. Frieda falls and lands on Ruth Wynyard, covering her in paste (p113/114). Louise Redfield and Margia make a formidable pair of tennis champions in the Fifth form (p147). Shortly after their visit to the Oberammergau Passion Play, Margia and her friends encounter Bridget O'Ryan, a young Irish orphan, and try to adopt her (p201/202/206). Margia is at Guide Camp at the Baumersee with her friends Cornelia Flower, Evadne Lannis and Elsie Carr in *Camp*. She is described as a bright-faced girl of fourteen, whose square chin and determined air give the key to her character, and in one place her surname is given as Stevenson (p47/54). The four girls form a quartette which sometimes becomes a quintette when Ilonka is about (p204/205). Elisaveta, Paula and Cyrilla arrive back at camp dripping wet and covered in green weed. On discovering that they are wearing their last change of clothes, Ilonka has the brilliant idea of doing some laundry with Margia, Evadne, Cornelia and Elsie's help (p205/210). Margia is Head of VA in *Exploits* and one of the leaders of the Middles. She decides that the School clock is wrong and needs fixing (p51/132). Margia has just turned fourteen and will give up most of her school subjects to spend her time on music lessons when she is fifteen. Her parents are able to attend the end-of-term Christmas Pageant (p194/289). Margia is in the Fifth form in *Lintons* and has a bright, interesting face that tells of great force of character. Gillian Linton joins her form and Margia is Head of Thekla von Stift's dormitory. She plays the part of Sleeping Beauty's Prince at the Sale (p59/250/291). Margia and Elsie Carr have become Seniors in *New House*. Margia has been appointed a sub-prefect and will help Carla von Flugen, the Music Monitress (p12/100). Slight, fifteen-year-old Margia re-forms the SSM to annoy Matron Besly. Margia is flushed with annoyance when challenged by Matron Besly who has insulted her over her enjoyment of practising. The girl is furious at being doubted, keeps her dignity, and manages to give Matron a look with her grey eyes that contains amazement, pity and disgust blended together (p160/183). Later in the term Margia and Elsie become stuck halfway up one of the tall pines in the forest (p247). Margia, the Chalet School's musical genius, is a prefect when Louise Redfield becomes Head Girl and is in the Sixth form in *Jo Returns* (p8/16). Margia stays at school at half term and dresses as Plato at the sheets and pillowcase party (p233/234). Margia and Berta Hamel help Nancy Wilmot with her French when she transfers to the Chalet School in *New CS*. Margia is destined to be a concert performer and we learn that she will be leaving at the end of term (p90/135/318). We are told in *Goes to It* that Margia has been on a concert tour of Australia and is now in South Africa completing another tour (p104). She is already making a name for herself as a pianist in *Highland Twins* (p127). We learn in *Lavender* that Margia was caught in South Africa by the war but reached Australia where she completed her concert tour and is now training to be a nurse in one of Sydney's big hospitals (p93). Joey tells Mrs Hart, the vicar's wife, about Margia's progress in *Rescue* (p159). Margia has composed the music for two songs in the Pageant in *Wrong* (p247/251). Nina Rutherford mentions in *Genius* that she has heard Margia play several times and thinks she is marvellous (p21). Margia arrives to open the School Sale in *Coming of Age* and is described as a slight, curly-headed person (p103/104). She is still pursuing her musical career in *N17* (p71).

STEVENS, PRIMROSE: Primrose is in IIIA at St Peter's School with Gerry Challoner and has difficulty with the hem she is sewing in *Gerry* (p195/197).

STEVENSON, SUE: Sue is in VA at St Peter's School in *Gerry* and plays the part of Tom in the end-of-term play, *The Water Babies* (p234).

STEWART, DR: After a severe attack of laryngitis in *Jo Returns* (p160/175) Miss Stewart is escorted home to Herefordshire by her doctor brother to recuperate (p210).

STEWART, CONSTANCE ELIZABETH (CON), 'CHARLIE' (MACKENZIE, CON): Miss Stewart replaces Miss Carthew at the Chalet School in *Rivals* (p33). She is the history mistress in *Eustacia* and it is explained that Joey gave her the nickname 'Charlie' as a shortened version of 'Bonnie Prince Charlie'. She is popular, young and pretty and also cheerful, possessed of a great sense of humour and is a great friend of Miss Wilson. The girls soon learn that she detests carelessness about one's personal belongings (p69/160). At half term a group of English and American girls go on an expedition to Fulpmes at the foot of the Stubai Glacier with Miss Wilson and Miss Stewart (p169/178). One morning they climb up to the glacier to watch the sunrise and, whilst returning down the mountain, encounter a snowstorm. Miss Wilson slips on a loose stone, damaging her foot. They manage to reach a mountain hut just as the snow is getting heavy but have to stay there overnight with Miss Stewart in charge because Miss Wilson is in great pain (p210/217/220). Miss Stewart has blue eyes and a soft Highland accent (p244/260). She moves all the lockers around in *And Jo* and Margia Stevens, who is in trouble with Miss Wilson for being untidy, blames it on 'Charlie's' reorganisation (p50). The Guide Company is well established and, thanks to Miss Stewart's Camper's Licence, they are able to begin camping this term, along with the new company at St Scholastika's (p70). Miss Stewart's name is C E Stewart, hence her nickname of (Bonnie Prince) Charlie, but in

fact her Christian names are Constance Elizabeth (p126). Miss Stewart, Miss Wilson and Miss Nalder take a group of Guides to camp at the Baumersee in *Camp*. Miss Stewart is a Lieutenant and is Catholic. She is described as big, with boyish prettiness (p79/92). News arrives with Jack Maynard that his sister Mollie and her new husband Alastair Macdonald are sailing for New Zealand, where they plan to live. Miss Stewart has brothers in New Zealand and is able to assure the girls that it is a civilised country (p175/176). Miss Stewart plays a viola in the Christmas Pageant orchestra in *Exploits* (p290). Tall, slim Miss Stewart is dressed as Prince Charlie for *Mrs Jarley's Waxworks* at the staff evening in *Lintons*. She is among those summoned by Mademoiselle to discuss Thekla von Stift (p118/257). Miss Stewart lives in the new Middles' house, St Clare's, in *New House*. She discovers the SSM plot to stare at Matron and, after scolding everyone in St Clare's, forbids it (p11/185). Miss Stewart has her curly, red-gold hair tumbling about her shoulders and is blessedly matter-of-fact, with an uncompromisingly downright manner, when dealing with Alixe von Elsen when she wakes up from sleepwalking. Miss Wilson and Miss Stewart take the Seniors up the Bärenbad on an excursion and help Joey to rescue Anne Seymour when she falls down a slippery rock face. Unfortunately Miss Stewart wrenches her shoulder muscles pulling Joey up (p202/257/259). Miss Stewart goes down with a severe attack of laryngitis in *Jo Returns*, and may possibly have to have her tonsils out before she can teach again (p160/175/199). Her doctor brother escorts her home to Herefordshire to recuperate. Miss Stewart has a peppery Scots temper (p210/254). Miss Stewart, the history mistress, is at a staff meeting in *New CS* when Hilda Annersley informs them of the new arrangements (p9). The girls visit Salzburg at half term and, on the return journey, some of them have to spend the night in a bus in the charge of Miss Stewart and Miss Wilson when they are marooned in a rising flood. Miss Stewart speaks Italian and is twenty-eight years old (p263/273/294). Con Stewart is a very pretty girl with wavy red-gold hair, delicate colouring and dark-blue eyes in *Exile* (p25/26/28). She visits relatives and then stays with Nell Wilson after the School closes down in Austria. Con wants to help to start the Chalet School in Guernsey because she will not be getting married for another year. She is engaged to Jock, who has just got a new appointment in Singapore (p173/174/175). When the Maynard triplets are born the following November, Joey asks Con and Eugen von Wertheimer to be baby Con's godparents. She names baby Con after Con Stewart (p281/282). Miss Stewart mentions in *Goes to It* that her sister Nancy was at school with Jack Maynard's sister-in-law Lydia (p11). Miss Stewart's marriage has been postponed due to the war but Mr Mackenzie unexpectedly arrives in Guernsey while she is packing books (p13/50/52). She finally marries her fiancé and goes out to Singapore with him (p105). She is in Australia when Miss Annersley, Miss Wilson, Mlle Lachenais and Miss Edwards are involved in a bus accident on holiday in Devon in *Gay* (p33). It is reported in *Island* that she is safely back in Singapore and now has twin boys and a small girl (p42). The Mackenzies are living at Manly near Sydney in *Shocks* and have met the Hopes, who decide to send their daughter Emerence to the Chalet School. The Mackenzies' twin boys Peter and Patrick are nine years old and their daughter Janetta is five (p15). In *Kenya* Con Maynard has not seen her godmother, 'Auntie Con', since she was a tiny girl because the Mackenzies are in Australia (p143). The Mackenzies are returning for a long holiday in *Genius* and breaking their journey in Madeira (p64). Con is mentioned as a former history mistress and Con Maynard's godmother in *Richenda* (p154). Madge and Jem Russell will stay with her in Sydney in *Future* (p202). She is mentioned in passing in *Reunion* (p17) and her marriage to Jock Mackenzie is referred to in *N13* (p57).

CHILDREN:
1/2) PATRICK: see MACKENZIE, PATRICK
1/2) PETER: see MACKENZIE, PETER
3) JANETTA: see MACKENZIE, JANETTA

STEWART, NANCY: We are told in *Goes to It* that Miss Stewart's sister Nancy was at school with Jack Maynard's sister-in-law Lydia (p11).

STIFT, THEKLA von (C): Thekla starts in the Fifth form at the Chalet School in *Exploits* and we learn that she does not want to mix with daughters of shopkeepers and the lower classes. Her father was an officer in the German Imperial army and aide-de-camp to Prince Oskar, one of the Kaiser's sons (p49/50). Thekla, a tall, fair Prussian girl of fifteen, is a distant cousin of Marie von Eschenau (p51/53). The von Stift family have been living on their country estate in North Pomerania and Thekla has been brought up to be a complete snob. We learn that Marie's great-grandmother had twin sons, one of whom married her grandmother and the other a Prussian girl named Thekla von Klavitz and became very much Prussianised. Thekla's father is of the old-fashioned Junker class. Her governess has recently married and she has been sent to school because her stepbrother Wolfram is coming home and her mother does not want the spirit of Young Germany infecting Thekla. Thekla's father, Graf Wolfram von Stift, found out about the Chalet School from Eva von Heiling's parents (p55/59). Bianca di Ferrara is on duty at the stationery cupboard when she is involved in a scene with Thekla demanding a new exercise book (p63). On a walk up the Bärenbad Alpe Thekla is snobbish and difficult and eventually makes her cousin so angry that Marie shakes her (p76/106/107). Thekla goes to Munich at half term to visit some cousins and her behaviour is beginning to improve. The prefects invite the girls to a late Hallowe'en party at the end of November and Thekla's frilly muslin petticoat catches fire when she jumps over some lighted candles. Miss Wilson and Miss Stewart put out the flames and Thekla is so impressed that she intends to ask her parents' permission to join the Guides (p228/270/273). Very tall, fair Thekla holds herself stiffly erect in *Lintons*, and does not pay much attention to the other girls. Simone Lecoutier catches Thekla passing notes with Joyce Linton and Kitty Burnett. Thekla and Joyce are impudent to Simone and Thekla makes rude comments about the French (p58/60/75). Thekla's contribution for a midnight feast is a parcel of raw smoked bacon rashers. Afterwards she has a fierce battle with Luise Rotheim who wants to confess about the feast. Thekla was the oldest girl present and is uncomfortable because she thinks that there will be trouble. She feels that she will receive a good share of blame and does not think she deserves it as Joyce had suggested it and she would never have thought of such a thing (p95/105/106). Miss Norman, who normally teaches Juniors, has an unpleasant time with Joyce and Thekla of the Lower Fifth when they are in her extra French classes (p185/186). Marie explains that Thekla's family changed their surname and also became Protestants in order to inherit property. Sixteen-year-old Thekla skips Miss Norman's lesson and Frieda finds her in the Third form room reading a novel that she has smuggled into School (p191/192/206). Thekla wakes Joyce up one night, takes her to the window seat outside the dormitory and tells her that she should not be friendly with Jo Bettany because she hates her (p238/239). The girls are discovered and Thekla is later expelled for unrepentant lying and venomous behaviour. She expresses no sorrow at the time but years later writes to Mademoiselle acknowledging that she deserved everything that had been said and it had been a safeguard to her (p242/259/261). Jo, who has almost forgotten about her, refers to her in *New House* as a 'poor little ass' who paid for her sins, but Frieda considers that she deserved her expulsion (p223). Jo thinks of Thekla in *Jo Returns* when she realises that the villain of her unpublished first book is unrealistic (p47). It is mentioned in *Island* that Thekla wrote an odd letter to Mlle Lepâttre after her expulsion, partly grateful, partly ashamed and very short (p50). Thekla is mentioned in *Bride* as one of only two pupils to have been expelled (p256). Simone mentions her in *Joey Goes* as the only real snob to have attended the Chalet School (p99). Joey remembers in *Kenya* that Thekla hated her with a deep and deadly hatred. Nobody has heard anything about the von Stift family since the war (p12). The occasion when Thekla's frilly petticoat caught fire is recalled in *New Mistress* (p134). Rosalie Dene comments in *Theodora* that Thekla and Betty Wynne-Davies were the School's only real failures (p11). Joey mentions Thekla's name to Stacie Benson in *Challenge* when they remember the time that the Middles boiled the School clock. Apparently the von Stifts vanished during World War II and even the von Eschenaus do not know what became of them (p166). EBD tells a reader in *N16* that Thekla vanished during the War (p68).

STIFT, WOLFRAM von (ESCHENAU, Wolfram von) (A): Marie von Eschenau explains in *Lintons* that her great-uncle Wolfram von Eschenau changed his name to von Stift to inherit an estate from an uncle of his wife with that name. He also became a Protestant although he had been brought up as a Catholic. We learn that Thekla's name should really be von Eschenau und von Stift (p191/192).

STIFT, GRAF WOLFRAM von (B): It is mentioned in *Exploits* that Thekla's father was

very important before the war as he was an officer in the German Imperial army and aide-de-camp to Prinz Oskar, one of the Kaiser's sons (p49/50). Marie von Eschenau mentions that the Graf's grandmother was also her great grandmother and that the Graf von Stift once stayed with the von Eschenaus. We learn that he married twice and that the first lady was timid and gentle and died during the war when their son Wolfram was born. His second wife is Thekla's mother, and Thekla's father Wolfram is a Prussian of the Prussians (p55/56). After Thekla's governess was married it was felt that it would be easier to send the girl to school rather than engage another governess. Thekla's mother agreed as she had been alarmed by her stepson Wolfram's absorption of the spirit of Young Germany and was anxious that Thekla should not be infected. Graf Wolfram von Stift found out about the Chalet School from Eva von Heiling's parents (p59). Marie von Eschenau mentions her cousin Wolfram in *Lintons* and explains that the Graf's father changed his name from von Eschenau to von Stift to inherit an estate from an uncle of his wife with that name. He also became a Protestant (p73/191). We learn in *Challenge* that the family disappeared during World War II (p166).

STIFT, WOLFRAM von (C): Wolfram, Thekla's half brother and Marie von Eschenau's cousin, is mentioned in *Exploits*. Thekla has been sent to school because Wolfram is coming home and her mother does not want his absorption of the spirit of Young Germany to infect Thekla (p56/59).

STONE, LINDA, 'ROCKY': Lower IVB's Form Mistress Miss Stone teaches German to Upper IIIA and is one of the new mistresses in *Feud* (p150). She is Lower IVA's Form Mistress in *Triplets* (p66). Miss Stone, Miss Andrews and Miss Bertram take the Juniors to play in the meadow behind the Élisehütte in *Challenge* (p76). Miss Bertram and Miss Stone, whose nickname is Rocky, are both stated to be the Lower Fourth's Form Mistress (p119/163/176). Miss Stone is responsible for literature in Upper IVB in *Two Sams* and her pupils call her Rocky amongst themselves. Upper IVB are games-crazy and mentally lazy according to the mistresses, and the Head decides to give the girls a shock by changing their Form Mistress from Linda Stone to Kathy Ferrars (p67/68/73). Miss Stone is manning the guardboat on Lake Thun in *Althea* when there is nearly a fatal accident with a runaway speedboat occupied by two young boys (p91).

STRATTON, EVE: It is mentioned in *Chudleigh Hold* that nineteen-year-old Eve stayed at the Rectory last year and ignored Ven and Crumpet (p35).

STRAUSS, MARC: Marc Strauss and Hansel Laneck are two of the oldest boatmen on the lake in *And Jo* (p255).

STUFFER, THE: Miss Maynard, Joey, Robin and Grizel are on a train from Paris to Basle in *Head Girl* when they meet a lady whom Jo christens 'the Stuffer' and her companion Maria, who are determined to sleep with the window closed (p24/28). The two ladies arrive at the Chalet School for the end-of-term summer garden party (p335). Joey and her friends meet 'the Stuffer' and Maria at the performance of the Oberammergau Passion Play in *And Jo* (p190). Joey donates a hideous tea and coffee set in repoussé silver to the School Sale in *Summer Term*. It was a wedding gift from the two ladies, who are now both dead (p161).

SUMMERS, MISS: Miss Summers is a mistress at The Gables in *Monica* (p10).

SUMMERS, WILMA: Wilma is in Upper IVB with José Helston and Jane Carew in *Jane*. Wilma is described as a sheep of a girl, running with the crowd and rarely voicing an opinion of her own (p34; p28 for form).

SUSIE: Susie is the Challoners' maid in *Gerry* (p19).

SUZANNE: see (OZANNE), SUZANNE

SUZETTE (SUSIE): Suzette is Mrs Lannis's French maid and she looks after Evadne, Joey, Grizel and Robin when they visit Salzburg in *Head Girl*. The hotel catches fire, and Suzette is completely unnerved and goes into hysterics (p225/238/239). She is also mentioned in *New CS* when the Chalet School visits Salzburg, and Evadne refers to her as Susie (p251).

SWANN, DR: Dr Swann leases his home, The Pantile, to his friend Mr Winterton in *Peggy* (p26/27).

SWANSON, MARY: Mary Swanson is a boarder at St Katharine's, Mélanie Lucas's previous school, in *Future* (p7).

SYBEL, LISA: Lisa is in Inter V in *Theodora* and partners Pen Grant on a walk (p105).

SYLVIA: Rosamund Lilley's sister Dorothy has a young daughter named Sylvia in *Theodora* (p63/64).

HALF TERMS AT THE CHALET SCHOOL

Mentions of half-term holidays vary throughout the series. Although school terms seem to follow the conventional pattern, with three per academic year, which starts in September and finishes in June/July, it would seem that EBD used the half-term holiday as a plot device as and when it suited her story. The different locations require different types of half-term break.

In the **Tyrol** years it would have been impractical (and expensive) for the pupils coming from countries other than Austria to go home for the few half-term days. However, the Austrian girls go home and often take friends with them. Those pupils who have relatives at the San spend their break on the Sonnalpe and sometimes also take friends. At this stage the school is still small and has a family feeling. Half term, in those books where it is described, concentrates on Joey and friends staying with Madge and Jem or on the group which contains Joey.

There are, in fact, only brief mentions of half term in the first five books. In *Princess* the possibility of dismissing Matron Webb at half term is discussed but there is no further mention. In *Head-Girl of the Chalet School* there is a chapter devoted to Joey and Grizel's visit to the Sonnalpe but no description about what happens to the other pupils. In *Rivals of the Chalet School* Joey expects to visit the Sonnalpe, weather permitting, but there is no further mention.

However, because of the 'short' Christmas holidays (*Jo of the Chalet School*) and Easter holidays (*Head Girl*) and the early breaking up because of chickenpox (*Rivals*), those pupils who are unable to travel home are sent in nationality groups with members of staff to nearer destinations such as Vienna, Munich and the Black Forest.

The first real description of a half term is in *Eustacia Goes to the Chalet School*; the Italian pupils spend it in the Black Forest with Miss Nalder and Miss Annersley whilst Mlle Lachennais takes a group to Salzburg. The English and American pupils, including Jo, travel to Fulpmes with Miss Wilson and Miss Stewart. In *The Exploits of the Chalet Girls* those who cannot go home stay at the Sonnalpe and in *The Chalet School and the Lintons* all pupils, except for Jo and her friends, go home. In *Jo Returns to the Chalet School* those pupils who cannot go home, including a visiting Jo, have to stay in school.

The tradition of celebrating Madame's birthday, initiated by Gisela in the School's first summer term, is a useful plot device for expeditions, and in some books (*The School at the Chalet, The Princess of the Chalet School, The New House at the Chalet School*) it replaces half term, even when there are brief mentions of this. There are only two instances of whole-school half-term expeditions: in *The Chalet School and Jo* (Oberammergau) and *The New Chalet School* (Salzburg).

The final half term of the Tyrol years (*The Chalet School in Exile*) is the most significant, as while the pupils are away the school is moved up to the Sonnalpe.

The school's stay on **Guernsey** is too short and actioned-packed for any half term.

A sentence from *The Chalet School and Rosalie* sums up how EBD sees half term in the **Plas Howell** and **St Briavel's** years: 'At the Chalet School it was the custom for most of the girls to stay at school for half term in the short term. Only those who lived near went home, the rest enjoying expeditions, tournaments, or dancing and games in Hall …' However it is not clear whether she is referring to the short term in that specific year or in general.

There are no half term mentions in *The Chalet School Goes to It* and *Bride Leads the Chalet School*.

Even in those books where there is a mention there is not always a description. Often the mentions are just used as markers in the term, although in some books there are descriptions of day trips and expeditions.

The Highland Twins at the Chalet School
Tom Tackles the Chalet School
Three Go to the Chalet School

The Chalet School and the Island: at the beginning of this book we are told half-term weekend is cancelled because of the long Easter holiday but there are still two references to it.

Peggy of the Chalet School: an excursion to Kester Bellever's bird sanctuary.

The Wrong Chalet School: Hilda Annersley plans at the beginning of the book to spend her half term with Edgar Mordaunt but there is no description of the holiday, although in the last chapter it is mentioned again together with Madame's birthday excursion to Bideford and Barnstaple.

Changes for the Chalet School: Half term is cancelled because of the coming move to Switzerland but Madame's birthday is celebrated with day trips, including the very detailed description of the excursion to the Bournville factory.

As well as in *The Chalet School and Rosalie* there are descriptions of arrangements in *Lavender Laughs in the Chalet School*, *Gay from China at the Chalet School*, *The Mystery at the Chalet School* and *Shocks for the Chalet School*. The most detailed description is the plot-led half-term excursion to the Bosherston Lily Ponds in *Carola Storms the Chalet School*, when Hilary Burn meets her future husband.

Barnstable

The **Swiss** books give EBD the opportunity to describe trips in more detail, no doubt drawing on guidebooks for information about the various places to which the girls are sent. Some are day excursions; others are half-term visits.

There is some mention of half term in all the school-based Swiss books. Even *Prefects of the Chalet School* has a mention although the book deals only with the second half of the summer term.

What is interesting is that we have more variety in the types of half-term references.

Half-term references as markers in the term occur in:

Mary-Lou: Halloween comes after half term
Summer Term: Silver Jubilee celebrations will take place at half term. Most of the pupils go on local expeditions on 'Jubilee Sunday' but these are not described.

Half terms which are a mixture of day trips, interspersed with school-based activities:
The Chalet School and Barbara
The New Mistress at the Chalet School
The Feud in the Chalet School
The Chalet School Triplets
Redheads at the Chalet School
A Leader in the Chalet School

Half terms with purely school-based activities because of circumstances:
Jane and the Chalet School: smallpox epidemic
Adrienne and the Chalet School: blizzards
Challenge for the Chalet School: inclement weather and Miss Annersley flies in from Copenhagen

Half terms where groups of pupils go away to another area of Switzerland:
A Chalet Girl from Kenya
A Genius at the Chalet School
A Problem for the Chalet School
The Chalet School and Richenda
Trials for the Chalet School
Theodora and the Chalet School
The Chalet School Wins the Trick
Althea Joins the Chalet School.

Details of some of the visits may be found in *Trips and Excursions* (see page 54).

Half terms when, for a variety of reasons, there is no half term but there are day expeditions:
The Chalet School Does It Again: disrupted term with an influenza outbreak and inclement weather as well as the term being a short one.
Excitements at the Chalet School: plans for the Coming of Age of the School in the next term.
Two Sams at the Chalet School: the term is short because Easter comes early and the holidays are extended to a month.

Half terms not fitting into the above categories:
The Coming of Age of the Chalet School: the actual 'half-term' weekend is the weekend of celebrations. Groups of pupils go off to the Tiernsee throughout the term.
Ruey Richardson—Chaletian: the Maynard/Bettany/Russell clan and invited members of staff go to Peggy's wedding but it is not clear how the rest of the school spends its break.

Evidence that EBD uses half terms as a plot device comes from the varying length of the half-term breaks and the flexibility of the dates. In *A Problem for the Chalet School* not only has the date been changed but an extra day added at Simone de Bersac's request. In *Adrienne and the Chalet School* half term has been 'put off already' by one week. In the event this does not matter as only a few local pupils brave the blizzard conditions to go home. In *The Chalet School Wins the Trick* the Kindergarten (St. Nicholas) half term is one week earlier.

When EBD started writing the series, she had no idea of how many books there would be. From her point of view she was not trying to replicate the reality of an academic year but to write interesting, fascinating stories for her schoolgirl audience. She tried to introduce a wide variety in her plots with gentle family scenes, colourful descriptions of everyday school life and local atmosphere, interspersed with comical mishaps, frightening accidents, exciting rescues, troublesome Middles' tricks, illnesses, enmity between pupils and feuds between schools. Her vivid descriptions of half terms and other excursions are another aspect of how well she has managed to captivate all her many fans.

Charmian Bilger

TALBOT, SIR JAMES and LADY: Mrs Linton's specialist Dr Talbot is described as a great physician in *Lintons*. He suggests that she should send her daughters to the Chalet School (p9/10). After a second consultation with the doctor, Mrs Linton takes tea with his wife, Lady Talbot, and accepts her offer to escort Gillian and Joyce on a shopping trip for their new school clothes. We learn that the Talbots' only daughter died when she was a baby and would have been the same age as Gillian Linton (p20/21). Sir James is called in from London for an opinion when Mlle Lepâttre becomes seriously ill in *New CS* (p13). Sir James Talbot opens the end-of-term Sale of Learning in aid of the Oberland branch of the Sanatorium in *Bride* but Lady Talbot is unable to be present as she is undergoing dental treatment. Sir James wins Tom Gay's model village and decides to give it to a hospital for very poor children suffering from TB (p288/289/294). This decision is mentioned in *Barbara* (p177) and *Does It Again* (p174). Joey Maynard visits England to consult Sir James and have an operation to correct a displaced organ in *Richenda* (p141/193). Mary-Lou Trelawney's mother, Mrs Carey, consults Sir James in *Triplets* and he orders her out to Switzerland for her health (p172).

TARENGO, SIGNOR: Nita Tarengo lives on the Platz in *Althea*, although her father, who is probably in the Sanatorium, is much better (p39).

TARENGO, NITA: Nita is in Upper IVB with Erica Standish in *Summer Term* (p51/53). She, Rita Quick and Catherine Leonard become wildly excited over the Jubilee plans (p68). Nita is on a ramble when Erica falls and breaks a bone in her ankle, and when Erica is criticised, speaks out in her defence in her native Italian (p105). Nita is in Upper IVA in *Challenge* when Jocelyn and Co decide to repeat the Lost Property prank to bring them down a peg or two (p121). Nita is a dark, Italianate girl who lives on the Platz at present in *Althea* although her father, probably in the Sanatorium, is much better. Erica introduces Nita to Althea Glenyon (p39).

TAYLOR, MR and MRS: Michael Taylor's parents take the news of their son's imminent death very pluckily in *Monica* (p149).

TAYLOR, MISS: We learn in *Steps In* that before Peter Chester lost his private fortune, Beth and Paul had an excellent governess named Miss Taylor for two years (p101/106).

TAYLOR, HILARY: Hilary is in Inter V's Evening of Tableaux in *Adrienne*. She appears as Eve in the Garden of Eden with her long brown tresses flowing around her (p161/162).

TAYLOR, MICHAEL: Sir William Borrodaile, a London surgeon and friend of Dr Marilliar, is called in to examine Michael Taylor, one of Dr Marilliar's young patients, in *Monica*. Michael is an only child and it is just a question of time before he dies (p141/142/149).

TEMPLE, MISS (i): Miss Temple, the Headmistress at Kingscote School, owns a handsome St Bernard dog called Woolly Bear in 'Woolly Bear' in *1st* (p100/101).

TEMPLE, MISS (ii) (A): We first meet the Temples in *Maids* and are told that Captain Michael Temple's first wife Giovanna caught a chill and died when her daughters, Elizabeth and Anne, were respectively four years old and five months old. As Captain Temple was a naval officer and away at sea, his young, unmarried sister, Miss Temple, volunteered to look after his young daughters. The girls lived with her in a flat in London surrounded by art students from the Slade School for the next five years. When Miss Temple wanted to get married and travel on the Continent, Anne became dangerously ill with pneumonia and Elizabeth too was fragile. Captain Temple married Agnes Weston because he needed a new home for his daughters. At the beginning of *Maids* Captain Temple's sister and her husband are in Australia with a large family (p12/13/15).

TEMPLE, AGNES (AGATHA) (née WESTON) (A) (2): We learn in *Maids* that Captain Temple's sister looked after his children after the death of their mother Giovanna. Miss Temple wanted to get married and travel on the Continent but the children had been ill and Anne nearly died of pneumonia. Captain Temple married Agnes Weston, who was very plain and three years older than he was. She had been kind to the children and he needed a home for his daughters. Captain Temple and his new wife had a baby they named Janie, and she was a tender mother to all of the girls, devoting her whole life to them. Unfortunately Agnes was killed in a carriage accident when Janie was still young. By this time Captain Temple had conceived a deep and true affection for his second wife. On her death bed she asked Captain Temple to send the girls to Miss Moulton's school at Hurst Ridge in Sussex, where they stayed until Elizabeth was eighteen, Anne fourteen and Janie nine years old (p13/14). Mrs Temple was a terrible sailor and was never able to go to sea (p31). Anne recalls in *Janie of* that her stepmother's care had saved her own life (p180). When Janice Agatha Chester is born in *Goes to It* she is named after Anne's mother, Giovanna, and Janie's mother, Agatha (p123).

TEMPLE, ANNE (CHESTER, ANNE) (B) (2): We first meet the Temple Family in *Maids*, and Anne is the second daughter of Captain Temple and his first wife Giovanna, an Italian girl. Anne is four years younger than her sister Elizabeth and is an exquisite contrast, with heavy, straight black hair, fair skin and grey eyes. We learn that when Elizabeth was four years old and Anne only five months old, their mother died from pleurisy. Captain Temple's young, unmarried sister looked after his young daughters in a flat in London surrounded by art students from the Slade School for the next five years. Miss Temple wanted to get married and travel on the Continent but Anne was dangerously ill with pneumonia and Elizabeth very fragile. Captain Temple proposed to Agnes Weston because he needed a home for his two daughters (p11/12/13). Agnes accepted and she provided Captain Temple with a third daughter, Janie, but Agnes was killed soon afterwards and the girls were sent to Miss Moulton's school at Hurst Ridge in Sussex, where they stayed until Elizabeth and Anne were eighteen and fourteen and Janie was nine years old. Miss Moulton's school closed (p14/15) and Anne and her sisters were then sent to Mme Ozanne in France, where they stayed for five years. Anne, who was artistic, had the best masters possible and her original sketches and paintings gave promise of something unusual in the future. They moved into a flat in London with their father and six weeks later received news of Mme Ozanne's death. Their father died shortly after and, as they were left badly off, the girls decided to live in Guernsey (p17/19/20). They rent a cottage, La Rochelle, near Rocquaine Bay in Guernsey, belonging to Javotte, Mme Ozanne's old nurse, and her son (p23/24). Twenty-year-old Anne and her sisters move to Guernsey and a fortnight later Anne has an encounter with a goat when she goes downstairs to have a cold tub one morning (p27/40/44). Anne meets Peter Chester, a young locum, when he calls on Mrs de Garis to look at her sick baby (p70/72). Mrs de Garis chases Anne down the road because the baby has died and she blames the Temple family (p97/98). Anne sells some of her exquisite watercolours but most of her time is devoted to her new painting, La Héroguïaze, with which she hopes to make her name. She is twenty-one (p151/152). Peter Chester helps her with her young sister Janie, who has scarlet fever during an epidemic and is very ill (p164). Anne's picture is hung at the Academy (p186). Peter wants to marry Anne as he has the chance of a country practice in Hampshire, and they decide to have a double wedding with Elizabeth and Paul Ozanne on 10th September. The Chesters travel to

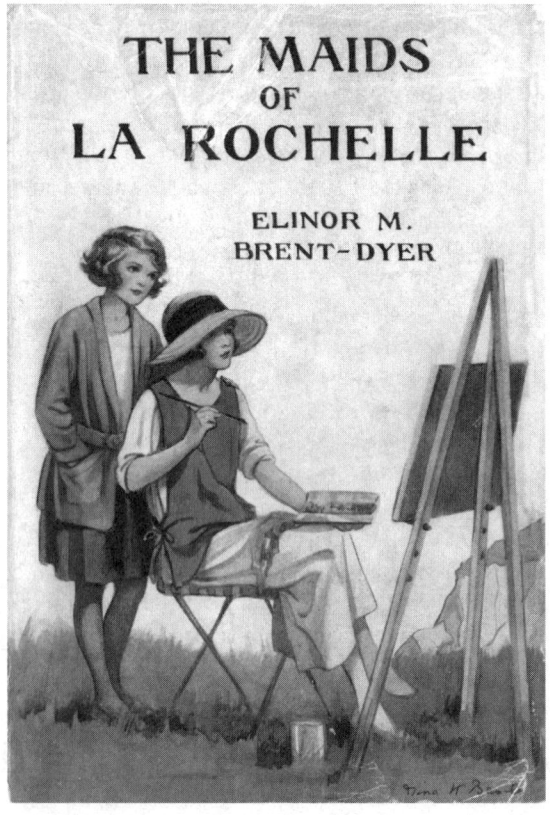

THE MAIDS OF LA ROCHELLE

ELINOR M. BRENT-DYER

Brittany in a fishing-smack belonging to Javotte's son for their honeymoon (p206/287/289). Anne and Peter are now married in *Scamps* and living in England. They visit Guernsey with their baby daughter Elizabeth, who is a fortnight younger than her cousin Michael Ozanne (p145/180). The Chesters return to Guernsey to stay with Paul, Elizabeth, baby Michael, Janie and Pauline in *Heather* (p57/58). We learn that the Temple girls had a French governess named Mme Mauray when they lived with Mme Ozanne (p70). The Chesters live in Hampshire (p114). They appear to live near Southampton in *Janie of*. Anne and Peter take their two children to Guernsey for Janie and Julian's wedding and their baby son is named as Paul (p20/25/41). Dr Fuzzey is retiring after Christmas and Peter Chester will take over his practice in Guernsey (p145). Javotte looks after Paul Chester while Anne is house-hunting, and soon afterwards they move into their new home, Pierres Gris, on St Sampson's road (p178/180). Beth and Paul catch chickenpox and Anne is unable to visit Janie when she is expecting a baby. Anne is present at La Rochelle for the birth of Juliet Lucy (p212/217). Anne and the children visit Devonshire in *Steps In* (p77) to stay with Mélie Lihou, and leave their maid Dulcie in charge at home (p94/97/99). Their house is beginning to look neglected as Peter's private income, left to him by old Mr Wedderburn, his godfather, was embezzled two years ago by Rennison, a lawyer in the north of England (p100/101). There are now six Chester children and they have had to dismiss their governess Miss Taylor, Nanny and the other maids. We are told that fifteen-year-old Lily, whom they employed, was a thief and had to be dismissed. Anne and Peter are horribly, loathsomely proud and will not allow Elizabeth Ozanne to educate Beth (p104/106/107). Janie and Nan Blakeney organise the house for Anne and the children returning home from Devon, and apples are ordered by different people, all meaning to help, from Le Marchant's, Rosomon's, Guérin's, Lemercier's and Tom le Martin. Anne returns home from Mélie's farm with even more apples (p125/126). Anne makes the rest of the family give way to baby Barbara's slightest whim (p148). Due to financial worries and concerns about Barbara's health Anne fails to deal with Beth properly. Janie tells her off for pride and warns Anne that she is warping Beth's character and that she must think of Beth as well as Barbara (p166/167/168/171). When Beth has mumps Anne is unable to visit her because Barbara is ill and Beth becomes convinced Anne does not love her (p198/207). Peter inherits a modest fortune from his old cousin and Anne and Beth visit Switzerland with Barbara, the Chesters' frail youngest child, to help improve her health so that she may be able to lead a normal life once she is into her teens. The Chesters and their Ozanne and Lucy cousins will go to the Chalet School, which is opening near Jerbourg (p240/241). Peter Chester is the leading Medico on the Island of Guernsey in *Exile* (p177/178). We are reminded that three years previously Peter lost his private fortune owing to the wrongdoings of a solicitor, and the shock made Anne, who had just given birth to her third daughter, Barbara, very ill. The Chesters live at Pierres Gris (p212/213/279). Janice is born soon after they settle in Armiford in *Goes to It* and we are told that they had another child, little Piers, who died when he was only a month old (p123). Peter is an Army Doctor in *Highland Twins* (p259). The Lucy family, together with the Chesters and Ozannes, donate one of the School boats in *Island* (p146). It is mentioned in *Bride* that the Chesters are a long family and a poor one into the bargain and that the Chester girls have known hard struggles (p150). Anne is prepared to let her frail daughter Barbara go to the Chalet School in *Barbara* because Joey will be next door to keep an eye on her and Beth will also be living there (p10). Jo mentions in *Does It Again* that she is responsible to Anne Chester for Barbara (p63). Anne goes to London for a few days at the beginning of *Coming of Age* for a shopping and theatre trip with Janie Lucy (p7). We learn in *Theodora* that Anne was never told about the time the girls were caught in a snowstorm in *Barbara* as it would have worried her too much (p45). Anne is in the South Seas for a year visiting her sister Elizabeth when Peter visits Switzerland in *Jane* and diagnoses Janice's cowpox (p152/153). Janice Chester mentions in *Adrienne* that her parents have never allowed their children to cheek people and are stricter in that way than her Aunt Janie and Uncle Julian Lucy (p116).

CHILDREN (GENERATION C)
1) ELIZABETH (BETH): see CHESTER, ELIZABETH
2) PAUL: see CHESTER, PAUL

3) **NANCY:** see CHESTER, NANCY
4/5) **DICKON:** see CHESTER, DICKON
4/5) **ROBIN:** see CHESTER, ROBIN
6) **BARBARA EMILY:** see CHESTER, BARBARA
7) **PIERS:** see CHESTER, PIERS
8) **JANICE AGATHA:** see CHESTER, JANICE

TEMPLE, ELIZABETH (OZANNE, ELIZABETH) (B) (1): We first meet the Temple Family in *Maids*, and Elizabeth is the eldest daughter of Captain Temple and his first wife, an Italian girl. Elizabeth has deep brown eyes and is a sweet, serious girl-child with her mother's exquisite face and father's fair curls. We learn that when Elizabeth was four and Anne was five months old, their mother Giovanna died from pleurisy. Captain Temple's young unmarried sister looked after his young daughters in a flat in London surrounded by art students from the Slade School for the next five years. When Miss Temple wanted to get married and travel on the Continent Elizabeth was fragile and Anne became dangerously ill with pneumonia. Captain Temple proposed to Agnes Weston because he needed a home for his two daughters (p11/12/13). When her daughter Janie was a baby, Agnes was killed. The three girls went to Miss Moulton's school at Hurst Ridge in Sussex, where they lived until Elizabeth was eighteen, Anne was fourteen and Janie nine years old. Miss Moulton closed the school as she was getting old and it wasn't paying enough, and Elizabeth, an exceptionally lovely girl, and her sisters were then sent to Mme Ozanne in France, where they stayed for five years. Elizabeth's talent for writing charming verses and fairy tales was noticed and she had a course in English, French and Italian classics (p14/15/17). Upon their father's retirement they went to live in London. Six weeks later they had news of their old friend Mme Ozanne's quiet death and shortly afterwards their own father died (p18). They were left badly off and Javotte, Mme Ozanne's old nurse, wrote and offered them the use of the little house belonging to her and her son, La Rochelle, at Rocquaine Bay in Guernsey (p19/23/24). Twenty-four-year-old Elizabeth, for all her steady common sense and quiet calm of mind, is an idealist (p28/47). Pauline Ozanne arrives unexpectedly at La Rochelle, having run away from home feeling bored, and Elizabeth meets her stepbrother Paul Ozanne when he arrives to collect her (p55/63). Elizabeth goes to the de Garis house to persuade Mrs de Garis to seek help for her sick baby but Mrs de Garis gets fearfully excited and shouts at Elizabeth in Norman French. Elizabeth and Anne decide that if her brother approves, they will give Pauline lessons with Janie (p74/76). Elizabeth discovers that Paul Ozanne's father was the cousin of Mme Ozanne's husband (p112). We are informed that on first meeting Elizabeth Temple, Paul was reminded of his mother, who died shortly before his tenth birthday. He proposes marriage to Elizabeth but is rejected. Elizabeth writes a book on the old Guernsey legends and a publisher in London accepts it (p141/148/187). La Sorcière Blanche starts a cliff fire that nearly engulfs the Athertons' holiday home and Elizabeth rescues José Atherton after battling with the old woman, who dies in the fire along with Peter de Garis (p268/272/274/275/277). Paul and Elizabeth finally decide to have a double wedding with Anne and her fiancé Peter Chester on 10th September. The Ozannes organise a honeymoon cruise round the French coast in a yacht lent by a friend of Paul's (p286/287/290). Elizabeth and Paul have a baby son named Michael in *Scamps*. They take a holiday house near the Athertons and Willoughbys and Anne and Peter arrive from England with their baby daughter Elizabeth (p154/180). The Raphaels visit Guernsey during the summer holidays in *Heather* and meet the Ozannes, who live in Peterport but are renting a summer cottage at Petit Bôt next door to the Raphaels' holiday cottage (p49/50/56). Baby Michael has Bonita de Garis to look after him as Elizabeth wants to help the de Garis family, who are awfully poor (p57). We learn that when the Temple girls were living with Mme Ozanne they had a French governess named Mme Mauray (p70). Elizabeth and Paul have two children in *Janie of*, four-year-old Michael and Billy. They are expecting an addition to the family in October, when Janie will look after the two boys (p26/127). Elizabeth gives birth to twin girls, Peronelle Jane (Nella) and Giovanna Anne (Vanna) (p147/148/173). We learn in *Steps In* that Elizabeth offered to pay for Beth Chester to attend a good convent school in Jersey, because the Chesters had lost money, but Anne would not hear of it (p107). We hear about Paul and Elizabeth again in *Exile* when the Chalet School is about to open in Guernsey and Joey Maynard meets Elizabeth and her two sisters. Paul, Robin and Dickon Chester's education is paid for by the Ozannes. The Ozanne twins are enrolled at the Chalet School along with Robin, Dickon, Nancy and Beth Chester and Julie and John Lucy (p187/213/214). The Ozanne family moves from Guernsey to Armiford in *Goes to It* where Paul, a lawyer, has the Recordership (p12). Elizabeth is mentioned in *Highland Twins* as a mother of twins (p41). Nancy Chester considers her too grown-up to be always laughing and teasing like Joey Maynard and Janie Lucy (p68). Vanna Ozanne mentions in 'New Flavouring' in *3rd* that Elizabeth taught them to make gingerbread and raspberry buns in the holidays (p130). Elizabeth is to be godmother to Aline Elizabeth Russell in *Rescue* (p236). Betsy Lucy says in *Three Go* that the family would confuse her with her Aunt Elizabeth Ozanne if they used her full name (p206). The Ozannes, Chesters and Lucys donate one of the boats to the Chalet School in *Island* (p146). It is mentioned in *Bride* that Paul Ozanne is a wealthy man who can give his girls all they want and that their mother has tended to keep them younger than their age (p150). Barbara and her cousins' fluent French in *Barbara* is the result of their mothers having spent so much of their girlhood in France (p112). Elizabeth wants Vanna and Nella to leave school and be company for her in Singapore in *Does It Again*. They are only in the Upper Fifth but she considers they are unlikely to progress further (p29). We are told in *Kenya* that Elizabeth employed Javotte to look after Vanna and Nella when they were small (p165). Vi tells Miss Annersley in *Genius* that they missed their aunt and uncle and all the rest of the Ozannes at Christmas as the boys had flown out for the holidays to join the rest of the family abroad (p38). They are still somewhere in the South Seas in *Problem* (p213), but have retained their house in Peterport, as we learn in *Ruey* (p123). It is mentioned in *Jane* that Anne Chester is in the South Seas for a year visiting her sister Elizabeth (p153).

CHILDREN (GENERATION C):
1) **MICHAEL:** see OZANNE, MICHAEL
2) **BILLY:** see OZANNE, WILLIAM
3) **NELLA:** see OZANNE, PERONELLE
4) **VANNA:** see OZANNE, GIOVANNA

TEMPLE, GIOVANNA (A) (1): We learn in *Maids* that Giovanna, a beautiful Italian girl, was Michael Temple's first wife, whom he adored,

and they had two daughters, Elizabeth and Anne, from their marriage. Michael married his first wife Giovanna when he was a twenty-three-year-old lieutenant and Elizabeth was born eighteen months later. He was sent to China for three years and Anne was born a year after his return. Unfortunately Giovanna caught a chill when Anne was five months old and died from pleurisy. She is buried in a Cornish graveyard (p11/12/13). When Elizabeth Ozanne gives birth to twin daughters in *Janie of* she names one of them Giovanna (Vanna) after her Italian mother (p173). Janice Agatha Chester is born in *Goes to It* and named after Anne's mother Giovanna and Janie's mother Agatha (p123).

TEMPLE, JANE AGATHA (JANIE) (LUCY, JANIE) (B) (3): Janie is Elizabeth and Anne Temple's half-sister and the daughter of Captain Michael Temple and his second wife Agnes. We first meet Janie in *Maids*. We learn that Agnes was killed in a carriage accident when Janie was small and the girls were sent to Miss Moulton's school at Hurst Ridge in Sussex, where they stayed until Elizabeth was eighteen, Anne was fourteen and Janie nine years old. Janie is a sturdy, healthy girl, plain, almost ugly but an exceptionally clever child. The girls were then sent to Mme Ozanne in France for five years and Janie's general education was attended to with thoroughness (p14/15/17). The three girls moved into a flat in London when their father retired and six weeks later received news of Mme Ozanne's quiet death. Shortly afterwards their father died, leaving them badly off, and they decided to rent La Rochelle near Rocquaine in Guernsey, which belonged to Javotte, Mme Ozanne's old nurse, and her son (p18/20/23). We are told that Janie thinks in French half the time, has learned fine needlework and does exquisite embroidery (p25/26). Janie is seasick on the boat over to Guernsey but recovers when they reach land. She is fifteen and brown-haired (p33/35/49). She becomes friendly with Mélie Lihou (p50). Héloïse de Garis hides Janie in the kitchen loft at Romaine to see La Sorcière Blanche cure her baby brother but the White Witch senses that Janie is there and orders her down (p79/80/83). Janie mildly objects to sharing lessons with Pauline Ozanne, who is only twelve years old. Janie is partly Irish and has lovely liquid brown eyes, never seen in those of purely Teuton blood (p95/114/123). The Temple sisters meet Julian Lucy and his parents, who have recently built a bungalow at Pleinmont. Julian, a big, handsome schoolboy and a prefect at Elizabeth College, nearly runs Janie down on his bicycle (p143). Janie becomes very ill during an epidemic of scarlet fever and Javotte arrives unexpectedly to nurse her. Janie recovers in time for her sixteenth birthday on 10th June (p166/172/186). Mr Atherton finds a holiday house for his family in Guernsey and Janie and Pauline meet his daughters on the beach when José Atherton falls into the sea and is rescued by Janie (p209/210/240). Janie tells them her full name, Jane Agatha Temple (p242). Elizabeth and Paul Ozanne have a double wedding with Anne and Peter Chester on 10th September. Julian and Colinette Ozanne bring Javotte over to Guernsey for the wedding and take Janie and Pauline back to Brittany with them (p287/290/291). Janie is with Pauline when she nearly cycles into Maidie Willoughby and her stepsister Britta Lundgren in *Scamps*. Janie was seventeen in June but looks three years younger (p144/146). Janie and Con Atherton become friendly with Marjolaine Willoughby. Elizabeth, Paul and their baby son Michael take a holiday house near the Athertons and Willoughbys and Anne and Peter Chester arrive from England to join them with their baby daughter Beth. We are told that Janie has not seen Anne and Peter since their wedding because Janie and Pauline have been living in France with Julian and Colinette (p151/180). Con Atherton, Julian Lucy, Janie, Pauline, and Maidie and Rex Willoughby take a boat out to Lihou Island late one night to pretend to be ghosts, but the boat drifts away and they have to wait for the tide to uncover the causeway before they can return home. Sigrid Willoughby meets the youngsters as she has found out about their adventure (p189/194/197). Miss Matthias, a neighbour of the Willoughbys, rents a cottage on Sark for a year and invites Janie, Maidie, Rex and Marjolaine Willoughby, the older Athertons, and Julian Lucy to stay for ten days. Janie takes a deep interest in the taunting of Mr Eltringham. We learn that Janie has recovered from a serious attack of scarlet fever in the spring of the previous year, and since then can do no wrong in Julian's eyes (p200/250/253). Janie and Pauline return to France at the end of the summer and Janie will go to the Paris Conservatoire. We learn that she intends to go to Florence for a year when she is twenty (p274/275). Janie and Pauline meet Heather Raphael and her family on a boat when they are crossing to Guernsey for the summer in *Heather* and we learn that Major Raphael knew Captain Michael Temple very well seven years previously. Janie is now at the

Paris Conservatoire studying the piano and it is mentioned that when the Temple girls were living with Mme Ozanne, they had a French governess named Mme Mauray. Janie is now eighteen (p48/52/70). Heather is rude to her father one morning but after a talk with Janie she apologises to him (p62/68/72). Janie, Pauline and the three Raphael girls have a picnic at Pleinmont and Raoul le Pelley and the Lemercier boys steal their shoes (p73/81/85). Janie and Pauline return to France at the end of the summer holiday (p94/96/163). The two girls visit the Raphaels at Christmas and meet Alured Saxon on the train (p180/181). Janie, Heather and Cressida Shakespeare are hurt fighting thieves who break into The Towers and Janie sprains her wrist (p230/232/237). Nineteen-year-old Janie is not pretty but is growing attractive and has Julian Lucy's engagement ring on her finger when she and Pauline visit the Raphaels in June (p244). Janie and Julian make their wedding preparations in *Janie of* and Julian buys La Rochelle, the house in which the Temple girls lived on first coming to Guernsey six years earlier (p9/11/16). The house is enlarged and includes a new dining room, a bigger kitchen and bedrooms for their maids Bonita and Michelle (p17/18). Janie has bright golden-brown hair and brown eyes and Pauline is to be her chief bridesmaid at her wedding to Julian Lucy in Peterport (p21/22/25). The twenty-three-year-old bride also has Heather Raphael, Con and Rosamund Atherton, and Maidie and Marjolaine Willoughby as bridesmaids and Beth Chester and Michael Ozanne as trainbearers. We are reminded that Janie received her mothering from her sister Elizabeth. Janie approaches beauty in her mid-Victorian wedding gown. Paul Ozanne gives her away (p27/33/37). Janie and Julian spend part of their honeymoon on Sark and stay with Fidelity (p44/45). They decide to stay on Sark rather than journey to Brittany. Janie is barely five foot two to her new husband's six foot one. They are on the beach when the Athertons, Willoughbys, Raphaels and Pauline Ozanne arrive to swim. The young couple hide in a cave until their friends depart (p51/56). We are informed that Miss Matthias is very fond of Janie (p63). Janie receives an unexpected visit from the formidable Mrs La Touche and has to improvise a lunch. Janie and Julian meet the four Clitheroe brothers, Mrs La Touche's nephews named after the northern saints, and later Janie has them picking fruit (p76/87/96). The Lucys visit the Raphaels at Shottery Towers when they go to England for Rosamund and Nigel Willoughby's wedding. Janie plays and sings for the Raphaels (p106/113). On returning home they discover that Julian's grandmother Mrs Orange has a chest infection and when she is well enough they move Mr Lucy and Mrs Orange to La Rochelle so that she can convalesce (p129/136). Janie's housekeeping endeavours lead her to bake a special cake when the Ozannes are invited to tea and she uses whitening instead of sugar (p137/141). Michael and Billy Ozanne visit La Rochelle when their mother gives birth to their twin sisters (p146/147). Janie falls asleep when she is looking after the boys and they set off to see their new sisters. Janie, Bonita, Michelle and Mrs La Touche search for the boys and Michelle finds them (p161/165/168). Janie, Pauline, Rosamund and Maidie become godmothers to Nella and Vanna Ozanne (p174). We are told that Janie's Parisian school was Sacré Coeur. She receives a visit from Rosamund and Nigel Willoughby at the time of the Ozanne twins' christening and it is evident that both Janie and Rosamund are expecting babies (p175/176). Allegra Atherton visits Janie after breaking off her engagement out of jealousy, but her fiancé Hugh finds her and they are reconciled. Michelle and Bonita attend Héloïse's wedding and Janie invites Miss Matthias to tea and burns her scones (p189/195/199). Janie gives birth to baby Juliet in May and Julian buys Les Arbres, just outside Peterport, from Harry le Martin with money left to him by Mrs Orange. There is enough space for his father to have his own rooms (p217/227/228). Janie is asked by Rosamund to be godmother for her first child, Harold Nigel. Janie and Julian keep La Rochelle as a holiday house (p231/233). Nigel Willoughby describes Janie in *Steps In* as being short with brown eyes and looking like Puck. Nan Blakeney, the Athertons' cousin, visits the Lucys and it is mentioned that Janie is the world's worst sailor (p35/53/55). Janie and Julian now have four children, six-year-old Julie, John who is five, two-year-old Betsy and baby Viola (p59; p27 for Vi's name). Janie and Nan get the Chesters' home ready for Anne's return from a visit (p94/97). We learn that Janie is Nancy Chester's godmother and looks after her education, as Peter's inheritance was embezzled (p102/107). Janie and Julian go away for a few days leaving Nan in charge, and Julie and John paint Betsy's face with nail varnish (p172/185). Julie, John and Betsy catch mumps from the Ozanne children and Janie takes baby Viola to La Rochelle (p188/190/191). Nan's father, Sir Charles Blakeney, is very ill and it is agreed that Nan will remain with the Lucys (p214/217). Nan is staying at La Rochelle with the four Lucy children, Nanny and Lucie when Janie gives birth to her second son, Barnabas Julian, and Nan becomes his godmother (p247/253). Joey Maynard meets Janie and her two elder sisters, Elizabeth Ozanne and Anne Chester, in *Exile* and we learn that Janie had another baby in June and hasn't been well. Her sisters are both lovely women but Janie is a puckish-looking individual with brown eyes and brown hair with glints of gold. Her husband Julian is good-looking and all the children except for Betsy have taken after him. Janie becomes fast friends with Jo Maynard (p187/188/189). When the Chalet School opens at Sarres, Julian and Janie pay for Nancy Chester's education, as she is Janie's goddaughter and only a few months younger than their eldest daughter Julie, who is also going there with her brother John and their cousins, the Ozanne twins (p213/214). The Lucys and Ozannes move to Armiford in *Goes to It* and Julian is in the RAF. Miss Everett, the school gardening mistress, who is also the Lucys' gardener, lives with them (p12/18/111). Joey Maynard has breakfast at the Lucys' house while waiting for the McDonalds' overdue train to arrive in *Highland Twins* and sees Janie's five children and also Nan Blakeney, who is newly engaged to David Willoughby (p39/40). Julie Lucy resists the temptation to quote Janie in *Lavender* as having said that the heroine of the Lavender Laughs series must be an awful kid (p48). Miss Wilson spends a night at Janie's on her way back to school after the motor accident in *Gay* (p118). Joey mentions to Simone in *Rescue* that Julian hasn't been home for two years (p90). Janie lives in Weonister Road on the opposite side of the city of Armiford to the cathedral in *Mystery*. A party of Chalet School girls have lunch at the Lucys' house before going to the cinema (p51). Janie has a new baby named Katharine Margaret in *Three Go*. It is mentioned that Janie is a great friend of Jo Maynard and is, like her, a matchmaker. She encourages a relationship between Gillian Linton and Clement Young (p72/208/209). The

Lucys, Chesters and Ozannes donate one of the Chalet School boats in *Island* (p146). Mr la Touche, a family friend, flies Janie Lucy to Cardiff in his private plane in *Bride* when Julie becomes very ill with peritonitis. We learn that although there is no lack of money in the Lucy family, they have brought up their family to help with the younger ones and as they grow older to take on responsibilities (p137/150). Julie's and her cousins' fluent French in *Barbara* is the result of their mothers having spent so much of their girlhood in France (p112). Janie and Julian go away for a few days at the start of *Coming of Age*, leaving Julie and Betsy to look after Kitten (p7). There is a passing mention of Janie in *Trials* when Vi has written to her mother but not yet to her sisters (p36). Janie has the keys to the Ozannes' house in Peterport in *Ruey* and is able to abstract Vanna and Nella's lacrosse crosses (p123). Janie informs Joey of Vanna Ozanne's engagement in *Future* (p203). Janice Chester mentions in *Adrienne* that her parents are stricter than her Aunt Janie and Uncle Julian Lucy about not cheeking (p116). EBD says in *N10* that all Janie's girls have attended the Chalet School (p39).

CHILDREN (GENERATION C):
1) **JULIET PAULINE (JULIE)** : see LUCY, JULIET
2) **JOHN:** see LUCY, JOHN
3) **ELIZABETH (BETSY)** : see LUCY, ELIZABETH
4) **MARY VIOLA (VI)** : see LUCY, MARY
5) **BARNABAS JULIAN (BARNEY)** : see LUCY, BARNABAS
6) **KATHARINE MARGARET (KITTEN):** see LUCY, KATHARINE

TEMPLE, CAPTAIN MICHAEL: Naval officer Captain Michael Temple is Elizabeth, Anne and Janie Temple's father and he has recently died at the start of *Maids*. We learn that he had fair skin, grey eyes and fair curls. He was newly retired from the navy and Elizabeth and Anne, his first two daughters, were the children of his first marriage, to Giovanna, an Italian girl. He married Giovanna when he was a twenty-three-year-old lieutenant and Elizabeth was born eighteen months later. Captain Temple was then sent to China for three years and Anne was born a year after his return. Unfortunately Giovanna caught a chill when Anne was five months old and died from pleurisy. Captain Temple's young unmarried sister looked after his young daughters in a flat in London surrounded by art students from the Slade School for the next five years, until Miss Temple wanted to get married and travel on the Continent (p9/11/12). Commander Temple then proposed to Agnes Weston because he wanted a home for his daughters, and became very fond of her after they were married. His new wife gave birth to a baby they named Janie but later Agnes was killed in a carriage accident. The girls were sent to Miss Moulton's school at Hurst Ridge in Sussex where they stayed until Elizabeth was eighteen, Anne was fourteen and Janie nine years old. Miss Moulton closed the school as she was getting old and it wasn't paying enough. Captain Temple was with the South Atlantic fleet and, as his sister and her husband were now in Australia, with a large family, he had nowhere to send the girls. Captain Temple's half-French Commander Julian Ozanne suggested that the girls should live with his widowed mother in France as his cousin Suzanne, who lived there, was about to be married. The three girls lived with her for the next five years, returning to England when their father retired (p13/15/17). Not long afterwards he died of a heart attack, and was buried in Cornwall in the same churchyard as his first wife. Like many sailors Captain Temple had spent every penny of his pay and there had been no chance to save from his pension (p18/19). His daughters later meet Peter Chester, who had been in the Navy and knew Captain Temple on the *Bellesaurus* (p89). The Raphael family visit Guernsey during the summer holidays in *Heather* and we learn that Major Raphael knew Michael Temple seven years ago (p52).

TEMPLETON, MR: Mr Templeton is an Australian neighbour of Emerence Hope's family in Manly, New South Wales, in *Shocks* (p17; p10 for location).

TERNIKAI, MAURÚS: Maurús Ternikai, a tall, dark Belsornian, would have liked to tell Prince Cosimo to do his own dirty work in *Princess* but has been blackmailed into working for Cosimo and does not dare defy him because Cosimo knows he was responsible for stealing secret papers from the Records Office and selling them to Belsornia's enemies (p142/180). He introduces himself to Madge Bettany as Signor Maurús Ternikai, lately Captain in the Royal Household Guards and Princess Elisaveta's bodyguard. He helps Prince Cosimo to kidnap Princess Elisaveta of Belsornia (p201/202/209/212).

TERRY, SHEILA: Sheila Terry appears to be an Australian friend of Beth Chester's in 'Beth's Diary' in *2nd* (p88).

THANE, SYLVIA: Sylvia starts at the Chalet School in *New Mistress* and is in Nancy Wilmot's form (p49).

THEO: Dorcas Brownlow's cousin Theo is mentioned in *Mystery* (p80/81/96).

THIRLBECK, MR AND MRS ALFRED: Alfred Thirlbeck and his wife are travelling by train with their five children, the children's Aunt Amy and Alfred's formidable mother-in-law when they meet Jacynth Hardy and Gay Lambert in *Gay* (p23/24/25/27). The family are taking over Mrs Parry's shop at Howells village. The children are Ethel, Maud, Stanley, Pansy and a baby boy (p26/190). Gay meets Mr Thirlbeck and Grandma, Rebecca Learoyd, when she runs away from school to see her brother Tommy before his departure to China (p168). 'Mr Thirlbeck's the shop' is mentioned by the triplets in *Joey Goes* (p10).

(THIRLBECK), AMY: Amy seems to be either Alfred Thirlbeck's sister or a younger daughter of

Rebecca Learoyd, Alfred's formidable mother-in-law, in *Gay* (p25/169).

THIRLBECK, ETHEL, MAUD, PANSY, STANLEY and unnamed baby BOY: Alfred Thirlbeck and his wife have five children, twelve-year-old Ethel, Maud, Stanley, who is about eight years old, Pansy, and a baby boy, in *Gay* (p23/24/25/190).

THIRTLE, MR and MRS: Reg Entwistle lives with his elderly widowed great-aunt Mrs Thirtle in *Rescue*. Mrs Thirtle's husband died, leaving her fairly well off, and she owns her cottage and the land and has two cows, a pig and some poultry. She is not the spending kind and can quite well afford to send Reg to Garnley Grammar but has no use for education. Mrs Thirtle accepts Jack Maynard's offer to pay for Reg's education on the understanding that until he goes to college he spends most of his holidays with her. She will provide his clothes and books but will not pay for his school fees (p150/151/239).

THOMAS: Thomas is a steward on board the cargo-boat on which Grizel Cochrane and Neil Sheppard meet in *Reunion* (p22).

THOMAS, EVAN: Evan and John Pritchard deliver the girls' trunks in their cart in *Shocks* (p25/26).

THOMAS, GWEN: Gwen is the Lower Fourth's Form Prefect when the girls are in trouble with Miss Wilmot for taking Upper IVA's possessions and putting them into other girls' desks and lockers in *Challenge* (p127).

THOMAS, JANE: Fifth former Jane forms a quartette with Jean Downes, Hilda Smith and Lorna Wills, and they make dolls' sheets for the School Sale in *Peggy* (p164).

THOMÉ, GABRIELLE: Gabrielle appears to be in Inter V with Ailie Russell and her friends in *Adrienne* and hopes to take up kindergarten work (p51).

THOMÉ, GHISLAINE: Ghislaine is a Middle and sits at the same table as Mary-Lou Trelawney's Gang in *Barbara*. Steady Ghislaine is friendly with Clare (Kennedy) and they visit Unterseen and the Rösleinalp (p59/91/139). She is in the Upper Fourth (p173/174). Ghislaine is in the Upper Fourth and is busy at a hobbies class in *Does It Again* (p173; p170 for form). She is from Belgium and may perform at the end-of-term concert in *Kenya* (p111).

THOMÉ, LIZETTE: Lizette is in Upper IVB with Samaris Davies in *Two Sams* (p99). Lizette is in the Pansy dormitory in *Althea* and we learn that she is French. She is in Upper IVB's art class when they are doing frieze design (p45/78/97).

THOMPSON, CAPTAIN: We are told in *Joey and Co.* that Ruey Richardson's maternal grandfather Captain Thompson was a captain in the Union Castle line, was married to Margaret and died when his youngest son Bertie was a baby. His youngest sister was Laurie Rosomon's mother (p204).

THOMPSON, DR: Dr Thompson is Phoebe Wychcote's local doctor at Garnham in *Rescue* (p210).

THOMPSON, MISS: see ROSOMON, MRS

THOMPSON (THOMSON), AILSA: Ailsa is friendly with Betsy Lucy and is at the staff party in *Barbara* (p193). Ailsa is a prefect or sub-prefect in *Mary-Lou* (although Vi Lucy fails to mention her when listing the prefects on p9) and, because she speaks decent German, is delegated to help buy prizes for the prefects' party (p93). Miss Wilson chooses her as one of the escort prefects for her own group on the expedition to the Falls of Rhine (p109). She is cast as Robin Hood in *Beauty and the Beast* (p152). Ailsa has been promoted to being a full prefect and is in charge of Music in *Genius* (p58/60). She plays the part of Simon in the St Mildred's pantomime *Puss in Boots* in *Trials* (p195).

THOMPSON, BERTIE: Bertie is mentioned in *Joey and Co.* as the youngest brother of Ruey Richardson's mother Evelyn (p204).

THOMPSON, EVELYN: see RICHARDSON, EVELYN

THOMPSON, MARGARET: We are told in *Joey and Co.* that Ruey Richardson's maternal grandmother Margaret Thompson came from Liverpool and was married to Captain Thompson, a captain in the Union Castle line. She was Evelyn Richardson's bossy mother. After the death of her husband, she was left to bring up their family, including baby Bertie, on her own and wanted her children to have no life apart from her. Her husband's sister was Laurie Rosomon's mother and we learn that Mrs Thompson died six years ago (p204/206/208).

THOMPSON, ROBERTA: Roberta arrives at the Chalet School after St Hilda's School has burned down in *Feud*. She is a friend of Phyllis Garstin and Katherine Rutherford and is probably with them in VB (p80; p55 for form).

THORA: see MADALE

THORNTON, CELIA (MORTON, CELIA): Celia is in Upper IVB and prefers games and gymnastics to schoolwork in *Two Sams* (p69). She may be the same person as Celia Morton in *Althea* (p79).

THORSBY, ANNE: Anne is from St Hilda's School and arrives at the Chalet School with Anne Crozier, Gillie Garstin and Mary Candlish after the disastrous fire that burns down their school in *Feud*. After school tests, Anne is sent down to Lower IIIA with Jane Mortimer and Susan Austin (p55).

THWAITES, MRS: Mrs Thwaites is the widowed cousin of Miss Holroyd, the headmistress of St Hilda's in *Feud*. She is an SRN and is the matron and housekeeper at St Hilda's until their school burns down and they move in with the Chalet School (p10/12). Mrs Thwaites settles in happily at the Chalet School and is content to accept difficulties and make the best of things. She strikes up a warm friendship with Matron Lloyd (p94/95/172).

TINAUREL, DR: Dr Tinaurel is a doctor whom Rex Willoughby consults at Nigel Willoughby's insistence when he has heart fluttering after Nigel, Rex and Julian Lucy have had a terrifying night on board Nigel's steam-yacht *Sea Dweller* in a storm in *Scamps* (p171/172).

TINGLE, MR: Bob Maynard's agent Mr Tingle is mentioned in *Rescue* (p141/145).

TIZZARD, MR and MRS: The Tizzards are servants of the Chudleigh family in *Chudleigh Hold* (p24).

TODD, LADY EVELYN: Lady Evelyn Todd's niece Georgiana is a young runaway in 'Joey Oar' in *1st* (p89/92).

TOINETTE, SOEUR: Soeur Toinette is one of the Sisters of St Vincent de Paul who help in the train crash rescue in *Summer Term* (p34).

TOM: Tom, Alice, Simmonds, Louie, Nancy and Sally are servants at the Raphaels' home, The Towers, in *Heather* and help search for Hazel and Honey when they are missing in the Monk's Passage. Tom is the boy who attends to the boots and knives and helps Barnes the butler with the silver (p140/141).

TOM, UNCLE: see (BETTANY), UNCLE TOM

TOMLIN, MRS: Mrs Tomlin is a local resident in Garnham in *Rescue*, with a daughter called Maisie (p30).

TOMLIN, MAISIE: Twelve-year-old Maisie lives in Garnham in *Rescue* (p30).

TOMSON, LILLIE: Lillie is a slim, fair girl in IIIA with Gerry Challoner at St Peter's School in *Gerry* (p75/80; p73 for form) and they are members of the Secret Society (p87). Gerry overhears Lillie mention that Mr Lorimer, master at the boys' school, is in love with Miss Hamilton, their form mistress (p148). Nell replies that Lillie is an awful little ass (p149).

TOT: Dark little Tot is in the Grange School tennis team playing against St Peter's School in *HG Difficulties* (p304).

TOTTON, MR: Mr Totton is the butler at the Dragon House in *Lost Staircase* (p21).

TOUCHE, MR la: Janie Lucy is flown from Guernsey to Cardiff by a family friend, Mr la Touche, in his private aeroplane when Julie becomes very ill with peritonitis in *Bride*. He is a great friend of Julian Lucy (p137/138).

TOUCHE, MRS la: Jacqueline and her mother, Mrs la Touche, spend a month in Brittany in *Steps In* and we learn that Mrs la Touche is frail (p97/205).

TOUCHE, MADAME (MRS) AMY la: Mme la Touche, a stern old lady, arrives unexpectedly at Janie Lucy's home, La Rochelle, in *Janie of*. She has four nephews, Wilfred, Ninian, Cuthbert and Aidan Clitheroe, named after the northern saints, and a niece named Margaret Hilda who is ten years younger and has scarlet fever. She is hoping that Julian will be able to take her nephews on expeditions (p76/78/79). We learn that Amy la Touche and Mrs Orange are old enemies and were at Miss Martin's school together (p92). Janie falls asleep when she is looking after Michael and Billy Ozanne and the boys set off to see their new twin sisters (p162/164). Mrs la Touche helps Janie search for the boys and baths Michael and Billy after they are found. She wisely prevents Janie from fussing over them (p165/169/170). Maidie Willoughby and Mrs la Touche's third nephew Cuthbert become engaged and Cuthbert and Maidie visit the old lady in Guernsey. Mrs la Touche mentions that she has seen Allegra Atherton in a London play (p182/183/187).

TOUCHE, JACQUELINE la: Jacqueline la Touche is Julie and John Lucy's governess in *Steps In*. She is a pleasant girl of about twenty-two with short dark curls, and lives with her mother (p57/58). Jacqueline also teaches the Lucys' cousins, Nancy Chester and Nella and Vanna Ozanne., The Chester twins will start after the summer holidays. Jacqueline and her mother have just spent a month in Brittany (p95/97). Jacqueline wants to come and help Nan Blakeney when she is nursing Julie, John and Betsy Lucy and four Chester children who have mumps, but Peter Chester forbids this because Jacqueline has not had mumps and her mother is frail. Miss la Touche is married at Easter (p205/241). Gillian and Joyce Linton meet Jacqueline in Guernsey in *Exile*, which takes place at about the same time. We are told that Jacqueline's charges will go to the Chalet School when it opens as she intends getting married in the summer (p175/176/181).

TOUCHE, NICOLE la: Nicole is Carol White's choice of partner for Joey's tea party in *Tom* and is prone to get into trouble (p29). Nicole is in the Lower Fifth with Betsy Lucy and Clem Barrass in *Peggy* and has no real love of lessons (p93; p92 for form).

TOUCHE, SYLVIE la: Sylvie is in the Upper Third with her friends Joy Bird, Marilyn Wynn and Hester Layng in *Lavender* and sides with Joy in her dispute with Lavender (p167).

TOURTELLE, MEDELEINE (MADELEINE): Medeleine Tourtelle helps Art Prefect Sally Winslow make invitations for the prefects' evening in *Mary-Lou* (p81). Her name was corrected to 'Madeleine' in the Armada editions.

TOUSSAINT, ANGÈLE: Canadian Angèle is about twenty years old when she is in the accident ward at the Görnetz Sanatorium in *Summer Term*. Angèle was mixed up in a bobsleigh accident and emerged with a compound fracture of the thigh (p107/116).

Interlaken

TOUVET, GHISLAINE (GHISELAINE): Ghislaine is an eleven-year-old French girl in the Pansy dormitory with Jack Lambert in *Leader*. She is in Lower IIIA, still with Jack (p19/68; p16 for Jack's form). Ghiselaine is walking with Gretchen von Ahlen and Rosemary Wentworth on a form walk in *Trick* (p70). She goes with the Junior Middles on an excursion to Neuchâtel in *Feud*. Ghiselaine shares a dormitory with Moira Baker and Helen Henderson, and Rosamund Lilley is their dormitory prefect (p119/133). Ghislaine is in Lower IVB with Jack in *Triplets* (p22). She is in IVA with Jack and her friends when they discuss their forthcoming entertainment in *Redheads* and suggests hopping races as part of a possible indoor gymkhana (p65). Ghislaine is in the Gentian dormitory with Arda Peik and initiates a pillow fight in *Adrienne*, and her treasured vase is broken. Afterwards Barbara Henschell mentions that Ghislaine's health must be improving (p191).

TOUVET, RENÉE: Renée starts at the Chalet School halfway through the term in *Theodora*. We are told that her only relative is an aunt who has been ill and is in the Sanatorium for treatment. Renée was at a convent school in Brussels before coming to the Chalet School. Ted Grantley moves up to VB to make room for Renée in Inter V (p97). Renée is in the Gentian dormitory where Len Maynard is Head in *Ruey*. Matey mentions that Renée spent most of the previous term in the School san so is practically new (p12/13). Renée has spent the holidays up at the Görnetz Platz because her aunt has been very ill. She stayed with Hilary Graves, who talked to her in English and German so that Renée understands them much better now (p14/33). Renée takes part in a Book Titles evening given by the Fifth forms in *Leader* and is the smallest member of both forms. She is in VB and because she is delicate she must not be overworked (p53/98).

TOVEY, MARIAN: Marian transfers from the Tanswick Chalet School in *Bride* and is in the Leafy dormitory. Fifteen-and-a-half-year-old Marian should have been in one of the Lower Fifths but is not up to standard. She is a year older than the other girls in her form and dormitory (p93/94) and is in Upper IVA with seven other girls from Tanswick (p95). She was not popular at her previous school (p101). Marian omits to stand when Miss Annersley leaves their formroom and bitterly resents being corrected (p104/105). Bride Bettany's study is ransacked and Marian admits to helping Diana Skelton do this after Diana threatened to expose her dishonesty, as she had caught Marian stealing sweets the previous term. Marian eventually reforms (p246/261/262). Marian is in the Leafy dormitory in *Changes* and her resentment of authority was too much for Gwen Jones as dormitory prefect, so Katharine Gordon has been moved there in her place (p43).

TOWNSEND, SIBYL and SYLVIA: The Townsend twins, Sibyl and Sylvia, are at Ripley Collegiate with Heather Raphael in *Heather* but standards of behaviour there have become unsatisfactory. Their parents remove them from the school and send them to a convent school in Edinburgh. Heather misses the fifteen-year-old Townsend twins, with whom she had been friendly at school (p16/18/123).

TRACY, DR: Dr Tracy, Princess Elisaveta's doctor in *Princess*, recommends that Princess Elisaveta should be sent to a school in the Austrian Tyrol that is run by an English girl. A friend of his has just sent his daughter there (p9/10/13). Dr Tracy approves of Elisaveta going to Guide Camp at the Baumersee in *Camp* (p12/26).

TRACY, MRS: Lady Carew is in the back seat of a car driven by Mrs Tracy when they meet with an accident in Australia in *Jane* (p175).

TRATSCHIN, HERR and FRAU: Joey Maynard knows the Tratschins very well and arranges for the Chalet girls to stay at their farmhouse near St Moritz during half term in *Trials*. Herr Tratschin startles the girls when he claims that the gaily coloured decorative artwork on the farmhouse is due to be repainted at any time, since they think it looks as fresh as if it had only been done the week before (p85). The house is so clean that Hilary jokes that they could eat their dinner off the floorboards (p86). Herr Tratschin and his wife have eight children, Johann, Paul, Kurt, Heidi, Lina, Maria, Arnold and Gaudenz. The girls are out tobogganing when an avalanche strikes and Herr Tratschin rescues them from a mountain hut in which they manage to shelter (p99/131/133).

TRATSCHIN, ARNOLD: Arnold is still at school in *Trials* but means to be a doctor (p99).

TRATSCHIN, GAUDENZ: Nine- or ten-year-old Gaudenz is the Tratschins' youngest child when the

Chalet girls visit their farmhouse near St Moritz in *Trials* (p90/99).

TRATSCHIN, HEIDI: Heidi and Lina Tratschin are nurses at the Burgspital in Lucerne in *Trials* (p99).

TRATSCHIN, JOHANN: The Tratschins' eldest son Johann is training to be a hotelier in Vienna in *Trials* and will then go to London to practise his English (p99).

TRATSCHIN, KURT: The Tratschins' third son Kurt is training as an engineer in *Trials* (p99).

TRATSCHIN, LINA: Lina and Heidi Tratschin are nurses at the Burgspital in Lucerne in *Trials* (p99).

TRATSCHIN, MARIA: The Tratschins' youngest daughter Maria is still at school in *Trials* (p99).

TRATSCHIN, PAUL: Paul will take over the Tratschins' farm when he finishes a course in pure science at Basle in *Trials* (p99).

TREDGOLD, MR and MRS: Mr and Mrs Tredgold, parents of Natalie and Nicola Tredgold, are involved in a ghastly motor smash in *Triplets*. Mrs Tredgold gets off with bad bruises and shock but Mr Tredgold is nearly killed and has to have an emergency operation. He is very ill and keeps calling for the twins (p149).

TREDGOLD, NATALIE: Natalie and Nicola Tredgold are twins at St Mildred's in *Triplets* and have come from Halidon House School. They have to drop out of the Welsen pantomime at the last minute when their parents are involved in a motor accident, and Clem Barras replaces Natalie as Fairy Nettlesting (p148/149).

TREDGOLD, NICOLA: Fair, pretty Nicola and her twin Natalie are pupils at St Mildred's in *Triplets* and they have come from Halidon House School. Nicola has the part of the Fairy Queen in the Welsen pantomime but the twins have to drop out at the last minute when their parents are involved in a motor accident. Barbara Chester asks Len Maynard to replace her, but Con eventually does as she is smaller than her sister (p148/149/150).

TREATT: Treatt is the postman in *Chudleigh Hold* (p86).

TREGASKIS, MR: Mélie Lihou marries a Cornish farmer, Mr Tregaskis, and they have one child when Anne Chester visits them in *Steps In* (p97/116).

TREGASKIS, MÉLIE: see LIHOU, MÉLIE

TRELAWNEY, PROFESSOR (B): We learn in *Three Go* that Professor Trelawney's brother was killed in the war (p62). Professor Trelawney, Mary-Lou's father and Doris's husband, is in South America on the Murray-Cameron Expedition exploring the Amazon. He has been away for seven years and is the expedition's entomologist, collecting butterflies and insects and writing books (p75/76). There has been no news of the expedition for nearly two years (p77/101). Later on word arrives that the Murray-Cameron expedition was attacked and that Professor Trelawney has been killed, with only two men surviving. Professor Trelawney was fair like Mary-Lou, who is also like him in character. Dr O'Brien and Verity-Ann Carey's father manage to escape (p173/176/177). Mary-Lou's father was not present when the expedition was attacked but rushed in to help his friends and was killed, so he died a hero (p223). He is one of Mary-Lou's heroes in *Shocks* and she hopes to grow up to be the kind of girl he would have wanted her to be (p139). The circumstances of his death are explained in *Changes* (p34). It is mentioned in *Mary-Lou* that Professor Trelawney, an exploring entomologist, was responsible for finding no fewer than seven different species of butterflies in the upper reaches of the Amazon (p1) Some of his collections are in the British Museum (p77). We learn in *Trick* that Professor Trelawney was an only child (p97). We are informed in *Adrienne* that Mary-Lou's father was a naturalist specialising in butterflies. He was noted for his additions to some of the great British collections and for his own private collection, which is considered to be one of the finest in the world. The collection is currently being lent to a museum because his wife refused to sell it, and it now belongs to Mary-Lou (p174).

TRELAWNEY (TREVELLYAN), DORIS (CAREY, DORIS) (B): Mrs Trelawney is introduced in *Three Go*, where she lives with her nine-year-old daughter Mary-Lou and her mother-in-law, referred to as Gran. Mrs Trelawney is not as strict as Gran and Mary-Lou would have ruled her mother if it were not for Gran. They live at Polquenel in Cornwall in a house called Tanquen (p7/8/9). Doris Trelawney has more and more frequent colds and because of her poor health they are advised by their doctor to move, while Gran is determined to separate Mary-Lou from her friends the Barras children, whom she considers unsuitable (p9/10/11/12/13). Mrs Trelawney and Gran teach Mary-Lou at home, although Mrs Trelawney herself went to school as a child and it sounds fun to Mary-Lou when she talks about it (p21). They move to Carn Beg in Howells village and we learn that Doris is a born gardener and is quiet and gentle (p37/39/60). Doris is an only child and there are no other relatives, as her husband's brother was killed in the war. Doris's husband has been away in South America on the Murray-Cameron Expedition exploring the Amazon for seven years (p62/76/77). Professor Trelawney is killed when the expedition is attacked and Mrs Trelawney becomes a widow (p173). Mrs Trelawney has dark hair, grey eyes and not much colour. She invites Clem and Tony Barras to spend Christmas with them (p176/219). She tells Mary-Lou about her first meeting with her husband about twelve years previously. Verity-Ann Carey's father, who was on the same expedition, meets Mrs Trelawney (p227/228/272). Clem refers to Mary-Lou's mother in *Island* as Auntie Doris. Slight, rather sad-looking Doris Trelawney attends the Regatta (p28/222). Joey refers to her on one occasion as Doris Trevellyan (p284). Clem mentions in *Carola* that her Auntie Doris gave her a new lacrosse stick for Christmas (p94). Mary-Lou has to ask her mother to post some missing socks to her in *Wrong* (p40). Mary-Lou has brought her mother's old cutting-out scissors to school to use in place of secateurs in *Shocks* (p124). Clem keeps an eye on Mary-Lou out of gratitude for the home provided by Mrs Trelawney in *Bride* (p264). We are told in *Changes* that Mary-Lou's mother is marrying Verity-Anne's father and Mary-Lou and Verity-Anne will become stepsisters. Mrs Trelawney has taken Verity-Anne to her heart and home, and the girl has stayed with them during the holidays because Verity-Anne's father is not well and the Careys have no home of their own. The wedding will take place in July and we are informed that Mr Carey is not fit enough to return to South America (p34/35). It is mentioned in *Joey Goes* that Doris Trelawney is ten years older than Joey (p42). Mary-Lou's early upbringing by her mother and grandmother is mentioned in *Does It Again* (p36). Mary-Lou recalls her mother and grandmother planting roses at their Howells house in *Kenya* (p90). We learn in *Mary-Lou* that the expedition's doctor, whose sight was damaged during the attack

Cornwall

on the Murray-Cameron expedition, now writes books. He often stays with the Careys and Mary-Lou's mother, a good shorthand typist, helps by acting as his secretary (p130). Later, Mrs Carey is in the throes of a severe attack of influenza and is too ill to be told of Mary-Lou's accident. She needs a complete change and it is decided that she and her husband should come out to Switzerland for a few months to stay at Das Haus unter die Kiefern (p174/189). The Careys are advised to stay longer in Switzerland and they manage to rent a chalet higher up the mountain at the Rösleinalp in *Genius*. Commander and Mrs Carey come to the School Sale (p101/196). Joey asks after Doris's health in *Problem* (p106). Mary-Lou is looking forward to spending the holidays with her mother, and with Clem and Tony who now make their home with them, in *New Mistress* (p218/219). Mrs Carey meets Miss Bubb up on the Rösleinalp in *Excitements* and informs her that the Chalet School is now in Switzerland (p189). Mary-Lou returns to England at Easter to open up Carn Beg for the Careys because her mother is well enough to go home (p222). Mary-Lou returns to school early in *Coming of Age* and stays at Joey's home with Verity, as their parents have gone to Edinburgh to see a specialist about Commander Carey's leg (p8). Mary-Lou's mother goes with her stepfather to see his specialist in Glasgow in *Richenda* (p28). Mary-Lou recalls in *Theodora* that her mother was ill and could not visit at the time of her accident (p139). Roland Carey's old wound has flared up in *Joey and Co.* and Doris and the girls are taking him to Glasgow to see Dr McKenzie (p11). Doris's health is much better in *Leader* and she has not had a single cold all winter (p139). Commander Carey dies after an operation in an Edinburgh hospital and Verity and Mary-Lou fly there to join Mrs Carey in *Trick*. Len Maynard mentions to her friends that this could mean the end of Mary-Lou's archaeological career because she may have to stay at home and look after her mother. Clem and Tony Barras still live with them (p95/96/97). Mary-Lou is still hoping to go to Oxford and Joey invites Mrs Carey to stay at Freudesheim. Doris is expected to spend the rest of the summer with the Maynards (p110/124). Mrs Carey is staying at Unter die Kiefern for the winter in *Feud* (p197). Mary-Lou takes her mother to see Sir James Talbot in *Triplets* and he confirms that her lungs are in a very poor state. Joey helps Mary-Lou and Verity close Carn Beg as Doris is going out to Switzerland. She is not in good shape when she arrives at the Sanatorium (p172/178/191). Doris Carey dies in *Reunion* and Mary-Lou is glad that her mother's years of suffering and sorrow are over. Mary-Lou mentions that her paternal grandmother mothered her mother and meant a lot to her, since she never knew her own parents (p75/76). Mary-Lou and Verity take Mrs Carey's body back to England for burial and Miss Annersley accompanies the girls. We learn that Mollie Bettany will stay at Carn Beg and help the girls with the arrangements (p78/80). We learn in *Adrienne* that Mary-Lou's mother refused to sell Professor Trelawney's butterfly collection but loaned it to a museum (p174).

TRELAWNEY, MARY (GRAN), 'MADRE' (A): Mary-Lou Trelawney's Gran is strict about obedience and tidiness in *Three Go* but is a dear, kind person and an absolute rock when you are in real trouble. Mrs Trelawney lives in Polquenel in Cornwall with her daughter-in-law Doris and grand-daughter Mary-Lou and moves with them to Howells village on the Welsh borders. She is a born gardener (p7/8/37/39). There are no other relatives as Gran's other son was killed during the war. Mary-Lou's full name is Mary Louise, after her Gran and Grannie (p62/73). After the death of Professor Trelawney on the Murray-Cameron Expedition, the old lady becomes ill (p173). Doris calls her mother-in-law Madre (Spanish for 'mother'). She tells Mary-Lou that Gran has bought Carn Beg (p221/227). Mary-Lou says in *Changes* that her grandmother told her years ago that she would remain at the Chalet School until she was eighteen. In Gran's opinion, no man is fit to bring up a girl properly on his own (p34/35). Mary-Lou tells Vi in *Barbara* that Gran says she will have to buy her own umbrella if she loses another (p32). Fifteen-year-old Mary-Lou returns late to school in *Mary-Lou* because her grandmother has recently died after a sudden illness. The old lady saw to it that Mary-Lou, her only grandchild, was not spoiled. She insisted on obedience, proper manners and a few other important virtues and remained with the family, extending her training to Verity-Anne, when Mrs Trelawney married Commander Carey (p1). Mary-Lou changes her hair from pigtails to one plait, remembering with a pang that Gran loved her Kenwigses (p24). It was Gran who insisted that Mary-Lou grow her hair when she was big enough, we are told in *Problem* (p34). She is mentioned again in connection with Mary-Lou's pigtails in *New Mistress* (p152). In *Coming of Age*, Mary-Lou says she is looking forward to telling her grandmother all that has happened when they meet again in heaven (p200). Mary-Lou mentions in *Trials* that her grandmother was fussy about tidiness, with a place for everything, and everything in its place (p140). Len says in *Trick* that Mary-Lou thought the world of her Gran and always looked up to her (p99). We learn in *Reunion* that Gran mothered Mary-Lou's mother and meant a lot to her, since she never knew her own parents (p75/76). Gran left Carn Beg to Mary-Lou (p78).

TRELAWNEY, MARY LOUISE (MARY-LOU) (C): Nine-year-old, blue-eyed Mary-Lou lives with her mother and her paternal grandmother at Polquenel in Cornwall and is friendly with Clem and Tony Barras in *Three Go* (p7/8/9). Mary-Lou is an only child and does lessons at home as the ten-mile bus ride to Melion is too much for her. Mary-Lou rejoices in her friendship with Clem and Tony and they are inseparable out of school hours. Mary-Lou has short fair plaits and a round tan-and-rosy face (p9/10/11). Because of her mother's poor health the Trelawneys move to Carn Beg in Howells village, where they have a kindly gardener (p12/37/40). Mary-Lou, who is just ten, meets the nearly-eight-year-old Maynard triplets and she informs them that her birthday is 30th June (p44/46/47). She has no other relatives as her mother was an only child and her father's brother was killed in the war. Mary-Lou adopts the elder Maynards and Russells as aunts and uncles and she starts at the Chalet School as a day girl in Upper IIA with Josette Russell to help her (p62/63/69). We are told that Mary-Lou's full name is Mary Louise, after both her grandmothers (p73). She meets Verity-Ann Carey, another new girl who has also never been at school before. They discover that both their fathers are in South America on the Murray-Cameron Expedition exploring the Amazon. Mary-Lou's father, Professor Trelawney, is collecting butterflies and insects and writing books and has been away for seven years (p75/76/77). Mary-Lou enjoys English subjects with Miss Linton but, not being mathematically inclined, and having been taught old-fashioned methods by her grandmother, drops nearly to the bottom of her form in that subject. However, she proves to be good at languages and is soon ahead of the rest in French (p95/96). Mary-Lou is told that she will start to board at school after half term because of the bad weather. She plays at Red Indians with the Maynard triplets and the Russell children at half term and they colour themselves with red ochre (p111/118/123). After half term Mary-Lou finds herself sharing a dormitory with Clem Barras, who has just started school (p129). Clem is in Upper IIIA and the two girls do school work together after going to bed at night in the hope that Mary-Lou will be moved up a form nearer to Clem (p136/152). Although her arithmetic improves, this strategy makes Mary-Lou ill (p154/164). Joey Maynard tells Mary-Lou that the Murray-Cameron expedition had been attacked and that her father is dead, with only two men surviving the attack (p173/174). We learn that Mary-Lou is like her father in looks and character, and that the survivors were Dr O'Brien and Verity-Ann Carey's father (p176/177). Mary-Lou is the

beating Tom Gay, who allows herself to be distracted (p90/92/223). She is twelve years old in *Peggy* and is one of the girls who stand up for Peggy Bettany against the malicious rumours. Mary-Lou is in the Third form and has another row with Phil Craven (p65/226/227). Twelve-year-old Mary-Lou is friendly to new girl Carola on the ferry across to the Island in *Carola* (p45). Later in the term she complains of feeling headachey and develops German measles (p185). Mary-Lou is described as a blue-eyed Junior in *Wrong* although she appears from the context to be a Middle. She seems to have attended the Catholic Prayers but this is not clear (p39/43). She is the Upper Third Form Prefect and is in the Poplar patrol at the overnight Guide Camp in Kittiwake Cove (p106/134). Mary-Lou is found in the corridor by Miss Annersley after having been sent out of maths by Miss Edwardes and is sent to the study. She confesses to tilting sideways on her chair after having been told not to tilt backwards and is punished by having to apologise and do her work standing up (p223/224). Thirteen-year-old Mary-Lou is in the Leafy dormitory with her friends Doris and Verity-Anne in *Shocks* and is in the Lower Fourth (p58/104/122). She smuggles some scissors into school to use during gardening and when required to show them to Miss Burnett becomes entangled in a rose bush. Peggy Burnett tries to disentangle Mary-Lou and disappears down a disused well (p124/129/130). Mary-Lou is the Lower Fourth's Form Prefect and Captain of the Junior Middles' netball team (p137/138/231). She is an imp who is bosom friends with Verity-Anne Carey in *CS Oberland* (p83). Mary-Lou is in the Leafy dormitory in *Bride* and wears her hair in long fair plaits. She wants to be an explorer when she grows up. She does not learn music and her special friends are Verity-Anne, Viola, Doris and Lesley Malcolm (p57/61/62). Mary-Lou has started calling her plaits 'Kenwigses' after reading an abridged version of *Nicholas Nickleby* the previous term. She is now in Upper IVA and it is mentioned that she was formerly a small, sturdily built creature, but last term had taken to growing and is becoming a leggy young thing (p73/86/95). She is thirteen years old (p261). Mary-Lou is the acknowledged leader of her clan in *Changes*. We learn that Verity-Anne and Mary-Lou will become stepsisters when Mary-Lou's mother marries

only person that Verity-Ann can confide in, resulting in a rather one-sided friendship between them. We learn that Mary-Lou's father was not present when the expedition was attacked but rushed in to help his friends and was killed, so he died a hero (p213/223). Mary-Lou tries to persuade Verity-Ann to overcome her prejudice against singing in German, but although Verity-Ann is secretly very fond of her, she will not back down. Mary-Lou feels so sorry for Verity that she is prepared, on Clem's advice, to ask Plato to allow her to sing non-German songs in the concert (p250/251/265). At the end of term Mary-Lou comes joint top of her form with Doris Hill and Vi Lucy and will go up a form (p282). Eleven-year-old Mary-Lou moves with the Chalet School to St Briavel's Island in *Island* and is in Lower IIIB with Verity-Ann (p28/82). Mary-Lou defends Ruth Barnes against Phil Craven's accusation, when playing Impertinent Questions, that she cheats, and is involved in the subsequent fight. Mary-Lou wins the open swimming race at the School Regatta,

Verity-Ann's father in July. Mary-Lou is the first to ask a question, wanting to know how they will get to the Görnetz Platz and wondering if they might fly (p32/34/39). Mary-Lou will be fourteen in July and is now a Senior Middle. She wins the under-sixteens' swimming race and gives promise of becoming the finest swimmer the Chalet School has ever known. She comes second in the open race, nearly beating eighteen-year-old Bride Bettany (p114/191). The comment is made in *Joey Goes* that Mary-Lou's mother never plays with her (p42). Mary-Lou moves with the Chalet School to Switzerland in *Barbara* and is a Senior Middle. Her mother is now Mrs Carey, having married Verity-Anne's father. Mary-Lou protects Verity-Anne and saves her from many scoldings by helping her to do things, while Verity-Anne acts as a brake on her stepsister's wilder notions (p29/34/35). Mary-Lou is in Leafy dormitory and has difficulty plaiting her hair straight (p52/56). There are eleven members in her Gang, including Barbara Chester, on the expedition to the Rösleinalp when they miss their path in a blizzard (p139/145). Mary-Lou misses the excursion to Berne as she hurts her ankle falling downstairs. She is the leader of the Children's Crusaders in the Christmas Play (p157/158/206). Mary-Lou is a Senior Middle in *Does It Again* and is a masterful-looking young woman of about fifteen with keen, blue eyes and long, light-brown plaits dangling on either side of a pink-and-white face full of character. Mary-Lou is Head of the Middle School (p15/27/28). Although she is a year younger than Betsy Lucy they have much the same interests and clicked during the last term. Mary-Lou will not be fifteen until July (p35/111). Mary-Lou is a tall, sturdy girl of almost fifteen in *Kenya* and she says that early practice is one thing that makes her glad she doesn't take music. She is on a moss-picking expedition when Emerence Hope falls over a cliff. Big, sturdy Mary-Lou offers her Guide cord to Miss Wilmot to help in the rescue and also holds Emerence by the leg while the mistress applies the cord (p37/174/179). Mary-Lou is in the Cornflower dormitory in *Mary-Lou* and returns to school a week late because her grandmother has just died (p1). She is a now a Senior in VB and is fifteen years old (p2/3/4). Mary-Lou is now the dormitory prefect and also Form Prefect (p14/15). She decides to get rid of her Kenwigses and have one plait instead, now that she is a Senior (p23). Joey Maynard asks her to help new girl Jessica Wayne who is jealous of her new, younger, disabled stepsister Rosamund and is very unhappy (p35/36/40). Mary-Lou signs up to go to the early service at the Anglican church in order to ask for God's help to deal with Jessica (p45). Mary-Lou can follow a tune but is not actually musical and angers Plato by singing flat, so that he is already annoyed when Jessica drones on two notes (p56). Mary-Lou wins a prize at the sheets and pillowcase party for being the most helpful Senior (p117). She tells Jessica about her connection with Verity-Anne and also about the expedition her father was on when he was killed (p128/129). Mary-Lou becomes stuck on top of a cupboard during the Feast of St Nicholas. She is involved in a very serious accident when Emerence Hope's sledge catches on a fallen tree and crashes into her. She fortunately survives although she has a severe head injury and the doctors fear spinal injury (p160/173/174). Mary-Lou's mother has not been well and it is decided that Commander and Mrs Carey should come out to Switzerland for a few

months to Das Haus unter die Kiefern. Mary-Lou thinks that her hair, cropped following the accident, will grow in curly (p189/198). In *Genius* it is mentioned that Mary-Lou was leader among her friends, but the Gang is now breaking up as some of the girls are still in the Middle School. She is in VA with Vi Lucy, Lesley Malcolm and Hilary Bennett and is the Cornflower dormitory prefect (p36/37/40). Mary-Lou is her old insouciant self despite last term's serious accident (p51). She is in St Clare's House. After an accident during leapfrog Mary-Lou becomes involved in trying to help Nina Rutherford develop a more balanced attitude to life. She finds Hilda Jukes crying in the art storeroom and, being a canny young person, refrains from comments and fetches Matron. She tries to coax Nina to forgive Hilda and is given permission to consult Joey about the situation (p72/80/83). The Careys have been advised to stay longer in Switzerland and manage to rent a chalet higher up the mountain from the School at the Rösleinalp (p101). Mary-Lou learns that Nina's cousin Alix is very ill and she is understanding and practical, advising Nina to inform her cousins about the Sanatorium (p108/110). She now appears to be in Ste Thérèse House (p178). Mary-Lou has her first article published in the *Chaletian* about a visit she and Verity paid to St Moritz during the Christmas holidays. She has also sent in a short composition of Nina's, which is included (p179/180). Mary-Lou is nearly sixteen in *Problem* and is in the Upper Fifth. She is a House Prefect and is one of the best tennis players in the School (p33/64/68). Mary-Lou is five-foot-eight in height, capable-looking, with blue eyes, and has a short crop of light-brown curls (p76). Mary-Lou goes to Freudesheim to consult Joey about the Joan Baker problem and ends up talking to Jack Maynard instead. She will be sixteen in July (p140/143/154). Mary-Lou invites Joan Baker for half term although it is the last thing she wants to do, but she is determined to do her best to help the other girl fit in at the School (p169/170). Mary-Lou is described in *New Mistress* as having thick fair curls and heavily lashed eyes. She is snubbed by Miss Ferrars when the mistress recalls her aunt's words about keeping her dignity. Mary-Lou is in the Lower Sixth and was sixteen at the end of the previous June (p69/73/119). Miss Ferrars objects to Mary-Lou's behaviour in her geography class and has difficulty understanding the girl when she is on an expedition with the prefects to a glacier above the Rösleinalp at Wahlstein (p124/154; p143 for location). Mary-Lou saves Miss Ferrars from a fatal accident when the rock that she is standing on breaks off and crashes down on to the glacier far below. Mary-Lou injures her back again while doing this (p161/163). She intends having a year at St Mildred's before going to Oxford to study for a career in archaeology (p217). Mary-Lou is the Library Prefect in *Excitements*. She returns to England at Easter to open up Carn Beg for the Careys, as her mother is well enough to go home (p9/222). She and Verity return to school early in *Coming of Age* and stay with Joey, as their parents have gone to Edinburgh to see a specialist about Mr Carey's leg. Mary-Lou is in the Gentian dormitory with Vi Lucy and represents VIB at the sale committee meeting (p8/11/66). She is among the group of prefects who visit the Tiernsee with Joey, Frieda, Simone and Marie, and are shown all the memorable places there (p139). Mary-Lou is the best swimmer in the School and races Joey, who wins. Mary-Lou and Joey lose an oar when out on the lake and have to climb the dripping rock

(p164/179/182). Mary-Lou accompanies Jessica Wayne to Basle when her stepsister Rosamund is dying. When she returns from the airport she is informed that she will be the next Head Girl (p198/199/204). Mary-Lou wins the half-mile race and is a finalist in the blindfold race. She wins the Josephine Maynard prize for the girl who most fulfils the ideal the pupils of the Chalet School always have held before them (p212/215/222). Mary-Lou is described in *Richenda* as exceedingly attractive, tall and slim, with a shapely head covered by a fuzz of brown curls that are full of golden gleams. Her blue eyes dance behind their long fringe of black up-curled lashes and she has a perfect complexion. She has spent part of the holidays in the Outer Hebrides with Clem and Tony Barrass (p27/28). Mary-Lou is Head Girl and also Head of Ste Thérèse. She helps Richenda deal with the weeping, home-sick Odette (p59/78). Mary-Lou is considered to be mentally older than her seventeen years in *Trials*. She is Head Girl and is going to St Mildred's for her final year. She has inherited Joey Maynard's mantle when it comes to butting in and helping people. Joey reckons that Mary-Lou will recognise the need for Naomi Elton to be helped and will do so on her own even if not specifically requested to do so (p11/12/15). Miss Annersley introduces Naomi to Mary-Lou, whose repulsion at Naomi's manner is mixed with pity for one so deformed (p23/24). Head Girl Mary-Lou reads the Parable of the Talents at the Protestant Prayers. She notices that Naomi cannot join the Sunday afternoon walk, being the only Sixth former who must miss out, and decides to stay at home with her (p33/35). Mary-Lou is able to be matter-of-fact in speaking of her faith (p49/50). She welcomed her release from all art lessons at the end of the previous summer term and music is not her strong point (p51/101). Mary-Lou knows what it is to have an aching back after her toboggan accident two years before, and uses her own experience to gain Naomi's confidence (p103). She is on the half-term expedition to the Grisons when there is an avalanche and Mary-Lou counsels Naomi during the night when they are sheltering in the mountain hut (p118/120/121). Mary-Lou loses her fountain pen and biro and this starts the investigation into the Lost Property prank. Later she confronts the miscreants (p139/164). Mary-Lou is still Head Girl in *Theodora* and is described as a tall, handsome girl of nearly eighteen, whose thick, golden-brown curls frame an oval face that is full of character. Her sensitive mouth is offset by a determined chin and steady blue eyes, and at a word from her even the twelve- and thirteen-year-olds become quiet and correct at once (p20). Mary-Lou informs Ted Grantley that engineering means nothing to her. She walks with Ted, impressing her without any intent to do so, and shows her a friendliness which she would not have expected from a prefect. Mary-Lou is among the Protestant prefects who join the Catholic girls at Vespers in the Catholic chapel when it is invaded by cockchafers (p45/54/85). Mary-Lou discovers that Margot Maynard's jealousy of her sisters' friends is causing her to be nasty to Ted Grantley (p117/140/162). Hoping to avert any problems, she accompanies them all on their trip to Zermatt (p158/165), becomes involved in a scene between them, and eventually helps them to sort out their relationship (p198/200/203). Mary-Lou intends to go to St Mildred's for a year before starting her training as an archaeologist. She is presented with a first-aid outfit in a leather case as a prize for all she has done for the School (p189/190/223). Roland Carey's old wound has flared up in *Joey and Co.* and it may mean amputation, from which he may not recover as he is frail now. The poor health of Mary-Lou's stepfather may jeopardise her career plans, because if he dies she will have to look after her mother (p11). Mary-Lou has moved on to St Mildred's in *Ruey* and she captains a team in a friendly lacrosse match with joint teams from the School and St Mildred's (p152/158). Mary-Lou plays the part of the Prince in the St Mildred's pantomime in *Leader* (p105). She is happier about her parents' health when she goes to inform Joey that Professor Richardson has gone off into space again. She also tells Joey that she does not intend to marry (p139/140/141). Commander Carey dies in *Trick* and Verity and Mary-Lou fly to Edinburgh, where his operation was performed. Clem and Tony Barras still live with the family but the death of Commander Carey may nonetheless mean the end of Mary-Lou's archaeological career because she may have to stay at home to look after her mother (p95/96/97). Mary-Lou still hopes to go to Oxford and Joey decides to invite Mrs Carey to visit Freudesheim (p110). Mary-Lou, Vi and Hilary are in charge of

Tom Gay's house competition at the Sale (p185). Len tells her father in *Future* that the girls look up to Mary-Lou and try to be like her (p125). It is mentioned in *Feud* that Mary-Lou has taken prizes in every class for which she entered in one of the well-known regattas. Mary-Lou has her hair up when she arrives for the Nativity Play but doesn't look very different (p34/197). She takes her mother to see Sir James Talbot in *Triplets* and he confirms that Mrs Carey's lungs are in a very poor state. Mary-Lou suspends her Oxford place to nurse her mother (p172/173). Joey helps Mary-Lou, now almost twenty, and Verity to close Carn Beg as their mother is coming out to Switzerland (p174/178). Mrs Carey dies in *Reunion* and Mary-Lou and Verity take her body back to England for burial. We learn that Carn Beg belongs to Mary-Lou, having been left to her by Gran, and Jack Maynard is her trustee until she comes of age. Mary-Lou intends to go back to Oxford and complete her degree course (p75/78). Mary-Lou and Grizel Cochrane help each other with their problems. Grizel provides sympathy and Mary-Lou shows courage and inspires Grizel. Mollie Bettany will stay at Carn Beg and help the girls with the arrangements (p79/80). Mary-Lou returns to Switzerland and, while visiting Grizel in the Sanatorium, mentions that Verity was married last week. Mary-Lou is much thinner and looks pale, with shadows under her eyes, and appears to be on the verge of cracking up (p190/193). After reminiscing about her mother with Joey, Mary-Lou is able to cry and afterwards feels much better. Grizel is married from Mary-Lou's house, Carn Beg (p197/198/205). Miss Annersley recalls in *Jane* that Joey was able to be there for Mary-Lou years ago when the news came of her father's death (p162). Mary-Lou turns up unexpectedly in *Adrienne* and is excited to hear news of Robin Humphries, now Soeur Marie-Cécile (p152/153). She helps Janet Henderson, who is annoyed with Adrienne Desmoines, to begin to see how selfish her own point of view has been. Mary-Lou identifies the likeness between Adrienne Desmoines and Robin Humphries (p155/156/179). It is mentioned in *Summer Term* that Joey and Jack are Mary-Lou's guardians and trustees and that she owns a house just outside Howells Village. We are informed that Mary-Lou will be invited to dig the first spadeful of earth for a new library building, to be presented by the Old Girls, at a private ceremony. She is a girl who has set her own indelible mark on the school (p18/125). Mary-Lou is at Oxford reading archaeology for her BA in *Challenge*. She appears unexpectedly and helps Stacie Benson, who is trying to comfort Evelyn Ross after her mother's relapse (p110/178). Mary-Lou is on sick leave following a cold that went to her chest. She rescues Jocelyn (Marvell) during a snowstorm, having been alerted by Stacie (p182/203/204). Con Maynard remembers the good advice Mary-Lou gave her in *Two Sams* (p95). Mary-Lou's hair becoming curly after her accident is recalled in *Althea* (p31). Mary-Lou arrives in Miss Annersley's salon when the School is roused by the sound of a riot happening further down the mountain in *Prefects*. She came up with the police. Five-foot-eight-inch-tall Mary-Lou is described as being almost a legend in the School (p126). Mary-Lou and her compeers are mentioned as a strong body of prefects in *N1* (p4). Although she is an exceptional girl, she is what her training has made her (p5). EBD asks her readers who they would like to replace Mary-Lou as leading character in the series when she leaves school (p6). Mary-Lou comes top in a competition for readers to choose their favourite Chalet School girl in *N4* (p17). EBD mentions in *N16* that Mary-Lou is C of E and she is reading history at Oxford (p68). Mary-Lou accompanies Joey to the television studio in 'Television' in *N18* (p76). In *N20* EBD comments that so far, Mary-Lou is unmarried (p84).

TRESKUS, SILAS: Silas is the handsomest man on the Raphaels' estate and he plays the part of St George in the Mummers play at Christmas in *Heather*. We learn that he saved Major Raphael's life on the Somme (p212).

TREVANION, EDMUND: Edmund is Eustacia Benson's uncle and trustee in *Eustacia* and is married to Margery, Eustacia's mother's sister (p11). The Trevanions have five sons ranging from fifteen down to three years old, named Ned, Humphrey, Gilbert, Walter and Frank, and they live in Taverton in Devonshire (p12/13). Eustacia, who is almost fourteen and a self-sufficient young person, lives with them when her parents die. She makes life unbearable for them, but her father has willed that she should be sent to school so she is enrolled in the Chalet School (p12/13/17).

Stacie's back is giving some concern in *Camp* (due to an accident in her first term) and Mr and Mrs Trevanion plan to come out to the Tyrol to visit her (p17/18). Stacie recovers and is the Spirit of Love in the Christmas Play in *Jo Returns*. Her aunt and uncle come to see the play and escort Stacie home to Devonshire, the first time that she has seen England for nearly two years (p275/300).

TREVANION, FRANK: Frank is the youngest of Eustacia Benson's five cousins who are mentioned in *Eustacia* as Ned, Humphrey, Gilbert, Walter and Frank, ranging from fifteen down to three-year-old Frank. Eustacia refuses to have anything to do with him (p12/13).

TREVANION, GILBERT: Eustacia Benson's five cousins are mentioned in *Eustacia* as Ned, Humphrey, Gilbert, Walter and Frank, ranging from fifteen down to three years old. Gilbert appears to be the third son (p12/13).

TREVANION, HUMPHREY: Humphrey is one of Eustacia Benson's five cousins who are mentioned in *Eustacia* as Ned, Humphrey, Gilbert, Walter and Frank, ranging from fifteen down to three years old. Humphrey makes Eustacia an apple-pie bed (p12/13).

TREVANION, MARGERY: Eustacia Benson goes to live with her mother's sister Margery, who is her guardian, and Margery's husband Edmund Trevanion, who is her trustee, after the death of her parents in *Eustacia*. The Trevanions have five sons ranging from fifteen down to three years old. Eustacia, who is almost fourteen and a self-sufficient young person, is very unpleasant to them all. The Trevanions live in Taverton in Devonshire and their sons are named Ned, Humphrey, Gilbert, Walter and Frank (p11/12/13). Mrs Cochrane recommends the Chalet School to Mrs Trevanion, and Eustacia is enrolled there. We are informed that Mrs Trevanion knew Madge Bettany and Mlle Lepâttre quite well when they lived in Taverton, and Madge remembers her as a pretty little woman with a swarm of small boys. Margery Trevanion was twenty years younger than her sister, Eustacia's mother (p16/25). Eustacia's Aunt Margery comes out from England to be with her niece when she is taken up to the Sonnalpe after hurting the muscles in her back badly, and Eustacia learns to value her kindness (p312). Stacie's back is giving some concern in *Camp* and Mr and Mrs Trevanion hope to come out to the Tyrol to visit

her (p17/18). Stacie recovers and is the Spirit of Love in the Christmas Play in *Jo Returns*. Her aunt and uncle come to see the play and escort Stacie home to Devonshire, the first time that she has seen England for nearly two years (p275/300).

TREVANION, NED: Eustacia Benson's five cousins are mentioned in *Eustacia* as Ned, Humphrey, Gilbert, Walter and Frank, ranging from fifteen down to three years old. Ned is the eldest and Eustacia scoffs at his prowess in Latin. Ned attended the same dancing class as Joey Bettany (p12/13/25). Stacie visits Cornwall at Christmas in *Lavender* when her cousin Ned, who is in the RAF, is missing. Joey is not too worried about him as she claims the Trevanion boys have as many lives as any cat. We later learn that Ned baled out of his plane over Zurich and is interned, but is quite all right (p101/111).

TREVANION, WALTER: Walter is one of Eustacia Benson's five cousins who are mentioned in *Eustacia* as Ned, Humphrey, Gilbert, Walter and Frank, ranging from fifteen down to three years old. Walter appears to be the fourth son and Eustacia refuses to have anything to do with him (p12/13).

TREVARN, MR: Dick Bettany's bailiff Mr Trevarn is mentioned in *CS Oberland* (p122).

TREVELLYAN, DORIS: see TRELAWNEY, DORIS

TREVENA (TREVENNOR), GERTRUDE: Gertrude is in IIIB at St Peter's School in *Gerry* and is chosen to be a delegate in the Third form strike. Her surname is given as Trevennor during a description of the prefects' meeting attended by the delegates (p186/191).

TREVENNOR, REVD ARTHUR (A): Mr Trevennor is the rector of Mordown in *Gerry* and he and his wife have ten children—five boys and five girls (p9/12/32). When Gerry Challoner comes to stay at the rectory, he is impressed by her standard of playing Schumann, as he is a great lover of music and the possessor of a fine bass voice. The rector's living at Mordown is not a large one and he is very worried about his financial position in view of all the demands on it, including sending Cecil abroad for health reasons (p104/105/123). Mr Trevennor witnesses Miss Catcheside's accident in *HG Difficulties* (p22/23). Gerry Challoner mentions her 'uncle' and 'aunt', Revd Arthur Trevennor and his wife Meg, when she visits the Chalet School with Grizel Cochrane in *Rivals* (p234).

TREVENNOR, BERNARD, 'BEAR' (B) (5/6): Bernard, the Trevennors' third son, plays the 'cello in *Gerry*. He is described as a jolly, brown-eyed boy of fourteen and is known as Bear (p31/35). Bernard attends St Peter's School and wants to go to Canada or Australia to do farming (p40/41). We learn that Bernard, who has a twin named Jill, has won a scholarship to St Peter's (p46/123).

TREVENNOR, CECIL (B) (7): Cecil has a delicate chest in *Gerry*, is musical and plays the viola (p12/31). He attends St Peter's Boys' School and wants to be an actor and may go to an acting school. His Uncle Hervey is his godfather and pays for his education (p40/42). Cecil's health is poor and Dr Nuttall hints that it will be unwise for him to stay in England during the winter (p123). Cecil is the first person to be diagnosed with diphtheria in *HG Difficulties* and later dies (p111/124).

(TREVENNOR), GREAT-AUNT ELINOR: The Trevennors have a Great-Aunt Elinor who apparently lives at Courdle Rigg in *Gerry* (p9).

TREVENNOR, ELIZABETH (BETTY), 'BETTS' (B) (10): Elizabeth, known as Betty, is the youngest Trevennor child in *Gerry*, not yet at school. Mrs Trevennor refers to her as Betts when working out where Gerry should sleep (p12). She is a small girl with brown eyes and brown hair (p35). Betty is in the Kindergarten at St Peter's School in *HG Difficulties* (p236).

TREVENNOR, GEOFFREY (B) (9): Geoffrey, the youngest son in the Trevennor family, is possessed of the most cheerful ugliness imaginable in *Gerry*. He has wide brown eyes, which are his only claim to good looks (p30/32). He wants to be a sailor and will be entered to St Peter's preparatory at Easter (p41/123).

TREVENNOR, GILLIAN (JILL) (B) (5/6): Gillian, known as Jill, has a little dark face that is hard and unfriendly when she meets Gerry Challoner in *Gerry*. She is fourteen years old (Bernard is fourteen and they are twins, p46) and has a vivid, impish face with a determined mouth and quick-glancing eyes (p11/35/38). Gillian is the Middle School Captain at St Peter's School. She is brainy and wants to be a doctor but it costs money (p40/41). Jill resents Gerry coming to live

in their home and she is a jealous creature where Bernard, her beloved twin, is concerned (p45/46). Gerry is disturbed when Jill creeps into her room one night to have a fight. Jill is brilliantly clever and works with girls whose average age is fifteen months older than her own (p108/204). Jill is bored one day and goes skating on Birkett's pond and Gerry follows her when she discovers it is unsafe. Farmer Birkett, Paul and Mr Maitland hear Gerry's screams and come to the rescue after Jill has fallen through the ice (p208/213/215). Jill repents afterwards and apologises to Gerry for behaving badly. Gerry's great-aunts remain in Madeira and pay for Jill's further education to study medicine in return for their niece living with the Trevennors permanently (p228/246/247). Jill has left school and is being coached in *HG Difficulties*. She is described as small, dark and impish-looking, with straight bobbed hair, when she and Gerry inform the Athertons about Miss Catcheside's accident (p10/21). Seventeen-and-a-half-year-old Jill was a sub-prefect last year (p66/98). Jill becomes ill with diphtheria but recovers (p131/133). She is in London in *Maids*, apparently at the university, and has not become superior or patronising (p289).

TREVENNOR, HELEN (NELL) (B) (3): Nell is the second daughter of Revd Mr Trevennor and his wife in *Gerry*. Tall, slender Helen is as fair as her older sister Margaret is dark, and her long, golden hair is plaited in one thick plait (p26/27). She has a good singing voice (p31). Nell has grey eyes and is Hockey Captain at St Peter's School (p38/39/40). Jem Gough, a ne'er-do-weel and drunkard, frightens Firefly, the Trevennors' pony, when her brother Laurence is driving Nell and Gerry home from the Comptons' house, and seventeen-year-old Helen keeps her head and looks after Gerry, though badly shaken. Nell plays the part of the Pierrot in the end-of-term play (p133/137/233). She is going to Lancashire to be a gym mistress in *HG Difficulties* and we are told that she played tennis during the Easter Holidays (p80/291).

TREVENNOR, LAURENCE (LAWRENCE), 'LARRY' (B) (4): Laurence, the Trevennors' second son, is musical and plays the double bass in *Gerry*. Larry is brainy and used to attend St Peter's Boys' School but won a scholarship to St John's, a big public day school at Greylands. He hopes to go to university (p31/40). Larry is driving Gerry and Nell home from the Comptons' house when Jem Gough, a ne'er-do-weel and a drunkard frightens Firefly, the Trevennors' pony, and they are all badly shaken (p133). Larry's name is given as Lawrence on p12.

TREVENNOR, MARGARET (MEG) (A): Mrs Trevennor has fair hair and dark eyes in *Gerry* (p30) and she and her husband have ten children—five boys and five girls (p32/33). Mr Trevennor calls her Meg. She is worn out with the anxiety of waiting for news when Jem Gough, a ne'er-do-weel and a drunkard, frightens Firefly, the Trevennors' pony, when Laurence is driving Gerry and Nell home from the Comptons' house (p123/133/138). Gerry Challoner mentions her 'uncle' and 'aunt', Revd Arthur Trevennor and his wife Meg, when she visits the Chalet School with Grizel Cochrane in *Rivals* (p234).

TREVENNOR, MARGARET (PEGGY) (B) (2): Margaret left St Peter's School six months ago in *Gerry* and is the eldest daughter of the ten Trevennor children. Nineteen-year-old Margaret is very pretty, with dark eyes and hair and delicately lovely colouring (p12/25). Mr Maitland, their father's curate, hears Gerry's screams and comes to Jill Trevennor's rescue when she falls through the ice on Birkett's pond, then finishes the day by proposing to Margaret Trevennor (p215/219).

TREVENNOR, PAUL (B) (1): Paul, the eldest boy of the ten Trevennor children, is musical and plays the violin in *Gerry* (p11/12). Tall, black-haired Paul is a brilliant pianist and plays the organ at church services, but it is the violin on which he excels. He wants to be a musician (p30/31/41). Gerry is disturbed when Jill creeps into her room one night to have a fight, and Paul intervenes (p111/112). He has left school, and but is earning very little (p123). He is the eldest born of the Trevennor children (p152). Paul hears Gerry's screams and comes to Jill's rescue when she falls through the ice on Birkett's pond (p215).

TREVENNOR, SHEILA (B): (8) Sheila is not musical and her practising is irritating in *Gerry* (p31). Fair-haired Sheila is in the Sixth hockey Eleven at St Peter's School (p32/38). Sheila signs the petitions when they decide to rebel against the Upper School (p176). She is very friendly with Allegra Atherton and Janie Ferrars in *HG Difficulties* and is in IVB (p68/70). Sheila becomes very ill with diphtheria (p111/123/125) but fortunately survives and the Burnhams take her to Mentone to recuperate (p136). Sheila, Diana Burnham and Kitty O'Connell return to school at the beginning of the summer term (p289/290).

TREVILLION, CAPTAIN: Captain Trevillion is asked by Crown Prince Carol to write to the Chalet School for a prospectus for Princess Elisaveta in *Princess* (p22/37). Captain Trevillion is one of Prince Carol's equerries. Prince Cosimo kidnaps Elisaveta during the term and Captain Trevillion helps Madge Bettany look for her and Joey (p254). Captain Trevillion flies the plane for King Carol when he visits Elisaveta at the Sonnalpe in *Camp* (p36).

TREVOASE, PRIMROSE: Primrose arrives from the Tanswick Chalet School in *Bride* and she is an enterprising young demon. She is from Cornwall and Miss Moore thinks that she is rather a nice brat with a cheeky little face (p121). She is in Lower IVA with the Dawbarn twins and Emerence Hope. Her father is a friend of Miss Annersley's cousin and he wants Primrose reformed. She only had one term at Tanswick (p120/123). Primrose is friendly with the Dawbarn twins in *Changes* and was at Tanswick with Peggy Harper. She will not be going to Switzerland until she has at least three good reports. Near the end of term, Primrose, Priscilla and Prudence Dawbarn and two friends decide to have a moonlight picnic in the Old Orchard where some pigs are living temporarily. Unfortunately Prudence trips over one of the pigs and the girls are chased over the gate by the squealing animals (p169/174/175). Primrose stays behind in England when the Chalet School moves to Switzerland. In *Excitements* we are told that Primrose, Prudence and Priscilla Dawbarn, Doris Hill and Gwen Jones will be coming from Pelham House in South Wales next term (p198/219). Fifteen-year-old Primrose appears in the Oberland with the Dawbarn twins in *Coming of Age*. Doris Hill is able to tell Blossom Willoughby that Primrose looks like being a decent bat at cricket. Primrose is five-foot-seven and in Inter V (p20/21/22). Primrose is a fair, pretty girl with hair as rampantly curly as Richenda Fry's and a wicked twinkle in her blue eyes in *Richenda*. She is in VB (p36/94). Primrose is in VB and described as a little pest in *Trials* (p45). Primrose and Eve Hurrell visit Jo Scott's home at half term in *Theodora* (p148). Fifteen-year-old Primrose is the Gentian dormitory in Ste Thérèse House with Len Maynard as Head in *Ruey* (p12/13). Matey asks Len to keep an eye on Primrose, who still wears a tunic so probably is not quite fifteen yet (p30). Primrose is voted Staff Monitress for VB (p35). She is one of the top four girls in VB in *Leader* (p99). She is keen at tennis in *Trick* and can sometimes have a demon service (p49). Primrose is in VIB with the Maynard triplets, Francie Wilford and Betty Landon in *Feud* (p106; p104 for form). She is described in *Jane* as having blue eyes, golden-brown locks and a pink-and-white complexion (p196). She is in VIB in *Adrienne* and is tall (p89/98). Primrose and Eloïse Dafflon in VIB help Frau Mieders to her feet in *Summer Term* when Emilie Laurent and her cousin Thérèse Parrais bump into her when she is carrying a bucket of buttermilk (p134). Primrose is the Second Games Prefect in *Challenge* (p141). She is still the Second Games Prefect in *Althea* (p64). Len mentions in *Prefects* that Primrose, Marie Hüber, Jeanne Daudet and at least fifteen members of VIB will be going on to St Mildred's next term. Primrose and Audrey Everett are good friends (p53/60).

TREVOR, ALAN: We learn in *Triplets* that Alan's sister Enid met Verity Carey at the Royal College in London. Enid introduced Verity to Alan, who was working in London, and he took the girls to concerts and the theatre. The Trevors live in Monmouth and visit Carn Beg. Verity is engaged to Alan Trevor when she visits Switzerland and she will be married in July from the Maynards' house, with Mary-Lou as her chief bridesmaid (p184/216/218). Mrs Carey dies during Joey's house party in *Reunion* and Verity and Alan get married while Joey and Jack are in England (p75/190). Mary-Lou informs the prefects in *Challenge* that Verity is going to have a baby in May (p183).

TREVOR, ENID: We learn in *Triplets* that Enid has become friendly with Verity Carey, who is in the same hostel. The girls are at the Royal College in London and Enid has introduced Verity to her brother Alan (p184).

TREVOR, VERITY: see CAREY, VERITY-ANN

TRINDER, MR and MRS BERT: Mr Trinder, the local policeman at Garnham, arrests two intruders trying to steal Phoebe Wychcote's 'cello from The Witchens in *Rescue*. At the time he is wearing pyjamas of violent orange and yellow stripes, purple slippers embroidered by Mrs Trinder, and his helmet (p127/134/135). The next day Bert breaks his left leg and is replaced by a taciturn deputy who keeps quiet about the burglary. Mrs Trinder shuts up their cottage and goes to stay with her sister in Garnley to be near her husband in hospital (p155).

TRUDA: Truda (no surname given) and Virginia (Adams) are new girls in *Does It Again* (p18). Truda is in the same form as Elsie Morris (p19).

TRÜDCHEN: Trüdchen is a maid at the Chalet School in *Feud* (p17).

TRUDI: Trudi and Gretchen serve hot drinks to the girls at Ste Thérèse when they are waiting for news of Mlle Lepâttre in *Jo Returns* (p268).

TUDOR, REVD MR: Mr Tudor, the rector of Medbury parish church, has seven children in *Monica* including Dilys and Myfanwy (p16/17/18/19). In *Goes to It* he is again described as the rector of Medbury, eighteen miles from Plas Howell (p77/109). He is referred to as the vicar at Medbury, with five children, no private means and living some twenty miles from Howells village, in *Highland Twins* (p127).

TUDOR, DILYS: Dilys and her younger sister Myfanwy are the daughters of the rector of Medbury parish church in *Monica*. The Tudor sisters are pretty, lady-like girls, who are being brought up to be useful both at home and in the parish. Dilys is fifteen and a half and the eldest of seven children. She is fair, with regular features, long flaxen plaits and blue-grey eyes, and has a pink-and-white colouring (p16/17/19). Dilys and Myfanwy attend Braemar House school and there are three tiny children at home. Dilys will stay at school for another eighteen months before leaving to help with her young siblings at home. She would like to go to Oxford but knows that her father cannot afford it (p20/65/106). It is explained in *Highland Twins* that Dilys went from Braemar House to Oxford as she gained a scholarship to read modern languages with a view to teaching. She is the eldest of a family of five and her sisters Myfanwy and Nesta (see p81) transferred to the Chalet School when it opened at Plas Howell (p127).

TUDOR, ELUNED: We are told in *Monica* that Dilys and Myfanwy's younger sister Eluned will start as a Junior at Braemar House school after Christmas (p21).

TUDOR, GWENSI: see HOWELL, GWENSI

TUDOR, MYFANWY (i): Myfanwy is a member of the Secret Society at St Peter's School in *Gerry* (p87) and is probably in IVB with Kitty O'Connell (p183).

TUDOR, MYFANWY (ii): Myfanwy and Dilys, the daughters of the rector of Medbury parish church, are pretty, lady-like girls, who are being brought up to be useful both at home and in the parish in *Monica*. Fourteen-year-old Myfanwy is fair with regular features, long flaxen plaits and blue-grey eyes. She has a pink-and-white colouring and is going to be a beauty later on. She attends Braemar House, a Medbury school, and hopes to teach music when she has all her diplomas (p16/19/65). Myfanwy is a pretty new girl at the Chalet School in *Goes to It* and joins the Fifth form with her friends Monica Marilliar and Jocelyn Redford from Braemar House, which is closing down. Her father is the rector of Medbury and she is his second daughter. Myfanwy wants to have a career in music and becomes one of Herr Anserl's music pupils (p77/109). Myfanwy has passed her public exams in *Highland Twins*, with credit in Latin and botany. She is a prefect, is in the Sixth form and has a young sister named Nesta (p9/65/81). She will be leaving at the end of the year to go to the Royal College of Music to study for her ARCM because she wants to teach. Myfanwy is a pretty, fair girl, rather shy and retiring. She is the School's musical genius although not a great concert performer like Margia Stevens (p127). Myfanwy is still at school in *Gay* and plays in a string trio with Amy Stevens and Ernestine Benedict at the end-of-term concert (p238).

TUDOR, NESTA: Myfanwy's younger sister, nine- or ten-year-old Nesta, is in the Upper Second with Bride Bettany and also Flora and Fiona McDonald in *Highland Twins*. An intruder looks through her locker searching for the Chart of Erisay (p80/81/168).

TUDOR, OLWEN: Olwen is a Lower Sixth prefect at St Peter's School in *Gerry*. Olwen plays the part of a gardener in the end-of-term play (p174/234).

TULLY, JOAN: Joan and her WAAF friends are travelling companions of the McDonald sisters in *Highland Twins* (p28).

TUNG, NAN: see NAN TUNG

TURNER, MARY: Mary is mentioned in *Rosalie* as she was Second Prefect the previous term. She has left the Chalet School and Jacynth Hardy has taken her place (p103).

TURNER, 'TOFFEE': 'Toffee' Turner is a science master at St James' School, which Gay Lambert's twin brother Mike attends in *Gay* (p126).

TURNOUR, VIOLET: Violet is in the Sixth form at St Peter's School in *HG Difficulties* (p148).

TWISS (TWIST), MARGARET (MEG): Margaret is in Lower IIIA with Jack Lambert in *Leader* and this is her second term (p27/44; p16 for clarification of form). When Margaret is singing she has a trick of going flat on high notes. Jack Lambert puts cobbler's wax on Margaret's chair in Miss Andrews's class after Margaret has annoyed her (p67/68). Margaret is not very popular with the rest of her form and has a gift for evading her share of any blame and punishment (p73). Miss Bertram faints after finding a toy snake in her desk and Jack is accused of putting it there by the majority of Lower IIIA. Margaret is a surprising exception and one of only a few girls who disagree, mumbling that Jack is not a liar so probably didn't do it (p175/182/183). After a terrible week for the form, Miss Andrews, recovering from a very severe bout of 'flu, explains that she put the confiscated snake there. Margaret later confesses to Miss Annersley that she saw Miss Andrews put it in the desk. Margaret apologises to Jack and is forgiven (p188/194/202). Margaret helps Renata, who is feeling faint after wrenching her arm, in *Trick* (p74). Margaret is in the Lower Fourth in *Feud* (p40; p38 for form). Margaret is now counted as one of Jack's gang in *Jane* (p182). She is in IVA in *Redheads* and Jack addresses her as Meg (p29). Margaret is in Inter V in *Two Sams* and, being musical, is disappointed when the new girl Samantha van der Byl is chosen to visit Nina Rutherford in hospital rather than someone of longer standing in the School who has an interest in music. However, she keeps silent about this (p137/138). The School devotes a day to making cakes and sweets for the confectionery stalls at the School Sale in *Prefects*. Margaret Twist, Wanda von Eschenau, Jack and Samantha have the task of shaking toffees up in a box of icing sugar before weighing them out (p113).

TYNDALL, DR: Laurie Rosomon is taking over Dr Tyndall's post at the Sanatorium in *Jane* (p101).

A LITTLE BRIEF AUTHORITY

The long Chalet School series provides its readers with a fair share of excitement, shocks and unexpected events. For me potentially one of the most puzzling of these occurs at the end of *The Coming of Age of the Chalet School*. Mary-Lou Trelawney has returned to school late at night after performing an errand of mercy. She is practically asleep when Miss Annersley visits her dormitory to give her some news: she is to be the school's next Head Girl. It is Mary-Lou's reaction to this that is—*perhaps*—surprising.

> 'Me!' Mary-Lou forgot the slumbering dormitory, and spoke in her usual clear clarion tones. 'But why me?' (p204)

Honestly, Mary-Lou, what a question!

Ever since she first appeared at the school, this girl has counted amongst its leaders. She set the pace in her form in her opening term (*Three Go to the Chalet School*, p149–50) and two years later, in *Shocks for the Chalet School*, generally ran her gang (p123). The school moved to Switzerland and Mary-Lou was soon given an official position as Head of the Middles (*The Chalet School Does It Again*, p35). Shortly after this she was singled out by Joey as the one person in her form mature enough to deal with Jessica Wayne (*Mary-Lou of the Chalet School*, pp36–8), and though she took on *that* task with some reluctance, in the next few terms she carried on giving out help to anyone in need.

Joey was not the only one to recognise Mary-Lou's special gifts in this period: the school prefects noticed them, too (*A Problem for the Chalet School*, p154). They were also quite clear about another thing: when Mary-Lou's time came, she would be Head Girl, even over and above Josette Russell, daughter of the school's founder.

> 'If any of the Russells is Head Girl, it'll be Josette …'
> 'It won't be Josette,' Katharine said with decision. 'She'll be Sixth with Mary-Lou and all the Gang and Mary-Lou's slated for Head Girl all right.'
> (*Mary-Lou*, p91)

EBD's readers all agree with Katharine: they know Mary-Lou *has* to be Head Girl—and their expectations are naturally met. Mary-Lou spends a whole year at the head of the school and, once her reign is over, we are none of us astounded to hear it being described in superlatives.

> 'She was one of the best in every way,' said Margot suddenly. 'Most of our crowd owe a lot one way and another to Mary-Lou—including myself.'
> (*Challenge for the Chalet School*, p110)

So we might well look back on that night in *Coming of Age* when Mary-Lou reacted with incredulity at her appointment and scratch our heads in bafflement—at least, we *might*, if it were not for the fact that there is more than a little precedent for her behaviour—for her inability to see that her nomination is correct.

As early as *The Head Girl of the Chalet School* (the fourth book in the series), we see a new Head Girl expressing dissatisfaction at her election: Grizel Cochrane would *much* rather someone else had been given the job (p12). A few terms later, Jo Bettany shows a similar distaste (*Eustacia Goes to the*

Chalet School, p38) and then at intervals throughout the chronicles of the school we observe history repeating itself. In the British period, for instance, Peggy and Bride Bettany both express qualms about their ability to fill the role (*Peggy of the Chalet School*, p61; *Bride Leads the Chalet School*, pp35, 38); and in Switzerland, not long after Mary-Lou's incumbency, the last Head Girl of the series, Len Maynard, does not even want to be appointed sub-prefect (*A Future Chalet School Girl*, p162).

Astonishment, dismay, trepidation: these seem to be the standard emotions felt by EBD's girls when offered posts of authority. It is tempting to conclude that in her world such positions were *per se* disagreeable or disgraceful—only bullies or sycophants need apply. But nothing could be further than the truth. A girl who is elected Head Girl or even a prefect immediately accrues honourable prestige. Rosamund Atherton, Head Girl in the Chalet School's companion La Rochelle series, knows she has become the 'undisputed queen' at St Peter's High School; Peggy Bettany's family are bound to be thrilled by news of her promotion; and Dora Robson is to be congratulated on her unexpected chance to serve as a prefect (*Head Girl's Difficulties*, p22; *Peggy*, p67; *Bride*, p185).

The Head Girl post is, therefore, at the very least *theoretically* desirable—and we should note that EBD never suggests that girls should not wish for honours as such. Bride informs us of Jo's thoughts on the matter of ambition:

'Auntie Jo says it's no use aiming low ... Aim at the sky and you may hit the top of the tree!'
(*Tom Tackles the Chalet School*, p103).

This is not just a passing whim on Jo's part. Throughout the Chalet series we are granted glimpses of girls who are inspired by legitimate goals. Girls are expected to work hard—in school and after they have left; good exam results and progress in careers are lauded (for example, *The Highland Twins at the Chalet School*, pp9, 62; *The Chalet School Goes to It*, p104); and scholarships are worth fighting for (see *The Chalet School and the Island*, p156; *The Chalet School Triplets*, p128). A lovely scene in *The Rivals of the Chalet School* shows us a group of girls in candid discussion about what they want to do after leaving school, and Mary Burnett's statement that she hopes to become a headmistress is treated with genuine respect, as is Simone Lecoutier's plan to teach for a while and earn some comforts for her parents before settling down to marriage and a family (p31). Hilary Burn reacts positively—if with a little doubt—to the suggestion that she might one day be Head Girl (*The New Chalet School*, pp318–19). And when Vi Lucy is suffering from a crisis of confidence, Mary-Lou cheers her enormously by pointing out that she is sure of promotion to a prefect's post very soon (*Excitements at the Chalet School*, pp127–31).

What is it, then, that causes Mary-Lou to be so very surprised by her own appointment and what influences her predecessors (and successor, Len) to express reluctance or concern about theirs? I think that the answer lies in the great responsibility the job brings. The Head Girl's post in EBD's world is no sinecure: there are many duties to perform.

'... here for a year she would be responsible for all that went on. St Peter's was wont to demand much of its head girls ...'

(*Head Girl's Difficulties*, p22)

'... the Head Girl is generally up to the eyes, anyhow, at the end of term—beginning, too, if you come to that.'

(*Bride*, p33)

The Head Girl—with her fellow prefects—is responsible for representing the headmistress: '... prefects ... are, in a sense, the Head's representatives' (*Bride*, p184). And if that were not enough, the Head Girl must represent the School, too, not just as the person who will respond for the School as a whole when a question is asked of it (for example, *The Wrong Chalet School*, p211), but as a prototype figure: the girl who embodies the School's ethos and provides a good example to the other girls—and, incidentally, to EBD's readers, too (for we know from *Jo Returns to the Chalet School*, pp157–8, that EBD believed that young people could be influenced by literature). Stacie Benson, full of admiration for Joey Bettany when she is Head Girl, puts it this way:

'All the girls look up to you, and follow you. You can do a tremendous lot with them if you like, because you are head-girl, as well as because they like you so much. It's a tremendous thing, really.'

(*The Chalet School and Jo*, p283)

A demanding task, indeed—perhaps it is not so surprising that its magnitude makes most appointees quail a bit. An analysis of their responses suggests that there are two typical sorts of reaction (and there is possibly some overlap between these). Girls either express reluctance to take on the job because they think it will be too heavy and will spoil their fun: Grizel complains, 'It *won't* be easy,' while Joey moans that she will have to be 'an angel without wings' (*Head Girl*, pp12, 43; *Eustacia*, p38; see also *And Jo*, pp12, 14). Or they hesitate because they are modestly unsure of their capability—why should the post have been given to them and not someone else?

Sometimes the girls feel that they are too young or too inexperienced.

'I suppose the truth of the matter is that you are afraid of your coming responsibilities.'
'Yes, I am! horribly!' confessed Rosamund. 'You see, it wouldn't be so bad if I weren't so young. But I shall be the youngest head girl that's ever been!'

(*Head Girl's Difficulties*, p10)

'Part of me is awfully bucked at the idea,' [Peggy] confessed. 'But I've had no real experience, and I'm afraid I may make an awful mull of it.'

(*Peggy*, p61)

Sometimes they worry that they can't live up to the standard set by previous Head Girls—Mary Burnett and Louise Redmond have this problem (*Head Girl*, p334; *Jo Returns*, p8). They think they may do the job badly (Peggy Bettany is afraid of making a 'mull' of it; while Bride thinks she may make a mess—*Peggy*, p61; *Bride*, pp37–8) or that they will make faulty decisions: 'And supposing I say things that go wrong?' (*And Jo*, p12).

We can appreciate their concerns. *Somebody* has to do the job, however, and advice is provided for all hesitant Head Girls. Those who are upset by their loss of freedom are encouraged to realise that their attitude is selfish. They have been given a great deal by the School and ought to be ready to give something back. Grizel's lesson is, of course, learnt very painfully, when her self-willed action in taking French Leave to visit the Falls of Rhine lands her in serious trouble (we will come back to this later). But Joey, too, has to be told that she must learn to be less selfish and stop running away from responsibility in a cowardly fashion. Gisela Mensch (herself a former Head Girl) puts it to her very strongly:

'The reason why you are so resenting this being head-girl is because you are afraid of it … Don't you think you are being very selfish …?'

(*And Jo*, p20)

Meanwhile the other girls, who hesitated through a mere lack of confidence, have to brace up and show a bit of courage as well. They, too, must think less of themselves and more of the community and what they owe it. Rosamund Atherton's father tells her that if she has a hard thing to do, she must set her teeth and 'go at it'. She encourages her fellow prefects by reminding them of their duty to serve the headmistress, their school and their country (*Head Girl's Difficulties*, p29). Miss Annersley speaks to Peggy Bettany in the same vein:

'Come, Peggy! The school has given you a good deal all these years. Are you going to refuse what it asks of you now?'

(*Peggy*, p61)

Of course, she doesn't refuse. *All* the girls we have mentioned so far eventually pledge themselves to do their best, and they keep their promises. They are, in consequence, excellent Head Girls—and that in telling contrast with the only 'bad' Chalet School Head Girl, Marilyn Evans.

Marilyn's case is an interesting one. It sheds further light on to the character and attitude of good Head Girls, by providing us with an insight into the management style of good *Headmistresses*. EBD only ever refers to Marilyn in passing: no book tells the story of her term of office. Nonetheless, we do learn that her problem was that she was very ambitious and became too wrapped up in her own work to put the school first (*Peggy*, p60). Ambition, as we saw earlier, is not a bad thing in and of itself: Marilyn was not fundamentally wrong in wanting to excel in her studies. For all we know, she may genuinely have wanted to do well in the Head Girl's post, too, but unexpectedly found herself unable to get the balance right between school and academic duties. But the important point for us is that the school authorities seem to have conceded that Marilyn was not completely to blame for her failure. The rules about eligibility for the Head Girl post were changed *after* she got into difficulties, the authorities having realised that it was unfair to ask certain people to put the school first (*Peggy*, p61).

The ability to recognise errors (even your own), to take advice and/or make adjustments, is an invaluable asset in a leader, whether you are prefect, Head Girl or Headmistress. Authority, when well exercised, is a fine thing and ought to be respected: EBD never wavers on that score. But she is also frequently at pains to demonstrate that good leaders are those who retain a sense of proportion—who don't lord themselves over others, assuming personal infallibility. They have learnt the lesson Shakespeare's Angelo is taught in *Measure for Measure*: dressed in 'a little brief authority', he has to become aware of his own 'glassy essence'—his human fragility (*Measure for Measure* Act 2, scene 2, 117–123). So it is not only Head Girls who display a certain modesty in EBD's world: successful staff members do so too.

The Heads of the school at the time of the Marilyn fiasco are Miss Annersley and Miss Wilson. They are used to working together and listening to each other (*Lavender Laughs in the Chalet School*, p25–6; *Gay from China at the Chalet School*, p159). And Miss Annersley herself, when originally appointed, reacted in a manner very reminiscent of the hesitant Head Girls.

> 'I'll do my best, and saints can't do more; but I'm not Madame, nor Mademoiselle. I'm glad to know you'll all back me up; I'll need it, I can assure you!'
>
> (*New CS*, p14)

If we consider other 'good' leaders in the series we see a similar pattern. The Chalet School's founder and first headmistress, Madge, is not so full of herself as to have no moments of doubt: before the School's first term, for instance, when she expresses her worries about her plan to Dick, and during the troubles with Matron Webb, when she confesses to Mademoiselle La Pattre that she feels as though she is becoming a preaching, bad-tempered headmistress and doesn't know what to do about it (*The School at the Chalet*, p47; *The Princess of the Chalet School*, p75). Mademoiselle herself becomes headmistress later on, but despite her evident wisdom, remains very willing to admit her limitations to her colleagues. 'What to do, I know not,' she says, when faced with the peculiar behaviour of Deira O'Hagan (*Head Girl*, p105). And Nancy Wilmot, temporarily appointed Headmistress in Miss Annersley's absence towards the end of the series, reacts in much the same way. She really *is* troubled by feelings of inadequacy (*Challenge*, p39)—and receives exactly the same sort of pull-yourself-together advice from Matron as a self-doubting Head Girl might get.

> 'How Hilda contrives to be so tranquil with it all is something I'd be glad to know. Of course,' she added hopefully, 'she's had years of it and this is my first experience. And I don't mind telling you that it'll be the last if I've any say in the matter.'
>
> Matey eyed her scornfully. 'Don't be so childish! You're talking like a sub-prefect suddenly landed with full prefect's duties!'
>
> (*Challenge*, p70)

It would, of course, be unrealistic to suggest that positions of authority only ever fall to persons well-suited to them. EBD is fully aware of this and so, as well as presenting us with a pleasing number of admirable leaders, also introduces a few over-confident adults and girls—people who tend to be persistently insensitive to other's opinions and feelings when exercising their powers. Amongst the staff, we have Matron Webb, who is foolish enough to show Madge scant respect (*Princess*, p106); Miss Browne, headmistress of St Scholastika's, who crassly assumes the superiority of her English school to one run by a Frenchwoman (*Rivals*, pp21, 68); Matron Besly, who exceeds her authority, refuses advice and makes herself ridiculous by thinking too much about herself (*The New House at the Chalet School*, pp

89, 115–16, 149, 178, 181); Miss Bubb, who is sure she knows better than anyone else (*Gay*, pp136, 159, 181); and even Miss Slater, initially portrayed as a good, if not an excellent, mistress (*Gay*, pp33, 42), indulges in unreasonable prejudice, despite Miss Annersley's cautions, and is over-assertive when challenged about her personal plans (*Changes for the Chalet School*, p92, 122, 124). And amongst the girls there is Eilunedd Vaughn, who acts very foolishly when she is *not* promoted to the Head Girl's position—a post she had thought

of as hers (*Peggy*, p208); that overbearing prefect, Ruth Wilson, who is rather too concerned about her dignity (*A Chalet Girl from Kenya*, pp95, 113–15); and Elaine Gilling, Head Girl at St Scholastika's, whose sense of self-importance is doubtless inflated by Miss Browne's unwise habit of confiding in her, and who consequently gives in to prejudice, nursing personal grievances and refusing to heed the advice of more sensible people (*Rivals*, pp119, 123, 124, 222).

A knowledge of these sorry cases is very useful. It helps explain further the mystery of Mary-Lou's cautious reaction to her own promotion. EBD had a definite purpose in writing that scene in *Coming of Age*: she wanted us to witness Mary-Lou beginning her job with humility—a state of mind that was bound to give her a far better chance of success than, for instance, Elaine Gilling. But it is worth noting the subtleties in EBD's characterisation. She does not content herself with supplying neat black-and-white demonstrations of 'how and how *not* to do it', revelling in the triumphs of her modest characters and exposing the folly of the proud. She gives her wise authority figures occasional moments of failure: Madge is inclined to misjudge Grizel over the row with Deira (*Head Girl*, pp110–12); Miss Stewart's bad temper causes problems amongst the girls in *Eustacia* (pp161, 172); Nancy Wilmot does not provide Evelyn Ross with adequate emotional support in *Challenge* (pp177,180); Gisela and Mary forget to lead by example, one speaking the wrong language for the day, the other entertaining the idea of playing tricks on Middles (*Jo of the Chalet School*, p140; *Rivals*, pp192, 211); Jo loses her temper with Matron Besly (*New House*, p123); Peggy Bettany risks her life unnecessarily in a storm (*Peggy*, p144). And the foolish authority figures are also given the opportunity to recognise their errors and to do better in the future.

Perhaps the most intriguing example of this is Miss Bubb. She reappears in *Excitements* and *Coming of Age* after many years' absence and, though she is still recognisably the same person is now ready to acknowledge her need for help and to accept some gestures of friendship—though perhaps not quite enough (*Excitements*, p193; *Coming of Age*, pp94, 109). Miss Browne and Elaine are seen to reform more thoroughly. The former acknowledges that her pupils are not better than the Chalet girls, listens to advice from one of her employees and finally acts admirably when dealing with Vera Smithers (*Rivals*, pp164–5, 262–4, 266–71). And Elaine suffers a shock, is punished and afterwards becomes a 'very different girl', proving her repentance by carrying on with her job and doing it properly, putting an end to the ill-feeling she had previously created against the Chaletians (*Rivals*, p270).

This leads us to consider a final point about EBD and her presentation of authority and authority figures. So far we have seen her demonstrate that positions of authority bring responsibility; that those responsibilities ought not to be selfishly shirked; and that they are better approached with humility rather than in pride. But EBD is also concerned to show that a job well done will bring its own rewards, not only to the community in general, but to the authority figure herself. To a certain extent this can be observed in Joey's experiences. Gisela and Gottfried agree that it will do Jo good to take on the role of Head Girl—she has remained a child too long—and are pleased with what they see after she has held the post for a term: the school has deepened and strengthened her, concludes Gottfried (*And Jo*, pp25, 285). But it is Grizel who perhaps provides us with the most extended and moving case study.

Grizel goes on a similar journey to Elaine, triumphing after an initial disaster, but we follow her history far more closely and for much longer. We first meet her as a troubled child. Her poor home background has made her unsure of herself, and, before her appointment as Head Girl, we see her go through a stage when she has an unfortunate habit of putting on superior airs, doubtless in an attempt to impress (*School at* p236, *Princess* p116, with perhaps some corroboration from *The Chalet Girls in Camp*, when Miss Wilson talks retrospectively about Grizel's conceit upon first becoming a prefect, p72). Then when she is offered the post of Head Girl, she tries to get out of it, afraid of the responsibility and the fact that she must put the School first and herself last in order to do the job well. But Madge, still very much in charge at the School, is not deterred. She is very aware of the girl's faults, but is also clear that there are only two more terms in which to influence her. She believes that the responsibility of being Head Girl may make all the difference to Grizel in later life and so persists in offering her the post (*Head Girl*, p42).

Grizel is persuaded: it is a good point in her character that she does feel affection for Madge and is not so wrapped up in herself that she remains uninfluenced by her. But she still hasn't quite managed to conquer her selfish tendencies nor her desire for the *wrong* sort of superiority. Piqued by Joey's disdain for her plan for a forbidden visit to the Falls of Rhine, she sets off by herself (pp43, 50, 51).

Fortunately, it is not long before her better self begins to get the upper hand again. Realising how badly she has behaved, she abandons her trip half way and returns to her party. She now knows she does not deserve to be Head Girl; she understands she had failed in her responsibilities—she has reached the correct position of humility.

Madge, of course, forgives her, allowing her to retain her position—because she *still* believes that this is the best thing she can do for the poor, complicated girl (pp55, 60, 74, 75). And Grizel rises to the challenge, beginning the job with an appropriate awareness of her own fallibility and yet determined to do her best—especially for Madge. Later on, towards the end of her reign, she wants Madge to know this. 'I've *tried*,' she says. 'You'll tell Madame, Joey.' (pp77, 78, 322) And she continues to feel humble, recognising her faults even after she has left the school—so much so that when Madge praises her for the work she did, she can only return thanks:

> Grizel flushed, and her grey eyes filled suddenly with tears. 'It—it was your doing, Madame,' she stammered. 'I don't think anyone else would have had the patience with me that you had. Even that last mad trick of mine you forgave, and gave me another chance. I'd have been a cad if I hadn't played up after that!'
>
> (*And Jo*, p278)

It is true that we then enter a period during which Grizel, the school's music mistress, does not appear in a favourable light. Embittered by her family problems and the fact that she never wanted to teach music, anyhow, she proves difficult to work with—an excellent teacher, but one with a 'nasty tongue' (*Island*, pp119–120). But we must not conclude that Madge's efforts with her and her time as Head Girl have taught her nothing. She continues to struggle with herself and her own character, acknowledging her faults in times of crisis—when she is distracted by more bad personal news in *Carola Storms the Chalet School* and causes an accident, for instance.

> 'An accident that should never have happened!' Grizel spoke almost harshly. 'Whatever I might have been feeling, I'd no right to go chucking matches around like that.'
>
> (*Carola*, p251)

And she doesn't give in: she keeps on trying. When we next meet her in *The Chalet School Reunion*, she is again in deep trouble. Her heart is broken and she has reached the point when she does not want to live any longer. But, writes EBD, Grizel resists the temptation to commit suicide.

> 'Grizel Cochrane had too much in her for that and her training at the Chalet School had deepened her character. She knew this. Somehow, she thought, she must live through this misery and trust to time healing her wounds.'
>
> (*Reunion*, p20)

Shortly after this EBD finally gives her an opportunity to find true happiness and to redeem herself. First she has an encounter with no other person than Mary-Lou, now a fellow former Head Girl, and is deeply impressed by her courage and selflessness in a time of bereavement. Grizel is humble enough to resolve to follow the younger woman's example (*Reunion*, p79). Then, at great personal cost, she takes on the responsibility for rescuing young Len Maynard after a cliff fall. It is a truly lovely touch that on the day in which this happens, Grizel assumes again the position of Head Girl amongst the group around her.

> 'She spoke with all the authority of the Head Girl she had been when all those present but Len had been Middles at the Chalet School …'
>
> (*Reunion*, p118)

Her brief authority, both in the past and in *Reunion*, was used for the general good—and for her own good.

Helen Barber

UILSELI, MARIA: Maria hears a rumour from her cousin Otillie Sneider about how Len Maynard became covered in oil paint in *Althea* and Maria tells Meta Gordon of IIIA (p148).

UNDERWOOD, MISS: Miss Underwood is one of the staff at Braemar House and teaches Junior Latin and French in *Monica* (p28).

UNSEL, HANNI: Hanni is in Lower IIIA with Jack Lambert in *Leader* (p171/172). Hanni is in Lower IVA with Rosemary Wentworth in *Redheads* and is a born giggler (p68/69).

UNSELI, FRAU: Frau Unseli discovers a viper's nest under the bank in her vegetable patch and a tiny viper is found by the Chalet kitchen staff in some spinach that she sends to the School in *Prefects*. The viper terrifies Mechtilde and two other maids but Gaudenz and Matey deal with it (p118/119).

UNSWORTH, MAYNA: Thirteen-year-old Mayna is in the Upper Fourth with Blossom Willoughby in *Peggy*. Dickie Christy rebukes Mayna for spinning a bucket of water around herself (p222).

UNWIN, HEATHER: Heather, Connie Winter, Nora Fitzgerald and Nancy Wadham manage to get lost in the wooded grounds of the Château Gutsch on an excursion to Lucerne in *Does It Again* (p123). Josette Russell rebukes Heather for pushing in the Speisesaal in *Ruey*. Heather is Upper IVB's form prefect. She asks about the age rule for learning lacrosse (p69/104).

UNWIN, JANET: Janet is in VB with Mary-Lou Trelawney and her Gang in *Mary-Lou* and is mathematically inclined (p53). Mary-Lou describes Janet as absolutely colourless and not suitable to be a prefect in *Excitements* (p129). No surname is given, so this could be Janet Youll.

URSULE: Ursule is one of Simone de Bersac's servants in *Joey Goes* (p107).

'Plas Gwyn'

VALENTI, CARMELA: Carmela is in Lower IVA in *Jane* when she informs Maeve Bettany that Jane and Jack are having a fight while they are washing Kathie Ferrars's car (p107/108).

VALENTINE, ANNE: Anne helps Sally Winslow, the Art Prefect, make invitations for the prefects' evening in *Mary-Lou* (p81).

VALERIE: Valerie is a big, pretty pupil at Campden House School who plays in a tennis match against Nancy Chester and Katharine Gordon in *Wrong* (p174/175).

VALLENS, MARY: Mary is at St Mildred's in *Coming of Age* but is living at the Chalet School because of all the visitors. Madge Watson mentions that Mary is friendly with Jocelyn Abbot. They were not at the Chalet School previously (p56).

Names beginning with 'van' are listed under the main part of the name, eg:

van ALDEN, MR: see ALDEN, MR van

VANE, URSULA: Ursula transfers from the Tanswick Chalet School with Maureen Grey and Hilary Bennett in *Bride*. They are put into Upper IVA with Mary-Lou Trelawney and are quick to follow the good example of the other girls, standing up when the Head enters the room (p102; p101 for form).

VARICK, MRS: American Mrs Varick is slowly dying up at the Sonnalpe in *Lintons* (p294).

VARICK, MARIE: Marie, an American, is the Frog Prince at the Fairy Tale Bazaar in *Lintons* and we learn that her mother is slowly dying up at the Sonnalpe, although Marie has no idea of this (p294). Marie is in the Brownies in *New CS* and her ambition is to be an elocutionist. The Brownies present the story of Grace Darling at an end-of-term entertainment and Marie is the narrator (p304). Marie sticks a pin into Marjorie Burn when Miss Phipps is teaching them bandaging in Guernsey in *Exile* (p285). Marie is in the Upper Fourth in *Gay* and is one of the group to whom Gay Lambert tells the story of her adventure in China (p134). Marie is in the Lower Fifth and still friendly with Gay in *Mystery*. Marie attends Catholic Prayers and she is one of the people who drag in the Yule log in the Christmas Play (p65/66/67/89).

VARLEY, MR and MRS: Mr and Mrs Varley take Lorraine and her friend Amandine Robinet to The Hague at half term in *Trials*, and Mr Varley, knowing them to be musical, has arranged to take them to two big concerts (p77).

VARLEY, LORRAINE: Lorraine starts at the Chalet School in *Kenya* and is a promising pianist (p75). Lorraine is in VB with Mary-Lou in *Mary-Lou* and is a very musical girl who usually stays in the background (p147; p146 for form). Lorraine and her friend Amandine Robinet visit Holland with Mr and Mrs Varley at half term in *Trials* (p76/77). Lorraine is among the early arrivals at school in *Theodora* and is the dormitory prefect in Margot Maynard's dormitory in St Clare's (p17/132).

VAUGHN, DILYS: Dilys gets colds easily. She steps into a hidden pool on a wintry walk in *Lavender* (p186).

VAUGHN, EILUNED (EILUNEDD): Welsh Eiluned is in the Sixth form in *Island*. She comes from near Howells village (p115; p113 for form). Eilunedd is in the Special Sixth in *Peggy* and is a small, very dark Welsh girl (p48/75). We are told that three years previously she fell out with Gwensi Howell and everything went wrong for Gwensi that term (p78). Eilunedd is not a particularly clever girl. She specialises in secretarial studies. She is jealous of Peggy Bettany as she had hoped to be the next Head Girl and tries to cause problems for her. We are told that her close friends left school unexpectedly the previous term and she now has no particular friend (p84). Eilunedd plots how to get her own back on Peggy Bettany for getting the Head Girl position instead of her (p207/208). She tells some younger girls Welsh folk tales and then spreads stories about Peggy Bettany, mentioning her late arrival at school to some of the girls including Blossom Willoughby, who starts to be rude to Peggy (p213/216/217). Joey invites Eilunedd to tea and teaches her that tales are like feathers and cannot be collected in easily. Eilunedd later apologises to Peggy (p245/252). Eilunedd has left the Chalet School by the beginning of *Shocks* (p69). Joey Maynard remembers in *Future* that Eilunedd made trouble for Peggy Bettany when Peggy was Head Girl because she expected to be Head Girl after Jacynth Hardy left school (p196/197).

VENABLES, DAISY: see VENABLES, MARGARET CECILIA

VENABLES, FRANKIE (C) (2): We are informed in *New House* that Stephen and Margot's middle son Frankie died when they were sugar-cane planting in North Queensland (p52/55/56).

VENABLES, JIMMY (C) (1): We are informed in *New House* that Stephen and Margot's eldest son Jimmy died when they were sugar-cane planting in North Queensland and he would now be nearly twelve years old (p52/55/75).

VENABLES, MARGARET (MARGOT) (MARGIE) (née RUSSELL) (MATRON VENABLES), 'VENNY' (B): Joey mentions Margot's name when they are thinking of a name for baby Sybil Russell in *Lintons* and we learn that Margot lives in Australia and has a daughter named Daisy (p169/170). Joey and Frieda meet Jem Russell's sister Margot and her two daughters, Daisy and Primula Mary, in Innsbruck in *New House*. We learn that Margot lost touch with her family when she married Stephen because they did not like her husband (p48). They had been living in Brisbane, Australia, and Stephen is now dead, having been bitten by a snake a year ago. Their three sons (Jimmy, Frankie and Steve) died when the family were trying sugar-cane planting in North Queensland. Her two-year-old daughter Primula Mary was born there but is not very strong. After her husband's death, Margot and her daughters moved to Brisbane, where she did a little teaching and lived with Nurse Rickards, an old friend. Unfortunately Nurse Rickards died of septic pneumonia so Margot decided to look for her brother Jem, starting at Innsbruck as the principal town of the Tyrol (p51/52/55/57/58/59). Margot is three years older than Jem and must be about thirty-eight (p64). Jem arrives in Innsbruck to meet his sister, whom he addresses as 'Margie', and learns that Margot's eldest son Jimmy would now be twelve (p70/71/72/75). Margot explains that Stephen would not let her write to her parents because he was jealous (p76). Jem escorts Margot and her daughters up to the Sonnalpe, where Margot collapses with exhaustion (p79/110). After a long rest Margot, a tiny woman, finally recovers and is offered the post of Matron at St Clare's when Matron Besly leaves at the end of term (p246/247). Margot is the Matron of St Clare's in *Jo*

Brisbane

Returns (p10). She has the girls well in hand and they like her. She is tactful and never says anything she does not mean (p87). Joyce Linton refers to her as 'Venny' (p134). It is mentioned that Margot was a nurse in a big sanatorium in England before her unfortunate marriage took her out to Queensland, though she is not as fully trained as 'Matey' (p145). Matron Venables and Daisy visit the Carrs up at the Sonnalpe at half term to see Primula Mary, who is staying with them (p209). Margot is apparently well but has very little reserve strength in *Exile* and Jem decides to send Margot and all of the children out of the country, with Rosalie Dene to help them. They will go to Guernsey, to La Rêve (p111/112/118). When the Chalet School's opening in Guernsey is planned, Margot has been dead for six months, having slipped away leaving her two girls with her brother and his wife. When the Maynard triplets are born, the youngest baby is named Mary Margaret, to be known as Margot, to please Daisy (p170/282). Joey explains this to Gwensi in *Goes to It* (p63). Margot's arrival at the Sonnalpe is recalled in *Highland Twins* (p105) and *Lavender* (p53). Joey introduces the Margot Venables Prize in *Gay* for the girl who has done most to help others, and Gay Lambert wins it (p234). Tom Gay wins the Margot Venables prize in *Wrong* (p247) and Jo Scott in *Kenya* (p200). It is renamed the Josephine Maynard Prize in *Coming of Age*, when Mary-Lou wins it (p222). We are reminded in *Joey and Co.* that Margot Maynard is named after Margot Venables (p201).

VENABLES, MARGARET CECILIA (DAISY) (ROSOMON, DAISY) (C) (4): Joey mentions Daisy, Jem Russell's niece in Australia, when they are thinking of a name for baby Sybil in *Lintons* (p170). Daisy is a small girl with blue eyes and thick, fair hair that is bobbed all round her head. She meets Joey and Frieda Mensch in Innsbruck in *New House*. Nine-year-old Daisy has a birthday in March (p47/53). Daisy is described as having a straight shock of fair silky hair and fearless blue eyes when she is introduced to her Uncle Jem. Daisy starts at the Chalet School Annexe (p72/73/110). She transfers to St Agnes' in *Jo Returns*. Daisy's mother Margot takes Daisy, Evadne Lannis and Elsie Carr up to the Carrs' home at the Sonnalpe for half term as Primula Mary, her younger daughter, is staying there during a measles and whooping cough epidemic at Die

Rosen (p11/209). Daisy and Robin Humphries are friends in *New CS* but will only manage to see each other for occasional weekends (p51). Jem intends to send Margot and her two children away at half term because of the political situation in *Exile*, but Daisy, a wide-eyed, yellow-headed irresponsible of twelve, goes down to Spärtz with a group of girls for a last shopping trip, and the girls try to rescue Herr Goldmann, the jeweller, from Nazi hooligans (p111/118/120). The girls manage to escape through a secret tunnel, but flight from Austria is necessary for them after their wild adventure. Little Daisy is taken by Joey to Otto Scheitzer, one of the mountain herdsmen, to escort home to Die Rosen, and she manages to get away to Guernsey with her mother and the nursery party (p128/129/131). There is a lapse of about a year before final plans are made to reopen the Chalet School in Guernsey and twelve-year-old Daisy is still grieving for her mother, who died six months before. We learn that she and Primula were sent to England for some months when her mother was dying as she did not wish them to be saddened. Daisy has grown and her thick honey-coloured hair is plaited into two plaits. Daisy looks very pretty in her brown tunic, shantung top and flame-coloured tie. She is living at Les Rosiers with Joey (p170/185/195). Daisy is Form Prefect for the Third form and makes friends with Beth Chester (p204/212). Gertrude Beck, or Gertrud Becker, a Nazi spy, questions thirteen-year-old Daisy about the School when it was in the Tyrol (p247/250). When the School moves to Plas Howell in Armishire in *Goes to It*, Third formers Daisy and Beth become friendly with Gwensi Howell, who has the same birthday as Daisy, 14th March. They are all thirteen (p88/63). The three girls go missing and explore a secret tunnel in the undergrowth, where they are waylaid by poachers (p171/172/178). They cause great alarm in the School by their prolonged absence (p183). Daisy and her young sister Primula Mary are two of Simone Lecoutier's bridesmaids when she marries her fiancé André, who is at home on leave (p239). Third formers Daisy, Beth and Gwensi decide to go ski-ing on home-made skis in 'Triumvirate' in *1st* (p115). Long-legged Daisy is almost sixteen and still lives with Joey in *Highland Twins*. Daisy, Beth and Gwensi have decided they will all have plaits (p7/9). Daisy is a clever girl and wants to be a doctor when she leaves school (p80). Daisy is in the Fifth form and is present when Jo gets a telegram about Jack being drowned. Because the telephone wires are down Daisy takes the bad news to the Round House (p100/225/228). Daisy is in the Lower Fifth in *Lavender*, is still growing fast and is a weekly boarder (p19/35). Robin, Daisy, Primula, Fiona and Flora McDonald normally live at Joey's home but the younger girls are full boarders during term and do not get their usual Saturday visits in the weeks before Stephen Maynard is born, especially after Jo's accident with some green dye (p202/203). Daisy is working towards School Certificate. She is worried that Jo may be growing away from them because they have not been allowed to visit or see the ten-day-old baby. She later learns that Joey didn't want Daisy and Robin to witness her green appearance (p217/222/227). Daisy, Lavender Leigh, Lilamani, Robin, Primula and the McDonald twins visit the Maynards' house at half term and are present at Stephen's christening service (p243/250). During the weekend they play at Consequences, listen to Fiona's stories and do a little cookery, with Daisy in charge (p257/259/262). Daisy, Beth and Gwensi are in the same dormitory as Gay Lambert, Gillian Culver and Jacynth Hardy in *Gay* (p52; dormitory Five, p50). Sixteen-year-old Daisy becomes Patrol Leader of the Swallows with Mollie Avery as her Second (p69). Daisy has a high, sweet soprano voice but is rather wild when it comes to piano accompaniments. She is one of the Fifth formers who visit Miss Bubb to ask her to change her mind about restricting them to the School grounds (p81/97). Daisy attends the Lower Sixth cookery lesson that Frau Mieders is taking in 'New Flavouring' in *3rd* (p135/136). Daisy, Primula and Robin visit the Chesters' home in *Rescue* and we are told that Daisy sings well and plays the violin (p172). Daisy is in the Lower Sixth and is one of the elected representatives of the Chalet School who attend Phoebe Wychcote's wedding in *Mystery* (p16/85). She has had chickenpox (p17). She owns a sweet and powerful soprano that gives promise of bringing her to concert work. Daisy plays the part of the Blessed Virgin in the Christmas Play (p91/92). While correcting Tom Gay about her behaviour and her badly drawn map in *Tom*, Daisy arouses Tom's dislike, and the new girl behaves rudely to Daisy, the Games Prefect, from then on, mistakenly believing that she has 'sneaked' to Miss Linton (p33/34/38/50). We learn

Smells of Soot

that Joey has dedicated *The Fugitive of the Salt Caves*, an adventure story set in the Tirol, to Daisy. She will be eighteen in March and is going to Oxford (p53/54/59). Daisy, Elfie Woodward and Tom Gay are returning to school from the Round House when a snowstorm starts and Elfie sprains her ankle badly. Daisy and Tom finally get Elfie home but Daisy wrenches her arm in the process. Tom is able to help Daisy with Elfie (p85/87/88). Daisy has to give up her violin for the rest of the term and cannot take her Final in the Associated Board Examinations. Madge Russell arrives at school with baby Ailie to help nurse Daisy back to health. Daisy and Primula will live with the Russell family again once the Bettanys go to their new home (p100/101/102). Daisy intends to go to Oxford in October to study medicine and hopes to do her practical work at a London Hospital. She wants to work entirely with children (p103/104). Beth mentions in 'Beth's Diary' in *2nd* that Daisy and Gwensi went crackers over the miserere seats inside Exeter Cathedral (p[ii]). Straight-haired Daisy mentions in 'Smells of Soot' in *2nd* that Jo and Madge object to her having a perm. She plans to go to Oxford and will perhaps have her hair permed then (p31). She stands down as Games Prefect in favour of Gay Lambert to work on important exams in *Rosalie*, though she still attends games meetings. One evening while Daisy is taking prep with the Upper Third she has toothache and upsets Rosalie Way, who runs out to hide in the rhododendrons (p121/124/140/144). We learn in *Three Go* that Daisy has been studying medicine in London for two years and has won the Ransome Gold Medal for a paper on infectious diseases of children (p82). We are informed in *Island* that Daisy is at present walking the wards of a big London hospital with the intention of working with children later on. She corresponds with Jacynth Hardy (p203/204/214). It is mentioned in *Peggy* that Daisy was in the Special Sixth when she was Head Girl (p225). Daisy is Jo Maynard's niece-by-marriage, and she and Primula are staying with friends outside Armiford in *Carola* (p21). She is a tall, fair girl in her early twenties and is engaged to a young doctor at her hospital. Daisy will be married in the summer and her bridesmaids will be Primula and the Maynard triplets (p151/234/250). We are informed in *Wrong* that long-legged Daisy, who is five-foot-nine, once had soup spilt on her, ruining her frock just before a tennis match (p169). Miss Annersley receives a letter from Daisy in *Shocks* (p14). Daisy spends a holiday at Welsen with Peggy Bettany and also visits Lugano before starting work at the Encliffe Children's Hospital in *CS Oberland*. Daisy's fiancé is Dr Laurence Rosomon, partner to a doctor in Devonshire, and their wedding has had to be postponed as they are waiting for Joey and Madge and their families to return from Canada before setting a date for the following June. Dr Rosomon will look for a home for them and Daisy will stay with Joyce Linton at weekends, as Joyce's husband has just been preferred to a living in the same place (p10/14). Daisy has rooms fairly near the Quadrant in Devon in *Bride* and is getting married soon (p29/36). Bride mentions in *Changes* that Daisy stayed with her family for Easter (p23). Daisy marries Laurie at the beginning of *Joey Goes* and Robin, Primula, Len, Con and Margot Maynard are bridesmaids. Daisy wears a white brocade picture frock, and the family veil of *point d'Alençon* lace is caught back with posies of pink-and-white daisies at either side. The wedding was to have taken place from the Round House, the Russells' home, but Madge Russell has German measles and so the reception is held in Howells village hall. Jack Maynard gives the bride away (p44/46). We learn when she signs the register that Daisy's full name is Margaret Cecilia Venables (p49). After a three-week honeymoon, Daisy will move into her new home with Laurence and Primula. Daisy and her new husband arrive at Freudesheim, but have to cut their honeymoon short because Laurence's locum has to leave suddenly (p53/192/196). It is mentioned in *Barbara* that Daisy, Beth and Gwensi visited Switzerland three years ago (p7). Daisy is mentioned in *Kenya* as Margot Venables' married daughter (p200). Len says in *Problem* that Daisy lives in Devonshire (p93). Joey informs everyone that she is now a great-aunt when Daisy produces a baby son named Richard Anthony in *New Mistress*. He is named Richard after Laurie's father and, as Joey never used Anthony, Daisy decides to use it instead as it is one of her favourite names (p167/169/170). Len Maynard calls the baby Tony in *Excitements* (p68). Daisy and Laurie will help Joey clear out Plas Gwyn ready to be sold in *Coming of Age*, and Joey is excited to be meeting little Tony (p172). The time when Daisy went missing along with Beth and Gwensi is remembered in *Trials* (p154). Joey mentions in *Joey and Co.* that Daisy and Laurie are coming out to the Tirol. They are bringing Joey's four younger children, who have been staying with the Russell family, and also Tony and their three-month-old baby (p172). The Rosomon family arrives at the Tiernsee and we learn that twenty-eight-year-old Daisy's second child is another boy. He is called Peter and is two months old (p199/201/202). Daisy informs Ruey Richardson that Laurie is the Richardsons' second cousin through their mother's side (p204). Daisy arrives with her sons and Madge Russell for the dedication of the Chalet School chapels in *Ruey* (p77). Daisy has a new baby daughter, Mary Margaret, in *Future* and the Richardsons are going to visit Daisy and Laurie in Devonshire at Christmas. Joey tells her family that Laurie will be coming out to work at the Sanatorium next summer (p192/204/205). The Rosomons have settled into their new house at Ste Cecilie in *Reunion* and Primula is engaged to a budding solicitor, Nicholas Garden, five years older than herself (p191). Daisy appears to be staying temporarily with Joey in *Jane* and we are told that the Rosomons have come out from England because Laurie is joining the Sanatorium and taking Dr Tyndall's place (p81/101). The Rosomons are settled in near St Hilda's school at Ste Cecilie in *Redheads*. Daisy is a doctor but has no time to work now she has two boys and a girl. Nancy Wilmot informs some girls on a ramble that Daisy was one of the wickedest Middles she ever knew but grew up to be an excellent prefect and Head Girl (p50/51). Laurie and Daisy have found a house on the Görnetz Platz in *Adrienne* and Joey will look after their three children for a few days while they settle in (p143). Ruey and Roddy Richardson spend part of each holiday with the Rosomons in *Althea* (p28). EBD tells us in *N17* that Daisy helps with the children's wards at the Sanatorium (p71). She answers two readers'

Pertisau

queries in *N20* by explaining that Daisy is Sir James Russell's niece (p84).
CHILDREN:
1) RICHARD ANTHONY (TONY): see ROSOMON, RICHARD
2) PETER: see ROSOMON, PETER
3) MARY MARGARET: see ROSOMON, MARY

VENABLES, PRIMULA MARY (GARDEN, PRIMULA) (C) (5): Margot Venables's younger daughter Primula Mary is described as a tired baby who draws back behind her mother with a whimper when Joey offers to carry her on first meeting her in *New House*. The shy little girl is the image of Jem Russell. We learn that she was a fragile baby of six weeks when her three brothers died (p49/53/55). Frieda comments that Primula is much fairer than Dr Jem but has his blue eyes and the same nose and mouth. She is pretty but very shy. Two-year-old Primula Mary's birthday is in November and she is fragile and has thick, primrose-coloured hair (p64/72/73). Jem Russell takes Margot and her daughters to live at Die Rosen at the Sonnalpe and Primula Mary settles down in the big nursery and becomes the sworn ally of her cousin David, who is a few months younger (p110). She remains at Die Rosen when her mother becomes Matron at St Clare's in *Jo Returns*, as she is very young (p11). Primula Mary is exceedingly delicate, with very little strength to fight any illness and fortunately manages to escape the measles and whooping cough epidemic at Die Rosen, as she sleeps in her mother's room. Later she is away from infection at the Annexe, and subsequently she stays with the Carrs (p25/30/209). She has kept well and is much stronger, responding well to the mountain air and Jem's strict régime. After the epidemic Joey notices that Primula Mary is blooming like a rose in the crystalline, bracing atmosphere and looks pounds better (p212/275). Primula Mary is a delicate member of the Russell family in *New CS* but is far stronger than she has been for some time. On the morning that Sybil is kidnapped, the little girl is in tears over the kidnapping (p108/156). Four-year-old Primula Mary is still terribly delicate when she leaves Austria with the nursery party and goes to live at La Rêve in Guernsey in *Exile* (p111/118). Tiny Primula Mary is described as having a straight shock of primrose-coloured hair. Primula Mary and Daisy are sent to England when their mother is dying and afterwards the former is too young to realise her loss. Daisy mentions that Primula Mary was at the Annexe during the School's last term in Austria (p170/171/249). Primula Mary is still in Guernsey and probably at school in *Goes to It* (p25/26). She is the youngest child in the Second form at Plas Howell and is one of Simone's bridesmaids (p154/239). Primula lives with Joey Maynard in *Highland Twins* and is nine years old (p33/50). She is a weekly boarder as she is not strong enough to cope with the daily journey. She is in the Upper Second with Bride Bettany and Julie Lucy and brains are not her strong point (p80/81). Primula is still with her friends in the Upper Second in *Lavender* and she spent Christmas with the Russells. She normally lives with Joey, along with Robin, Daisy and the McDonald twins (p32/34). The girls are boarders when Stephen is born (p223). Lavender and Lilamani are invited to the Maynards' house at half term with Daisy, Primula, Robin, and Fiona and Flora McDonald, and they are present at Stephen's christening service (p243/250). During the weekend they play

at Consequences, listen to Fiona's stories and make waffles and a fruitcake (p257/259/262). Jo has invited Daisy and Primula for half term in *Gay* but they cannot go as they are in quarantine for German measles (p193/197). Daisy, Primula and Robin visit the Chesters in *Rescue* and we are told that Primula is beginning to play the piano very prettily (p172). It is mentioned in *Mystery* that Primula has had chickenpox in the past (p17). Madge mentions in *Tom* that Primula and Daisy will be living with the Russells once the Bettanys move to their new house. Nine-year-old Primula is a tiny girl whose primrose-fair hair is cut short and very straight (p102/150). Primula is nearly fourteen in *Three Go* when she meets Mary-Lou (p59). Her cousin Sybil Russell is a little younger than Primula, who is to be a full boarder this term. Primula, a tiny, slender girl with fine, silky, primrose-coloured hair and big blue eyes, becomes friendly with Clem Barras, who is a nature lover like herself (p61/64/149). The Russells go to Canada in *Island* and Primula will spend her holidays with the Maynards (p17). Clever, frail Primula is in the Lower Fifth with her special friend Betsy Lucy in *Peggy*. Hockey is too strenuous for her and she plays netball (p93/94/95). It is explained in *Carola* that Primula and Daisy are nieces-by-marriage of Jo Maynard. After Christmas they are staying with friends outside Armiford, near their old home (p21). Primula and the Maynard triplets will be Daisy's bridesmaids when she gets married in the summer (p250). We learn in *CS Oberland* that Primula has been spending the summer holidays in Canada with the Russells and will be staying there until next spring. Canada has done Primula a tremendous lot of good. She will make her home with Daisy and Dr Rosomon during her holidays (p12/14). Tiny, dainty, eighteen-year-old Primula is as fair as her sister in *Joey Goes*. She and Robin Humphries are Daisy's two grown-up bridesmaids (p44). Primula is invited to accompany Jo and her family out to the Platz and stay with them until Daisy and Laurence finish their honeymoon, instead of staying at the Round House. Primula will go to Welsen when term starts (p56/57/197). Primula is still at Welsen in *Kenya* (p200). Con Maynard tells Ruey Richardson that Primula is twenty in *Joey and Co.* (p201). Twenty-four-year-old Primula is engaged to a budding solicitor, Nicholas Garden, in *Reunion*. He is five years older and they will live at Etherleigh in Devonshire (p191/192).

VENABLES, STEPHEN (B): Stephen, Margot Venables's late husband, is mentioned in *New House* and we are told that they ran away to get married. Stephen died from a snake-bite a year before the date of the story, when they were trying sugarcane planting, and their three sons had died before that. Stephen was a weak man, a waster, who could be the delight of company, but a tyrant at home. He never accomplished anything, though he was always going to do wonders. He had no idea of the value of money, and would order largely without considering how he was going to pay. He later took to drinking, and his wife had the care of him as well as the children (p51/52/55).

VENABLES, STEPHEN (STEVE) (C) (3): We learn in *New House* that Steve was Stephen and Margot's youngest son and he died when they were sugarcane planting in the cruel climate of North Queensland (p52/55/56).

VENETTA: Venetta is a maid at the Belsornian court who helps Juliet Carrick dress for Joey's Presentation at Parliament House in *Princess*, and then shows Joey the way to the White Salon (p298/300).

VENN, JOY: Joy is an extremely pretty girl at St Mildred's who plays the part of Beauty in their pantomime, *Beauty and the Beast*, in *Genius*. Joy came from another school (p89).

VERDIN, DI: Lavender Leigh hits Anne Montague's hand forcefully when she is on the hockey field in *Lavender* and Anne's young cousin Di hears about it and is very upset. Di's father is a doctor in the same village where Anne's father is the vicar (p118/119).

VIDLER, URSULA: Ursula is described as a fat podge of a girl in *Barbara* and is dismayed to find many of the magazines in the common room are in French or German (p61). She is by way of being artistic and is in the Upper Fourth when they discuss gardening in *Kenya* (p90; p89 for form). Ursula is in VB and sits beside Jessica Wayne in *Mary-Lou* (p28/29). Hilary Bennett hears Joan Baker talking 'mush' to Sarah Hewitson and Ursula Vidler in *Problem* and Mary-Lou describes Sarah and Ursula as gigglers at the best of times (p146).

VIENNE, ANDRÉE de: New girl Andrée is French and in the Pansy dormitory in *Does It Again* (p17).

VIGNES, (two unnamed SISTERS) de: The two de Vignes sisters are new girls and come from Paris in *Shocks*. They spend half term in France and fly there with Mlle de Lachenais (p75/171).

VIGORS, MR: see BOURNE, MR

VINCENT, CHRISTINE: Christine is a mop-headed, wide-eyed innocent who gets into scrapes by taking everything literally in *Bride*. She is in the Leafy dorm with Mary-Lou Trelawney (p60; p57 for dormitory). Christine is in Upper IVA in *Changes* and learns that she will move to Switzerland with one of her friends, Catriona Watson. Her other friend, Gwen Jones, will not be going to Switzerland but will stay in England at St Agnes' until she is seventeen. The three girls have been at school together since they were eight (p45/120; p47 for form). Christine, an attractive-looking girl with wavy, brown hair, grumbles that she is not in Leafy dormitory with Catriona in *Barbara*. She is a Senior Middle (p53/58/62) and later appears to be in Leafy dormitory with Mary-Lou Trelawney and Barbara Chester, although this may be intended to be Christine Dawson. Christine is a member of the Gang and is in the group supervised by Miss Dene when they visit Unterseen (p81/93). Christine is in the Fourth form in *Does It Again* and she and Catriona Watson are in the Gang when the girls visit Lucerne (p68/115/122). Christine is in the Bluebell dormitory with Catriona in *Kenya*. She is learning to play the piano. Christine is with the Gang when they discuss their show (p35/37/167). In *Mary-Lou* we learn that Christine comes from Leeds (p100). She is one of the Seniors who visit Vevey in *Genius* (p120). Christine and Catriona come third in the wheelbarrow race by steady plodding in *Coming of Age* (p214). Christine is a sub-prefect when Mary-Lou is the Head Girl in *Richenda* (p59). The two inseparables, Christine and Catriona, are in VIB in *Trials*. Miss Annersley mentions that they have minds of their own and have important public exams ahead (p10/11). Christine is one of the few prefects who will still be at school next year (p153). Christine is among the prefects at Vespers in the Catholic chapel when there is an invasion of cockchafers in *Theodora*, and is terrified (p86). She is chosen to be the Stationery Prefect when Josette Russell is Head Girl in *Ruey* and we are informed that she is always on the spot and will not issue anything that has not been ordered by a mistress (p59). Christine is one of the prefects when Josette Russell is Head Girl in *Trick* and their meeting is interrupted by someone throwing stink-bombs (p51).

VINNIE, AUNT: Rita Quick's Aunt Vinnie sends her a scent-spray, which is unfortunately sprayed over Erica Standish and attracts a swarm of bees in *Summer Term* (p119/120).

VINTON, FATHER: Father Vinton officiates at Simone and André de Bersac's wedding in Armiford in *Goes to It* (p243).

VIOLA: Viola and Rosalind, the Shakespeares' cousins, play netball at their school in *Heather* (p118).

Unnamed VISCOUNTESS: The person officially opening the Sale in *Carola* is a Viscountess who has three little girls at home (p234/235).

VIVALANTI, DOMENICA: Domenica and her sisters Giulia and Fiamma are at St Peter's School in *HG Difficulties*. Domenica and her friends hide during a private display of gymnastics given by Miss Benson and Miss Handley to the Fifth form. The seven girls from IIIB become locked in the gym and Rosamund finds them (p34/38/47). Domenica becomes very ill with diphtheria (p123/124) and

later dies and is buried in the old churchyard at Dawley (p132/136).

VIVALANTI, FIAMMA: Fiamma is in the Second form at St Peter's School in *Gerry* and is a gorgeous dragonfly in the end-of-term play (p234). She is IIIA's Form Captain in *HG Difficulties* (p30). Fiamma's name is mentioned after the incident in the gym, when the prefects interview members of the Second form, but this is probably an error. It is mentioned that Fiamma kicks Madge to stop her crying (p52). Fiamma is a member of IVB and buys Cambridge paper from the stationery room. Fiamma, Althea Southern and Allegra Atherton bring out a Junior School Gazette and Fiamma is a sub-editor (p72/74). Fiamma and her sisters become ill with diphtheria and little Domenica dies (p123/132). Fiamma has written a letter about adoring Vivien and later Fiamma and Giulia are in mischief over some cobbler's wax (p225/266). Fiamma is in IVB with Sheila Trevennor and plays the part of a prince in the Juniors' end-of-term play, *The Oyster Princess* (p266/290/311).

VIVALANTI, GIULIA (GEMMA): Giulia and her sisters Fiamma and Domenica are at St Peter's School in *HG Difficulties*. Giulia, Nicola, José and Madge are some of the girls determined to watch a private display of gymnastics that Miss Benson and Miss Handley give to the Fifth form (p34/35). The girls hide in the gym and seven members of IIIB become locked in (p38/47). Later, Giulia is referred to as Gemma when she is the first person to see Rosalind Atherton's notice, posted in response to their magazine (p92). Giulia and her sisters become ill with diphtheria and little Domenica dies (p123/132). Giulia is one of the girls involved in the writing of sentimental notes. She is in IIIA and Miss Lawrence is her form mistress. Giulia and Fiamma are in mischief over some cobbler's wax (p183/256/259/266).

Names beginning with 'von' are listed under the main part of the name, eg:

von AHLEN, ANDREAS: see AHLEN, ANDREAS von

VOS, MÉLANIE de: Mélanie is a good little French girl at the Annexe who was very shy when she started school. She takes part in a snowball fight at the Sonnalpe in *Exploits* and loses some of her shyness. She is in the annexe party who are entertained at Herr Anserl's house in Spärtz on their way to the main Chalet School (p222/281).

VRENELI: Vreneli is a maid at the Chalet School who has violent toothache in *Althea* (p52).

WADHAM, NANCY: Nancy is a Middle in *Barbara* (p58/59). She manages to get lost in the wooded grounds of Château Gutsch with Connie Winter, Heather Unwin and Nora Fitzgerald on an excursion to Lucerne in *Does It Again* (p123). She is in the Alpenrose dormitory with Con and Margot Maynard in *Ruey* (p14). Nancy is a Senior at Joey's sheets and pillowcase party in *Adrienne*. She is dressed as a frog and wins a prize for the funniest costume (p120).

WAGSTAFF, SIMEON: We learn in *Lost Staircase* that Simeon supervised the building of parts of the Dragon House (p187).

WAKE, TERRY: Terry is a younger Middle who has more or less of a character in *Shocks* (p58).

WALKER, ANNE: Anne starts school in *Mystery* and is in the Upper Fourth. She becomes friendly with Esme Béranger and takes her to Joey's new girls' tea party. Anne's father is an organist at Leston Parish Church (p18/29).

WALLACE, REVD MR: Ernest Howell's locum Mr Wallace has two daughters who join the Chalet School when it opens at Plas Howell in *Goes to It* (p16/100). Mr Wallace, the current vicar of Howells, is going to a parish in one of the London suburbs in *Changes* and Ernest Howell is retiring from the Navy and taking over Howells church again (p69).

WALLACE, BARBARA: Ernest Howell's locum Mr Wallace has two daughters who go to the Chalet School when it opens at Plas Howell in *Goes to It* (p16/100). Barbara and her younger sister Ursula are mentioned in *Highland Twins*, and Barbara is in the Fifth form (p83).

WALLACE, URSULA: Ernest Howell's locum Mr Wallace has two daughters who go to the Chalet School when it opens at Plas Howell in *Goes to It* (p16/100). Ursula has an elder sister, Barbara, and is in the Upper Fourth in *Highland Twins* (p83).

WALLER, MISS: Small, plump Miss Waller is in charge of the orphaned Erica Jane Standish when they meet Joey Maynard in Oxford Street in *Summer Term*. We learn that she has been Erica's governess and also a companion-housekeeper to Mrs Standish. Miss Waller is about to be married to a Mr Parker and has brought Erica to Britain to find Joey (p9/11/12).

WALLIS, MR: We are told in *HG Difficulties* that Mr Atherton was Mr Wallis's secretary before the war. Mr Wallis died about the time that Noel Atherton was born and left them shares in a copper mine in Texas, which unfortunately is not doing well (p12).

WALTERS, DR: Dr Walters is Rosalie Way's doctor. He has two daughters, Gertrude and Winifred, in *Rosalie* (p107).

WALTERS, REVD MR and MRS: Mr Walters is the vicar at Pwllylleyn in Carnarvonshire, and we learn in *Peggy* that he and his wife are the parents of Mary Winterton and the grandparents of Polly and Lala (p12/24).

WALTERS, GERTRUDE: Gertrude and Winifred Walters have been sharing their tutor, Miss Miller, with Rosalie Way and the Herbert girls from the rectory, in *Rosalie*. Jonny Agnew, whose father Wing-Commander Agnew was stationed at the aerodrome, also had lessons with them. Gertrude and Winifred's father is the local doctor and they are going to stay with their grandmother and go to school at Bexhill (p107).

WALTERS, MARY: see WINTERTON, MARY

WALTERS, WINIFRED: Winifred and Gertrude Walters shared their tutor, Miss Miller, with Rosalie Way, Jonny Agnew and the Herbert girls in *Rosalie*. Their father is the local doctor and the sisters are going to stay with their grandmother and go to school at Bexhill (p107).

WALTHER, CARMELA: Carmela is a new girl in the Pansy dormitory in *Richenda* (p45; p44 for dormitory) and she speaks fluent English with a strong German accent. Carmela comes from Bonn and is in a group with three Swiss girls in VB (p58/94). She is sub-prefect of Pansy dormitory in *Trials* and fetches Emerence Hope when Margot Maynard is running a temperature. Carmela is a gangling mop-headed creature with eyes like blue saucers (p58/59). Carmela goes on a ramble with VB in *Theodora* and has improved considerably in reputation since she moved up to VB. Kathie Ferrars mentions that Carmela is one of the stormiest petrels in the School, along with

Margot, Emerence, Francie Wilford and Heather Clayton. Carmela is Swiss and is on VB's trip to Zermatt at half term (p50/147/183). She is interested in learning all about lacrosse from Ruey Richardson in *Ruey* and plays in a friendly lacrosse match with joint teams from the Chalet School and St Mildred's (p126/127/158). We learn that Marie Walther is her cousin (p223). Carmela is in VA in *Leader* and plays the piano when the Fifth forms entertain (p49). She helps Jo Scott, Rikki Fry, Sue Mason and the Maynard triplets clear up pepper in the Speisesaal after the tennis match in *Trick* (p90). Carmela is a prefect in charge of the Junior Middles at Hobbies Club in *Feud* and her black hair is in a coronal of plaits. Her discipline is always excellent (p126/127). She is a favourite prefect in *Redheads* but it is best not to play any tricks when she is in charge (p69). Carmela, whose home is near Geneva, is dressed as a nun at Joey's sheets and pillowcase party in *Adrienne*. We learn that, as a Middle, she was famed for being a demon with a trick of looking angelic when she was at her wicked worst (p80/120). Carmela plays tennis with Francie Wilford in *Summer Term* and later is in a group of prefects who survey the cricket pitch when it has been ruined by a thunderbolt (p112/179). She is the Hobbies Prefect in *Challenge* (p76/107). Sixth formers Carmela, Priscilla Dawbarn and Henriette Zendl are experienced ski-ers and are at the top of a steep run in *Two Sams* when Samantha van der Byl reaches the top. They tell the younger girl about the difficulties and snags of the run but despite their warnings she has a ski-ing accident. Carmela goes after her and speaks in her native tongue of Swiss German (p84/85). Miss Annersley sends for Carmela, Priscilla and Henriette and blames them for Samantha's accident, stressing that the mistresses rely on the prefects to ensure that rules are kept. Emotional Carmela is seventeen years old (p88/89/90). Carmela is still a prefect in *Althea* and helps to arrange a Seasons Sale of Work (p60/66). She is one of the twelve Sixth form girls who go on an art expedition to paint some views to sell at the end-of-term Sale, when Len trips and falls on her oil painting (p133). It is mentioned in *Prefects* that curly-haired Carmela will be going to university after this term at the Chalet School. She is clever at modelling and organises artistic girls to model marzipan into flowers and fruit for the Sale of Work (p9/53/111).

WALTHER, MARIE: A Swiss girl named Marie is on a walk with VB in *Theodora* and this may be Marie Walther (p107). Marie is in the Alpenrose dormitory with Con and Margot Maynard in *Ruey*. We learn that Marie was born in Geneva and is Carmela Walther's cousin. She has spent most of her life in England because her father is the Swiss representative of his firm there (p14/223).

WALTON, BARBARA: Barbara is sent on a message by Hilary Burn in *Wrong* (p52). Barbara is at St Mildred's in *Excitements* and plays the part of Abanazar in their pantomime, *Aladdin* (p136).

WALTON, BOB: see COWLEY, MR
WALTON, CYRIL: see COWLEY, CYRIL
WALTON, MARGARET JOSEPHINE: see COWLEY, MARGARET
WALTON, MARGARETTA (MEG): Meg has a red pigtail, is about the same age as Jack Lambert and is probably in the Anemone dormitory in *Feud*. We learn that when Meg was in IIIB she was involved in a squirt battle in the splashery. The girls were caught by Mary-Lou Trelawney and sent to Matron. As a punishment they had to help with household mending instead of playing progressive games (p27/54). Meg is on a walk

with the Lower Fourths and later visits Neuchâtel with some of Lower IVB (p63/68/116). A pupil named Meg is mentioned in *Triplets* (p77). Meg is friendly with Angela Carton in *Jane* and is moved out of her cubicle in the Violet dormitory to go to Alpenrose so that Jack can have her cubicle. Meg plays tennis with Celia Everett, Val Gardiner and Corinne Sambeau (p9/34). She is in IVA and has a long red pigtail in *Redheads* (p32). She is a shining light of Inter V in *Two Sams* and her real name of Margaretta is given. It is explained that very few of the girls are allowed shortened names by the staff. On a visit to Stans we learn that Meg is deeply interested in Pestalozzi's theories and educational methods as she intends to be a Kindergarten mistress (p25/111).

WALTON, MAY: see CARTHEW, MAY
WALTON, PETER: see COWLEY, PETER
WALTON, SUSAN: see COWLEY, SUSAN
WANDA: see ROTH, WANDA
WARD, DR and MRS: Dr Ward is a neighbour of the Athertons and has a rheumaticky wife. He gives Allegra Atherton a puppy in *HG Difficulties* (p14/19). Dr Ralph Farringford finds it reassuring that Dr Ward lives next door to his sister, Anita, when there is an outbreak of diphtheria in Lasterby. Dr Ward uses prussic acid and a syringe when he has to put down José's kitten (p124/125). He later runs from his house next door and helps to extinguish a fire in the Athertons' home (p204). The young Athertons' Uncle Aubrey is married to a lady named 'Jack' (p38), and in *Janie of* we learn that Jack is the Wards' daughter. The young people gather at the Wards' home before Rosamund and Nigel Willoughby's wedding in *Janie of* and Dr Ward is persuaded to dance at their wedding despite being eighty years old (p116/118).
WARD, MISS: Miss Ward is the headmistress at Redfearn School, Jack Lambert's previous school in *Leader* (p12).
WARD, FRANK: In *HG Difficulties* we are informed that Frank Ward was the Head Girl at St Peter's School when Peggy Trevennor was a pupil there (p142).
WARD, JACK: see FARRINGFORD, JACK
WARNER, HEATHER: Heather is in IVA with Connie Winter in *Trials* (p150).
WARREN, ELIZABETH: Elizabeth Warren may be an alternative name for Elizabeth Wren in *CS Oberland*. She is at the Welsen Branch of the Chalet School in the Oberland when it opens as a finishing school. She is one of the younger girls and fishes for rhinestones in a stream (p8/108).
WATSON, LADY (i): We are told in *Trials* that Sir Edgar Watson's first wife died of polio seven years previously, when their youngest child Marcia was only a few months old (p191).
WATSON, LADY (ii): see LANNIS, EVADNE
WATSON, ANNE: Anne has a twisted ankle and is unfit to go for a walk in *Peggy* (p214/216).
WATSON, BARBARA: Barbara and her younger sister Kathleen are from Orkney and stay at school at half term in *Carola*. Barbara is in the Lower Fourth (p145/146). She is on the expedition to the Bosherston lily ponds and wonders if St Govan's well is a wishing well (p156).
WATSON (SATSON), CATRIONA: Catriona is in the Lower Fourth's gardening class when Miss Burnett disappears down an old well in *Shocks* (p123/130). Catriona appears to be in the Leafy dormitory with Mary-Lou Trelawney in *Bride* (p57/59). Dark-haired and grey-eyed Catriona moves up to Upper IVA (p81/86). It is mentioned in *Changes* that Catriona has been at the Chalet School with Christine Vincent and Gwen Jones since they were eight but Gwen will not be going to Switzerland until she is seventeen. Catriona is the cox in St Clare's boat in the Seniors' inter-house race in the Regatta (p120/188). Catriona moves with the Chalet School to the Görnetz Platz and is in the Leafy dormitory with Mary-Lou in *Barbara*. Catriona and Christine are partners on an excursion to Unterseen (p52/53/93). Catriona and Christine are in Nancy Wilmot and Biddy O'Ryan's group of girls on a visit to Lucerne in *Does It Again* and are present when Margot Maynard has an unexpected plunge into the lake (p122/126). Catriona is in the Bluebell dormitory in *Kenya*. She is in Upper IVB and still trips up in her French. Catriona is Scottish and comes from Lewis. She is a shy girl but agrees to sing the Hebridean spinning song at the school concert (p35/61/166). Catriona sits at the same table as Mary-Lou and the rest of the Gang in *Mary-Lou* (p29). Catriona and Christine go to Vevey with the Seniors in *Genius* (p120). Catriona and Josette Russell are in VA in *Coming of Age* and create an enormous golliwog for the Sale (p113). Christine and Catriona come third in the wheelbarrow race by steady plodding. Catriona's surname is here misprinted as Satson (p214). The

two inseparables Catriona and Christine are in VIB in *Trials* and have important public exams ahead (p10/11). The prefects visit the Auberge in *Ruey* and Catriona produces a toy accordion and plays some excruciating notes that come back to them transmuted to fairy music, much to the surprise of some tourists. She is chosen to be the Staff Prefect at a prefects' meeting and accepts the post with resignation. Catriona suggests that they should start a debating society (p57/59/62). She is at a prefects' meeting in *Trick* when Val Gardiner and Celia Everett throw stink bombs (p52/54).

WATSON, DOROTHY: Dorothy is a prefect at the Swiss branch of the Chalet School in *Barbara* and is elected Art Prefect (p34/72). She is given a ride back to school after their first ski lesson because she is not very strong. At the staff party when the girls are masked she is recognised because her front teeth are banded in gold (p186/192). Dorothy is in the Poppy dormitory in *Does It Again* (p14). She is at St Mildred's in *Genius* and is one of the Merchant's daughters in their pantomime *Beauty and the Beast* (p89).

WATSON, SIR EDGAR: Evadne Lannis informs Joey in *Trials* that she is going to become Lady Watson. Edgar, her fiancé, is a widower and Evadne will be a stepmother to Edgar's three children, Ned, Thea and Marcia. His previous wife died of polio when Marcia was only a few months old. Edgar's mother has been living with the family but she died last year. Edgar and Evadne have known each other for three years and are planning a June wedding (p191/192). The Swiss party meet Evadne in Paris in *Ruey* when they are going to Peggy Bettany's wedding in England. Evadne is married and expecting a baby at the end of April. Edgar is a tall, grey-headed man, very straight backed, with a well-drilled look. He has a humorous mouth and very kind eyes and Joey can see that he thinks the world of Evadne (p172/175). Evadne and her family stay at the Villa Caramie for Joey's houseparty in *Reunion*. Their baby boy is a year old (p34/35). Evadne hopes that her stepdaughters will start at the Chalet School in September, as Marcia is nearly ten years old (p45). Later we learn that Evadne will be bringing the

St Govan's well

girls to school and will stay at Freudesheim (p202).

WATSON, EDGAR (NED): Twelve-year-old Ned and his two sisters, Thea and Marcia, are the children of Sir Edgar Watson, Evadne Lannis's future husband, in *Trials*. Ned is described as a fine boy (p191).

WATSON, GILLIAN: Gillian is at St Mildred's in *Triplets* and is the tallest pupil. She is stately with her height and has a somewhat stand-offish manner. Gillian is quite a good amateur actress and plays the part of the Beast in their pantomime *Beauty and the Beast* (p150/157).

WATSON, KATHLEEN: Kathleen, who is from Orkney, is in Lower IIIA in *Carola* (p145/146). Kathleen and her elder sister Barbara are on the expedition to the Bosherston lily ponds (p156).

WATSON, MADGE: Madge is in the Upper Fourth with Sybil Russell and Blossom Willoughby in *Peggy* when the Fourth formers decide to improve their vocabularies after they have been given fines for talking slang (p178; p176 for form). Madge is good at tennis and hopes to represent Ste Thérèse in the inter-house tennis matches in *Wrong* (p149). Madge is in Lower VB in *Shocks* (p156). She is in Lower VA in *Bride* and friendly with Katharine Gordon, Hilary Wilson and Betsy Lucy (p77). Madge moves to the Görnetz Platz in Switzerland with the Chalet School and is the Music Prefect in *New Mistress*. She plays the piano for dancing at the Staff Evening and is described as a quiet girl who usually has little to say (p134/135/156). Because Madge is sitting General Higher Certificate in July she is only in the tableau at the end of the school play, playing the part of St Joseph (p193). Madge is still the Music Prefect in *Excitements* and has to play the piano for the St Mildred's pantomime *Aladdin* when Nina Rutherford has to take over as conductor (p123/131). Madge is still a prefect in *Coming of Age* and presumably visits the Tiernsee with Joey and her friends Frieda, Marie and Simone. She takes part in a wheelbarrow race with Elinor Pennell (p55/214).

WATSON, MARCIA: Marcia and Thea and their brother Ned are the children of Sir Edgar Watson, Evadne Lannis's future husband in *Trials*. We are told that the first Lady Watson died of polio seven years earlier when Marcia was only a few months old (p191). Marcia is nearly ten years old in *Reunion*. Evadne hopes that her stepdaughters Marcia and Thea will start at the Chalet School in September (p45). Later we hear that she will be bringing her stepdaughters in September (p202).

WATSON, THEA: Thea and Marcia and their brother Ned are the children of Sir Edgar Watson, Evadne Lannis's future husband in *Trials* (p191). Evadne hopes in *Reunion* that Thea and Marcia, her stepdaughters, will start at the Chalet School in September (p45). Later we hear that she will be bringing her stepdaughters in September (p202).

WAY, MR and MRS: Anxious Mrs Way meets Tom Gay and her mother at the station in *Rosalie* and puts her daughter Rosalie into Tom's care as she has never been to school before. Mr Way is a wealthy man and provides his daughter with pretty garments, which come in useful at a fancy dress party (p101/177). Rosalie and Tom have been visiting Laugharne with Rosalie's parents just before term starts in *Shocks* and Mr Way drove them to Carnbach and gave them tea in a café (p63).

WAY (BROWNE), ROSALIE: Rosalie Way starts at the Chalet School in *Rosalie* never having been at school before. Blue-eyed Rosalie has a pink-and-white face and is a very feminine little person (p101/105/106). She has been sharing her tutor Miss Miller with the Rectory girls—thirteen-year-old twins Madge and Bess, eleven-year-old Nan, and seven-year-old Ruth Herbert; Gertrude and Winifred Walters, the local doctor's daughters; and Jonny Agnew, whose father is a Wing Commander stationed at the aerodrome. Rosalie, who meets Tom Gay on the journey to school, will be thirteen in June (p107/108). Rosalie is in the Upper Third with Tom and in St Clare's House. She is in the North Yellow dormitory with Nora Bird, Amy West and Anne Webster. Rosalie is described as having long fair ringlets tied back with brown ribbons (p112/113/115). She plays the piano (p116) and, because Tom Gay is a cricketer, wants to play cricket too, although she is good at tennis (p118/126/131). Daisy Venables has toothache when she is taking the Upper Third's prep and upsets Rosalie, who runs outside to hide in the rhododendrons (p140/143/144). After being sent to bed early, she gets up before the rising bell the next morning and, ignorant of the rules, goes for a walk without permission and without drinking some milk. She then eats very little breakfast and consequently faints during a lesson (p149/155). Tom and Rosalie are at the School half-term fancy-

dress party dressed as Solomon and the Queen of Sheba and Rosalie has suitably pretty garments for her role because her father is wealthy (p177). During the weekend they visit Stratford to see *As You Like It* (p157). The following day Rosalie is tired and squabbles with her friends before disappearing into the shrubbery (p183/185/187). Unfortunately her hair gets caught on the bushes and Tom has to hack at it with her knife when she goes to her rescue (p201/202). Rosalie moves with the Chalet School to St Briavel's Island in *Island* and is in Lower VA with Tom and Bride Bettany (p60; p58 for form). She writes good stories and is sending her book home to be typed at her father's office (p183/190/191). The following term in *Peggy*, Rosalie's surname has changed to Browne. She is Tom's own protégée and they are in the same dormitory. Rosalie is pretty and fair, with fluffy golden locks that are glossy and in perfect order. Tom appears to have been promoted to the Upper Fifth (p156) and it is possible that Rosalie is in that form with her, since they leave the dormitory together to get their books ready for prep (p98/150/156). However, it is possible that the reference to Upper Fifth applies only to the formroom they use for Hobbies. When Rosalie Browne is next mentioned, in *Carola*, she is taking part in a cookery lesson with the Lower Fifth (p200; p198 for form) and is also with members of that form during the Sale (p230). Rosalie's surname is Way in *Shocks* and she is above average at tennis but not at hockey, lacrosse or netball. Although they are opposites in every way, Rosalie is still friendly with Tom Gay and they have both been staying with Rosalie's parents at Laugharne just before term starts (p62/63). Rosalie is in the Sixth form and, although she is charmingly pretty, has very little influence on her fellows so would not make a prefect. Tom plays King Herod in the Christmas Play and Rosalie, an exceedingly pretty girl, plays the part of Queen Elpis (p67/264). Rosalie is given the surname of Browne again in *Bride* and is the prettiest girl in the Sixths, with cloudy fair hair, a perfectly featured face and deep blue eyes. She has the part of Love at the end-of-term Sale based on the *Crown of Success* (p78/79/279). The games committee decides in *Changes* that although Rosalie Browne plays a very pretty game of tennis, she lacks the stamina needed for matches (p101). Rosalie Way goes on the Senior girls' expedition to Bourneville (p133). Rosalie moves to Switzerland with the Chalet School and is a prefect in *Barbara*. Her ideas on art infuriated the art master, Herr Laubach, and her lessons were stopped the previous term. She is elected Staff Prefect (p71/72). Rosalie is a prefect in *Does It Again* and is destined to appear in Society when her school days are over (p85/86/105). Rosalie helps Jo Scott on to the dais when she receives the Margot Venables Prize in *Kenya* (p201).

WAYNE, MR: We learn in *Mary-Lou* that Jessica Wayne's father died in an accident when Jessica was two years old (p40).

WAYNE, MRS: see SEFTON, MRS

WAYNE, JESSICA: Jessica starts at the Chalet School in *Mary-Lou* and is about the same age as Mary-Lou Trelawney (p2). Hazel-eyed Jessica refuses to go to Kaffee und Kuchen and is finally brought in by Matron. She appears to be very unhappy (p3/5/11/12). Jessica is in VB with Mary-Lou (p15). Jessica wishes that she had not been sent to school. She is in the Leafy dormitory. Her aunt is a friend of Katharine Gordon's aunt, Lucia

Gordon (p29/32). Joey Maynard asks Mary-Lou to help Jessica because she has heard from Miss Gordon, through whom Jessica has been sent to the Chalet School (p36/39). We learn that Jessica's widowed mother married again and has a young disabled stepdaughter, Rosamund Sefton, who is a little younger than Jessica. Jessica was entered as a weekly boarder at her school because the Seftons' home on the south coast of England was too far from town for daily travel, and she became very jealous of Rosamund. Jessica became so unbearable at home that she was sent to a boarding school in Devon and behaved so badly that the Head asked for her to be removed. She has been accepted at the Chalet School and is on trial for one term (p40/41/42). Jessica is tone deaf and this infuriates Mr Denny, causing a commotion in his singing lesson. Mary-Lou explains to Miss Annersley what has happened and Jessica later apologises to Mr Denny for losing her temper and speaking so rudely to him (p56/61/70). Mary-Lou makes sure Jessica is with the Gang on the trip to Schaffhausen. Jessica is puzzled by the way she has been treated since the affair with Mr Denny and feels that at another school she would have been severely punished (p95). Jessica asks if Mary-Lou resents sharing her mother with Verity and during the conversation Mary-Lou helps the girl to see Rosamund's point of view (p130/134/135). Jessica is given the task of handing out programmes at the end-of-term concert. She tells Mary-Lou that she plans to apologise for being horrid to Rosamund. She has started writing to her and hopes it will help to show her mother she is sorry (p192/196). Mary-Lou sits between Jessica and Verity on the bus on the half-term trip to Lac Léman in *Genius* (p115). Sybil Russell mentions that Jessica is turning into a very decent girl in *Problem* (p155). Jessica is very worried about Rosamund's health in *Coming of Age*. She explains to Mary-Lou that Rosamund has had to stop knitting and is even more helpless now (p25). Jessica and Josette Russell dress up as Puck and Oberon at the School Sale, at which Jessica wins a beautiful wool shawl knitted by Frau Bertoni, which she intends to give to Rosamund (p98/112). Mary-Lou accompanies Jessica to Basle airport when she is called home just before the end of term and the girl arrives home in time to see Rosamund before she dies (p198/199/203). Mary-Lou's befriending of her is mentioned in *Richenda* (p30). Jessica is in VIB in *Trials* and has important public exams ahead. She is good at maths (p10/11/42). She is not a prefect, but with the remainder of VIB she is brought into the prefects' council to discuss the Lost Property prank (p151/152). Jessica is still in VIB in *Theodora* and is possibly a prefect as she is leading a walk with Mary-Lou and Josette (p106). She is elected Hobbies Prefect with Marie Zetterling to help her when Josette is Head Girl in *Ruey*. Jessica seconds a motion to introduce lacrosse into the Chalet School as she played the game during the holidays with a team run by the vicar's daughter (p59/64). She is one of the prefects on escort duty for Lower IIIA's walk in *Leader* (p173). Jessica is still the Hobbies Prefect in *Trick* and is Head Girl of St Hild's, Margot Maynard's house. Jessica is sitting advanced level examinations in maths and science (p49/182/194).

WEATHERBY, DORIS: Doris is Music Prefect at St Peter's School in *Gerry* and in the Upper

Sixth. She is not really suited to be a prefect, and in practice Concetta Donati actually runs the Musical Club (p174/178).

WEAVER, ALMA: We learn in *Gay* that Miss Bubb plans to join her friend Alma Weaver as partner in her boarding school after leaving her temporary post at the Chalet School (p179/181/184).

WEBB, MATRON: see MATRON WEBB

WEBSTER, ANNE: We learn that Anne is in the Lower Third with Bride Bettany during a French lesson with Mlle Berné in *Lavender* (p84; p31 for form). Anne is in Blue South dormitory in *Tom* and is going to Joey's new girls' tea party with Moira Fitzpatrick (p14/29; p13 for dormitory). During Upper Third prep, Anne makes a sign to Tom Gay, as she wants to borrow a rubber. Nobody is allowed to talk and Tom sees making signs as dishonest, believing that Anne should have asked for what she wanted, and speaks to her (p32). Anne is in the Upper Third and is the North Yellow dormitory prefect in *Rosalie*. She has a pleasant manner when she takes Rosalie Way under her wing. Brown-haired Anne is the oldest of her crowd, being almost fourteen, and knows the difference between 'telling' and 'sneaking' (p113/147/191). Anne moves with the Chalet School to St Briavel's Island in *Island* and is apparently a house prefect in St Agnes' when the boats are handed over. We are informed that Anne can row. Anne appears to become one of Mary-Lou's contemporaries although she is back among the Seniors later and probably in Lower VA with Annis and Bride (p148/161/182; p63 for form). Anne later appears to know nothing about boats but is keen to learn. She is in the Cricket Eleven (p201/215). Anne is a motherly girl and becomes the Juniors' prefect in *Shocks*. It is well known that any Junior who is in trouble or wanting help or comfort makes a bee-line for Anne if she is anywhere near (p83). Anne is becoming friendlier with Loveday Perowne and they are both artistic. They are out with the prefects on an early evening walk when Julie Lucy becomes stuck in the mud. Anne attends the Catholic Prayers taken by Miss Derwent (p154/155/159/203). Anne helps with the younger girls in *Bride* and is a quiet prefect (p47/208). It is mentioned that Anne is a very quiet girl at a prefects' meeting in *Changes* (p57).

WEDDERBURN, MR: Peter Chester's godfather Mr Wedderburn left him everything when he died but unfortunately we learn in *Steps In* that Rennison, a lawyer in the north of England, embezzled it two years previously. Rennison was caught in Paris and given twelve years in prison but Peter lost his private fortune (p100/101/102).

WEILEN, AIMÉE: Aimée is from Lorraine and is a St Mildred's pupil in *Coming of Age*, although the pupils from St Mildred's are in practice living at the Chalet School because of all the visitors. Aimée was not at the Chalet School previously (p56).

WEISEN, HERR: Herr Weisen is out fishing and rows Jem Russell, Joey, Marie, Evadne and Irma across the lake on their way home from a weekend trip to the Sonnalpe in *And Jo* (p108).

WEISSEN, MARIE: Marie is a Senior who dresses as Rapunzel at Joey's sheets and pillowcase party in *Adrienne* and is awarded a prize for one of the most original costumes. She is blessed with a mane of flaxen hair reaching to below her hips. She normally wears it plaited and doubly looped by ribbons at her neck, and is looking forward to having it bobbed when she is grown up (p120/121).

WELDON, HARRIET: Naomi Elton's guardian Mrs Weldon is going to Nigeria to be with her daughter, who is expecting her first baby, in *Trials*. She first flies out to Switzerland with Naomi, who is slightly deformed following an accident. Aunt Harriet can never make up her mind which religious denomination to attend (p9/28/31). Naomi makes headway slowly after an accident and we are informed in *Theodora* that her Aunt Harriet is expected early the following month. We are told that Mrs Weldon will stay until Naomi's second operation in September before returning to make her home near her own daughter in Johannesburg (p139).

WELLAND, HARRIET, 'THE RIVER': Mrs Welland is the Willoughbys' housekeeper in *Scamps* and is known as 'the River'. She has been at Steyne Winting since before Sir Piers was born and cannot control the Willoughby children any longer. Mrs Welland goes to Guernsey with two of the maids to get the Willoughbys' rented house ready for the summer (p18/38/132).

WELLS, MISS: Miss Wells is Miss Stewart's assistant in the history department at the Chalet School in Austria in *Exile* (p50).

WELLS, IRIS: Iris is in Upper IIA in *Three Go* with Mary-Lou Trelawney (p73; p70 for form). She moves with the Chalet School to St Briavel's

Island and is in Lower IIIB with Mary-Lou in *Island* (p87; p82 for form).

WENDL, BERTA: Berta is a new pupil in VA in *Richenda* and her native language is German. She is a rosy, flaxen-haired girl of about sixteen. No surname is given in this book (p64; p63 for form). Maeve Bettany mentions in *Triplets* that Berta Wendl and Marie Dupont are slated for Basle University (p130).

WENDT, HILDA: Hilda is in Upper IVB and prefers games and gymnastics to schoolwork in *Two Sams* (p69).

WENTWORTH, COMMANDER and MRS: Nan Wentworth's mother died just after Christmas and her father, Commander Wentworth, is in the Navy in *Does It Again*. Her mother's death took place at the Sanatorium (p14/15/55).

(WENTWORTH), GRANNY: We are informed in *Does It Again* that Nan Wentworth's granny is awfully old and has done nothing but cry since Mrs Wentworth died (p15).

WENTWORTH, DOROTHEA: Dorothea starts at the Chalet School in *Mystery* and is in the Upper Fifth with Gillian Culver. She tells Joey at a tea party for new girls that she has a younger sister, Frances, who will come to the Chalet School when she is fourteen (p18/22/23).

WENTWORTH, FRANCES: Frances is Dorothea's younger sister and it is mentioned in *Mystery* that she will come to the Chalet School when she is fourteen (p23).

WENTWORTH, JOAN: Joan is a tall, quiet Sixth former in *Island* who starts wearing glasses due to eyestrain (p115; p113 for form). Eighteen-year-old Joan sits for the Thérèse Lepâttre Scholarship. Joan intends to gain a degree in pure science and then take a course at one of the agricultural colleges, possibly Cirencester, and take up farming (p157/158).

WENTWORTH, NAN: Nan is one of the younger girls in *Barbara* and is nervous about learning to ski (p185). Nan has moved from the larger Poppy dormitory to the Primrose dormitory in *Does It Again*. We learn that her mother died just after Christmas and her father, Commander Wentworth, is in the Navy. She is ten months older than Len Maynard (p14/15; p12 for dormitory name). Nan is a frail, timid little creature. Her mother's death has deepened her timidity (p55). Nan will probably be able to sew her own costume for the sheets and pillowcase party in *Mary-Lou* (p84). Nan is in Upper IVB in *Problem* and Miss Annersley mentions that she is not a clever child and they should ride her lightly because of her family medical record (p60).

WENTWORTH, ROSEMARY: Eleven-year-old Rosemary is English and in the Pansy dormitory with Jack Lambert in *Leader*. She has been at the Chalet School for more than two years and is Lower IIIA's form prefect (p19/44/45; p14 for form). Rosemary tells Jack Lambert in *Trick* that they never go swimming on Sunday as there are too many weekenders around (p79). She is in the Lower Fourth in *Redheads*. Her mother is half-French and she can speak fluent French. Rosemary missed most of the summer term due to measles complicated by bronchitis and so missed her form promotion (p68).

WERTHEIMER, GRÄFIN von und zu (A): It is mentioned in *Exile* that Eugen's mother Gräfin von und zu Wertheimer was an American (p26).

WERTHEIMER (WERTHEIM), CARL von und zu (C) (3): Marie and Eugen's second son Carl is mentioned in EBD's *N11* (p48).

WERTHEIMER (WERTHEIM), BARON EUGEN von und zu (von) (B): The Baron von und zu Wertheimer, the local lord of the manor,

presents the big silver cup donated to the Chalet School by the King of Belsornia to Marie von Eschenau after the Chalet School boat wins the boat race in *And Jo*. The Baron is a pleasant young man of twenty-two who has been educated at Oxford and he greatly admires Marie (p259/260). The Baron is present at the Fairy Tale Sale in *Lintons* (p292). We learn in *New House* that Marie will be betrothed in August to Eugen von und zu Wertheimer at Wanda and Friedel's home in Salzburg and hopes that her three friends Joey, Frieda and Simone will be present. They hope to get married at Christmas time (p241/242/243). Marie says in *Cook Book* that Eugen loves Joey's special gingerbread, and ate four slices last time she made it (p137). It is mentioned in *New CS* that Marie's husband the Baron is a wealthy young man (p257). We learn in *Exile* that Eugen's mother was American, and after the death of Marie's mother and birth of their son Wolferl he takes Marie and Wanda and their children to America (p26/27). Eugen has been ordered home by the Nazis but refuses to return to Austria and the Nazis requisition their castle. Marie and Eugen arrive in Guernsey with their two children, Wolferl and baby Josefa, and also Wanda and her family, around the time that the Chalet School opens there (p172/185). Con Stewart and Eugen von Wertheimer become baby Con's godparents when the Maynard triplets are born in Guernsey (p281/282). Marie and Wanda and their babies live with Madge Russell at the Round House in *Goes to It* (p86). Their visit to America at the time of the Anschluss is recalled in *Highland Twins* (p95). Wolferl is seven, Josefa is five and Eugen is fighting in Italy when Marie, Joey, Frieda and Simone are at Garnham in *Rescue* (p22/26). We learn that the Wertheimer family, now named Wertheim, were in America visiting Eugen's American relatives and Eugen refused to return home and lost all his Austrian possessions. They were in America for nearly three years (p102/183). In *Island* Marie and her family live in their wonderful old castle in the Tirol (p221). Marie and Eugen are living in the Count's old castle of Wertheim with their rampageous family in *Joey Goes* (p62). Marie arrives from her home near Salzburg for the celebration weekend at the Görnetz Platz in *Coming of Age* (p84/127). Frieda informs Herr Braun that Marie has five girls and two boys. Marie and Eugen's eldest girl is at the Chalet School and their youngest child is now five years old (p151/156). Joey informs Irma von Rothenfels in *Future* that Marie has six children (p95). EBD states that Marie has four sons and two daughters in *N11*. Wolferl and Josefa were born in America. Carl, Friedrich and Otto were born in the Tirol after Marie and Eugen were able to claim the castle and estate of Schloss Wertheimer back, and they also have a five-year-old daughter, Ilse (p48).
CHILDREN: Wolfram, Josefa, Carl, Ilonka, Friedrich, Otto, Ilse
WERTHEIMER (WERTHEIM), FRIEDRICH von und zu (C) (5): Marie and Eugen's third son Friedrich is mentioned in EBD's *N11* (p48).
WERTHEIMER (WERTHEIM), ILONKA von und zu (C) (4): Marie has four children in *Changes* and Ilonka, her second daughter and youngest child, is only eighteen months old (p86/127). Ilonka is not mentioned in EBD's *N11* although it is written after *Changes*.
WERTHEIMER (WERTHEIM), ILSE von und zu (C) (7): Frieda informs Herr Braun that Marie has five girls and two boys in *Coming of Age*. Marie's youngest child is now five years old (p151/156). Marie's youngest daughter Ilse is mentioned in EBD's *N11* (p48).
WERTHEIMER (WERTHEIM), JOSEFA von und zu (C) (2): Josefa is born in America in *Exile* and is a sunny little person of five months when she arrives in Guernsey. She is very like her pleasant-faced father although, along with his black hair and dark skin, she has inherited her mother's lovely violet eyes (p172/185/186). Josefa is five years old and able to dress herself when Marie, Joey, Frieda and Simone stay at Garnham with their children in *Rescue* (p22/40). Josefa has a fright when she stirs up a wasp's nest with a stick. She is now described as having her mother's golden locks, violet eyes and delicate features (p158/163/164). There is an oblique reference to her in *Mystery*, as a member of the Kindergarten (p87). Josefa is in Upper IIA with Mary-Lou Trelawney and her friends in *Three Go* (p80; p70 for form). The Wertheimers live in a wonderful old castle in the Tirol in *Island* (p221). It is mentioned in *Peggy* that Josefa and her brother Wolferl are having friends to stay at the holiday cottage in Garnton, Yorkshire, in the summer (p12). Frieda informs Herr Braun, the owner of the Kron Prinz Karl, that Marie has five girls and two boys in *Coming of Age*. Marie's eldest girl is at the Chalet

School and her youngest child is now five years old (p151/156). Josefa is listed among Marie's children in *N11* (p48).

WERTHEIMER, COUNTESS MARIE von und zu: see Eschenau, Marie von

WERTHEIMER (WERTHEIM), OTTO von und zu (C) (6): EBD mentions in *N11* that Marie and Eugen's fourth son Otto was born in the Tirol after the family were able to claim their castle and estate, Schloss Wertheimer, back from the Nazis (p48).

WERTHEIMER (WERTHEIM), WOLFRAM (WOLFERL) von und zu (C) (1): Wolferl or Wolfram is born during his maternal grandmother's last illness and before the family evacuates from Austria in *Exile* (p27). When Simone marries André de Bersac in *Goes to It*, Wolferl is one of her trainbearers (p239). Wolferl is seven years old when Marie, Joey, Frieda and Simone and their children stay at Garnham in *Rescue* (p22/23). Wolferl is at the Chalet School in *Mystery*, in the Second form, and rides on the Yule log in the Christmas Play (p87/89). We are told in *Peggy* that Wolferl and his sister Josefa are having friends to stay at holiday cottage in Garnton, Yorkshire, in the summer (p12). It is mentioned in *Coming of Age* that Wolfram was a complete little American, accent and all, when they first returned to England (p167). EBD mentions in *N11* that Wolferl and Josefa were born in America (p48).

WEST, AMY: Amy is an English Junior in the Upper Second with Flora and Fiona McDonald when an intruder searches her locker seeking the Chart of Erisay in *Highland Twins* (p168/158). Amy is moved into the Yellow dormitory in *Lavender* (p40). She is ten or eleven years old in *Gay* (p42). Amy is in the Upper Third in *Rosalie* and the North Yellow dormitory with Nora Bird and Anne Webster (p113). Amy has a gentle little voice and is described as a small, round-faced person of twelve, with a rosy face. She goes to the half-term fancy-dress party dressed as a granny (p148/174/175).

WEST, JANE: Jane is in the Upper Third and is one of Peggy Bettany's special cronies in *Lavender* (p166/167).

WEST, VALERIE: Valerie is Lesley Malcolm's partner on a walk in *Mary-Lou*. Valerie is in V$_B$ and her tastes lie more towards maths than history (p49/53).

WESTCOTT, SHIRLEY: Shirley is a new girl in the Lower Third in *Peggy* and is unfit to go for a walk as she has earache. Brown-eyed Shirley is slightly older than her cousin Althea (Mordaunt) at Branscombe Park, who met Peggy Bettany at the start of term (p212/215/216).

WESTON, AGNES: see Temple, Agnes

WESTON, DOROTHY: Dorothy Weston from Frent Farm is training to be Miss Christopher's lieutenant in a Guide Company that the Raphaels and Shakespeares join in *Heather* (p162/163).

WESTON, MARY: Mary appears to be one of the younger girls in *Leader* (p49).

WHICHCOTES: Peggy Primrose mentions in *Monica* that the Whichcotes have invited her to go with them to a new exhibition of watercolours in the city museum in Malestone (p180).

WHITE WITCH: see Sorcière Blanche

WHITE, CAROL: Carol is a pretty, fair-headed twelve-year-old with only average brains when she starts in the Upper Second at the Chalet School in *Tom*. She becomes friendly with Nicole la Touche and takes her to Joey's tea party for new girls. Carol has been a Guide at home and transfers to the Chalet School Guide Company (p28/29/30; p22 for Carol's surname).

WHITE, MARJORY: Marjory is a pupil at the Chalet School in 'Midnight' in *2nd* (p153).

WHITLOCK, PAMELA: Pamela is in the Special Sixth in *Peggy* (p48). She sits with Frances Coleman during a tennis match in which Blossom Willoughby would have been playing if she had not been locked in the art room in *Wrong* (p172).

WHITNEY, ANNE: Anne is in LV$_B$ with Carola Johnstone and Clem Barrass in *Carola* (p41; p83 for form).

WHYTE, MEG: Meg is in the Upper Fourth with Hilary Wilson, and plays at noughts and crosses during prep in *Peggy*. The two girls are boon companions (p102/177). Meg is unfit to go out for a walk as she suffers from chilblains (p212/215). Plump, fourteen-year-old Meg works in the Upper Fourth's rock garden in the evening in *Wrong*. She is in Leafy dormitory with Katharine Gordon and helps her get ready for a tennis match (p15/154/170; p29 for name of dormitory). Meg is in the Fifth form with Blossom Willoughby and Hilary Wilson in *Shocks* (p132; p131 for form). When the games committee discuss a possible tennis six in *Changes* they suggest that

Meg should be tried as a second string, and she is later appointed (p103/104/105). Meg helps the prefects provide folding desks so that the girls can sit their examinations in the garden in shady spots. She is one of the girls taking General Certificate (p160/161). Meg is at the Swiss Chalet School in *Genius* and is with Hilda Jukes, her great friend, when they visit Lac Léman. We learn that Meg is not gifted in languages (p118). Meg and Hilda are in the Lower Sixth in *New Mistress* and we are informed that Meg has no brains (p118; p117 for form). Meg is the leader of the second violins for the St Mildred's pantomime, *Aladdin*, in *Excitements*. Mary-Lou later describes Meg as a complete scatterbrain (p122/129). Meg is a prefect in *Richenda* when Mary-Lou is the Head Girl (p59). Meg is the only prefect overlooked by the practical jokers during the Lost Property business in *Trials* and her blank expression when she realises this makes everyone laugh (p149). Meg is at Vespers in the Catholic chapel with the other prefects when there is an invasion of cockchafers in *Theodora*, and she is terrified (p86). Meg is at St Mildred's in *Ruey* and is a reserve in a friendly lacrosse match with joint teams from the Chalet School and St Mildred's (p152).

WILFORD, MR: In *Excitements* we learn that Francie Wilford's mother died when she was born and two years later her father married a lady who became a mother to Francie. Mr Wilford died in a yachting accident on the Norfolk Broads when Francie was eight, and about eighteen months later her stepmother married an old sweetheart (p19).

WILFORD, MRS (i): We learn in *Excitements* that Francie Wilford's mother died when she was born (p19).

WILFORD, MRS (ii) (BOURNE [VIGORS], MRS): We learn in *Excitements* that Francie Wilford was two years old when her father married a lady who became Francie's stepmother. Mr Wilford died in a yachting accident on the Norfolk Broads when Francie was eight and about eighteen months later her stepmother married an old sweetheart, Mr Bourne (p19). Mr Bourne's name is changed to Mr Vigors in *Ruey* (p23).

WILFORD (WILMOT), FRANCES (FRANCIE) (FRANCESCA), 'FRAN': Frances is in Lower IVA with Priscilla Dawbarn in *Shocks* and is a girl who might make a nuisance of herself (p227). Francie moves to Switzerland with the Chalet School in *Barbara* and is a Middle (p59). She is Heather Clayton's boon companion and is in Upper IVB (p91/108; p107 for form). Francie is a mischievous-looking girl who does not want to be addressed as Francesca in *Does It Again* (p24). She is in Upper IVB in *Kenya* and needs help understanding maths in French. Francie is on a moss-picking expedition when Emerence Hope has a near-fatal fall. Both girls have well-deserved reputations for being thoroughly naughty (p61/174/175). Brown-haired Francie, Emerence Hope, and Connie Winter are in trouble for continually speaking in English on French days in *Genius*. Francie has been in trouble many times during the term and refuses to apologise for her rudeness (p154/155/156). She is friendly with Margot Maynard who is two years younger. Francie is roused out of her sullen mood by Nina's enthusiasm for a poem and she apologises to Betsy (p157/158/162). Francie is in the Tulip dormitory with Heather in *Problem*. She is in Upper IVA with Rosamund Lilley (p115/160; p23 for form). Francie is in Inter V with Heather Clayton and Emerence Hope in *New Mistress* and is in trouble with Mary-Lou and Miss Ferrars for misbehaving during prep (p64/65/91). Francie is still in Inter V in *Excitements* and we are informed that she is a young woman who seems to go around bearing an eternal grudge. It is explained that her mother died when she was born and two years later her father married a lady who has been a mother to Francie. Mr Wilford died in a yachting accident on the Norfolk Broads when Francie was eight and about eighteen months later her stepmother married an old sweetheart, Mr Bourne. He was prepared to be kind but found Francie unbearable and packed her off to boarding school (p9/19). Grey-eyed Francie starts a campaign against bossy Seniors. We learn that her French is fluent enough but her accent is poor (p22/24). She attends Protestant Prayers, although in a distinctly unprayerful mood. Francie and Eve Hurrell are Chinese frogs in the St Mildred's pantomime *Aladdin* (p32/123). Francie is particularly affected by the sneezing powder that Prudence Dawbarn releases in prep in *Coming of Age* (p131). Francie is still in Inter V in *Richenda* and described as a scaramouche. Francie and Primrose Trevoase are going to Paris with the Dawbarns at half term (p136). Francie is in VB in *Theodora* and has improved considerably in reputation. We are told that she has bobbed hair (p50/174). Francie is in the Alpenrose dormitory with Con and Margot Maynard in *Ruey* (p14). She is in VB and her grey-green eyes have a look of bitter resentment when Margot introduces her to new girl Ruey Richardson (p18/19). Francie is a clever girl who can turn out brilliant work on occasion. She would like to be Margot's special friend now that Emerence has left but finds that Ruey is in the way. The name of her stepmother's husband Mr Bourne has now changed to Mr Vigors (p20/23). Francie is named as a reserve in a friendly lacrosse match with joint teams from the School and St Mildred's. She has a gift for acting but is displeased with the part of an old woman that she is given in the Christmas Play (p152/181). During an argument, Francie and Ruey have an unexpected bath when they are out for a walk and end up in a very wet ditch. The girls finally get together at a staff evening and start to sort out Francie's problems. Francie wins VB's voucher for a new school uniform (p188/218/221). Ruey and Francie go to the gym to talk the following day and afterwards they are well on the way to becoming real friends. This is far better for Francie than the one-sided adoration of Margot that she had previously. We are informed that Francie's thoughts now turn outwards and when she goes home at Christmas she is prepared to be pleasant. We are told, in a foreshadowing of the future, that by the time Francie leaves school she has lost her permanent black dog and is an attractive young woman and Miss Annersley feels she is one of the School's successes (p224/225). Francie is in VB in *Leader* and spends half term at Freudesheim as Ruey's guest. (p99/103). Her surname changes temporarily to Wilmot. Her fortnightly average is 70 per cent and she is planning to do art (p113/114). She is entered for GCE in *Trick* and forms a trio with Margot and Ruey (p150). Francie becomes a prefect in *Feud* and is in VIB with the Maynard triplets (p82/104). She visits Lausanne with the prefects at half term in *Triplets* (p124). She is on duty for Upper IVB's prep in *Jane* (p45; p29 for form). She is a prefect in *Redheads* and congratulates the Upper Fourth on their play (p74). Francie is the Library Prefect in *Adrienne* and is in VIA. She dresses as a snowman at Joey's sheets and pillowcase party and wins a prize for the funniest costume (p67/93/120). Ted Grantley mentions that Francie will not be leaving school at the end of *Summer Term*. She is still the School librarian. Margot addresses her as 'Fran' (p64/91). Francie plays the part of the Cat in the St Mildred's pantomime, *Dick Whittington*, in *Two Sams* (p206).

WILHELM, HERR and FRAU: Frau Wilhelm has smallpox in *Theodora* and her husband sends their young daughter Margrit out of their chalet (p69/71).

WILHELM, MARGRIT: Frau Wilhelm has smallpox in *Theodora* and Herr Wilhelm sends his young daughter Margrit outside. Len Maynard, Ted Grantley and Rosamund Lilley find Margrit there and have to go into isolation at the Sanatorium (p69/71/72).

WILHELM, MARTA: Marta is a Junior Middle with Felicity Maynard in *Prefects* and they and some other girls develop a mysterious infectious illness that means the Chalet School Regatta has to be cancelled (p68).

WILKINS, MISS: We learn in *Carola* that Miss Wilkins was one of Carola Johnstone's former governesses and taught her botany (p80).

WILLIAM, GREAT-UNCLE: see (BETTANY), GREAT-UNCLE WILLIAM

WILLIAMS (i): Williams drives Peter and David

Willoughby to St Peter's School in Scamps. Williams is Sir Piers' chauffeur (p38/96/108).

WILLIAMS (ii): Williams is one of the bus drivers on the Bourneville expedition in *Changes* (p133).

WILLIAMS, MR and MRS EVAN, TEDDY, ARTHUR and BABY: Evan Williams is the Gatekeeper at the Lodge in *Highland Twins* and lives there with his wife and three children: Teddy, Arthur and the baby (p173). Daisy Venables and Tom Gay attempt to get help from the Williams family when they are carrying injured Elfie Woodward back to school in *Tom*, but they realise they have mistaken their way in the snow and instead of reaching the Lodge, have ended up at Fairmeads, which belongs to the Jesmonds (p93).

WILLIAMS, FLORENCE, 'FLOPPY BILL': Seventeen-year-old Florence, an empty-headed, fluffy-haired girl, is a particular friend of Betty Wynne-Davies in *Highland Twins* and is rapidly becoming a pale shadow of her (p107/112). She is in the Sixth form and comes from Birmingham, and tries to dissuade Betty from getting hold of the Chart of Erisay to upset the twins. She is described as stout and not in the least pretty (p127/130/133). Florence has too shallow a nature to recover from the shock of the behaviour which led to Betty's expulsion and refuses to say goodbye when her former friend leaves school in disgrace (p265/272). Florence is in the Fifth form in *Gay*. She doesn't even qualify for the Second Eleven in cricket, and it is mentioned that Floppy's tennis is a legend (p90). Florence is a Sixth former when she snatches a book from Fiona, saying Millie Allen wants to read it, in 'New Flavouring' in *3rd*. Millie Allen's father is the senior partner in Florence's father's firm. Florence's great friend is Hilda Hope and she is in the Lower Sixth (p128/129/135).

WILLIAMS, IRENE: Catholic Irene is in the School sanatorium for a week with a bronchial cold in *Mystery* and Daphne informs Roosje Lange that Irene is getting better (p68).

WILLIAMS, NESTA: Nesta is a Middle in *Barbara* (p59). Twelve-year-old Nesta is in the Primrose dormitory in *Does It Again* and came with the Chalet School from England (p14/55; p12 for dormitory). Nesta is in the same form as Con Maynard in *Mary-Lou* and, like Con, completes all her proverbs correctly in a class exercise (p141).

WILLIAMS, NINA: Nina sits beside Anne Montague at meals in *Lavender* (p130). Nina is in the Sixth form in *Peggy* (p57; p50 for form) and is a sub-prefect, responsible for stationery (p58/85). She is at a geography lesson with Miss Stephens in the annexe when they evacuate the building due to storm winds (p134). Nina is present at an inter-school tennis match in *Wrong* and shares a small dormitory with Nita Eltringham (p172/207). Nina goes to the Welsen Branch in the Oberland when it opens in *CS Oberland*. French is not her strongest point (p67). Lesley Malcolm mentions in *Genius* that Nina was a prefect when their gang were in the Third form (p21).

WILLIAMS, ROSAMUND: Rosamund is a new girl in Upper IIA with Mary-Lou Trelawney and Josette Russell in *Three Go* (p78; p70 for form).

WILLIAMSON, JOY: Joy is a new girl in *Does It Again* (p22).

WILLIAMSON, VIOLET: It is mentioned in *Monica* that Violet was one of Monica Marilliar's friends at The Gables (p130).

WILLOUGHBY, SIR — and LADY (AA): We learn in *Scamps* that the Willoughbys' eldest child is Sir Piers and his younger brother Nigel is eighteen years younger. When Nigel was ten months old their mother, Lady Willoughby, and some of their siblings including a sister, Madeleine, died of diphtheria. Their father had been killed hunting when Nigel was a tiny baby (p133). We learn in *Janie of* that Piers is a baronet, having inherited his title, presumably, from his father (p163).

WILLOUGHBY, LADY (i) (A): We learn in *Scamps* that Sir Piers Willoughby's first wife was a sweet, gentle lady who died when Tim was seventeen months old. She had seven children, listed now as seventeen-year-old Madeleine, sixteen-year-old Rex, fourteen-year-

old Marjolaine, thirteen-year-old Peter, eleven-year-old David, Bernadine and five-year-old Tim (p9/10/11/12). Lady Willoughby was an Australian and her three sisters and two brothers all live in the Antipodes. Sir Piers was twenty-two when they married and their daughter Madeleine was born the following year. Sir Piers's orphaned brother Nigel, who is five years older than Madeleine, came to live with them after their marriage (p14/133).

WILLOUGHBY, unnamed BABY (B) (11): Sir Piers Willoughby and his second wife Sigrid have three small sons in *Steps In*: Axel, Rolf and an unnamed baby (p14/245).

WILLOUGHBY BOYS (i) (C) (1–2): We are told in *Steps In* that Con and Rex Willoughby are going to Ceylon and will leave their two sons with Sigrid (p12/13/14).

WILLOUGHBY BOYS (ii) (C) (1–4): Nan and David Willoughby's first four children are all boys, aged eleven to four years old in *Genius*. They have a younger sister, Christine (p38).

WILLOUGHBY GIRL (B) (5): We learn in *Problem* that Blossom is going to help her mother at home when she leaves school because her young brother Aubrey is very frail and they have a year-old baby rounding off the family (p214). Blossom is needed at home in *Coming of Age* to help with her baby sister and Aubrey, who is now stronger but still very frail (p198).

WILLOUGHBY, AUBREY JULIAN (B) (4): We are informed in *Wrong* that Nigel and Rosamund's fourth child Aubrey was born just before Easter. He is awfully delicate, sweet but very tiny and white and named after his two godfathers, who must be Aubrey Farringford and Julian Lucy (p57). Nigel and Rosamund have their frail little son Aubrey with them at the School Regatta in *Changes* (p186). Blossom is going to help her mother at home as her young brother Aubrey is very frail and they have a year-old baby rounding off the family in *Problem* (p214). Aubrey is stronger in *Coming of Age* but still very frail, and Blossom is needed at home to help with Aubrey and her baby sister (p198).

WILLOUGHBY, AXEL (B) (9): Janie Lucy mentions that Sigrid Willoughby has three small sons by her second husband, Sir Piers, in *Steps In*. She names the eldest as Axel and says he is Julie's age, six years old (p14/245). No mention is made of Frithiof, Sigrid's son, who was about two years old when Julie was born in *Janie of* (p182). It is possible that he and Axel are actually the same person.

WILLOUGHBY, BERNADINE (DINA) (B) (6): Bernadine—Dina for short—is blessed with a sensitive conscience, unlike her siblings, in *Scamps*. Her mane of red-gold hair helps to hide the fact that one of her shoulders is higher than the other as a result of a fall when she was a baby (p12/17). The Willoughby children sneak out of their house one night to sleep in hammocks in the orchard, with bad effects on some of them. Rex and Dina suffer most as Rex has rheumatic pains and Dina is scared by the owls and has some back pain (p25/34). It is suggested that Dina should see a spinal specialist, Sir James Canning (p36/43). Sir Piers and Maidie are sent for when Dina is to have an operation. When Dina is coming round after the operation she believes that her sister is her dead mother and Maidie stays at her bedside throughout the long night (p96/102). The family visit Guernsey for the summer to help Dina get strong again after her operation and Nurse Austin accompanies them. Dina becomes friendly with Allegra Atherton and Pauline Ozanne (p130/132/151). Dina gives Julian Lucy an elaborate tie-case for a wedding present when he marries Janie Temple in *Janie of*. Dina and her stepsister Britta are at St Peter's High School but are leaving at Easter to go to a boarding school on the Hampshire Downs where Rosamund Atherton was until recently the Senior Mistress. Thirteen-year-old Dina is one of Rosamund's bridesmaids when she marries Nigel Willoughby (p61/72/117). Dina is one of the younger Willoughbys who have measles, but fortunately not badly (p182).

WILLOUGHBY, BLOSSOM (B) (2): Nigel and Rosamund Willoughby's second child Blossom is mentioned in *Steps In* and she has an exquisite face (p17/19). Her brother Toby is a plain boy and all the good looks have gone to the young girl, who is the prettiest child of the younger generation. Blossom has a temper that is the limit when it is roused and is a little monkey sometimes. Her eyes, complexion and features are those of her mother and she has lovely golden hair. Julian Lucy is her godfather (p22/74/80). Blossom and Toby catch measles and Rosamund's cousin Nan Blakeney has to stay longer with the Lucys in Guernsey (p163). Blossom must have been at the Chalet School in Guernsey, perhaps in the Kindergarten, before the

Willoughbys move to Surrey in *Goes to It*, as they want to keep Toby and Blossom on at the School (p12). Blossom is in the Lower Second with Sybil Russell in *Highland Twins* (p123). She has an angelic little face and an imp-like disposition and leads her small sister Judy into awful scrapes when she is at home. Blossom is a clever little girl and is nine years old, the same age as John Lucy (p150; p40 for John's age). It is mentioned in *Lavender* that Blossom is like her father Nigel in character as but gets her looks from her mother. Blossom helps to create an explosion when she and her friends put snow on a boiling hot radiator (p219/220). Blossom, Betsy and their friends decide to have a midnight feast in 'Midnight' in *2nd* (p150). Blossom and Julie Lucy are to be bridesmaids to Nan Blakeney in *Gay* (p65). Blossom moves with the Chalet School to St Briavel's Island and is presumably taken there on her father's yacht with the Lucys, Chesters and Nita Eltringham in *Island* (p25/32). Blossom is in the Upper Fourth and friendly with Sybil Russell in *Peggy*. She plans that her form should talk like Jane Austen and Georgette Heyer heroines, as pay-back for too many slang fines (p91/173). Blossom develops toothache. She is thirteen and is used by Eilunedd in a plot against Peggy Bettany (p212/214/216). Blue-eyed Blossom slides down the banisters, landing in a heap at Peggy's feet. She is rude to the Head Girl and starts spreading Eilunedd's rumours about her (p217/218/224). Blossom is one of the prettiest girls Katharine Gordon has ever seen when they play tennis with Elinor Pennell and Madge Watson in *Wrong*. Blossom hopes to represent Ste Thérèse in the inter-house tennis matches (p53/149). She is in the Upper Fourth and suggests that Jennifer Penrose and her friends should help in their form garden. Blossom is in the Garden dormitory (p154/158/170). She does not appear at the start of an inter-school tennis match against Campden House in which she is reserve, and is missing when she is required (p172/181). Jennifer has locked Blossom into the art department but Blossom finally succeeds in escaping by breaking the window with Clytie, a plaster bust she finds in the art room (p184/189). Blossom is sent for when Jennifer has nightmares and believes she has seen her cut and bleeding. Being a good-hearted girl despite her faults, she shows Jennifer that she is not cut. Jennifer confesses about locking Blossom up, but Blossom has already guessed (p235/236). Blossom is in the Fifth form in *Shocks* (p132; p131 for form). Pretty Blossom is friendly with Katharine Gordon and Hilary Wilson and moves up to Lower VA with them in *Bride* (p76/87). Blossom's tennis has come on enormously and her drive is as swift as a man's in *Changes*. Blossom, Katharine and Carola Johnstone bring out ink to place on the folding desks that have been set up so that the girls can sit their examinations in shady spots in the garden (p99/161). Blossom moves with the Chalet School to the Görnetz Platz in Switzerland in *Barbara*. She makes her début as a soloist in the Christmas Play with beautiful deep alto notes (p202/203). Blossom is still friendly with Sybil Russell in *Kenya* and it is mentioned that she has the potential to become a Wimbledon tennis player. She is in the Lower Fifth and suggests school sports for the end-of-term entertainment (p36/72/106). Blossom helps Katharine Gordon with games in *Mary-Lou* although she is not a prefect. She is in VIB and takes charge of a group of Middles on a family sledge (p9/171). Blossom is a prefect in *Genius* and becomes the

third Games Prefect. She will provide necessary help in coaching the Juniors in ski-ing and tennis (p60). Blossom takes part in an exhibition game of tennis with Katharine Gordon in *Problem* and her excellent play and fierce service are said to result partly from a lot of practice at home with her father (p70/72). She admits to not being a scholar but has scraped through to the Sixth form. She is going to help her mother at home as her young brother Aubrey is very frail and they have a one-year-old baby rounding off the family (p214). Blossom is the Games Prefect in *New Mistress* and she is fair and lovely with perfect features and complexion and golden curls (p55/147). Blossom is Head of Games in *Excitements* and has trouble with Inter V (p9). Doris Hill reports to Blossom in *Coming of Age* on the progress made in games of Prudence and Priscilla Dawbarn and Primrose Trevoase when they were at the English branch (p21). Blossom acts the part of Caliban at the School Sale. The normally easy-going prefect takes prep the night that Prudence behaves badly (p97/130). Blossom intends to go to St Mildred's for a year before going home to help her mother with frail Aubrey and her baby sister. She appears to be in St Clare's team during the tug-of-war (p198/219/220). Blossom has curly brown hair and is the Principal Boy in the St Mildred's pantomime *Puss and Boots* in *Trials* (p195). She is mentioned in connection with a tug-of-war disaster in *Theodora* (p66). Blossom is still at St Mildred's in *Ruey* and is consulted about the joint lacrosse match (p148/150). Blossom's younger sister Judy is like her for carelessness in *Adrienne* (p61).

(WILLOUGHBY), BRITTA: see LUNDGREN, BRITTA

WILLOUGHBY, CHRISTINE NATALIE (C) (5): Nan and David Willoughby's fifth child Christine Natalie was born on Christmas Day and is mentioned in *Genius* (p38).

WILLOUGHBY, CONSTANCE (CON): see ATHERTON, CONSTANCE

WILLOUGHBY, DAVID (B) (5): Sir Piers' third son, eleven-year-old David, is fair-haired and has a habit of thinking aloud with embarrassing results in *Scamps*. He takes lessons with Mr Eltringham, the curate, for three hours every morning (p12/13). The Willoughby children sneak out of their house one night to sleep in hammocks in the orchard, with bad effects on some of them, and their father is informed by letter. Mr Eltringham sends Peter and David to St Peter's Boys' School in Dawley (p25/34/35/38). One hot Sunday afternoon, Peter, David and their stepsister Britta encourage a donkey to enter the church whilst Mr Eltringham is preaching but they are discovered by Sir Piers (p126/128). The Willoughbys go to Guernsey for the summer holidays and David and Britta become friendly with José Atherton (p131/151). David is frightened by a newspaper headline, 'The Day of Judgment is at hand', which refers to the following day. David has a clear, sweet voice and suggests that the children should all sing different songs simultaneously when they are on the beach (p206/258/259). At the end of the holidays they picnic at Petit Bôt and during an argument with Peter at the top of the cliffs, David falls and is caught on a jutting-out bit of rock. Mr Eltringham climbs up the cliff face and reaches him just before he passes out. David is finally rescued when Mr Atherton returns with a rope and two local men who help haul the boy up the cliff (p274/283/284/287). Some soldiers help with six-foot-tall Mr Eltringham as he is too heavy for the picnic party to haul up (p288/291). Fifteen-year-old

David is at Winchester with Peter and doesn't care much about any games in *Janie of* (p72/183). Tall, fair David meets seventeen-year-old Nan Blakeney after she has fallen into the sea during a picnic at La Rochelle in *Steps In* (p153/157). Twenty-two-year-old David is in the Navy and is commissioned to the North Atlantic Fleet (p156/182). He writes from HMS *Lothian* and asks Nan to accept his engagement ring. He is going to be tied up in the West Indies for the next eighteen months and Janie advises Nan to wait. Nan learns from David that he is returning home from Jamaica as his ship is damaged and requires a refit (p241/254). David is newly engaged to twenty-year-old Nan Blakeney, Janie Lucy's adopted sister, when Joey Maynard has breakfast at the Lucys' house in *Highland Twins* (p40). David and Nan are married in June in *Gay* and their bridesmaids are Nigel's daughter Blossom and Julie Lucy (p65). Vi Lucy mentions to Miss Annersley in *Genius* that her Auntie Nan had a fifth baby on Christmas Day to be called Christine Natalie. Nan's husband is Commander Willoughby and they already have four boys aged eleven to four years old (p38).

CHILDREN: Four unnamed boys, Christine

WILLOUGHBY, FRITHIOF (B) (8): We are informed in *Janie of* that Sir Piers's eighth child Frithiof was born two years after Sir Piers married his second wife Sigrid, who is Norwegian. Frithiof was named after his maternal grandfather. Marjolaine takes two-year-old Frithiof to stay at the Athertons' home when the younger Willoughby children have measles (p100/182).

WILLOUGHBY, HAROLD NIGEL (HAL) (TOBY) (B) (1): Rosamund and Nigel's first child is a son named Harold Nigel after Mr Atherton and Nigel in *Janie of*. He has a mop of fine, fair hair and Janie Lucy is invited to be his godmother. Rex Willoughby and Rosamund's Uncle Ralph Farringford are his godfathers (p230/231). Six-year-old Toby is plain with a wide mouth, over-big nose, a chin like a ramrod and freckles in *Steps In*. Toby and his younger sister Blossom catch measles while Rosamund's cousin Nan Blakeney is visiting the Lucys (p22/163). Toby and Blossom must be at the Chalet School in Guernsey in *Goes to It*, as their parents, who are moving to Surrey, want to keep the children at the School if it is at a suitable place (p12). Blossom mentions Toby when listing her siblings in *Wrong* (p57).

WILLOUGHBY, LADY JULIANA (ANCESTOR): Lady Juliana, a Willoughby ancestor who married Sir Reginald Willoughby during the Regency days, is mentioned in *Scamps*. Maidie's second name is Juliana after her, by family tradition (p63).

WILLOUGHBY, JULIANA JANE (JUDY) (JUDITH) (B) (3): Nigel and Rosamund's third child is born in *Steps In* and is given the old Willoughby name Juliana. She will be known as Judy (p239). Judy's elder sister Blossom leads her into awful scrapes when she is at home in *Highland Twins* (p150). Judy is a pupil at the Chalet School on St Briavel's Island in *Island* (p221). Nine-year-old Judy is a Junior in *Peggy* when she overhears a conversation the Middles are having and relays it to her friends, including Janice Chester (p192/226). Judy is in the Upper Second and in the Wallflower dormitory where the girls practise jiu-jitsu after lights out in *Wrong* (p57/103/112). Judy, Janice and Ailie Russell are in the Third form in *Kenya* and the three friends are good swimmers (p28/143). Judy is still in the Third form in *Mary-Lou* (p84). Ten-year-old Judy is in the Upper Third in *Problem* (p36). Judy is described as having short, straight hair with a fringe in *New Mistress*. She stands beside Ailie and new girl Tessa de Bersac (p54). Barbara Chester refers to her as 'Judith' in *Excitements* (p97). Judy is the rider for Hilda Jukes when they win a horseback race in *Coming of Age* (p213). She is in the Lower Fourth in *Trials*. She, Ailie and Janice confess to collecting items to put in Lost Property, but Judy is keen to explain that Janice was very unwilling to take part (p162/164). She has a passion for new words (p169). Judy and her boon companions Janice and Ailie go on a trip to Lake Constance with Lower IVA and B at half term in *Theodora* (p144). Judy is one of the girls called to order by Head Girl Josette Russell in *Ruey*. Judy, Ailie and Janice write a play that they intend to act during a midnight feast (p69/147). Judy has hazel eyes, and she, Ailie and Janice are leaders of the Senior Middles in *Jane* (p94/95). Judy is in Inter V and her real name is given as Juliana Jane in *Adrienne* (p35/37). She has short, brown curls and is keen on maths, detests art and rubs along in her other subjects. It is a rare week in which Judy does not contribute at least one fine to the fines box for the sin of speaking English instead of German. Len mentions that Judy is like Blossom over again for carelessness (p45/50/61). Judy is in the Fifth form in *Challenge* and plays right inner in a practice game of hockey (p143). She is probably in VB in *Two Sams* with her friends Ailie and Janice and is said to be artistic (p170). Judy is talking to Flavia Ansell, Val Gardiner and Jack Lambert in *Prefects* and is amused at the idea of Jack as mentor. She sleeps in the Crocus dormitory with Jane Carew and Copper (p30/124).

WILLOUGHBY, MADELEINE (A): We learn in *Scamps* that Sir Piers's mother and most of his siblings, including his sister Madeleine, died of diphtheria when he was nineteen (p133).

WILLOUGHBY, MADELEINE JULIANA (MAIDIE), (CLITHEROE, MADELEINE) (B) (1): Seventeen-year-old Madeleine, known as Maidie, has been the mistress at Steyne Winting since her mother's death (p9/10). She looks younger than her age with her long, floating, dark brown curls and brown eyes, and is supposed to have finished with lessons in *Scamps* (p11/13). The Willoughby children sneak out of the house one night to sleep in hammocks in the orchard, with ill effects on some of them, and their father, Sir Piers, is informed by letter. Maidie develops a bad cold. Dr McAllister suggests that she should be sent to a good boarding school (p25/34/36). Maidie complains to Miss Matthias about Mr Eltringham, the boys' tutor, and says she loathes and detests him (p46/47). Sir Piers arrives home unexpectedly, bringing with him his children's new stepmother, Norwegian Sigrid Lundgren, and her daughter Britta (p58/60/61). We are informed that Maidie's second name follows the tradition that the first Willoughby daughter is always given the name of Juliana after a Regency ancestor (p63). Maidie is hostile towards the newcomers, especially when Britta breaks a Dresden figure that Maidie's mother had given to her shortly before she died (p75/76/77). Signor Donati teaches Madeleine to play the piano and Marjolaine the 'cello and often speaks about Geraldine Challoner, a former pupil of his (p86). Sir Piers and Maidie are sent for when her young sister Dina has to have a spinal operation urgently, and Sigrid helps the girl to pack a case. Dina thinks when she is coming round that Maidie is her dead mother and Maidie stays at her bedside throughout the long night (p96/98/102). The family visit Guernsey and rent a house for the summer

to help Dina get strong again after her operation. Maidie no longer detests Sigrid, who was kind to her when Dina was so ill, and they become friendly (p130/134/140). Pauline Ozanne and Janie Temple meet the Willoughbys when Pollie nearly cycles into Maidie and Britta. The Willoughbys also meet the Atherton family and Maidie makes friends with Rosamund and Francesca Atherton very quickly (p144/151). Maidie is worried about Nigel, Rex and Julian when they are out in the boat without her father's permission, as she thinks there is a gale blowing up (p158). Maidie and Con Atherton plan to pretend to be ghosts and, accompanied by Julian Lucy, Janie, Pauline and Rex, take a boat out to Lihou Island late one night. Unfortunately they do not tie the boat up properly and have to wait for the tide to uncover the causeway before they can return home to their beds (p176/189/194). Sigrid finds out about their escapade through Peter and meets the adventurers on their return (p197/198). Miss Matthias, a neighbour of the Willoughbys, rents a cottage on Sark for a year and invites Maidie, Rex and Marjolaine Willoughby and their friends Francesca, Rosamund, Con and Allegra Atherton, Janie Temple and Julian

Lucy to stay for ten days. Maidie is upset to hear that Mr Eltringham is joining the holiday party (p200/234/235). She is horrified when Cesca spends time with Mr Eltringham and her attitude earns her a gentle reproof from Rosamund. At the end of the summer Maidie is ready to go to London to study music in earnest. She tells the children how sorry she feels that they have been such beasts to Mr Eltringham after his brave rescue of David (p256/274/293). Maidie is in Paris in *Janie of*. The Willoughbys journey to Guernsey for Janie and Julian Lucy's wedding and Maidie is one of the bridesmaids (p12/32/33). Maidie is in the party that visits a beach on Sark during Janie and Julian's honeymoon, thus unwittingly forcing the newlyweds to hide in a cave (p56/59). Cuthbert Clitheroe sees a photograph of Maidie at Janie's home and he is very taken with her (p99/100). Maidie is one of Rosamund Atherton's bridesmaids when she marries Nigel Willoughby. We are informed that Rex has introduced Cuthbert to Maidie at Oxford. Elizabeth and Paul Ozanne invite Janie, Pauline, Rosamund and Maidie to be Nella and Vanna's godmothers (p117/162/174). Maidie and Cuthbert become engaged although her father is not very pleased about her marrying a Catholic. Maidie visits Cuthbert's aunt, Mrs la Touche, in Guernsey and is present at Anne and Peter Chester's house-warming party. Maidie and Cuthbert intend to live in Oxford when they are married (p180/182/185). Sigrid is looking after Maidie's daughter, Con's two sons and her own three babies, in *Steps In*. Rosamund visits Maidie in Oxford when she is convalescing after a serious operation and is still very frail (p13/14/29).

WILLOUGHBY, MARJOLAINE (B) (3): Piers's third child, fourteen-year-old Marjolaine, is little, dark, dainty and very matter-of-fact in *Scamps*. Marjolaine takes lessons from an elderly lady every day and she loves music (p11/13). The Willoughby children sneak out of their house one night to sleep in hammocks in the orchard and this is reported to their father in letters (p25/34). Signor Donati teaches Marjolaine music, and her preferred instrument is the 'cello. Marjolaine marches her young brother Tim out of church and tells him off for making a noise during the service (p86/115). The Willoughby family travel to Guernsey for the summer and Marjolaine makes friends with Con Atherton and Janie Temple. Miss Matthias, a neighbour of the Willoughbys, is renting a cottage on Sark for a year and invites Maidie, Rex and Marjolaine Willoughby and their friends Francesca, Rosamund, Con and Allegra Atherton, Janie Temple and Julian Lucy to stay for ten days (p151/200). Marjolaine is one of the people involved in thinking up mischief to do with spoof cigars and Mr Eltringham. Marjolaine is hoping to persuade her father to send her to the Athertons' school, St Peter's (p264/274). The Willoughbys travel to Guernsey for Janie and Julian Lucy's wedding in *Janie of* and Marjolaine is one of their bridesmaids (p32/33). Marjolaine is in the party that visits a beach on Sark during Janie and Julian's honeymoon, thus unwittingly forcing the newlyweds to hide in a cave (p56/59). Marjolaine is a bridesmaid when her Uncle Nigel marries Rosamund Atherton. Janie mentions that Marjolaine was to be presented at court but sprained her ankle and must wait for the next season. Marjolaine takes her two-year-old stepbrother Frithiof to stay at the Athertons' home when the younger Willoughbys have measles (p117/163/182).

WILLOUGHBY, NAN: see BLAKENEY, ANITA

WILLOUGHBY, NIGEL (A): We learn in *Scamps* that twenty-two-year-old Nigel is the youngest brother of Sir Piers and is currently at Oxford. The Willoughby family journey to Guernsey and Nigel takes them there in his new steam-yacht *Sea Dweller*, anchored at Weymouth (p14/131/132). Maidie explains that her father, Sir Piers, is the eldest child of his family and Nigel, the youngest, is eighteen years younger. Nigel was a tiny baby when their father was killed hunting and he was ten months old when their mother and some of their siblings, including their sister Madeleine, died of diphtheria. His brother Sir Piers was twenty-two when he married his first wife and they looked after Nigel, who was then about four years old. Madeleine, the Willoughbys' first child, was born the following year and is five years younger than Nigel (p133). Nigel is a slim, fair young man, very like Rex, and the two of them make friends with Julian Lucy (p134/151/152). The three young men are caught in a storm when out sailing but they finally reach land in Bordeaux. When they return to Guernsey three days later it is discovered that Nigel had not taken Captain Polperran but took only Smith and Wilson as his crew (p159/165/169).

Nigel is about to start his final year at university and goes to Cornwall to join a reading party (p236). Nigel is engaged to Rosamund Atherton in *Janie of* and is the best man when Julian Lucy marries Janie Temple (p13/33). Nigel has been engaged for three years and is to be married in August. He is one of the people who visit a beach on Sark during Janie and Julian's honeymoon, thus unwittingly forcing the newlyweds to hide in a cave (p54/56/59). Jack Eltringham officiates at Nigel and Rosamund's wedding service at Lasterby (p109/117). Elizabeth and Paul Ozanne invite Nigel and Julian Ozanne to be godfathers to their twin daughters Nella and Vanna. Rosamund and Nigel are living in a small flat in London (p174/176/185). Rosamund and Nigel have a son whom they name Harold Nigel after Mr Atherton and Nigel. They are moving out of their London flat in October into a house outside the city (p230/235). Nigel is tall, fair-haired and slim, with mischievous hazel eyes, in *Steps In*. Rosamund's cousin Nan Blakeney is visiting them after the death of her mother in an accident eight months previously. Her father was badly injured in the accident and is advised to take a long sea-voyage (p9/11/16). Nigel and Rosamund have two children, Toby and Blossom. Because Rosamund has to go away to help Maidie Clitheroe they decide to send Nan to the Lucys in Guernsey (p17/29). Nigel intends taking Nan over to Guernsey but is prevented by a sudden crisis in a big lawsuit on which he is working as Junior Counsel. Nigel puts Nan on to a train at Paddington and she remembers being told that he was very irresponsible when he was younger, and is amused by his solicitude. Nigel and Rosamund live at Whitelade by the Thames (p34/36/38). Nan's father Sir Charles Blakeney's health becomes very poor and he is put ashore at Madeira, where he is expected to die; Nigel becomes Nan's guardian and trustee (p214/217). Toby and Blossom are at the Chalet School in Guernsey in *Goes to It*. The Willoughbys move from Guernsey to Surrey as both Nigel and Rosamund's families live there. Rosamund and Joey Maynard are close friends and

St Peter's Church, Guernsey

the Willoughbys now have three children. Nigel takes Joey and her young triplets, Miss Wilson and Frieda to England on his yacht *The Sea Witch*. They have an adventurous voyage and finish the journey on a naval destroyer. The Navy commandeer Nigel's yacht and, much to his distress, his eyesight is not good enough for him to go too (p12/28/43). Miss Wilson recalls the awful voyage across the Channel in Nigel's yacht in *Lavender* (p219). The Chester and Lucy children are taken to school on St Briavel's Island on Nigel's yacht in *Island* (p25). Blossom mentions in *Wrong* that her father is keen on tennis and she has played many times with him. His younger daughter Judy is nine years old and he has a new, delicate son named Aubrey (p57). Nigel and Rosamund travel by yacht to visit Kester Bellever on Brandon Mawr in *Peggy* (p89). The summer term finishes in *Changes* with a regatta and Nigel's yacht, *The Sea Witch*, is used as the judges' boat (p183/184). Nigel and Rosamund have their frail little son Aubrey with them. We learn that Nigel rowed for his college at Oxford and spends all his spare time on the water (p186/187). Blossom has developed a fierce service at tennis in *Problem* by playing so much against Nigel when she is at home (p72). The Willoughbys now have a one-year-old baby (p214) and we learn in *Coming of Age* that this is a girl (p198).

CHILDREN: Harold (Toby), Blossom, Judy, Aubrey, unnamed daughter

WILLOUGHBY, PETER (B) (4): Thirteen-year-old Peter is always in mischief and despises his own fair good looks in *Scamps*. Peter and his brother David have lessons with Mr Eltringham for three hours every morning (p11/13). The Willoughby children sneak out of their house one night to sleep in hammocks in the orchard and Mr Eltringham, the curate, decides to send Peter and David to St Peter's School for Boys in Dawley (p25/34/38). One hot Sunday afternoon, Peter, David and their stepsister Britta are caught by Sir Piers after they have encouraged a donkey to enter the church whilst Mr Eltringham is preaching (p126/128). The Willoughbys visit Guernsey for the summer holidays and Peter spends a great deal of time on the beach reading. He tries smoking one of his father's cigars, with dire results (p151/184/185). Peter rolls out of bed and falls into a bath of cold water left there by Mr Eltringham during an interchange of pranks (p270). At the end of the holidays they picnic at Petit Bôt and during an argument with Peter, his brother David falls at the top of the cliffs and is caught on a jutting out bit of rock (p283/294). Peter is in the party that visits a beach on Sark during Janie and Julian's honeymoon, thus unwittingly forcing the newlyweds to hide in a cave in *Janie of* (p56/58). Seventeen-year-old Peter is at Winchester with fifteen-year-old David and is a keen cricketer (p72/183). Peter is engaged to a girl he has met in Kelowna in *Steps In*. He has a good job and a bungalow where they will live (p244).

WILLOUGHBY, SIR PIERS (A): We first meet the Willoughby family in *Scamps* and learn that Sir Piers Willoughby, the Squire, is rarely at home and his motherless children are allowed to run wild in the neighbourhood. His home is at Steyne Winting and his wife died when their youngest child Tim was seventeen months old. He has seven children, seventeen-year-old Madeleine, known as Maidie, sixteen-year-old Rex (Reginald), fourteen-year-old Marjolaine, thirteen-year-old Peter, eleven-year-old David, Bernadine (Dina) and five-year-old Timothy, known as Tim (p9/10/11/12). Sir Piers spends his time wandering over the Continent and leaves his family to take care of itself (p13/14). He has a twenty-two-year-old brother, Nigel. Sir Piers is a tall, thin man with brown hair that curls crisply over his head, clear blue eyes and a deep tan. Sir Piers's servant Achmet brings letters from home that inform him that his children have sneaked out of the house one night to sleep in hammocks in the orchard (p33/34). He returns home unexpectedly with his new wife, Sigrid, and her ten-year-old daughter, Britta. We are informed that Sir Piers met Norwegian Mrs Lundgren in Algiers two years ago. They were married in Cairo and had a short honeymoon on the Nile (p60/62/84). Dina, Sir Piers's youngest daughter, has to have a spinal operation and Sir Piers and Maidie go to London with her. After Dina's operation, the Willoughby family travels to Guernsey on Nigel Willoughby's steam-yacht to spend the summer on the island, hoping that this will help Dina become strong again (p96/130/131). We learn that Sir Piers was twenty-two when he married his first wife, and their daughter Madeleine was born the next year. Sir Piers is eighteen years older than his brother Nigel and he cared for Nigel, who was ten months old when their mother died from diphtheria along with some of her children. Their father had been killed in a hunting accident when Nigel was a tiny baby (p133). Rosamund Atherton mentions that Sir Piers is a famous explorer and has been to many places including Mecca and Lhasa. Sir Piers is an old friend of Mr Atherton, whose family they meet. Sir Piers reminds Nigel that he is under his guardianship until he is twenty-five (p148/150/173). We learn in *Heather* that the Willoughby family are spending the summer at Sigrid's home in Bergen (p48). Sir Piers is the Member of Parliament for Mordown in *Janie of* and we learn that Frithiof was born two years after Sigrid married Sir Piers and is named after her father. Sir Piers is a baronet, one of the oldest baronetcies in England. He is perturbed by the fact that Cuthbert Clitheroe is a Roman Catholic, but Sigrid persuades him to allow Maidie's engagement to him (p100/163/180). Sigrid has three babies of her own, besides Maidie's daughter and Con's two sons, to look after in *Steps In* (p14).

WILLOUGHBY, SIR REGINALD (ANCESTOR): Sir Reginald Willoughby, a Willoughby ancestor who married Lady Juliana during the Regency days, is mentioned in *Scamps* (p63).

WILLOUGHBY, REGINALD PIERS (REX) (B) (2): Sixteen-year-old Reginald, known as Rex, is a tall, lanky fellow with short yellow hair and blue eyes in *Scamps*. He had a severe attack of rheumatic fever six months after he started at a public school and is still too delicate to return to school. He is supposed to be reading classics three mornings a week with Mr Eltringham, the curate (p10/11). The Willoughby children sneak out of the house one night to sleep in hammocks in the orchard, with ill effects on some of them. Letters to their father inform him about the incident. Unfortunately Rex becomes ill again with rheumatic pains (p25/34/35). Rex has a Regency ancestor, Sir Reginald Willoughby, after whom he may be named. Rex's younger sister Dina has to have an operation and he accompanies his father, Maidie and Dina to London (p63/97). The family visits Guernsey for the summer and Rex is not allowed to swim at first because of his health. Rex and Nigel make friends with Julian Lucy, who is living with his parents in their summer bungalow (p144/151/152). Nigel, Rex and Julian sail Nigel's steam-yacht, *Sea Dweller*, in a storm (p159) and, after a terrifying night on board, the boys finally reach land in Bordeaux. Nigel insists on Rex seeing Dr Tinaurel as his heart is fluttering (p165/171/172). Con Atherton, Julian, Janie Temple, Pauline Ozanne, Maidie and Rex take a boat out to Lihou Island late one night to pretend to be ghosts. Unfortunately they don't tie the boat up properly and have to wait for the tide to uncover the causeway before they can return home to their beds. Sigrid finds out about the adventurers through Peter and meets them on their return (p189/194/197). Miss Matthias, a neighbour of the Willoughbys, rents a cottage on Sark for a year and invites Rex, Maidie and Marjolaine Willoughby and their friends Francesca, Rosamund, Con and Allegra Atherton, Janie and Julian to stay for ten days (p200). The Athertons and Willoughbys visit Guernsey for Janie and Julian Lucy's wedding in *Janie of* and Con Atherton is one of the bridesmaids (p32/33/42). Janie suspects that twenty-one-year-old Rex is in love with twenty-three-year-old Con and says that his casual air is only superficial. He has steadied down now that he is at The House (Christ Church), Oxford, and is the heir to Willoughby Chase (p53/54/55). Rex is in the party that visits a beach on Sark during Janie and Julian's honeymoon, thus unwittingly forcing the newlyweds to hide in a cave (p59). It is noticed that Rex and Con have been going on long rambles together (p109/110). Six-foot-three Rex meets Con at Rosamund and Nigel's wedding and proposes to her (p118/119/121). We learn that Rex is a keen polo player. Rex insists on being one of the godfathers when Rosamund's son Harold is born (p183/231). Con and Rex, now married, are going to Ceylon in *Steps In*. Sigrid will look after their two sons, her own three babies, and Maidie's daughter (p12/13/14).

CHILDREN: Two unnamed boys

WILLOUGHBY, ROLF (B) (10): Rolf is the second of the three small sons mentioned as Sir Piers and Sigrid's children in *Steps In* (p14/245).

WILLOUGHBY, ROSAMUND: see ATHERTON, ROSAMUND

WILLOUGHBY, LADY (ii), SIGRID: (LUNDGREN, SIGRID) (A): Sir Piers's second wife Sigrid is a widow, and he marries her on impulse so that she can take over the running of his household and look after his family in *Scamps*. Sigrid has a ten-year-old daughter named Britta and we learn that Sigrid's old nurse Thora looked after Britta when her mother and Sir Piers were on their honeymoon. Norwegian Sigrid's first husband Mr Lundgren was an artist and he married his greatest friend's daughter when he was forty and she was a girl of seventeen. Britta was born on her mother's eighteenth birthday and Mr Lundgren died when Britta was five months old. Sigrid was left well off and had no wish to return to her native Bergen. She travelled about the Continent with Britta her baby, Julie her French maid and her own old nurse, Madale (p62/83/84). Sir Piers and Maidie are sent for before Dina's spinal operation and Sigrid helps Madeleine pack a case (p97/98). Because of Dina's poor health, the family travels to Guernsey on Nigel's steam-yacht *Sea Dweller* and we learn that Sigrid is used to boats as everyone has them at home in Bergen. Her father's home is large, as he was one of fourteen children growing up in it, and Sigrid invites Maidie to visit him with her. When the children are missing Sigrid comes out to meet them and is angry that they have dragged Pauline into the escapade (p137/197). The Willoughbys go to Lady Willoughby's home in Bergen for the summer holidays in *Heather* (p48). We learn in *Janie of* that Frithiof was born two years after Sigrid married Sir Piers and is named after her father. Sigrid persuades Sir Piers to allow Maidie's engagement to Cuthbert Clitheroe, a Roman Catholic. Marjolaine takes two-year-old Frithiof to stay at the Athertons' home when the young Willoughby children have measles (p100/181/182). Sigrid is looking after her own three children, Maidie's daughter and Con's two sons in *Steps In*. The three children are named as Axel, Rolf and a baby (p14/245).

WILLOUGHBY, TIMOTHY (TIM) (B) (7): We first meet the Willoughby family in *Scamps*. The youngest child, Timothy, is five years old and we learn that his mother, Lady Willoughby, died when he was seventeen months old. The Willoughby children sneak out of their house one night to sleep in hammocks in the orchard (p9/10/25). Tim goes missing while the other children are making a welcome home arch for their father and when he is found he mentions he has been eating red berries, which they assume are poisonous. In fact they were only loganberries. His father spanks him when he discovers Tim throwing stones into the lake (p52/56/88). Lady Sigrid, his new stepmother, decides that Tim should start going to church but he misbehaves. The Willoughbys visit Guernsey during the summer holidays and Tim, who is newly six years old, becomes friendly with Noel Atherton (p109/115/151). The Willoughbys visit Guernsey for Janie and Julian's wedding in *Janie of* and Tim and Noel are among the group who go to welcome the Athertons on their arrival. Tim is in the party that visits a beach on Sark during Janie and Julian's honeymoon, unwittingly forcing the newlyweds to hide in a cave (p33/56). Ten-year-old Tim is at a big preparatory school with Noel Atherton and is furious to be missing football when the young Willoughbys have measles (p72/183). Tim is mentioned as one of the Willoughbys' dependent children, together with his three young stepbrothers, in *Steps In* (p245).

WILLS, LORNA: Fifth-former Lorna forms a quartette with Jean Downes, Hilda Smith and Jane Thomas, and they make dolls' sheets for the School Sale in *Peggy* (p164).

WILLS, SUSANNAH: Susannah is in the Upper

Fourth and is friends with Blossom Willoughby and Sybil Russell in *Peggy* (p91).

WILLY: see (GRANTLEY), MARY and WILLY

WILMOT, MR: Mr Wilmot is a retired lawyer and he and his sister Jane are Polly Heriot's elderly guardians in *Jo Returns* (p48/59). They are staying at Garmisch when Polly decides to run away (p49), and when seventy-three-year-old Mr Wilmot arrives at the Chalet School it is arranged that Polly will become a pupil (p57/59). In *Goes to It* we are informed that Mr Wilmot's eighty-seven-year-old sister Jane died the previous year (p47). Mr Wilmot dies and Polly closes up the house in *Lavender* (p101).

WILMOT, MR: Nancy Wilmot refers to her father in *New CS* as a flying enthusiast who does mad stunts and tries to thrash about in the stratosphere (p71).

WILMOT, FRANCIE: see WILFORD, FRANCES

WILMOT, HILDA: Hilda is a dreamy, artistic girl at St Scholastika's who lets Elaine Gilling do her thinking for her in *Rivals* (p118/119). Hilda is present at the snow fight in *Eustacia* but is called away as she is not very strong (p152/154). Hilda and the Head Girl, Gipsy Carson, are in the lead when the girls from St Scholastika's School come to set up their stalls for the Bazaar in *Lintons*. Hilda is dressed as Fatima at the Fairy Tale Bazaar (p268/290).

WILMOT, IRIS: Iris is a new girl in Inter V in *New Mistress* and her work is below standard for this form (p80).

WILMOT, JANE: Mr Wilmot and his sister Jane are Polly Heriot's elderly guardians in *Jo Returns* (p48/57/59). In *Goes to It* we are told that eighty-seven-year-old Jane died the previous year (p47).

WILMOT, NANCY, 'WILLY', 'WILLIE': Nancy Wilmot and Ida Reaveley dress in full Turkish male costumes at the Fairy Tale Bazaar in *Lintons* because they are the two biggest girls in the Fifth form at St Scholastika's (p291). Nancy transfers to the Chalet School in *New CS* with her great chums Hilary Burn and Ida Reaveley (p25). Nancy has a younger cousin who was also at St Scholastika's. She was looking forward to a lazy term with no responsibilities and is not keen on the thought that she might be made a prefect at the Chalet School. Her friends tease her for being fat but she points out that her sister was fat in her teens and is now slim and elegant. Hilary wishes that maths had never been invented and Nancy agrees that all maths people are the extreme edge (p26/28/29). Nancy is in the Green dormitory at Ste Thérèse with Cornelia Flower and Evadne Lannis. She would have liked to fly to school and thinks her father should encourage this as he is a flying enthusiast and does mad stunts. Nancy, Hilary, Ida and Irene Silksworth become Chalet School prefects (p67/71/80). When the girls are out for a walk, Margia Stevens and Berta Hamel help Nancy with her French as she describes herself as the world's worst dud at languages. Nancy undertakes to be in charge of the Junior Library (p90/103). After some of the Middles have been out on their flat roof at night rehearsing a play, Nancy suggests that they should make them perform it to the whole School as a punishment. Gillian Linton mentions that Nancy will be leaving at the end of the Christmas term (p235/318). Nancy is in the WRNS in *Goes to It* along with Anne Seymour, Elsie Carr, Ida Reaveley and Irene Silksworth (p104). EBD mentions in *N14* that after Nancy's career in the WRNS ended she taught in various schools (p60). Plump, very pretty Nancy becomes the Senior maths mistress at the Chalet School when it opens at the Görnetz Platz in Switzerland in *Barbara*. She becomes Upper IVB's form mistress and takes over maths from Miss Slater, who has left the Chalet School. On a visit to Berne she gives the keeper at the bear-pit a tin of condensed milk for the bears and the bears' response is very entertaining. Miss Wilmot has seen this done at Regent's Park Zoo with a tin of golden syrup. When the snow comes Nancy skis with a skimming, easy, bird-like movement (p107/166/181). Miss Wilmot visits Lucerne in *Does It Again* and she and Miss O'Ryan are jointly in charge of a group of girls that includes prefects Clem and Julie and also Margot, Emerence, the Gang, Con, Prunella and Len. She is present when Margot takes her unexpected dip (p115/126). Nancy mentions in *Kenya* that she was a Junior when Jo Scott's mother Maisie Gomme was a Senior (p74). Miss Wilmot, who is generally easy-going, accompanies the girls on a moss-picking expedition where Emerence Hope is involved in a near-fatal accident. Nancy, who grew up among a horde of brothers, knows how to fling a lasso. She uses Mary-Lou's Guide cord in the rescue (p174/175/179). Nancy is dressed as a demon at

the St Nicholas's feast in *Mary-Lou* (p158). Winifred Silksworth, now Mrs Embury and the mother of seven sons, recognises Nancy when they are on a boat trip in *Genius* (p127). Miss Wilmot teaches Joan Baker's first Chalet School lesson and is cheeked by her in *Problem*. She is notoriously easy-going, although she can be very much on her dignity when she wants to be (p120/178). Miss Wilmot is House Mistress of Ste Thérèse in *New Mistress*. She remembers that Miss Wilson's sarcasm used to make her writhe when she was a pupil at the School, though it made her learn (p64/114). It is mentioned in *Excitements* that Nancy Wilmot and Kathie Ferrars are very good friends (p165). The girls go down to the lake and Nancy persuades Miss Bubb to join them for coffee and cakes when they land at Thun in *Coming of Age*. Nancy later barges into a changing hut, disturbing a bald woman (p93/95/96). The present-day prefects visit the Tiernsee with Joey and are told of the roof-top playacting and Nancy's punishment suggestion (p155). Miss Wilmot is Va's form mistress in *Richenda* (p97). Plump, sturdy, five-foot-nine Miss Wilmot takes charge of Vb's excursion after a river bursts its banks and the girls have to wade with her help (p126/128/130). She is a plump, pretty young woman and is easy-going to a degree, although she has her limits, in *Trials* (p47). Nancy visits Zermatt with Vb in *Theodora* and has an adventurous ride when a pig collides with her and carries Nancy on its back, but her weight, since she is five foot ten and plump, is enough to slow the animal down (p186). It is mentioned in *Ruey* that Vb is the lowest form that Nancy usually takes for maths. Ruey Richardson has an accident and hurts her finger during Nancy's lesson. Nancy goes to Basle one weekend to attend some lectures at the university (p78/81/183). She helps spread blankets over sleeping girls when the heating fails in the night in *Leader* and witnesses the half-awake Richenda Fry nearly throttling Matey (p37). Miss Wilmot helps to clear up the mess resulting from the pepper incident in *Trick*. She is Va's form mistress (p91/149). Irma von Rothenfels is astounded to hear in *Future* that Nancy Wilmot teaches maths (p198). Miss Wilmot, Miss Ferrars and Miss Ashley are in charge of a group of Junior Middles who visit Neuchâtel at half term in *Feud*. Miss Wilmot's sense of humour has got her into trouble at intervals for most of her life. Miss Annersley asks at the end of Frühstück which girls painted golden syrup on the doors leading to the kitchens the previous evening and Nancy drops her handkerchief and grovels under the table for it, and does not come up again until she can control herself. Several other people are biting their lips to keep from laughing aloud (p114/164). When Nancy helps in the rooftop rescue of Minette we learn that she has long arms, powerful shoulders and is six feet in height. She has done a fair amount of mountain climbing (p186/187/189). Big, sturdy Miss Wilmot carries Michelle Cabràn back to school when the girl gets caught in a snowstorm in *Triplets*. Matron wakes Miss Wilmot, Miss Ferrars and Miss Yolland to help search for Con Maynard, who is sleepwalking after the snowstorm incident (p48/58). Nancy Wilmot receives a passing mention in *Reunion* (p68). It is mentioned in *Jane* that Miss Wilmot and Miss Ferrars are joint owners of a car. Nancy is tall and broad, fair with blue eyes and has honey-coloured hair. She is a placid, happy-go-lucky creature who can be icily dignified on occasion (p108/124/125). Miss Wilmot and Miss Ferrars meet Flavia Ansell from the train at Besançon in *Redheads* and Miss Wilmot drives them to school in a small dark-blue Citroën (p12/13). Miss Wilmot has pansy-blue eyes (p17). According to Kathy Ferrars, Nancy does not have an ounce of imagination (p48). Miss Wilmot rescues Matron Lloyd when she manages to get stuck in a bathroom late one night due to a faulty lock in *Adrienne* (p191). Miss Wilmot is the maths mistress and also Form Mistress of the Lower Fifth in *Summer Term*. Her sense of humour prompts her to suggest to the prefects that they could use the crater on their hockey pitch as the start of a swimming pool (p67/68/179). Miss Wilmot is about thirty years old in *Challenge* and becomes the temporary Headmistress when Miss Annersley is away inspecting other schools. She has been teaching for ten years, eight of them with the Chalet School and is a tall, rather plump woman, and very good-looking with her shining waves of golden-brown hair and fresh complexion (p11/33). We are reminded of Emerence Hope's accident and also that Nancy grew up with five brothers and learnt to use a lasso (p83/84). Miss Wilmot is very worried when Kathy Ferrars is taken ill in Upper IVA's form (p100). Nancy tells the present Chalet School staff that she used to be a pupil at St Scholastika's School and transferred to the Chalet School when Miss Browne, their headmistress, retired (p114/115). Miss Wilmot deals with the girls of the Lower Fourth who have been playing tricks with Upper IVA's property (p123/124). She tells Evelyn Ross that her mother has had a relapse. She thinks it will be best for Evelyn to go into lessons but later, after a talk with Joey, she is full of remorse at how she handled the situation (p177/180). Nancy says that she will rejoice when Hilda comes back again to take over. She feels that she is not cut out to be a headmistress because there is too much correspondence for her liking. She hands over to Miss Annersley with a joyful heart (p184/185/214). Miss Wilmot is in charge and is organising walks in the aftermath of Nina's car crash in *Two Sams*. She instructs the Seniors to suppress any gossip about the accident. Miss Wilmot realises in the middle of a lesson that she needs another book and sends Samantha to the staffroom. As a result Samantha rescues a cat (p43/152/153). Miss Wilmot and Miss Ferrars take the Fourths on a half-term excursion to Zurich and Zug in *Althea*. Miss Wilmot becomes involved when a man sneaks into the girls' room during the night to steal their belongings and she sits her entire ten stone odd on the intruder's feet (p152/169). Nancy reports to the Head in *Prefects* that a flood has occurred because of the storm. They are cut off from the valley as the waters have got into the railway generators and everything is held up (p159). A brief biography of Nancy Wilmot is given in *N14* (p60).

WILSON: Wilson is the Willoughbys' gardener in *Scamps* (p54). Wilson and Smith are acting as crew on board Nigel's steam-yacht *Sea Dweller* when it is driven to France in a storm. The two men are responsible for saving the lives of all on board, since Nigel left Captain Polperran behind in Guernsey (p169/172).

WILSON, MR and MRS (i): Mr Wilson's wife has died, leaving him with three boys and a tiny girl, and we learn in *Princess* that Matron Wilson has left the Chalet School to help her brother (p40/43).

WILSON, MR and MRS (ii): Nell Wilson mentions her parents in *Gay* when she tells Jacynth Hardy that she is from a musical family, although she doesn't play herself. She was twenty-two when she lost her mother, father and sixteen-year-old sister Cherry within a year (p229/225).

WILSON, MR and MRS (iii): Hilary Wilson mentions in *Problem* that her father used to be a traveller for his firm, which has a lot of continental business and used to send him abroad. She sends a postcard to her mother (p190/191).

WILSON, MISS (i): see MATRON WILSON

WILSON, MISS (ii): When Katharine Gordon mistakenly joins the Chalet School in *Wrong*, the Principal of the Tanswick Chalet School is a Miss Wilson, who has recently had a major operation in Birmingham and is too ill to help solve the puzzle created by Katharine's arrival at St Briavel's. Later we are informed that Katharine's mother was at school with Miss Wilson, who has now given up teaching and gone out to Kenya to join her brother (p70/225/227).

WILSON, CHERRY: We are told in *Gay* that Miss Wilson's sister Cherry was very musical. Everyone said that Cherry would have a great career but she died when she was sixteen years old (p191/229). Nell gives Jacynth Hardy her father's 'cello and Jacynth calls the 'cello 'Cherry' in memory of Nell's dead sister (p132/191/229).

WILSON, GREAT-AUNT ELLA: We are informed in *Scamps* that Miss Wilson, the Willoughbys' Great-Aunt Ella, lives in Melbourne and is a former beauty. Julian Lucy's grandmother, Mrs Orange, lends Francesca Atherton some clothes so that she can dress up as Miss Wilson for a joke (p218/219/226).

WILSON, HELENA MARGARET (NELL), 'BILL': We first meet Miss Wilson in *Princess* and she teaches geography and science. EBD jumped a year at this point and it appears not to be Miss Wilson's first term (p53). She teaches general subjects in *Head Girl* and advises that Madame should be sent for to deal with Deira (p105). She helps to organise the snow fight and rings for Dr Jem when Grizel is injured (p141/145). She and Miss Annersley provide a church service for the non-Catholic girls (p274). She is an Alpinist and is on an unexpected trek in *Rivals* when the path breaks up (p101). It is mentioned in *Eustacia* that 'Bill' was her old name at the School of Economics (p71). A group of English and American girls go on an expedition to Fulpmes at the foot of the Stubai glacier at half term with Miss Wilson and Miss Stewart in charge (p169/178). On their descent from the glacier they encounter a snowstorm and Miss Wilson has the misfortune to slip on a loose stone and break one of the bones in her foot when Eustacia Benson jerks her arm. They manage to reach a mountain hut just before the snow becomes really heavy and have to spend the night there (p217/246). The Guide Company is well established in *And Jo* and Miss Wilson is the Chalet Guide Captain. St Scholastika's have started Guides this term and she hopes that they can help the new Guides when they go off for weekend camps (p68/69/70). Miss Wilson, who is Catholic, is in charge when the Chalet Guides spend two weeks camping at the Baumersee in *Camp* (p79). Along with her other duties, she rescues Joey when she falls down a pit. Joey, who has not recognised Miss Wilson, calls her an idiot (p106/111/113). Miss Wilson is referred to in *Exploits* as the Science and Geography Mistress. She has been at the Chalet School four years and the girls treat her with affection and respect. She is tall and athletic and has a pleasant face, although not as pretty as one or two of the staff. She deals with Thekla von Stift when she causes a fuss on a walk, and with biting sarcasm threatens to leave her behind. Miss Wilson is very friendly with Miss Stewart (p57/111/255/256). Miss Wilson plays the part of Mrs Jarley at the Staff Evening in *Lintons* (p118/119). Con Stewart addresses her as Nell, and we are told that this is short for Helena (p210). One night she hears Thekla, Joyce Linton and Cornelia Flower and investigates. This makes her the first mistress to become involved with Thekla in the final row that leads to her expulsion. Cornelia observes in passing that Miss Wilson's hair must be naturally curly (p242/243). We later learn that Bill's hair goes down to her waist. While they are preparing for a Sale Jo falls off a ladder and lands on Miss Wilson, who takes Jo's full weight on her chest and is winded. When she recovers she teases Jo by asking why she has a grudge against her, as in the summer she was roundly abused by Jo, who had fallen into a pit, and now she tries to extinguish her by falling on her (p279/282/284). Jo later comments that it is the first time since the mistress came to the School that anyone has succeeded in

completely suppressing Bill (p285). Miss Wilson is in a boat with Joey on the Tiernsee in 'Joey Oar' in *1st* (p82). She is in charge of St Clare's, the new Middles' house, with Miss Stewart and Miss Nalder in *New House* and is twelve years older than Joey and her friends, who are now about eighteen (p11/25). After a disturbed night during which Alixe von Elsen walks in her sleep wailing like a Banshee, Miss Wilson is able to guess the chief culprit, saying that as sure as her name is Helena Margaret Wilson, Biddy O'Ryan must have frightened Alixe with tales of Irish spooks (p199/205/206). She is Head of St Clare's in 'Woollen Measles' in *3rd* (p152). Madge and Bill once ordered one Pfannkuchen each in a restaurant in Innsbruck in *Cook Book*, not realising how much bigger they would be than English pancakes (p112). Miss Wilson and Miss Nalder spend half term in Innsbruck in *Jo Returns* (p209). It is mentioned in *New CS* that Miss Wilson's writing might easily be more legible. Miss Wilson, who is now first mistress in the School, is described as a very tall, athletic-looking woman, with a clean-cut face and dark brown hair that ripples over her head in silky waves and is fastened in a great knot at the nape of her neck. She has keen grey eyes and a chin that rivals Cornelia Flower's. She is a great favourite with her pupils despite her reputation for sarcasm, which miscreants dread, and has a clear, rather deeply pitched voice (p24/78/79). The girls visit Salzburg at half term and Miss Wilson and Miss Stewart are in charge when they have to spend the night in a bus which is marooned in a rising flood on the return journey. Grey-eyed Miss Wilson can speak Italian, although not always correctly, and is thirty years old (p264/273/294). Nell is described as a tall, clever-looking woman in *Exile*. Miss Wilson is in charge of a last shopping trip to Spärtz, when a group of girls attempt to rescue Herr Goldmann the Jeweller from Nazi hooligans (p26/27/118/119). They escape through a secret passage under the altar in Vater Johann's church, and when they emerge, her hair is discovered to have turned white. Jack Maynard and Gottfried Mensch accompany Miss Wilson, Joey Bettany and seven girls when they flee from Austria, eventually reaching Switzerland (p124/127/128/158). Miss Wilson tells their hostess that she has no family left. She still has black brows and eyelashes despite her snowy hair, so it does not age her (p166). While the school is closed, Con Stewart visits Nell Wilson at her little cottage (p174). Bill returns to resume classes in science and geography when the Chalet School opens in Guernsey. When the Maynard triplets are born in November Joey names her firstborn daughter Helena after Nell, who becomes the baby's godmother (p190/281/282). Miss Wilson is now thirty-three years old (p320). The Channel Islands become unsafe and once again the Chalet School moves. Bill helps Joey with her babies in the evacuation from Guernsey to the mainland on Nigel Willoughby's yacht in *Goes to It*. She then resumes her science and geography teaching at Plas Howell (p27/94). Miss Wilson's face is a study when she sees Beth, Gwensi and Daisy with their home-made skis in 'Triumvirate' in *1st*, although she would have given a good deal to have seen the beginning of that affair (p125). Miss Wilson is a Guide Captain in *Highland Twins* when Emmie and Joanna Linders tell the Guides of their adventurous escape. She is famed for staying up late and wakes first on the night of the burglary (p103/154). Miss Wilson's little cottage in the wilds of Dartmoor is being lent to a cousin from Portsmouth for the duration in *Lavender*. Miss Wilson and Miss Annersley discuss all school affairs together and although Miss Annersley is Head, Miss Wilson has an equal right of veto on what they do (p19/26). Catholic Miss Wilson is the Second Mistress and always takes Prayers for the Catholics. She is the Staff Head of the Peace League because of all she has suffered in its cause (p62/64). Nell breaks her leg when she is involved in a bus accident in Devon with Hilda Annersley, Jeanne de Lachenais and Dollie Edwards in *Gay* (p31/32). In response to an urgent letter from Joey about Miss Bubb, the temporary headmistress, who is upsetting everyone, Nell returns to school early. She mentions to Matey and Joey how much Hilda Annersley means to her (p107/114/122). Miss Wilson intends to lend Jacynth Hardy her father's 'cello. When Gay Lambert runs away, Miss Wilson takes over authority and is angry when she learns that Miss Bubb refused Gay permission to go home to see her brother before he travels to the Far East (p132/154/163). Miss Wilson has been at the Chalet School for twelve years, takes over running the School and interviews Mrs Learoyd, who has helped Gay (p184/187). Miss Wilson insists on hearing Jacynth play the 'cello and afterwards promises that she will give Jacynth her father's 'cello in memory of her sister Cherry when Jacynth is good enough to be taught by Mr Manders. We learn that Miss Wilson is from a musical family although she doesn't play herself. She later tells Jacynth that when she was twenty-two she lost her mother, father and sixteen-year-old sister Cherry within a year (p191/225/229). Miss Wilson sends Flora McDonald on an errand to the cookery room in 'New Flavouring' in *3rd*, thus giving her an opportunity to spike Floppy Williams's shepherd's pie with cod-liver oil (p135/136). Simone is woken from a deep sleep in *Rescue* and thinks for a moment that she is back at school and must be careful not to be heard by Bill's sharp ears (p67). Miss Wilson tells the girls in 'Beth's Diary' in *2nd* that Exeter Cathedral is unique in having transept towers instead of one central one (p[i]). Miss Wilson is Acting Headmistress of the Chalet School in *Mystery*. She visits Miss Annersley at half term, near Chepstow (p32/56). She is Headmistress when Tom Gay appears at school in *Tom* and we are informed that Miss Wilson prefers girls with character but objects to discussing them in front of themselves. Miss Wilson is the Guide Commissioner for the District (p9/10/30). A burglar steals Acting Head Miss Wilson's silver rose bowl in 'Midnight' in *2nd*, but accidentally runs away with Moira's clothes instead (p154). Miss Wilson and Miss Annersley are co-Heads in *Rosalie* (p136). Miss Wilson has recently returned from an educational tour in America in *Three Go*. She has clear-cut features, kindly dark grey eyes and perfect white teeth (p66/67). Nell is helping to find new premises for the School in *Island*. She moves with the Chalet School to St Briavel's Island and is the joint Headmistress with Miss Annersley (p8/29). We are informed that she still has broad streaks of red in her hair and needs to do her hair carefully to avoid a patchy effect. Nell and Hilda are going to Gillian Linton's wedding and stay at Dick Bettany's home (p47/49). Peggy Bettany mentions to Nell Randolph in *Peggy* that the School has two Heads, Miss Annersley and Miss Wilson. Bill was staying at the Quadrant six weeks previously for Gillian's wedding (p39/54). Miss Annersley and Miss Wilson are both Headmistresses in *Carola* and Miss Wilson is described as the Second Head (p51/83). Nell is the District Guide Commissioner for Carnbach in *Wrong* but is not present at the Guide Camp at Kittiwake Cove as she has a Commissioners' meeting at County Headquarters. Miss Wilson deals with Jennifer Penrose after the girl has locked Blossom in the art room and we learn that Nell is the younger Head (p129/233/239). Miss Wilson is in charge of the new Swiss branch whose first term is about to start in *Shocks* (p14). *CS Oberland* takes place in the same term and Miss Wilson becomes Headmistress when the Chalet School opens a new finishing branch at Welsen in the Oberland. Peggy Bettany refers to Miss Wilson as having been a co-Head of the School in the Tirol after the death of Mlle Lepâttre but this is an over-simplification. Miss Wilson deals with the problem of Elma Conroy when she receives letters from the undesirable Stuart Raynor (p7/35/136/139). Miss Wilson is in charge of the branch in the Oberland in *Bride* and we are informed that Mlle de Lachennais has taken over the Catholic Prayers at the main School (p55). Nell Wilson has let Jack Maynard know in *Changes* about a derelict hotel in Switzerland, which he has bought so that they can move the San out there (p11). Miss Wilson persuades the younger sister of a maid at Welsen

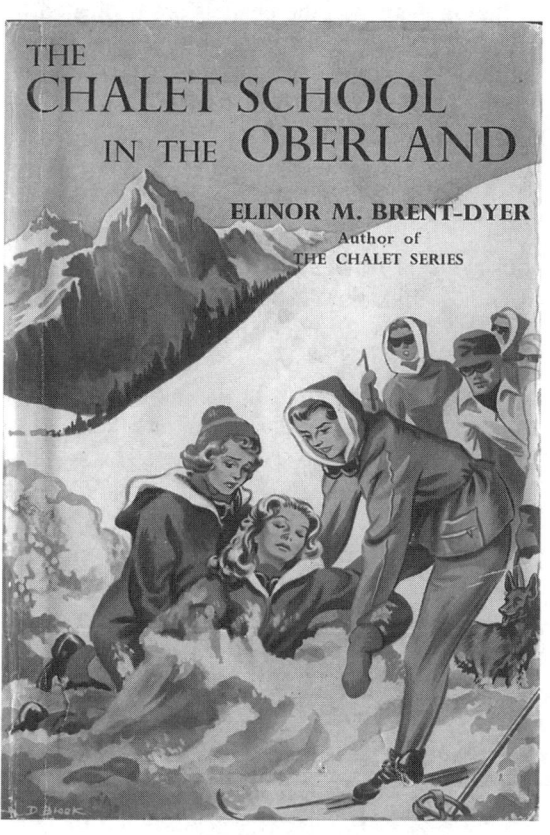

to come and work for Jo as a coadjutor for Anna in *Joey Goes* (p151). Miss Wilson, the Head of the finishing branch at Welsen, arrives in *Barbara* on a very early train to discuss the maths curriculum with the new teacher (Nancy Wilmot) at the main School, which has moved to the Görnetz Platz (p106). She wins a multicoloured blanket at the Sale in *Does It Again* which Anna from Freudesheim has knitted (p188). The Chalet School Sixth formers visit Welsen for science lessons with Miss Wilson in *Kenya*. Bill accompanies the Welsen girls when they join the rest of the School at Thun for bathing (p117/141). The finishing branch moves up to the Görnetz Platz in *Mary-Lou* and is now named St Mildred's. Miss Wilson is able to teach science to more of the school (p20/28/21). She joins her co-Head and close friend Miss Annersley for the trip to Schaffhausen (p95). After Mary-Lou's accident, Miss Wilson and Miss Annersley make sure that one of them visits the invalid every day. Bill is spending a fortnight or so with the Russells in their new home in the mountains at Christmas and will write and send photos to Mary-Lou (p189/197). Miss Wilson is the producer of the St Mildred's pantomime, *Beauty and the Beast*, in *Genius* (p92). The staff have been having trouble with Upper IVB in *Problem*, but Miss Wilson has brought them into line with her renowned sarcastic tongue (p60/61). She interviews Kathie Ferrars for the post in *New Mistress*. Bill, who can be very sarcastic, has white hair with a good deal of copper mixed in it and very black eyebrows and lashes (p12/42/43). Miss Wilson rebukes Mary-Lou in a clear-cut voice for overloading a sledge in *Excitements* (p37). Miss Wilson finds Prudence outside the door at prep in *Coming of Age* and the punishment she gives the girl is to be treated as a Junior for the rest of the week (p135). In *Richenda* Bill still takes Prayers for the Catholics when she is at the main School, although most of the time she is at St Mildred's (p43). Miss Wilson is feeling pessimistic about the coming term in *Trials* (p7). Mary-Lou advises Theodora to ask Miss Wilson if she wants to know how the electric trains work in *Theodora* (p44/45). In *Joey and Co.* Joey remembers Bill driving up to the Sonnalpe at the time of the Anschluss with the school car loaded with folding desks (p77). Miss Wilson donates the east window of Our Lady of the Snows when the chapels are dedicated in *Ruey*. She joins the Swiss party going to Peggy Bettany's wedding (p73/171). EBD states in *Leader* that Miss Wilson started at the Chalet School a term before Miss Annersley. When Miss Wilson moved to Welsen, science lessons at the Chalet School were taken over by Miss Armitage. After St Mildred's moved to the Platz a young cousin of hers, Davida Armitage, shared the science teaching with Miss Wilson, taking all forms below VA while Miss Wilson took back the senior classes (p96). Rosalie Dene goes over to St Mildred's at the start of *Trick* to consult Miss Wilson, as Miss Annersley is in Interlaken. One or other of the Heads is always on tap at this stage (p9). Joey tells Irma von Rothenfels in *Future* that she will let Bill and the Abbess know at the first opportunity that they have made contact (p96). Miss Wilson, Miss Dene, Marie, Joey and Frieda represent the Chalet School at Herr Laubach's funeral in Innsbruck in *Feud* and Miss Wilson and Miss Dene stay with Sophie Hamel (p111/112). Miss Wilson is in the rescue party when Cecil Maynard is kidnapped in *Triplets* (p216). Nell stays at school for Joey's houseparty in *Reunion* and goes on an expedition to Wahlstein (p40/61). In *Jane* Miss Wilson

remembers the time when Gay Lambert brought German measles into the School and everyone had to be quarantined, meaning no expeditions (p118). Miss Annersley wishes she could ask Nell Wilson's advice about the intrusive American in *Redheads*, but Miss Wilson is away (p56). Miss Wilson is described as Hilda Annersley's partner and co-Head in *Adrienne* (p163). Miss Wilson is involved in the plans for the School's jubilee celebrations in *Summer Term*. She lives at St Mildred's but a room is always ready for her in the Head's wing in the main School. She predicts the storm that brings the Sale to an early end (p73/83/157). Miss Annersley explains at the beginning of *Challenge* that Miss Wilson will not be able to take over the headship in her absence, as she can't be spared from St Mildred's (p9). Bill phones the School when a shed at St Mildred's is on fire in *Two Sams*. It contains all the costumes for their pantomime, *Dick Whittington*, being staged later in the day. Unfortunately the costumes are all destroyed but they manage to stage the production later in the term (p159/206). Miss Wilson, Head of St Mildred's, joins the stately procession for the opening of the Chalet School Sale in *Prefects* (p135). Miss Wilson is mentioned in *N9* as having joined the School in *Princess* (p37). There is a short biography of her in *N11*, describing her as one of the best-loved mistresses despite her biting tongue, and mentioning that she has visited the USA and Australasia on a tour of educational establishments on two occasions (p48). EBD answers a reader's query about when Miss Wilson's hair went white in *N15* (p63).

WILSON, HILARY (LESLEY): Hilary is in the Upper Fourth in *Peggy* and plays at noughts and crosses with Meg Whyte during prep (p102). We learn that Meg is Hilary's boon companion. Blue-eyed Hilary's cousin Anthea Barnett later scolds her for her involvement in the Regency English prank (p177/178/192). Hilary is a leggy fourteen-year-old in *Wrong*, whose round pink-and-white face wears a perpetually cheeky look owing to a pert nose. Katharine Gordon is put into Hilary's charge on the journey to school and they are both in Leafy dormitory (p15/28/29). Hilary mentions that she is C of E. She is in the Upper Fourth (p41/49/50). Hilary is in the Cherry patrol at an overnight Guide Camp in Kittiwake Cove. She works in the Upper Fourth's rock garden in the evening and it is revealed that Hilary's father is a nursery gardener in a very large way (p132/154/157). Hilary has curly dark hair (p170). She sits next to Emerence Hope in *Shocks* but doesn't consider it her business to tell her to eat. She is in Lower V<small>B</small> (p92/170). Hilary moves up to Lower V<small>A</small> in *Bride* and her friends are Katharine Gordon and Blossom Willoughby (p77/87). Hilary helps the prefects provide folding desks so that the girls can sit their examinations in shady spots in the garden in *Changes* (p161). She accidentally knocks over Mademoiselle in an indoor boat race at the staff evening in *Barbara* (p197). Hilary is friendly with Betsy Lucy in *Does It Again* (p35). She is a prefect in *Mary-Lou* and is the Stationery Prefect (p9/81). Hilary gives up stationery to become the Senior Library Prefect in *Genius* so that she can help her friend Peggy Adams, who finds that the Junior Library takes up all her time (p59/60). She is one of Robin Hood and his Merry Men in the St Mildred's pantomime and is in Ste Thérèse House (p89/178). It is mentioned in *Problem* that seventeen-and-a-half-year-old Hilary is five foot eight. She visits Basle at half term and is looking after Rosamund Lilley, who has toothache, when they meet Joan Baker, who is running away (p187/193). Hilary moves on to St Mildred's and is with the finishing branch for a spot supper party at the Chalet School in *Excitements* (p213). Hilary is with the St Mildred's girls who are living temporarily at the School because of an influx of visitors in *Coming of Age*. Blossom Willoughby hopes to put her in the School Tennis Six (p60/72). Hilary, who is here referred to as Lesley, agrees to play for the Tennis Six (p76).

WILSON, LESLEY: see W<small>ILSON</small>, H<small>ILARY</small> and M<small>ALCOLM</small>, L<small>ESLEY</small>

WILSON, ROSEMARY: In *Two Sams* Rosemary tells Samaris Davies about the landslide involving Erica Standish. She is in Upper IV<small>B</small> (p49/139; p138 for form).

WILSON, RUTH: Ruth is in the Sixth in *Shocks*. She is inclined to use a bullying manner with her juniors and has not been made a prefect (p67). Ruth is on the Seniors' expedition to Bourneville in *Changes* (p133). She takes part in the Senior pair-oars in the Regatta and comes third (p184). Ruth is the Hobbies Prefect in *Barbara*. She is quite a pleasant girl on the whole but apt to be domineering and hard on those she dislikes (p72/77). Ruth is still the Hobbies Prefect in *Kenya* and we learn that she is an only child. She has little sympathy and understanding for the younger girls and has a great opinion of the dignity of prefects. She has the reputation for holding on to grudges. Her hat is damaged when Jo Scott bursts out of Upper IVB's room without looking, and Jo is advised by her friends to avoid the prefect, who, like the elephant, never forgets (p95/96/113/116). Ruth is the Merchant in the St Mildred's pantomime, *Beauty and the Beast*, in *Genius* (p89).

WILTON, HILARY: Hilary is a Junior who is mentioned in *Challenge* (p13).

WINCHBY, ANNE: Anne is one of the St Hilda's pupils who arrive at the Chalet School in *Feud* after their disastrous fire and she is in VIB with the Maynard triplets (p105; p104 for form).

WINDT, MR van der: Arda van der Windt's father is in the Sanatorium in *New CS* but expects to be completely cured in six months' time (p68).

WINDT, ARDA von (van) der: Arda is a new girl and is in the Amber dormitory at the Chalet School in *Eustacia*. Arda von der Windt is involved when a plate is broken during break (p55/274). Arda van der Windt is in the Sixth form in *Exploits* (p48). Sixteen-year-old Arda van der Windt is a pleasant-faced Dutch girl and prefect who helps Sophie Hamel with the library in *New House* (p101). She is a prefect when Louise Redfield becomes Head Girl in *Jo Returns*. Arda is the Junior Librarian (p8/156/157). Seventeen-year-old Arda is a pretty Dutch girl with long black curls and black-lashed grey eyes in *New CS*. Her father is in the Sanatorium but expects to be completely cured in another six months (p68). She spent her holidays in Haarlem. Arda is leaving school at the end of term (p72/318). Arda's two young daughters, Lysbet and Grietje, start at the Chalet School in *Shocks* (p75). They have no surname and as Arda has been married for twelve years they must be only eleven and ten years old at most. In *New Mistress* Peggy Burnett has been staying with an Old Girl, Marie Drooglever, in Leyden and has also seen someone called Arda, who may be Arda van der Windt. Arda has three children and intends to send her daughter Roosje to the Chalet School when a younger class is started (p20/32).

(WINDT), GRIETJE and LYSBET (van der): Arda van der Windt's two young daughters, Grietje and Lysbet, start at the Chalet School in *Shocks* (p75). No surname is given for the girls. As Arda has been married for twelve years, they must be eleven and ten years old at most.

(WINDT), ROOSJE (van der): see ROOSJE

WINKELSTEIN, FRAU (ANNICH, FRAU): Frau Annich is Joey, Frieda, Marie and Simone's landlady at the Gasthaus at Buchenhaus where Joey and the friends have a holiday soon after they leave school in *Cook Book*. Joey mentions that she is a romantic soul (p71/72). She is later called Frau Winkelstein (p126/131). She supplies hot chocolate and fancy bread for elevenses (p152/153).

WINKELSTEIN, KURT: Kurt is the young son of the landlady at Buchenhaus who has mumps and causes the girls to go into quarantine for four weeks in *Cook Book* (p153).

WINSLOW, SALLY: Fifteen-year-old Sally has previously been at the Tanswick Chalet School when she joins the Chalet School at St Briavel's in *Bride*. She is one of the best of the former Tanswick pupils and, disliking its lack of timetabled games, had managed to arrange for at least the younger girls to play hockey there. Sally and Iris Drew organise a Christian names competition for the School Sale (p177/286). When the games committee discuss a possible Tennis Six in *Changes* they mention that Sally should be tried for a second string. She is very steady and occasionally sends over an untakeable service. Sally is rather young and small but she's wiry. She later helps the prefects set up folding desks in the garden so that the girls can sit their examinations in shady spots (p104/160). Sally moves with the Chalet School to Switzerland and is a sub-prefect in *Mary-Lou*. She is the Art Prefect and is the most artistic member of VIA (p9/81). Sally is still the Art Prefect in *Genius* and is a prefect in Ste Thérèse House (p59/178). Sally and Jill Ormsby beat Vi Lucy and Sybil Russell at a practice tennis match in *Problem* (p70). Sally is in her second term at St Mildred's and plays the part of the widow in their pantomime *Aladdin* in *Excitements* (p133).

WINSLOW, ZENA: Zena wears spectacles, is about the same age as Mary-Lou Trelawney and is a wizard at languages in *Barbara* (p61). We don't discover her surname until *Mary-Lou*, where Zena Winslow is a great friend of Gwen Parry (p27).

WINTER, MISS: Miss Winter is in charge of

handwork and takes the Lower Second for a snowy walk with her great friend Miss Norman in *Lavender* (p171).

WINTER, CONNIE: Connie is a Middle in *Barbara* and is deemed to be one of the worst lot in the Chalet School, with Peggy Harper and Barbara Kitson (p59). Connie is a mischievous thirteen-year-old with wicked blue eyes shining in a face freckled like a plover's egg in *Does It Again*. She is a Junior Middle in the same form as Len Maynard (p11/12/16). Connie gets lost in the wooded grounds of the Château Gutsch with Nora Fitzgerald, Heather Unwin and Nancy Wadham on an excursion to Lucerne. She is dressed as a Chinese boy when she helps at Chang's boat lucky dip at the Sale (p123/180). Vi Lucy mentions Connie, Isabel Drew and Margot Maynard as 'kids' in *Mary-Lou* (p20). Connie, Emerence Hope and Francie Wilford are in trouble for continually speaking in English on French days in *Genius*. Connie is in Ste Thérèse House with her boon companion Emerence Hope and they make up a quartette with Francie and Margot Maynard (p154/155/157). Connie is in the Upper Fourth in *Coming of Age*. She takes part in a frog race and upsets the next girl (p212). Connie is in IVA with Heather Warner in *Trials* (p150). She is in Inter V in *Ruey* and has the reputation of being an imp. She wins her form prize of a voucher for a new uniform at the staff evening for making a nurse's uniform. Connie is at school on the Thérèse Lepâttre Scholarship as her people are very poor. There is no money for extras and she was resigned to wearing skirts while the other girls flaunted the new uniform. She has a younger sister named Lulu, who Connie expects will come to the Chalet School. She intends to look after her prize of the new uniform so that it will do for Lulu in due course (p136/221). Connie is a Senior in *Leader* and is mentioned as too old to be suspected of the prank when Peggy Burnett's bath overflows with bubbles (p76/77). She is in charge of a ping-pong ball game at the Sale in *Trick* (p189/190). She is in VA in *Summer Term* and wishes Miss Wilson would pay more attention to the bell and not make them late (p86/87). Connie is a prefect and helps to arrange a Seasons Sale of Work in *Althea* (p66). She helps colour marzipan fruit and flowers that Carmela Walther and her artistic team make in *Prefects* (p111).

WINTER, LULU: Lulu is Connie Winter's younger sister, and Connie expects in *Ruey* that she will come to the Chalet School in due course (p221).

WINTER, MARJORIE: Marjorie is a pupil at Kingscote School in 'Woolly Bear' in *1st* (p99).

WINTER, POPPY: We learn in *Adrienne* that Adrienne Desmoines's late mother's artist friend Poppy Winter did design and also painted pot-boilers (p144).

WINTERTON, MR: We are informed in *Peggy* that Mr Winterton has a son named Giles from his first marriage and three children from his second marriage, fifteen-year-old Polly, thirteen-year-old Lala and ten-year-old Freddy. Mr Winterton is a well-known journalist and is the Far East foreign correspondent for his newspaper (p14/23). He returns home after ten years to find his children undisciplined (p25) and moves them from Yorkshire to The Pantile at Channing St Mary on

the north Devon coast near the Bettanys' home, The Quadrant (p26/27/29). Lala Winterton's father insists on her taking Latin as an exam subject in *Coming of Age* (p58).

WINTERTON, MRS : It is mentioned in *Peggy* that Mr Winterton's first wife died of bronchitis when their son Giles was about three, and Mr Winterton married again a few years later (p14).

WINTERTON, unnamed BABY: Peggy Winterton, née Bettany, is expecting her next baby in June, so she will be able to be matron of honour at Bride Bettany's wedding, planned in *Adrienne* for early September (p198).

WINTERTON, ALAN: Peggy Bettany marries Giles Winterton and they live in Jamaica with their baby son in *Triplets*. Maeve shows some snap-shots of her nephew, now five months old, to Len. Mollie visits Peggy and her new grandson and mentions that although Peggy is fit, she is going to Canada to escape the heat (p74/174). Alan's name is given in *N18* (p75).

WINTERTON, ALICE (LALA) (LALLA) (3): Peggy Bettany first meets the Winterton girls in *Peggy* when Polly is pretending to be Lady Acetylene Lampe and Lala is her faithful attendant. Lala is Polly's younger sister and her real name is Alice. They have been living in Channing St Mary for six weeks, having previously lived in the Yorkshire Pennines, on the moors (p8/10/12). Lala is almost fourteen as her birthday is in September. She is small and daintily made, with brown eyes and straight brown hair parted in the centre and brushed smoothly down either side of her small three-cornered face. We are informed that Lala and Polly were previously taught by their mother's friend in the mornings, with no lessons in the afternoon and prep in the evenings (p14/15/16). As the result of a lack of discipline the girls have ended up lazy, impudent and disobedient and it is decided to send them to the Chalet School (p25/32). Lala is put in the Lower Fourth and she has plenty of brains, but is lazy and needs some prodding (p91/92). She is in the beginners' group for hockey and is one of the Lower Fourth girls who read Regency books to 'improve' their vocabularies and have to go on a formal walk as a consequence (p94/175/185). Lala sits next to Carola Johnston at her first meal at the Chalet School in *Carola* and makes a few friendly remarks (p50). Lala is good friends with Bess Appleton in her form in *Wrong*. She camps with the First Chalet Guides at Kittiwake Cove and passes her swimming test (p106/137/138). Lala is in the Fifth form in *Shocks* with Blossom Willoughby and Hilary Wilson (p132; p131 for form). She moves up a form with Carola Johnston in *Bride* and shares a dormitory with Betsy Lucy (p87/141/142). Lala moves with the Chalet School to Switzerland and takes part in an indoor boat race at the Staff Evening in *Barbara* (p198). Lala is a sub-prefect in *Mary-Lou* and described as an attractive-looking girl of nearly eighteen with her golden-brown hair wreathed round her head in a coronet of plaits. She is older than the other girls, has been at school just over three years and has to make up back work. She is the Bank Prefect (p9/72/73/94). Lala is made a full prefect in *Genius* (p58). She is a good all-round player in tennis in *Problem* and is apparently leaving school at the end of term (p73/166). Lala is on the prefects' trip to Wahlstein in *New Mistress* when Miss Ferrars has an accident (p145/161). Red-haired Lala is matter-of-fact, has no imagination and is less upset

than the others following the accident. She offers practical advice on getting back to the Gasthaus (p149/163). Lala is responsible for stationery in *Excitements* (p10). Lala, who has Miss Bubb for Classics and in consequence is losing confidence, intends to go to London University to work for a degree before plunging into journalism in *Coming of Age* (p58/197). Lala's brother Giles becomes engaged to Peggy Bettany in *Joey and Co.* and Len, Con and Margot Maynard, Sybil, Josette and Ailie Russell, Bride and Maeve Bettany and Polly and Lala will be their bridesmaids (p15/171). The wedding takes place in *Ruey* (p176).

WINTERTON, FREDDY (4): Polly and Lala Winterton's younger brother Freddy will be eleven at the end of December in *Peggy*. The family have recently moved to Channing St Mary and Freddy is going to prep school in September (p14/27).

WINTERTON, LIEUTENANT GILES (1): Giles Winterton is introduced as Polly, Lala and Freddy's elder stepbrother. We learn in *Peggy* that Giles's mother died of bronchitis when her son was about three years old and a few years later his father married again. When the family moved to Yorkshire, fourteen-year-old Giles went with them. Giles was then at public school and later entered the Navy and spent most of his leave with friends (p14/23). Peggy Bettany becomes engaged to Lieutenant Giles Winterton in *Joey and Co.* and they intend to be married early in October. Peggy will make her home in the West Indies as Giles is in the Atlantic fleet. Len, Con and Margot Maynard, Sybil, Josette and Ailie Russell, Bride and Maeve Bettany, Polly and Lala will be Peggy's bridesmaids. We are informed that Peggy will be living in Canada at first (p15/171). Peggy and Giles are married at half term in *Ruey* with all the bridesmaids wearing gold dresses, and the autumn tints of flowers and dresses suit every one of the bridesmaids (p125/176). Peggy and Giles have a five-month-old baby boy in the photos that Maeve shows to Len in *Triplets*. Mollie Bettany visits Peggy, Giles and her new grandson in Jamaica and mentions that although Peggy is fit she is going to Canada to escape the heat (p74/174). Bride's wedding is planned for early September in *Adrienne* and Peggy will be able to be matron of honour as her next baby is expected in June (p198). Peggy's marriage to Giles is mentioned in *N19* (p81).

WINTERTON, MARY (née WALTERS): Mrs Winterton is the mother of Polly, Lala and Freddy and stepmother of Giles in *Peggy*. We learn that Mrs Winterton does not like boarding schools, as she was bitterly unhappy at hers, and is against sending the girls to one. An old friend of hers who used to be a high-school mistress gave the Winterton children lessons (p14/16/17). We are informed that Mrs Winterton is a thin, worried-looking woman. The three younger children were born in London but Mr Winterton was sent to the Far East as foreign correspondent to his paper; and his wife and children, including Giles, who is fond of his stepmother, moved to a big old house at Thoreston in Yorkshire which they had inherited (p19/23). Mrs Winterton's father, Mr Walters, is the vicar at Pwllylleyn in Carnarvonshire (p12) and has nothing but his stipend, so when Mary was fourteen, a friend of her mother offered her a place at her exclusive boarding school. Mary was bullied by the other girls, two of whom were then expelled, but this was too late for Mary who was seen as having told tales. Mr Winterton returns home after ten years abroad to find his children undisciplined and moves them to the north Devon coast, overturning his wife's decision that they should not go to a boarding school (p24/25/26). Mrs Winterton comes to the pageant with Mrs Bettany in *Wrong* (p254).

WINTERTON, MARY (POLLY) (2): Peggy Bettany meets the Winterton girls in *Peggy* when Polly is pretending to be Lady Acetylene Lampe and her younger sister Lala is her faithful attendant. Polly's real name is Mary. She is a tall, lanky girl with a wavy shock of very dark red hair, a fresh pink-and-white skin liberally freckled and heavily lashed hazel eyes (p7/8/10). The Wintertons have recently arrived at Channing St Mary in Devon from Yorkshire and their maternal grandfather, Mr Walters, is the vicar at Pwllylleyn in Carnarvonshire (p10/12). Fifteen-year-old Polly's birthday is in January and she has a younger brother, Freddy, who will be eleven in December and also an older stepbrother named Giles. We are informed that Polly freckles or burns but never tans. An old friend of their mother taught the children in the mornings when they lived in Thoreston in Yorkshire and they were allowed too much freedom (p14/15/16). We learn that Mr Winterton was sent to the Far East as a foreign correspondent for his newspaper when

Freddy was a year old and the family moved from London to Yorkshire at that time. When their father arrived home to write a book he discovered his children were undisciplined (p23/25). It is decided that the girls will go to the Chalet School with the Bettany girls (p31). Polly is placed in the Lower Fifth with Clem Barrass and is in the beginners' group for hockey. Polly goes to Miss Burn for remedial exercises because she is growing very quickly (p91/94/150). Tom Gay is making a dolls' house mansion at a Hobbies Club evening and encourages Polly to paint miniature pictures for it as she has an artistic bent. Polly's delighted mother admires her paintings at an end-of-term hobbies show (p153/154/255). Polly goes on an icy walk with some of the Fifth formers and Miss O'Ryan in *Carola* and ends up at the bottom of a hill in a gorse bush (p120/124). We are informed in *Wrong* that Polly has an outsize conscience, perhaps because it had wakened late, and when told of the Wallflower incident by Lala, mentions the matter to Bride Bettany, who is a chum when they are at home (p107/108). It is mentioned in *Shocks* that Polly is a great friend of Caroline Soames, who has been staying with the Wintertons during the holidays (p38). Sixteen-year-old Polly is described as a lanky redhead and appears to be in the Daffodil dormitory (p42/108; p105 for dormitory). Polly helps the prefects set up folding desks in the garden so that the girls can sit their examinations outside in shady spots in *Changes* (p160). She moves with the Chalet School to Switzerland in *Barbara* and is six feet tall (p192). Red-haired Polly is a gangling member of the Lower Sixth and a sub-prefect in *Does It Again* (p102). She is a prefect in *Kenya* (p103). Polly is at St Mildred's in *Mary-Lou* (p73). She is one of the Merchant's daughters in the St Mildred's pantomime, *Beauty and the Beast*, in *Genius* (p89). Polly arrives with the St Mildred's girls for the Chalet School spot supper in *Excitements* (p213). We are told in *Coming of Age* that Lala thinks she and Polly did far too much fooling around before they joined the Chalet School, and have had a lot to make up (p90). Polly and Lala's brother Giles becomes engaged to Peggy Bettany in *Joey and Co.* and Polly and Lala, Len, Con and Margot Maynard, Sybil, Josette and Ailie Russell, Bride and Maeve Bettany are to be their bridesmaids (p15/171). Tall Polly and Bride are the leading pair of bridesmaids at the wedding in *Ruey* (p176).

WINTERTON, PEGGY: see BETTANY, MARGARET

WINTERTON, POLLY: see WINTERTON, MARY

WISHART, MRS: Mrs Wishart is a resident at the Görnetz Platz in *Kenya* and is described by Jo Maynard as the finest example of a leaky cistern she has ever met (p161).

WITHERS, JEAN: The Withers are the family to whom Mlle La Pâttre was governess in Taverton at the start of *School at*. Mademoiselle was not too happy there, and Madge rebuked Jean Withers for being rude to her (p19/20). Mademoiselle remembers with gratitude in *Head Girl* the day Madge came to the Withers' to offer her a place in her new venture, the setting up of the Chalet School (p128).

WITT, PROFESSOR CHRISTIAN von der: Joey and Grizel first encounter big, hairy Professor Christian von der Witt of Wien, a fresh-air fiend, in a train travelling from Paris to Basle in *Head Girl* (p30/31). We learn that he is interested in finding the caves under the Tiernsee (p196/197). Cornelia Flower runs away to discover them and is captured by Herr Arnolfi, a madman (p313), and Herr von der Witt later organises the opening up of the caves (p326/327/330). When Jem Russell is concerned about his sister Margot's health in *New House*, he decides to let Herr von der Witt take a look at her (p111/112).

WOLFRAM (von STIFT): see (STIFT), WOLFRAM von

WOOD, ANNE: Anne is in Inter V in *Theodora* and Miss Moore, her form mistress, remarks that she is like a sheep (p38).

WOOD, BERYL: Beryl starts at the Chalet School in *New Mistress* and is in Nancy Wilmot's form. She has connections with the Sanatorium although she herself is healthy (p49).

WOOD, MATRON: see MATRON WOOD

WOOD (WOODS), VICTORIA: Victoria Wood is in Upper IVB in *Summer Term* and is a very superior young person (p70; p68 for form). She dislikes Erica Standish who is six months younger but is higher in their form. Erica is friendly with a set of girls that Victoria has always wanted to be her friends. Victoria has been at the Chalet School over two years (p84/85). Victoria's unkindness to Erica when she falls and breaks her ankle on a ramble increases her unpopularity with the other girls. The conflict is resolved when a bottle of sweet pea scent sent to Rita Quick is accidentally sprayed over Erica, who is immediately the target of a bee swarm. Victoria's father is an enthusiastic amateur beekeeper and she holds Erica to keep her steady until Herr Antonelli is able to remove the swarm (p104/120/121). Later Victoria and Erica toboggan down the stairs together on a tray (p175). Victoria Woods is in Upper IVA in *Challenge* when Kathy Ferrars becomes ill in their class with appendicitis while trying to sort out their missing possessions. Victoria has been overheard talking about the brats in the Lower Fourth and this persuaded the younger girls to annoy Upper IVA (p97/121). Victoria Wood is a Middle in *Althea* and is with Erica when they are told the tale of Len being covered in paint (p146).

WOODLEY, IRIS: Iris is in Inter V in *New Mistress* and was hoping to be tried as goal defence for the School's second netball team but will miss the trials as the girls are given detention (p101). Iris is still in Inter V in *Excitements* and it is mentioned that her father is a keen gardener (p73).

WOODLEY, MARGUERITE: Marguerite is a new girl in Inter V in *New Mistress* and her work is below standard for this form (p80).

WOODLEY, MARY: Mary is in Upper IVB with Barbara Chester in *Barbara* and is a dull girl (p110; p107 for form). Fifteen-year-old Mary, the oldest girl in the form, is a rather heavy, dull girl and has a trick of sulking when she is annoyed by anything. She should be in a still lower form because her work is very poor. Since coming to the Chalet School, Mary has admired Vi Lucy, who is unaware of this, and is jealous of Vi's friendship with Barbara. Mary hears a conversation between Barbara Chester and Caroline Sanders about a book and she hatches a plot to make Barbara unpopular with everyone, especially Vi (p116/119/120). We learn in *Does It Again* that Mary, who lives in Newbury, has left the Chalet School because her father has got a job in Launceston in Tasmania (p17/18).

WOODS, MOLLIE: Mollie is in Upper IVA with Mary-Lou Trelawney in *Changes* and is sure her father will not let her go to Switzerland with the Chalet School (p46). Her father must have relented as Mollie is a Senior Middle at the Görnetz Platz in *Barbara* (p59).

WOODS, VICTORIA: see WOOD, VICTORIA

WOODWARD, MR and MRS: Elfie's mother, Mrs Woodward, and elder sister, Joan, come to the Chalet School concert in *Gay* (p237). Elfie mentions a younger sister in *Tom* (p131/132). However, in *Shocks* Elfie is forced to leave the School temporarily because her stepmother died during the holidays, leaving two young boys, nine-year-old Geoff and seven-year-old Peter. Another son, Michael, who would have been thirteen, is mentioned as having died as a baby, but no reference is made to either sister (p42/44). Elfie states that she never knew her own mother (p43). For a while she appears to be the only person left in the family who can run the home for her father, but eventually a cousin writes offering her services and Elfie returns to school (p44/193).

WOODWARD, ELFRIDA (ELFIE): Eleven-year-old Elfie is in the Lower Third with Bride Bettany in *Lavender* and is a small girl with curly fair hair and wide blue eyes which give her a kittenish look (p76/77; p75 for form). Elfie is a shining light at gym and games but struggles to keep at sixth or seventh place in form. She knows she must work hard as her ambition is to be a games

mistress. Later in the term we are told that Elfie is thirteen years old. Mollie McNab invites Elfie and Anne Montague to visit her home at Easter because their people have been bombed out on the northeast coast (p88/182/276). Elfie's mother and elder sister Joan are present at the end-of-term concert in *Gay* (p237). Elfie joins Bride in trying to convince Tom Gay that girls are not sentimental in *Tom* (p23). When Elfie is returning to school during a snowstorm after a visit to the Round House with Daisy Venables and Tom Gay, she slips in the snow and sprains her ankle badly. As a result she is forbidden all games and gym until after Easter. At their Hobbies Club evening she hopes to buy a scrapbook, made by Primrose Day, for her kid sister (p85/102/131). Thirteen-year-old Elfie is described as fairylike in *Rosalie* and she is Upper Third's Games Prefect (p117/118). Unfortunately she is not allowed to play games in the first half of the term. Elfie goes to the half-term fancy-dress party as Sport (p124/173). She moves with the Chalet School to St Briavel's Island in *Island* and is a prefect in St Scholastika when the boats are handed over but we are told that she cannot row (p149). Dickie teaches her not to dig her oars in too far (p201). She is in the Cricket Eleven with Tom Gay and Anne Webster. Elfie wins the Junior single-oars race in the Regatta (p215/229). Elfie is in the Upper Fifth in *Peggy* (p149). She is still in the Upper Fifth in *Carola* and suggests that they should get on with their work in Hobbies instead of wasting time while a delegation goes to the Heads about the naming of Tom's dolls' house (p215). Elfie appears to be Patrol Second of the Laburnums but is also mentioned as a Poplar when the First Chalet Guide Company camps at Kittiwake Cove in *Wrong*. She is very friendly with Bride Bettany. Elfie is the first reserve for the School Tennis Six but misses an important match as she is at home for the weekend (p130/131/145). Elfie is described as a small, slenderly built girl with big blue eyes in a quaintly triangular face and she has short brown waves of hair that give her a kitten-like look in *Shocks* (p41). Sixteen-and-a-half-year-old Elfie, one of Bride's closest friends, is not returning to the Chalet School because her stepmother died during the holidays, leaving Elfie to take charge of her two young stepbrothers, nine-year-old Geoff and seven-year-old Peter. Their older brother Michael, who would have been thirteen, died as a baby. The family lives in a little modern house of just eight rooms with one elderly servant who needs to be told what to do (p43/44/45). Elfie does return to school after half term as a distant cousin offers to come and help. Elfie takes over as the Games Prefect and Bride becomes Bank Prefect, a new post because the Bank Mistress Miss Edwards is now at St Agnes' on the mainland (p193/197). We are informed in *Bride* that Elfie's young brothers had chickenpox during the holidays and she has been staying with friends. She has been hoping to be a games and drill mistress since she was ten (p46/67). Elfie is in the Rose dormitory and is the Games Prefect (p133/134/139/155). She has been a close friend of Bride Bettany and Nancy Chester for ten years. Elfie has the part of Duty at the Sale based on the *Crown of Success* (p205/279). It is mentioned in *Changes* that Elfie has been motherless from birth. She has slightly displaced a bone in her ankle due to slipping on some stairs and needs to go into hospital in the summer, and cannot do anything strenuous this term (p22/99). She is on the Seniors' expedition to Bourneville. Elfie leaves school at the end of term to have a year's work at massage and remedials before going to Chelsea to train as a PT mistress (p142/200). She arrives for the celebration weekend in Switzerland in *Coming of Age* (p83). EBD states in *N17* that Elfie's real name is Elfrida (p73).

WOODWARD, GEOFFREY (GEOFF): Elfie does not return to school in *Shocks* because her stepmother died during the holidays leaving two young boys, nine-year-old Geoff and seven-year-old Peter, and Elfie will look after them (p44). We learn in *Bride* that the two boys had chickenpox during the holidays (p46).

WOODWARD, JOAN: Elfie's mother and elder sister Joan are present at the end-of-term concert in *Gay* (p237). Joan is not mentioned in *Shocks* when Elfie is obliged to leave school to look after her young half-brothers (p44).

WOODWARD, MICHAEL: Elfie's oldest half-brother Michael would have been thirteen in *Shocks* but died when he was a baby (p44).

WOODWARD, PETER: Elfie is to look after her young half-brothers, nine-year-old Geoff and seven-year-old Peter in *Shocks* (p44). We learn in *Bride* that the two boys had chickenpox during the holidays (p46).

WOOLLY BEAR: Woolly Bear is a St Bernard

belonging to the Headmistress of Kingscote in 'Woolly Bear' in *1st*. He is nine months old and is ill and in danger of being put down. Miss Laing has a grudge against him because at four months he got into her room and made a mess of her shoes, hat and powder-puff before racing through the grounds with a card of curling pins, thus exposing the fact that she does not, as she tried to tell people, have naturally curly hair. He is rescued by Miss Maynard, Jo Bettany and Robin Humphries when they discover some Kingscote girls trying to hide him, and Miss Maynard diagnoses his illness as distemper (p99/100/107/108).

WORMALD, MARY: Mary is the youngest pupil at the Welsen Branch in the Oberland when it opens in *CS Oberland* and is from Dulverley High School. Mary is discontented with the continental breakfast and makes signs instead of speaking French. She is later very upset when Peggy Bettany disappears in the snow when they are ski-ing. The girls produce a pantomime, *The Sleeping Beauty*, for the staff and Mary plays the part of a black Imp (p64/177/239). Mary is at Welsen in *Kenya* and takes part in a flowerpot race (p197).

WORSLEY, VERONICA: Veronica is a Senior in *Barbara* (p160). She is a prefect in *Does It Again* and plays the piano for the Catholic Prayers when there is a 'flu epidemic. Veronica also plays the piano when the School assembles afterwards in the Hall. She helps to tell Rosalind Wynyard the story of the Willow Pattern when the Sale is being planned (p66/67/91). Veronica attends Catholic Prayers and is the Second Prefect in *Kenya* (p42/68). She helps to organise a tennis tournament (p70). We are told that she has been at the School two years longer than Ruth Wilson (p104). She is heavily involved in the organisation of the end-of-term celebration, showing the other prefects how the best suggestions can be combined and suggesting a 'tilting' race (p107/169).

WORTH, JANE: Jane is a new girl in *Does It Again* and is in the Upper Fifth with Nella and Vanna Ozanne when there is an epidemic of 'flu (p60).

WORTH, SYLVIA: Sylvia is in Upper IVA with Mary-Lou Trelawney and her friends and is the ink monitress in *Bride* (p101).

WOTHERSPOON, MISS: We learn in *Joey and Co.* that Miss Wotherspoon was Professor Richardson's housekeeper at his home near Croydon but left in June to make her home with a sister (p49/50/54). It is mentioned in *Ruey* that Miss Wotherspoon was efficient at managing the housekeeping but unable to cope with Ruey and her brothers (p10). We are reminded in *Future* that Professor Richardson closed their house when Miss Wotherspoon left and took his children to Austria (p157).

WOTTON, ANGELA: Angela is in the Upper Fourth with Blossom Willoughby and Katharine Gordon in *Wrong*. She is sitting in the garden with Jennifer Penrose and some other girls instead of working in their form's garden but heeds a warning from Blossom and goes to work in the garden. Angela is persuaded by Felicity King to own up to listening to Jennifer Penrose's illicit reading and is moved to another dormitory for the rest of term (p160/167).

WREN, MRS: Mrs Wren asks to send her daughter Elizabeth to the finishing branch of the Chalet School in *CS Oberland* (p8).

WREN, ELIZABETH: Elizabeth was at Red Gables with Susan Marriott and Gwynneth Hughes and starts at the Chalet School finishing branch at Welsen in the Oberland when it opens in *CS Oberland* (p8). Elizabeth may be the same person as Elizabeth Warren (p108).

WYATT, HILARY: Hilary is in the Upper Fifth with her Dutch cousin Lysbet van Lange and they win a jigsaw competition at half term in *Gay* (p199).

WYCHCOTE, MR and MRS (i): Phoebe's grandparents are mentioned in *Rescue* (p11/12).

WYCHCOTE, MRS (ii): We are informed in *Rescue* that Phoebe Wychcote's mother married her husband Nicholas against the wishes of both their families and she died when Phoebe was six months old (p11).

WYCHCOTE, NICHOLAS: Phoebe still mourns her father Nicholas in *Rescue*. He died eighteen months before the start of the story when he was beginning to make his name as a 'cellist. He owned a valuable Lott 'cello which came to him from his godfather. He refused to play at the village concert and referred the vicar's wife to his agent to deal with the engagement (p11/12/13). Nicholas paid for handcraft lessons for Phoebe after her illness and bought her silks and materials when he was on his concert tours. Joey mentions that he played at a concert at which Vanna di Ricci also performed as a soprano soloist (p16/19). Frieda remembers that he was a giant of a man, with a bush of hair and eyes rather like Cornelia Flower's. Nicholas taught Phoebe to play the 'cello from the time she was eight years old until she became ill with rheumatism (p24/46). Gay Lambert mentions in *Mystery* that it was hearing Nicholas play that inspired her to work hard at the 'cello (p27).

WYCHCOTE, PHOEBE (PETERS, PHOEBE): We first meet Phoebe, who is an invalid, and her young friend Reg Entwistle in *Rescue*. Phoebe lives at Garnham near the village of Garnley on the Yorkshire moors and is still mourning her father Nicholas who died eighteen months ago when he was beginning to make his name as a 'cellist. Phoebe's mother died when Phoebe was six months old and, as she has no family connections, her grandmother's old cook Debby looks after her (p7/8/11). Mr Burthill wants to buy her father's Lott 'cello for his daughter (p12). Phoebe lives at Many Bushes when Joey, Frieda, Marie and Simone arrive to stay with all their young children in a house across the road called The Witchens (p14/15). She manages to earn a little money from her knitting and embroidery. Phoebe has a broad brow from which her thick brown hair with its golden lights springs back to give a square effect, a pointed chin with a deep cleft, wide-set large eyes and a long sensitive mouth. Joey mentions that Phoebe's father played at a concert at which her friend Vanna di Ricci performed as a soprano soloist (p16/19). We learn that Phoebe was twelve when she had rheumatic fever very badly and, unknown to Phoebe, her specialist doctor, Leaver Mitchell, has recently died. She now suffers from rheumatism (p20/21/25). Phoebe is almost twenty-three and has been ill since she was caught in a thunderstorm (p39/52). Jack Maynard has Phoebe admitted to the Welsh Sanatorium where she meets Dr Peters, who has made a special study of rheumatism in America (p98/104/216). Phoebe becomes engaged to Frank Peters and her health improves. She plans their wedding, which will take place from the Maynards' home with the triplets as her bridesmaids (p218/229/230). Phoebe is asked to be one of the godmothers for Aline Elizabeth Russell. Frank and Phoebe will let out Many Bushes and move into Ty-Gwyn, which is nearly next door to Frieda's house in Howells village. Debby will live with them there (p231/232). Phoebe marries Frank in *Mystery* and some of the Chalet School girls are present, one from each form, to represent the School (p84). Dr Peters says in *Carola* that Phoebe will be thrilled to hear that Con Maynard has won the dolls' house competition. All the girls know Phoebe well (p237). The Peters have been married for seven years in *Joey Goes* and have moved to Switzerland. Frank is on the staff at the new Görnetz Platz Sanatorium and they have adopted a little girl named Lucy who is two and a half (p200/201). Miss Burnett tells the girls in *Barbara* that Dr and Mrs Peters are sharing a former guest-house on the Platz with Dr and Mrs Graves (p36). Phoebe and Frank share a house with Hilary and Phil Graves at Sonnenhofen and it has four tennis courts that they are able to let the Chalet School use in *Kenya* (p69). Phoebe will help provide prizes for the Sale in *Genius* (p66). Biddy mentions in *New Mistress* that although Phoebe is not an old girl, she counts as one of them. The Peters now have a son (p24/33). Miss Annersley writes to Joey about the new Kindergarten in *Joey*

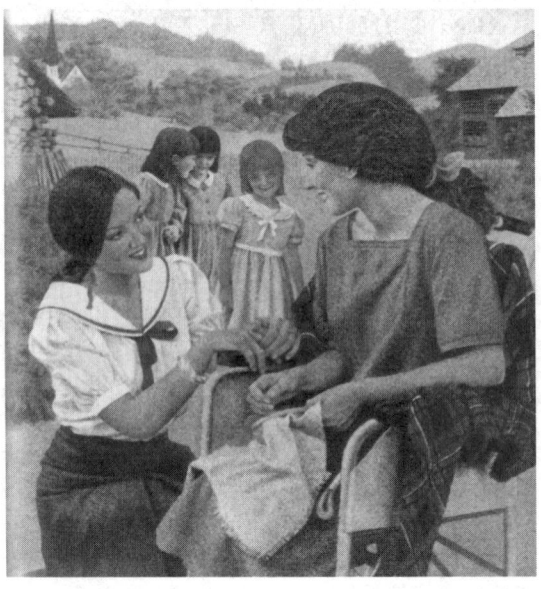

and Co. and mentions Phoebe's daughter Lucy as a prospective pupil (p219). Phoebe and Frank arrive for the lacrosse match in *Ruey* with their two adopted children and Phoebe is pushed in her invalid chair. She is able to walk a short distance but the School is a good mile and a half away from their home (p160). Peggy Burnett mentions in *Feud* that the Peters' elder two are at St Nicholas (p90). Phoebe still has Debbie, her maid, living with them at their home, Cordelliers, in *Reunion*. Phoebe is amazingly well and can even use her 'cello sometimes, although she tires easily (p39). Phoebe is very well and will be asked to help with making new costumes with the fabric brought by Sophy Hamel in *Althea* (p127).

CHILDREN:
1) LUCY: see PETERS, LUCY
2) BOY: see PETERS, UNNAMED BOY

WYLIE TWINS: The Wylie twins are in the Upper Fourth with Blossom Willoughby and Katharine Gordon in *Wrong* and they are friendly with Jennifer Penrose (p159). We never learn their Christian names, although it is possible that Zoë is one of them. However, no twin is mentioned in connection with her.

WYLIE, ZOË (ZOE) (ZOÉ): When Bride is reading out the removes in *Bride*, she accidentally forgets to announce that Zoë is to go up a form, along with Carola Johnstone and Betsy Lucy (p87). This girl may be Zoe Wylie who, after the Chalet School has moved to Switzerland in *Barbara*, is the Stationery Prefect (p72). We discover that Zoé has ski-ed before (p183). Zoë is still a prefect in *Does It Again* and enjoys weaving on a handloom (p85). She remembers when they used the Willow Pattern theme in a previous Sale (p93). Zoë is at a prefects' meeting with Pat Collins in *Kenya* (p101). Zoe represents St Mildred's at a sale committee meeting in *Coming of Age* and proposes a Water Babies Sale (p64).

WYMAN, MR: In *Gay* Madge Russell mentions Mr Wyman, a former patient of Jem's who suffered from duodenal trouble, and annoyed Sybil Russell so much that, as a small girl, she was once very rude to him (p40).

WYNNE, SURGEON-COMMANDER: Surgeon-Commander Wynne examines Joey on *The Sea Witch* during their voyage to England and safety in *Goes to It* (p41).

WYNN, MARILYN: Marilyn is friendly with Joy Bird in *Lavender* and is in the Upper Third with Hester Layng and Sylvie la Touche (p167).

WYNNE, KAY: see HILLIS, KAY

WYNNE, TESSA and unnamed BROTHERS: Juliet Carrick's niece Tessa has a reputation for practical joking when she starts in the Upper Fourth, Biddy O'Ryan's form, with nine other new girls in *New Mistress*. Tessa and her brothers have been allowed to run wild, and their invalid mother, Kay, is Donal O'Hara's sister (p49/50).

WYNNE-DAVIES, MR and MRS: We are informed in *Highland Twins* that Mr and Mrs Wynne-Davies, Betty's parents, died of influenza within a few days when their daughter was five years old. Mrs Wynne-Davies' name was Jessie (p273).

WYNNE-DAVIES, BEATRICE (BETTY): Betty and her friend Elizabeth Arnett transfer to the Chalet School from St Scholastika's in *New CS*. Hilary Burn describes Betty as a regular gipsy of a kid with black eyes, black curly hair and a brown skin. Betty does the bad things but Elizabeth thinks of them (p26/32). Ida Reaveley discovers that the Middles are getting out on to St Clare's roof garden at night (p190). The prefects and Joey investigate and find that they have organised a dramatic society led by Elizabeth and Betty. They also discover a packet of cigarettes with one missing. The girls visit Salzburg at half term and Betty is among the girls who spend a night in a bus that is stuck in a rising flood on the return journey (p218/226/268). Betty is fourteen when the School leaves Austria in *Exile* (p49). Betty is impudence and mischief incarnate, from the tip of her furthermost black curl to her pointed toes. She and her special friend Elizabeth go to the Chalet School when it reopens in Guernsey (p214). Gardening lessons are introduced and Miss Everett, the Lucys' gardener at Les Arbres, comes once a week to teach the girls (p215). Fourth formers Elizabeth and Betty hide her tools (p218/220). They are still in the Fourth form at Plas Howell in *Goes to It* when Betty is nearly fifteen (p124/167; p123 for form). Elizabeth is becoming more thoughtful and Betty, who is still almost childishly tiresome, realises that her friend is beginning to grow away from her. We learn that they have been together since they started at St Scholastika's (p192). Seventeen-year-old Betty has fallen out with Elizabeth in *Highland Twins* and is embittered. Betty has a strong character (p14/15/99). Betty's particular friend is Florence or 'Floppy Bill' Williams. Betty annoys the Juniors and ends up boxing Fiona McDonald's ears (p107/108/109). Betty is in the Sixth form. She plans to pay back a grudge on Robin, Daisy, Flora and Fiona and writes to Phyll Graves, a friend of her dead mother, for help with translating a message into Gaelic (p112/190/191). A spy blackmails Betty after she has allowed her hatred for the McDonald twins get the better of her. She was sure that all she told him would not harm anyone. Elizabeth comes to her support after Betty is discovered to have had contact with the spy and given information about the Erisay Chart to the enemy, making it inevitable she will be expelled (p262/266/267). Betty is an orphan and has a stern guardian, Mr Irons, who has little time or sympathy for her. Betty's former friend Florence refuses to say goodbye to her when she leaves the school and is described as having too shallow a nature to recover from the shock (p268/271/272). We are informed that the Graves were out in India at the time of the death of Betty's parents from influenza and the child became the responsibility of another Trustee, Mr Irons, who is unmarried and sent Betty off to boarding school at the age of five. After being expelled, Betty goes to live with Mrs Graves, a former friend of her mother Jessie, and her husband, Betty's other Trustee. Betty's Christian name of Beatrice is mentioned. Fiona McDonald sends Betty a letter after their Christmas Play to say that she is sorry that she annoyed her (p273/274/275). Joey says in *Gay* that, in her opinion, Miss Bubb's repressive style of discipline would have been able to keep even Betty Wynne-Davies in order (p111). Betty and her friends Floppy Williams and Hilda Hope are mentioned in 'New Flavouring' in *3rd* (p129). Rosalie Dene says in *Shocks* that even Betty Wynne-Davies at her worst was not as bad as Emerence (p92). Miss Wilson remembers the breach between Betty and Elizabeth when dealing with another broken friendship in *CS Oberland* (p220). It is mentioned in *Bride* that Betty was more sinned against than sinning and made good later (p256). Joey tells Rosalie Dene in *Theodora* that Betty did pull up when she got into kind hands at home. We are informed that Joey met Betty years later and she was really a nice girl (p11). EBD states in *N20* that Betty and Elizabeth did not meet again (p84).

WYNYARD, ROSALIND: Rosalind is the Chalet School Music Prefect in *Barbara* and plays the part of the landlord's wife in the Christmas Play (p72/205). Rosalind is still a prefect in *Does It Again*. She is musical and takes extra lessons in harmony, counterpoint and thoroughbass (p90/105). Rosalind is a prefect in *Kenya* when Julie Lucy is Head Girl and helps Edris Young look through suggestion slips (p101).

WYNYARD, RUTH: Ruth Wynyard goes on the expedition to Fulpmes at the foot of the Stubai glacier at half term with Miss Wilson and Miss Stewart in charge in *Eustacia* (p169/170). She has straight brown hair that is bobbed with a fringe, and she is a tomboy and full of mischief. Thirteen-year-old Ruth and her friend Violet Allison do not have permission to attend the Catholic church (p197/206). Ruth is the Third form's stationery monitress in *And Jo* and she is a jolly, downright young person of about twelve (p111/112). She drops some stationery in the middle of the corridor and Margia Stevens trips over it and falls, clutching at a stepladder that Frieda Mensch is standing on. Frieda lands on top of Ruth, covering her in paste (p113/114). Ruth goes to Guide Camp at the Baumersee in *Camp* with Violet Allison, Greta Macdonald and Lilli van Huysen (p57). Ruth is in the Fourth form in *Exploits* and is present at a snowball fight at the Sonnalpe at half term. Ruth is one of the last girls to finish a French exercise given by Mlle de Lachenais (p16/225/243). Ruth and Violet go up to the Sonnalpe hotel to stay with their families at half term in *Lintons*. Tomboyish Ruth surprises the other girls at a naming party by suggesting Esmeralda as a lovely name (p150/175). Ruth and Violet are both excellent Heads of Garden dormitory in *New House*. Ruth is not musical and is given the castanets to play in the band formed by Evadne and Cornelia (p188/189/218). Ruth is at prep one evening in *Jo Returns* when Alixe von Elsen makes unearthly screeches with a balloon creature outside the window under the ventilator (p187). The girls visit Salzburg at half term in *New CS* and fourteen-year-old Ruth is among the girls who have to spend a night in a bus that is stuck in a rising flood on the return journey (p268). Ruth is in the Sixth form when the Chalet School opens in Guernsey in *Exile* (p245).

X marks the Spot wherein lies the pit into which Joey Bettany falls and from which Miss Wilson rescues her in *Camp* (p109, 112).

YARNOLD, JENNIFER: Jennifer is in VA with Evelyn Ross and tells her about the Nativity Plays in *Challenge* (p150; p149 for form).
YATES, MARY: Mary is in VA with Nina Rutherford in *Genius* (p79; p78 for form).
YEATES, CHLOË: Chloë is a new girl in *Does It Again* (p22).
YETTERS, IANTHE: Swiss Ianthe is in Inter V in *Two Sams*, and Samantha van der Byl asks her about Stans because their form will be visiting that area. Ianthe, Michelle and Emilie shriek when the little funicular train in which they are travelling suddenly stops and begins to slide downward (p109/115).
YOLLAND, MR and MRS: We learn in *Joey and Co.* that Rosalind left school to go home and help her mother but she must work now as the Yollands have had money losses (p220). Prudence Dawbarn expresses surprise that Rosalind has become a teacher in *Ruey*, as she remembers the Yollands as being frightfully rich, with a gorgeous place somewhere in Devonshire (p48).
YOLLAND, ROSALIND, 'YOLLIE': Rosalind is very pretty and has an aunt who lives in Cheltenham in *Shocks* (p54/55). We discover her surname when her name is read out in Prayers in a list of girls who subsequently turn out to be prefects (p66/69). Rosalind was in the Lower Fifth last term and is now in the Sixth (p67). She volunteers to help Tom Gay with the knitting and needlework side of the Hobbies Club. She becomes the Art Prefect, as she is good at art, and is described by Nancy Chester as being one of Herr Laubach's blue-eyed darlings (p81/82/85). Rosalind is condemned to an all-day trip to visit the dentist in Cardiff. She is a day older than Julie, the youngest prefect, and attends Catholic Prayers taken by Miss Derwent (p153/194/203). Rosalind is a member of the School netball team (p241). She is in charge of the art rooms in *Bride* and returns to school late as she has had a bad cold. She is the youngest of the sub-prefects, and expects to have another year at school (p44/47/161). Rosalind is still a prefect in *Changes* and is now the youngest but one (p54). Joey learns from Hilda Annersley in *Joey and Co.* that Rosalind will replace Herr Laubach as the new art teacher in the autumn term. She left school to go home to help her mother but now must work as the family have

had money losses. She was an excellent prefect and taught well in Hobbies Club (p220). Margot Maynard reminds Prudence Dawbarn in *Ruey* that Rosalind was a prefect at St Briavel's when Bride Bettany was the Head Girl. Prudence remembers that the Yollands were frightfully rich and had a gorgeous place somewhere in Devonshire (p47/48). Rosalind volunteers to help with lacrosse as she played in a private club when she left school. She is one of the three mistresses who model the new School uniform at the Staff Evening (p100/214). Rosalind comments in *Leader* that the problem with VB is simply laziness, apart from one or two delicate girls and the fact that many of the girls are games mad (p98). Rosalind is the art mistress in *Trick* and takes VA and VB out sketching. We are informed that she is a sweet-tempered, patient creature and was a capable prefect (p152/153). Miss Yolland is a real help to the girls over their painting, and all with a gay cheerfulness which they find most encouraging (p154). Rosalind helps deal with the problem when Win goes missing and Len later mentions that she took charge of the situation as well as Bill could have done (p163/167). Miss Yolland's comment for art on Len's school report in *Future* is 'Conscientious' (p35). Miss Yolland and Miss Carey undertake to produce extra scenery for the Nativity Play in *Feud* (p140). Miss Yolland, Miss Wilmot and Miss Ferrars sleep in adjoining rooms in *Triplets* and are woken by Matey to help search for Con Maynard when she sleep-walks (p58/59). Rosalind mentions in *Jane* that she was in IVA when the staff performed *Mrs Jarley's Waxworks* one half term when the whole School was in quarantine for German measles. It was when Mademoiselle, Hilda and Teddy were absent (p118) (ie during *Gay*). 'Yollie' takes Inter V for an art lesson in *Adrienne* (p51). Miss Yolland's lessons are regarded as real joys in *Summer Term* and she is described as tall, slim and graceful, and very good-looking, with a keen sense of humour that appeals to all her pupils (p58). Miss Yolland visits Interlaken with the Sixth forms in *Challenge* (p77). Rosalind Yolland helps to entertain the girls at an unexpected St Patrick's celebration in *Two Sams* (p173). Miss Yolland is still teaching art at the Chalet School in *Althea* when a group of Sixth form girls go on a painting expedition (p133). She is teaching Jocelyn Marvell design in *Prefects* and almost turns her out of the art room for inattention (p52).

YOULL, JANET: Mary-Lou describes 'Janet' as absolutely colourless and not suitable to be a prefect in *Excitements* (p129). No surname is given, so this could be Janet Youll or Janet Unwin. Janet Youll becomes a prefect in *Richenda* (p59). Lizette Falence mentions in *Ruey* that she deputised for Janet, the Music Prefect, when she had a dreadful throat the previous year (p60). Janet is at St Mildred's and plays in a friendly lacrosse match with joint teams from the Chalet School and St Mildred's (p161).

YOUNG, MR: Edris Young's father has a big slum parish in a north-country city in *Does It Again* and Edris is looking forward to helping him with it (p105).

YOUNG, two unnamed BOYS (2–3): Gillian and Peter Young have three boys and a new baby daughter in *Summer Term* (p79). Two of the boys remain unnamed.

YOUNG, unnamed GIRL (4): Gillian gives birth to a baby daughter in *Summer Term* (p79).

YOUNG, CLEMENT PETER: Clement, a portrait painter, is Clem Barras's godfather from whom she received her name, Clemency. He is a tall, lean man with deep-set dark eyes in *Three Go*. He meets Gillian Linton when she takes Clem and Mary-Lou Trelawney into Armiford to see him (p189/198). Clement settles down in Howells village for the winter to paint a picture called 'The Shepherdess'. Miss Linton is the Shepherdess and all the Juniors who live in the area are her 'lambs'. The painting is hung at the Academy and then goes to a big Australian picture gallery. Clement is also known by his second name, Peter. He becomes engaged to Miss Linton at the end of term (p272/273/285). We are informed in *Island* that Gill is to be married from her sister's house in August and Jack Maynard will give her away when she marries Peter (p49/118). In *Peggy* we learn that the Youngs are living near Plas Gwyn. They were married during the holidays (p52/54). It is mentioned in *Carola* that Mr Young, who married Miss Linton the previous summer, has undertaken to do lightning portraits at the Sale (p223/224). Joey informs the Chalet School staff in *Changes* that Gillian has a baby boy, Robert Clement, who was born that morning, and he is named after Gillian's father, whose name was Robert, and Peter, whose first name is Clement (p125). Gillian has three boys in *Summer Term* and a new baby daughter born the previous night. The Chalet School staff ask Peter to paint a portrait of Madge Russell for the Silver Jubilee and he agrees to do so (p79/80/88).

CHILDREN: Robert Clement, two unnamed boys, unnamed girl

YOUNG, DOROTHEA: Dorothea manages to spill ink on every possible occasion in *Mary-Lou*. She is one of the youngest Juniors at the Feast of St Nicholas (p158).

YOUNG, DOROTHY: Dorothy is the Tennis Captain at St Peter's School in *Gerry* (p174).

YOUNG, EDRIS: Edris is the Magazine Prefect in *Barbara*. She makes a charming barmaid in the Christmas Play (p72/200/201). Edris is still Magazine Prefect in *Does It Again* and is looking forward to giving her father help in his big slum parish in a north-country city (p101/105). Edris is still the editor of *The Chaletian* in *Kenya* (p100). Betty Landon mentions in *Excitements* that Edris lives near her and is training to be a nurse (p68).

YOUNG, ENID (i): Enid is in the Sixth in *Shocks* but is not a prefect as she is delicate and spends at least a week of each term in the sanatorium (p67).

YOUNG, ENID (ii): Enid is at the Welsen Branch in the Oberland when it opens in *CS Oberland* and is at the Feast of St Nicholas, where her sin of heedlessness is mentioned (p195).

YOUNG, GILLIAN: see LINTON, GILLIAN

YOUNG, ROBERT CLEMENT (1): Joey informs the Chalet School staff in *Changes* that Gillian has a baby boy who was born that morning. The baby is named after Gillian's father Robert and his own father Peter, whose first name is Clement (p125).

YOUNGE, ZOE: Zoe is a Senior when the Chalet School girls devote a day to making cakes and sweets for the confectionery stalls at their Sale of Work in *Prefects* (p115).

YOUNGER, CAROL (CAROLE): Carol is one of Mary-Lou's Gang of Senior Middles travelling on a train in *Barbara*. She is inclined to be sallow and has mousey-brown hair and grey-green eyes, so the new uniform does not suit her. It is later noticed that Carol is not so sallow any more, as she has acquired a colour in Switzerland (p29/30/182). She is in the Upper Fourth in *Does It Again* (p172; p170 for form). Carol is kept down in Upper IVA in *Mary-Lou* because she is lazy (p7/8). She is in the Tulip dormitory with Joan Baker in *Problem* (p86). Carole is in VB in *Coming of Age* and wins the Senior hundred yards race (p212). She is in VA and very friendly with Rosemary Lambe and Monica Caird in *Trials*. We are informed that Carol is a student, and is never happier than when she has her teeth into a really stiff problem (p77). She is described as a most literal young person. Carol is on a half-term expedition to the Grisons when they are caught in an avalanche. Later that term, Carol appears to be in the Sixth form when the girls discuss the St Mildred's pantomime (p109/118/135).

YVONNE: Yvonne is at the Chalet School with Francie Wilford and Connie Winter in *Barbara* (p59).

ZARAGOVA, DOLORES: When the prefects discuss the Sale of Work in *Althea*, Len suggests that Spanish Dolores could be the Gypsy Queen and tell fortunes, as she is dark enough for any gypsy. Miss Annersley later recommends that someone else should do the job, because it would make the rather retiring Dolores too nervous (p67/69). Dolores is in VA in *Prefects* and hints to Len that Reg Entwistle may be fond of her, but receives a severe snub (p67).

ZENA: see WINSLOW, ZENA

ZENDL (ZENGAL), HENRIETTE: Henriette is in VA in *Challenge* and she and Mélanie Lucas are the leaders on an excursion to the Auberge (p79; p78 for form). Henriette Zendl is in the Sixth in *Two Sams* and is an experienced skier. Henriette, Priscilla and Carmela warn Samantha van der Byl about the difficulties and turns of a run. We are informed that Henriette's native tongue is Swiss German (p84/85). After Samantha's ski-ing accident Miss Annersley blames the three Sixth formers for not enforcing the rules. Henriette is newly eighteen (p88/90). Henriette Zengal and two other Swiss girls, Odile Paulet and Nina Konstam, donate a beautifully dressed doll to the School Sale in *Prefects* (p149).

ZETTERLING, HERR: Herr Zetterling runs a big hotel in Berne in *Triplets* and his daughter Marie will train with a hotelier friend of his in Vienna for a couple of years before going in with her father (p130).

ZETTERLING, MADAME: Mme Zetterling is one of the visitors at the School Sale in *Jane* and she enters a competition to win Tom Gay's dolls' houses (p205).

ZETTERLING, MARIE: Marie is in VA in *Trials* and unable to go out for a walk as she twisted an ankle during the holidays (p35). She is the prefect on dormitory duty at the start of term in *Ruey* when Matey has twisted her ankle. It is Marie's first term as a prefect and she is steady and responsible. She is the Second Hobbies Prefect and helps Jessica Wayne by looking after the needlework. Marie shows promise at lacrosse and plays in a friendly match with joint teams from the Chalet School and St Mildred's (p24/59/151). Gwen Parry is soaked after Jack Lambert fills her boots with water in *Leader*, and Marie lends her a towel (p160). We are informed in *Trick* that Marie comes from Berne. She is chosen for the Tennis Six. Marie and Aimée Robinet lose their set by two games (p48/88). She is a prefect in *Feud* when Maeve Bettany is the Head Girl (p82). A girl named Marie helps Rosamund Lilley in the library in *Triplets* and this will be either Marie Zetterling or Marie Dupont. Marie's father runs a big hotel in Berne and she will train with his hotelier friend in Vienna for a couple of years before going in with her father (p61/130).

ZIEGLER, MARIE: Little Marie is last in alphabetical order on the Chalet School register in *Richenda* (p58).

ZINKEL, HEIDI: Heidi goes on the Lower Fourth ramble with Arda Peik and Renata van Buren in *Feud*. We later learn Heidi's surname (p66/131; p63 for form).

ZINKEL MARIA: Maria is in the Gentian dormitory where Len is the Dormitory Head in *Ruey* (p13; p12 for dormitory). Swiss Maria is in VB with Margot Maynard and Ruey Richardson. Initially Mary Allen is VB's Form Prefect and Margot Maynard her second, but later that term Maria, who is from Geneva, is VB's Form Prefect (p31/33/79). Maria is one of the people in VB who has good marks in *Leader* (p146). She is a prefect in *Challenge* and plays the part of St Joseph in the Nativity Play (p77/217). Maria is still a prefect in *Althea* when they arrange a Seasons Sale of Work and she thinks that she might be able to tell people's character through palmistry (p68). Maria is described as a Swiss girl who looks as if she had stepped out of a bandbox in *Prefects*. She recalls a day when she upset the flour in domestic science and emerged with white hair instead of black. Maria and some of her friends take charge of all the visiting children beyond babyhood and up to the age of five at the Sale (p10/141).

ZINKEL, VRENELI: Maria's small sister Vreneli is a Junior or Kindergarten pupil in *Althea* (p70).

ZITA: Zita is the mother of Joey's dog, Rufus, in *Jo of* (p90/93/279), *Head Girl* (p183), *Rivals* (p26), *Exploits* (p34), *N7* (p29).

ZOË: see WYLIE, ZOË

THE CHALET SCHOOL SERIES BY LOCATION

AUSTRIA
The School at the Chalet
Jo of the Chalet School
The Princess of the Chalet School
The Head Girl of the Chalet School
The Rivals of the Chalet School
Eustacia Goes to the Chalet School
The Chalet School and Jo
The Chalet Girls in Camp
The Exploits of the Chalet Girls
The Chalet School and the Lintons
The New House at the Chalet School
Jo Returns to the Chalet School
The New Chalet School
The Chalet School in Exile chs 1–12

GUERNSEY
The Chalet School in Exile chs 13–end
The Chalet School Goes to It chs 1–4

ENGLAND (PLAS HOWELL)
The Chalet School Goes to It chs 5–end
The Highland Twins at the Chalet School
Lavender Laughs in the Chalet School
Gay from China at the Chalet School
Jo to the Rescue
The Mystery at the Chalet School
Tom Tackles the Chalet School
The Chalet School and Rosalie
Three Go to the Chalet School
Joey Goes to the Oberland chs 1–5

WALES (ST BRIAVEL'S)
The Chalet School and the Island
Peggy of the Chalet School
Carola Storms the Chalet School
The Wrong Chalet School
Shocks for the Chalet School
Bride Leads the Chalet School
Changes for the Chalet School

Switzerland

The Chalet School in the Oberland
Joey Goes to the Oberland chs 13–end (chs 6–12 are in transit)
The Chalet School and Barbara
The Chalet School Does It Again
A Chalet Girl from Kenya
Mary-Lou of the Chalet School
A Genius at the Chalet School
A Problem for the Chalet School
The New Mistress at the Chalet School
Excitements at the Chalet School
The Coming of Age of the Chalet School (chs13–17 are back in Austria)
The Chalet School and Richenda
Trials for the Chalet School
Theodora and the Chalet School
Joey and Co. in Tirol (school still in Switzerland but book takes place in Austria)
Ruey Richardson—Chaletian
A Leader in the Chalet School
The Chalet School Wins the Trick
A Future Chalet School Girl (school still in Switzerland but book takes place in Austria)
The Feud in the Chalet School
The Chalet School Triplets
The Chalet School Reunion
Jane and the Chalet School
Redheads at the Chalet School
Adrienne and the Chalet School
Summer Term at the Chalet School
Challenge for the Chalet School
Two Sams at the Chalet School
Althea Joins the Chalet School
Prefects of the Chalet School

Lavender's bath

CHARACTER INDEX BY CHRISTIAN NAMES

CHALET GIRLS:

A

Adrienne Desmoines
Adrienne Didier
Adrienne Rousselle
Agneta Gabrielli
Ailie Russell (Aline)
Ailsa MacDonald
Ailsa Thompson
Aimée
Aimée Béranger
Aimée Diderot
Aimée (Mercier)
Aimée Robinet
Alicia Landon
Alicia Leonard
Alison Grant
Alison Rutherford
Alixe von Elsen
Alixe McNab (Alexandra)
Althea Glenyon
Amalie Hamel
Amandine Robinet
Amandine St Michel
Amarilla van der Kock
Amy Dunne
Amy Stevens
Amy West
Andrée de Chaumont
Andrée Lecoutier (Renée)
Andrée de Vienne
Angela Carter
Angela Carton
Angela Sartori (Sartou, Angèle)
Angela Wotton
Angèle Roverie
Angèle Sartou
Angélique Ste Barbe
Anita Donati
Anita Rincini
Ann Morell
Anna Engels
Anna Hoffman
Anne Carter
Anne Chappell
Anne Charlot
Anne Cooke
Anne Crozier
Anne Francis
Anne Gordon
Anne de Guitry
Anne Harrison
Anne Lambert
Anne Montague
Anne Seymour
Anne Thorsby
Anne Valentine
Anne Walker
Anne Watson
Anne Webster
Anne Whitney
Anne Winchby
Anne Wood
Anne-Marie
Anneli Bertoni
Annelise Richet
Annette Orange
Annis Lovell
Anthea Barnett
Anthea Rutherford
Arda Peik
Arda van (von) der Windt
Armine Brown
Astrid Anderssen
Astrid Carlsen
Astrid Helgersen
Audrey Everett
Audrey Simpson

B

Babette Rolland
Barbara
Barbara Chester
Barbara Craven
Barbara Gow
Barbara Henschell
Barbara Hewlett
Barbara Holmes
Barbara Kitson
Barbara Smith
Barbara Wallace
Barbara Walton
Barbara Watson
Bernhilda Hoffman
Bernhilda Mensch
Berta
Berta Hamel
Berta Wendl
Beryl Lester
Beryl Wood
Bess Appleton
Bess Herbert
Beth Chester (Elizabeth)
Beth Lane
Betsy Lucy (Elizabeth)
Bette Rincini
Bette Schmaltz
Betty Burnett (Kitty)
Betty Landon (Bettina)
Betty Wynne-Davies (Beatrice)
Bianca di Ferrara
Bianca Meracini
Biddy O'Hara (O'Ryan) (Bridget)
Biddy O'Ryan
Blossom Willoughby
Bobbie McQueen (Robina)
Bride Bettany (Bridget)
Bridget (Bridgie) O'Connor
Brigit Ingram
Briony Quest

C

Carla von Flugen
Carlotta von Ahlen
Carlotta von Eschenau
Carlotta Kieffen
Carmela Valenti
Carmela Walther
Carol White
Carol Younger
Carola Johnstone
Caroline Carlyon
Caroline Sanders
Caroline Smith
Caroline Soames
Catherine Leonard
Catriona Watson
Cecil Maynard (Marya Cecilia)
Cecile le Brun
Cécile Rolland
Cecilie Auber
Celia Everett

Celia James
Celia Morton
Celia Thornton
Céline
Charles Maynard
Charlotte Harrison
Charlotte Müller
Charmian
Charmian Spence
Cherry Christy
Chloë Yeates
Christine Dawson
Christine Vincent
Claire Duhammel
Clare
Clare Danvers
Clare Fenton
Clare Kendal
Clare Kennedy
Clare (Claire) Kynaston
Clarissa Dendy
Clem Barras
Con Maynard (Mary Constance)
Connie Winter
Copper Ansell (Flavia)
Corinne Sambeau
Cornelia Flower
Cyrilla Maurus

D
Daisy Venables (Margaret)
Daphne Russell
Daphne (Williams)
David Russell
Deira O'Hagan
Della Armstrong
Della Bailey
Di Verdin
Diana Skelton
Dickie Christy (Delicia)
Dickon Chester
Dilys Edwards
Dilys Enderby
Dilys Owen
Dilys Vaughn
Dolores Gonsalez
Dolores Zaragova
Dora Ripley
Dora Robson
Dorcas Brownlow

Doreen O'Connor
Doris Bratsby
Doris Hamblin
Doris Hill
Dorota Heilinge
Dorothea (Doro) Buck
Dorothea Fletcher (Forsyth)
Dorothea le Martin
Dorothea Wentworth
Dorothea Young
Dorothy Brentham
Dorothy Hatcherd
Dorothy Ruthven
Dorothy Watson

E
Edelgarde von Rothaus
Edmund Eltringham
Edris Lyall
Edris Young
Eileen Johnson
Eileen Osborne
Eiluned Vaughn
Elfie Woodward (Elfrida)
Elinor Pennell
Elisaveta Arnsonira
Elise Kramer
Elizabeth Arnett
Elizabeth von Arnim
Elizabeth Gregory
Elizabeth Kemp
Elma Conroy
Eloïse Dafflon
Elsa Behrens
Elsa Fischer
Elsie Carr
Elsie Morris
Elspeth Macdonald
Elspeth McTavish
Emerence Hope
Emilia Casabon
Emilie Gabrielli
Emilie (Emelie) St Laurent
Emmie Linders
Emmy Friedrich
Enid Matthews
Enid Roberts
Enid Sothern
Enid Young
Erica Jane Standish

Ernestine Benedict
Ernestine Emery
Esme Béranger
Esther Collins
Eustacia Benson
Eva von Heiling
Evadne Lannis
Eve Hurrell
Evelyn Ross

F
Faith Barbour
Felicity King
Felicity Maynard
Felix Maynard
Fiona McDonald
Flavia 'Copper' Letton (Ansell)
Flora McDonald
Florence 'Floppy Bill' Williams
Frances Carew
Frances Coleman
Frances Grey
Frances Wentworth
Francesca (Frankie) Richardson
Francie Wilford (Francesca)
Françoise Richet
Freda Kendal
Freda Lund
Fredrika von Gerling
Frieda Mensch
Frölich Amundsen

G
Gabrielle Meynolles
Gabrielle Thomé
Gay Lambert (Gabrielle)
Gay Spencer
Gaynor Christie
Geneviève Rosier
Gerda Nordheim
Gertrud Becker (Gertrude Beck)
Gertrud Steinbrücke
Gertrude Beck
Gertrude Blenkinsop
Ghiselaine St Amant
Ghislaine (Ghiselaine) Thomé
Ghislaine Touvet
Gianetta di Patelli
Gillian Culver
Gillian Linton

Gillian Moggeridge
Gillie Garstin (Gilbertine)
Giovanna Celli
Giovanna Donati
Giovanna Pecci
Giovanna Rincini
Gisel Mensch
Gisela Marani
Giulia di Ricci
Greta Harms
Greta McDonald
Gretchen
Gretchen von Ahlen
Gretchen Braun
Gretchen Mensch
Gretel Hamel (Gredel)
Grietje
Grizel Cochrane
Guita Foncé (Marguérite)
Guita Levasseur (Marguerite)
Gwen Davies
Gwen Evans
Gwen Jones
Gwen Parry
Gwen Thomas
Gwensi Howell
Gwladys Evans
Gwynneth Jones

H
Hanni Unsel
Heather Clayton
Heather Unwin
Heather Warner
Heidi Blaser
Heidi Zinkel
Helen Henderson
Helen Reeves
Hélène Förster
Henriette Zendl
Hester Layng
Hilary Bennet
Hilary Burn
Hilary Simpson
Hilary Taylor
Hilary Wilson
Hilary Wilton
Hilary Wyatt
Hilda Bhaer
Hilda Davies
Hilda Hope
Hilda Imray
Hilda Jukes
Hilda Matthieson
Hilda Pinosch
Hilda Smith
Hilda Wendt
Hildegard Johanssen
Hortense Romande

I
Ianthe Yetters
Ida Reaveley
Ilonka (Lonny) Barcokz
Ilonka Maïco
Ingeborg (Inga) Eriksen
Irene Allison
Irene Silksworth
Irene Williams
Iris Drew
Iris Harris
Iris Stephens
Iris Wells
Iris Wilmot
Iris Woodley
Irma Ancokzky
Irma Barcokz (Barkocz)
Irma von Rothenfels
Isabel Allan
Isabel Drew (Isobel)

J
Jack Lambert (Jacynth)
Jacky Bettany (John)
Jacqueline (Jack) le Pelley
Jacynth Hardy
Jane Abbott
Jane Carew
Jane Mortimer
Jane Thomas
Jane West
Jane Worth
Janet Forster
Janet Graham
Janet Grant
Janet Henderson
Janet Ingham
Janet Kemp
Janet Lee
Janet Overton
Janet Scott
Janet Unwin
Janet Youll
Janice Chester
Janice Richards
Jaquetta de Henezell
Jean Abbot
Jean Ackroyd
Jean Allison
Jean Callendar
Jean Donald
Jean Downes
Jean McGregor
Jean Mackay
Jean Morris
Jeanne le Cadoulec
Jeanne Daudet
Jeanne Dubois
Jeanne d'Élie
Jeanne de Marné
Jeanne Romande
Jeanne Sarazin
Jennifer Bell
Jennifer Hughes
Jennifer Penrose
Jennifer Yarnold
Jesanne Gellibrand
Jessica Wayne
Jill Ormsby
Jo Bettany (Josephine)
Jo Scott (Josephine)
Joan Baker
Joan Damer
Joan Dancey
Joan Fitch
Joan James
Joan Leeming
Joan Sandys
Joan Wentworth
Joanna Kiefen
Joanna Linders
Joanna Reay
Jocelyn Fawcett
Jocelyn Marvell
Jocelyn Redford
Joey Bettany (Josephine)
John Bettany
John Lucy
José Helston (Joséphine)
Josefa von und zu Wertheimer

Josette Russell (Josephine)
Joy Bird
Joy Leigh
Joy Williamson
Joyce Linton
Judy Carew
Judy O'Connor
Judy Rose
Judy Willoughby (Juliana Jane)
Julia Hudson
Julie
Julie Lucy (Juliet)
Julie Pierre-Bonnet
Juliet Carrick
June Orde

K
Kâtchen Melnarti
Kate
Katharine Gordon
Katharine James
Katharine Lucy
Katharine Norman
Katherine Rutherford
Kathie Robertson
Kathleen Norman
Kathleen Watson
Kester Russell
Kevin Russell
Kirsten Johanssen
Kitty (Kate)
Kitty Anderson
Kitty Burnett
Kitty Gordon
Klara Melnarti

L
Laila Semple
Lala Winterton (Alice)
Laure Olivier
Laurens Istar
Laurenz Maïco
Lavender Leigh
Leila Norris
Len Maynard (Mary Helena)
Léoline Marmont
Léonie Dubois
Léonie St Denis
Lesceline Prideaux
Lesley Anderson

Lesley Bethune
Lesley Malcolm
Lesley Pitt
Liebchen von Bruling
Lieschen von Hoffman
Lilamani
Lilias Hume
Lilias Mackay
Lilias Robertson
Lilli Andries
Lilli van Goeschen
Lilli van Gruneveldt
Lilli van Huysen
Linda
Linda Sonnenschein
Lisa Bernaldi
Lisa Grünbaum
Lisa Sybel
Lizette Falence
Lizette Thomé
Lois Bennett
Lois Kynaston
Lonny Barcokz (Ilonka)
Lorenz Maïco (Laurenz)
Lorna Wills
Lorraine Varley
Louise Grünbaum
Louise Redfield
Loveday Perowne
Loyola de Manselle
Lucy Peters
Luigia di Ferrara
Luigia Meracini
Luise von Rotheim
Luise von Starken
Lulu (Louise Redfield)
Lydia Sackett
Lysbet
Lysbet Alsen
Lysbet Brandt
Lysbet van Lange

M
Madeleine
Madeleine de Lisle
Madge Dawson
Madge Herbert
Madge Watson
Maeve Bettany
Margaret Anstey

Margaret Benn
Margaret Browne
Margaret Hart
Margaret Jones
Margaret Twiss
Margery
Margia Stevens
Margot Maynard (Mary Margaret)
Margritta Ajockz
Marguerite Camben
Marguérite (Guita) Foncé
Marguerite (Guita) Levasseur
Marguerite Woodley
Maria Ileana von Glück
Maria Marani
Maria Uilseli
Maria Zinkel
Marian Hadaway
Marian Tovey
Marie Anderson
Marie Angeot
Marie Bellever
Marie le Cadoulec
Marie Drooglever
Marie Dupont
Marie von Eschenau
Marie Hüber
Marie Lemprière
Marie (Rambeau)
Marie Varick
Marie Walther
Marie Weissen
Marie Zetterling
Marie Ziegler
Marie-Mélanie le Cadoulec
Marie-Thérèse Dubosc
Marilyn Evans
Marilyn Wynn
Marion Orde
Marjorie Burn
Marjorie Graves
Marjorie Jenkyns
Marjory Keith
Marjory White
Marney Jennings
Marta von Eisingau
Marta Semerling
Marta Wilhelm
Mary Allen

Mary Anstey
Mary Brown
Mary Bruce
Mary Burnett
Mary Candlish
Mary Charlton
Mary Elliot
Mary Everitt
Mary Garth
Mary Hume
Mary Ireson
Mary Leigh
Mary Lowe
Mary Murrell
Mary Shand
Mary Shaw
Mary Turner
Mary Weston
Mary Woodley
Mary Yates
Mary-Lou Trelawney
Mathilde (Mathilda) Dauray
Maureen Grey
Maureen O'Toole
Maxine de Moné
Mayna Unsworth
Medeleine Tourtelle
Meg Farrant
Meg Lyall
Meg Walton (Margaretta)
Meg Whyte
Mélanie Kerdec
Melanie de Lisle
Mélanie Lucas (Marie-Mélanie)
Mélanie de Vos
Mercy Barbour
Meta Gordon
Meuda Melnarti
Michelle Cabràn
Millie Allen
Moira Baker
Moira Carroll
Moira Damer
Moira Fitzpatrick
Moira Redmond
Mollie Avery
Mollie Carew
Mollie McNab (Mary)
Mollie Rossiter
Mollie Woods

Monica Caird
Monica Carr
Monica Garstin
Monica Marilliar
Muriel Abbey
Myfanwy Davies
Myfanwy Tudor

N
Nan Herbert
Nan Lambert (Anne)
Nan Wentworth
Nancy Canton
Nancy Chester
Nancy Hatton
Nancy Wadham
Nancy Wilmot
Naomi Elton
Natalie Mensch
Natalie Mercier
Natasha Patrovska
Nella Ozanne (Peronelle Jane)
Nénette
Nest Owen
Nesta Parry
Nesta Tudor
Nesta Williams
Nicole de Saumarez
Nicole la Touche
Nina Konstam
Nina Rutherford
Nina Williams
Nita Eltringham (Anita)
Nita Tarengo
Noel Bettany (John)
Nora Bird
Nora Penley
Norah Fitzgerald
Norah O'Connor

O
Odette Bertoni
Odette Mercier
Odette Paulet (Odile)
Odile Badrutt
Odile Paulet
Olga Petrovska
Olwen Hughes
Ottilie Paulet
Ottillie Sneider

P
Pamela
Pamela Jackson
Pamela James
Pamela Morton
Pamela Oliver
Pamela Whitlock
Pat
Pat Collins
Paula von Rothenfels
Peggy Adams
Peggy Bettany (Margaret)
Peggy Burnett
Peggy Harper
Penelope Drury
Penelope Grant
Phil Craven (Phillida)
Phyllis Amberley
Phyllis Garstin
Polly Heriot
Polly Winterton (Mary)
Primrose Day
Primrose Trevoase
Primula Mary Venables
Priscilla Dawbarn
Prudence Dawbarn
Prunella Davidson

R
Renata van Buren
Renée Lecoutier
Renée Touvet
Richenda (Ricki) Fry
Rita Anderson
Rita Quick
Rix Bettany (Richard)
Roberta Thompson
Robin Chester
Robin Humphries (Cecilia)
Robina McQueen
Ronnie Pertwee (Véronique)
Roosje
Roosje Lange
Rosa van Buren
Rosalie Dene
Rosalie Way
Rosalind Wynyard
Rosalind Yolland
Rosamund Lilley
Rosamund Williams

Rosemary King
Rosemary Lambe
Rosemary Smith
Rosemary Wentworth
Rosemary Wilson
Roswitha Saxon
Ruey Richardson (Evelyn Ruhannah)
Ruth Barnes
Ruth Herbert
Ruth Lamont
Ruth Wilson
Ruth Wynyard

S
Sally Godfrey
Sally Winslow
Samantha van der Byl
Samaris Davies
Sancia
Sandra Johnson
Sara Carlyon
Sarah Akerman
Sarah Hewitson
Sarah Lomax
Sarah Ridley
Selma Khrakhovska
Shirley Westcott
Signa Björnessen
Signa Johansen
Sigrid Alvarsen
Sigrid Bjorneson
Simone Lecoutier
Simonetta d'Angeli
Solange (Solly) de Chaumontel
Sophie Hamel
Sophie Rincini
Stacie Benson (Eustacia)
Stella Porter
Stéphanie
Sue Mason (Susan)
Sue Meadows
Susan Austin
Susan Barnett
Susan Dagleish
Susan Dickie
Susan Gibbs
Susan Holmes
Susan James
Susan Lane
Susannah Leslie
Susannah Wills
Suzanne Élie
Suzanne Kiefen
Suzanne Mercier
Swanhild Alvarsen
Sybil Russell
Sylvia Curling
Sylvia Peacock
Sylvia Thane
Sylvia Worth
Sylvie la Touche

T
Ted Grantley (Theodora)
Terry Prosser (Theresa)
Terry Wake
Tessa de Bersac (Thérèse)
Tessa Wynne
Thea Harding
Thekla von Stift
Thelma Johansen
Theodora Grantley
Thérèse de Grammont
Thérèse Parrais
Thérèse Rambeau
Thora Helgersen
Thyra Björnessen
Thyra Eriksen
Thyra Jespersen
Thyra Lund
Tina Harms
Toby Willoughby (Harold)
Tom Gay (Lucinda Muriel)
Truda

U
Ursula Nicholls
Ursula Vane
Ursula Vidler
Ursula Wallace

V
Val Gardiner (Valerie)
Val Pertwee (Valencia)
Valerie Arnott
Valerie Ford
Valerie West
Vanna Ozanne (Giovanna Anne)
Vanna di Ricci
Verity-Ann(e) Carey
Veronica Worsley
Vi Lucy (Mary Viola)
Vicky McNab (Victoria)
Victoria Wood
Viola Emery
Violet Allison
Virginia Adams
Vivien Allen
Vivien James
Vreneli Zinkel

W
Wanda von Eschenau
Wanda von der Kock
Wanda Roth
Wendy Robson
Wilma Summers
Win Everett (Winifred)
Winifred Etheridge
Winnie Silksworth (Winifred)
Wolferl von und zu Wertheimer

Y
Yolanda di Maladetta
Yolande le Cadoulec
Yolande de Saussure
Yseult Pertwee
Yvette Mercier
Yvette Olivier
Yvonne
Yvonne de Gramont
Yvonne Robinson

Z
Zena Winslow
Zita Rincini
Zita Roselli
Zoë Wylie
Zoe Younge

CHALET SCHOOL STAFF:
Miss Alton
Miss Ames
Miss Anderson
Miss Andrews
Miss Sharlie Andrews (Charlotte)
Miss Hilda Annersley

Herr Karl 'Vater Bär' Anserl
Miss Cicely Armitage
Miss Vida Armitage (Davida)
Miss Mirian Ashley
Miss Barton
Miss Renie Bell
Matron Bellenger
Dr Eustacia Benson
Mlle Julie Berné
Miss Joan Bertram
Matron Besly
Miss Josephine Bettany
Miss Madge Bettany
Herr von Borken
'Bracey'
Miss Mabel Bubb
Miss Hilary Burn
Miss Mary Burnett
Miss Peggy Burnett
Miss Beth Carey
Miss Juliet Carrick
Miss May Carthew
Miss Rosemary Charlesworth
Miss Grizel Cochrane
Miss Nest Davidson
Miss Rosalie Dene
Miss Sarah Denny
Mr Tristan 'Plato' Denny
Miss Ruth Derwent
Matron Duffin
Miss Marjorie Durrant
Miss Dorothy (Dolly) Edwards
Miss Elliott
Miss Betty (Rhyll) Everett
Herr von Falck
Fräulein Felsen
Miss Kathie Ferrars (Kathleen)
Matron Gould/Gowland
Miss Greene
Herr Franz Helfen
Matron Barbara Henschell
Miss Holroyd
Miss Howard
Miss Johnson
Miss Edith Kent
Mlle Jeanne de Lachenais
Herr Laubach
Miss Dorothy Lawrence
Mlle Simone Lecoutier
Mlle Céline Lenoir

Mlle Elise Thérèse Lepâttre
Miss Kit Leslie (Katherine)
Frau Linders
Miss Gillian Linton
Matron Gwynneth Lloyd
Herr Mahler
Mr Manders
Mlle le Martin
Miss Mollie Maynard
Frau Anna Mieders
Miss Rosalind Moore
Miss Morley
Miss Grace (Phyll) Nalder
Miss Ivy Norman
Miss CV Oldroyd
Miss Biddy O'Ryan (Bridget)
Miss May Phipps
Miss Nell Randolph
Matron Gertrude Rider
Miss Kathie Robertson
Miss Robinson
Miss Pam Slater
Miss Smith
Miss Deborah Smith
Miss Soames
Herr Steinach
Miss Ivy Stephens
Miss Stephenson
Miss Constance Stewart
Miss Linda Stone
Mrs Thwaites
Matron Margot Venables
Matron Webb
Miss Wells
Miss Nancy Wilmot
Matron Wilson
Miss Nell 'Bill' Wilson
  (Helena)
Miss Winter
Matron Wood
Miss Rosalind Yolland

**CHALET SCHOOL
DOMESTIC STAFF:**
Andreas/Andry
Anna
Anna Pfeiffen
Anneli
Annette

Berta
Dulcie
Eigen/Eitel Pfeiffen
Eitel
Eitel Pfeiffau
Elsa
Emil
Evan Evans
Fritz Pfeiffen
Gaudenz;
Gertlieb
Getterl Pfeiffen
Gladys/Gwladys
Gredel
Gretchen
Gretchen Angbach
Gretel
Griffiths
Gwladys
Hans Pfeiffen
Hanserl
Hansi
Hansi Pfeiffen
Jenks
Joan
Jockel
Karen/Karin (Pfeiffen)
Klara
Klara Pfeiffen
Liesl
Lisa
Luise Pfeiffen
Margeli
Maria
Marie
Marie Pfeiffen
Mary
Mechtilde
Megan
Michelle
Miggi
Moida
Nansi Evans
Nette
Olivette
Olwen
Otto
Owen Owens
Pieter Koch
Rhoda

Rosa Pfeiffen
Rösli Pfeiffen
Trudchen
Trudi
Vreneli

CHALET SCHOOL FINISHING BRANCH WELSEN/ST MILDRED'S:
Mlle Julie Berné
Miss Gillian Culver
Herr Freibach
Frau Lehmann
Miss Grace (Phyll) Nalder
Miss Violet Norton
Matron Gertrude Rider
Miss Nell 'Bill' Wilson (Helena)
Gertiebl
Karen
Marie
Ailsa Thompson
Aimée Weilen
Alison Power
Anne Purdey
Anthea Barnett
Antoinette Duval
Auriel Herbert
Barbara Chester
Barbara Henschell
Barbara Smith
Barbara Walton
Bess Appleton
Bess Herbert
Blossom Willoughby
Bride Bettany (Bridget)
Charmian Spence
Clare Kennedy
Clem Barras (Clemency)
Daphne Russell
Deborah Mitchel
Diana Laking
Dickie Christie (Delicia)
Doris Hill
Dorothy Watson
Edna Purdon
Elinor Pennell
Elizabeth Warren
Elizabeth Wren
Ellison Holmes
Elma Conroy
Enid Young
Frances Coleman
Francie Wilford (Francesca)
Gabrielle Fournet
Ghiselaine St Georges
Gillian Watson
Gwen Parry
Gwynneth Hughes
Heather Clayton
Hester Layng
Hilary Bennet
Hilary Wilson
Hilda Jukes
Janet Youll
Jean Henderson
Jeanne Daudet
Joan Sandys
Jocelyn Abbott
Josephine Bellenger
Joy Venn
Judy Rose
Julie Lucy (Juliet)
June Amery
Katharine Gordon
Lesceline St Georges
Lesley Bethune
Lucy Holmes
Madeleine de Lisle
Marie Hüber
Marie Kauffmann
Marie-Thérèse Georges
Marie-Thérèse de Maurignac
Mary Elliot
Mary Vallens
Mary Wormald
Mary-Lou Trelawney
Meg Whyte
Mollie Carew
Muriel Abbey
Nancy Canton
Nancy Chester
Natalie Mensch
Natalie Tredgold
Nell Randolph
Nicola Tredgold
Nina Williams
Nita Eltringham (Anita)
Pamela Burton
Pat Collins
Patricia Binney
Peggy Bettany
Phyllis Gurney
Primrose Trevoase
Primula Mary Venables
Ruth Wilson
Sally Winslow
Stella Johnson
Susan Branning
Susan Marriott
Tatiana Khavasky
Tom Gay (Lucinda Muriel)
Valerie Herriot
Verity Carey
Vi Lucy (Mary Viola)

BRAEMAR HOUSE:
Miss Brewer
Miss Burchell
Miss Cundell
Miss Everett
Miss Simpson
Miss Underwood
Alixe McNab (Alexandra)
Clare Danvers
Dilys Tudor
Dorothy Saunders
Eileen Smith
Eluned Tudor
Enid
Ernestine Benedict
Gwen Evans
Gwladys Evans
Iris Stephens
Ivy Leighton
Jill Austin
Jocelyn Redford
Lavender Norton
Louise Gardner
Margery Bruce
Marie Gardner
Monica Marilliar
Myfanwy Tudor
Nancy Austin
Peggy Reid
Terry Prosser (Theresa)
Vicky McNab

BRANSCOMBE PARK SCHOOL:
Althea Mordaunt
Lucy Holmes
Nell Randolph

CAMPDEN HOUSE:
Miss 'The Bun' Baker
Jessica Mallory
Joyce Lemon
Marian
Mary Martin
Valerie

CWYST HIGH SCHOOL:
Gwladys Pugh
Margiad Evans
Myfanwy Griffiths

DULVERLEY HIGH SCHOOL:
Miss Emmeline Bliss
Miss Grace Nalder
Alison Power
Angela Morton
Elma Conroy
Mary Wormald
Pamela Burton

GABLES SCHOOL:
Miss Burnside
Miss Cuthbertson
Miss Evans
Miss Innes
Miss James
Miss Morgan
Miss Summers
Mary Somers
Monica Marilliar
Violet Williamson

GRANGE SCHOOL:
Audrey
Tot

IVY LODGE:
Miss Kendal
Miss Doris (Kendal)
Anne Harper
Jacynth Hardy
Margaret Harper

KINGSCOTE SCHOOL:
Miss Laing
Miss Temple
Madeleine Fawcett
Marjorie Winter
Mary Severn

MORAY HOUSE:
Miss Elspeth Henderson
Edna Purdon
Valerie Herriot

PENSION DAUBENY SCHOOL:
Madame Daubeny
Gerda
Jennifer

PENSION DE MADAME GRUNAT:
Madame Grunat
Doreen Fitzgerald
Mollie Fitzgerald

RED GABLES SCHOOL:
Elizabeth Wren
Gwynneth Hughes
Olwen Hughes
Susan Marriott
Thelma Lord

REDFEARN SCHOOL:
Miss Ward
Anne Lambert
Jack Lambert (Jacynth)

RIPLEY COLLEGIATE:
Miss Blakeney
Miss Hardy
'Maitie'
Miss Ross
Miss Slater
Doreen Fitzgerald
Gwen Ferrars
Heather Raphael
Millicent Edwards
Mollie Fitzgerald
Roma Colwyn
Rory Colwyn (Aurora)
Sibyl Townsend
Sylvia Townsend

SACRED HEART CONVENT:
Genevieve Leycester
Josephine O'Donovan

ST HILDA'S SCHOOL:
Miss Mirian Ashley
Miss Bethia Holroyd
Miss Edith Kent
Mrs Thwaites
Anne Crozier
Anne Thorsby
Anne Winchby
Doris Bratsby
Gillie Garstin (Gilbertine)
Helen Henderson
Hilda Matthieson
Jane Mortimer
Jean Callendar
Katherine Rutherford
Kitty Anderson
Marian Hadaway
Mary Candlish
Mary Elliott
Mary Murrell
Moira Baker
Monica Garstin
Pamela Oliver
Phyllis Garstin
Roberta Thompson
Susan Austin
Susannah Leslie

ST KATHARINE'S SCHOOL:
Mother Mary Joseph
Sister Angela
Sister Bonaventure
Sister Clare
Sister Mary Margaret
Anne Kaye
Margaret James
Mary Swanson
Mélanie Lucas
Rosalind Kaye
Susan James

ST MARGARET'S HOUSE SCHOOL:
Miss Coulson
Miss Hilton
Richenda Fry
Sue Mason (Susan)

ST MATTHEW'S SCHOOL:
Miss Keatinge
Joan Baker
Rosamund Lilley

ST PETER'S SCHOOL:
Mademoiselle
Mr Allison
Miss Beddoes
Miss 'Benny' Benson
Miss Rotha M Catcheside
Miss Denham
Signor Donati
Miss Jean 'Hammy' Hamilton
Miss Handley
Miss Hildreth
Madame Karanski
Miss Kennedy
Miss Lawrence
Miss Mitchell
Miss Motley
Miss Nesfield
Miss Phillips
Miss Rose
Adelicia 'Blossom' Smyth
Alicia Brett
Allegra 'Lal' Atherton

Althea Southern
Annette Fairless
Aveline Gladwin Meredith
Bernadine 'Dina' Willoughby
Bettina Isherwood
Betty Oliver
Britta Lundgren
Christine Brett
Claire Ashe
Concetta Donati
Constance Atherton
Daphne Hethcote
Daphne Ruffell
Deirdre O'Farrell
Diana Burnham
Domenica Vivalanti
Doria Compton
Doris Weatherby
Dorothy Cornwall
Dorothy Ellis
Dorothy Erwin
Dorothy Hannay
Dorothy Young
Edith Oliver
Eileen Kearney
Eirene Maynard
Elaine Hannay
Elizabeth Hilton
Elizabeth Trevennor
Elsie Meredith
Fay Meredith
Fiamma Vivalanti
Florence Anderson
Francesca Atherton
Frank Ward
Gerry Challoner (Geraldine)
Gertrude Trevena
Giulia Vivalanti
Gloria Fitzgerald
Gwenna Compton
Hazel Burnham
Hester Brown
Jacynth Newton
Janet Burton
Janet Grant
Janie Ferrars
Jean Ross
Jessie Mackay
Jill Trevennor (Gillian)
Joan Hannay

Joan Hethcote
Josie/José Atherton (Josephine)
Judith Fitzgerald
Kathleen Raby
Kitty O'Connell (Kathleen)
Leo Fairless (Leonora)
Letty Harrison
Lilian
Lilian Dudley
Lilian Ellis
Lillie Tomson
Louie Baker
Madeleine Carew
Madeleine Ruffell
Madge Halloran
Madge Hannay
Maeve O'Farrell
Maidie Penrose (Madrigal)
Marcia Compton
Margaret Trevennor
Marjolaine Willoughby
Mary Anderson
Mavie Dunne
Molly Kearney
Molly O'Farrell
Muriel Ellis
Muriel Hatherley
Muriel Joyce
Muriel Purvis
Myfanwy Owen
Myfanwy Tudor
Naïda Ashe
Nancy Hethcote
Nell Trevennor (Helen)
Nesta Owen
Nicola Carewe
Nina Ruffell
Olive Purvis
Olwen Tudor
Pamela Hethcote
Pauline Norton
Peggy Hughes
Peggy Trevennor (Margaret)
Philippa Southern
Primrose Stevens
Rachel Naylor
Rosalie Southern
Rosamund Atherton
Rosemary Drewe
Sheila Trevennor

Stella Newton
Sue Stevenson
Sybil Forsyth
Sylvia Newton
Tessa Donati
Veronica Seton
Viola Dawnay
Violet Turnour
Vivien Ashe

ST SCHOLASTIKA'S SCHOOL:
Miss Anderson
Mlle Julie Berné
Miss 'The Fawn' Browne
Miss Elliott
Miss Harris
Miss May Phipps
Matron Gertrude Rider
Miss Soames
Ailsa MacDonald
Betty Wynne-Davies
Bride Donovan
Doris Potts
Dorothy Hatcherd
Elaine Gilling
Elizabeth Arnett
Elspeth Macdonald
Ernestine Emery
Gipsy Carson
Hilary Burn
Hilda Imray
Hilda Wilmot
Ida Reaveley
Irene Silksworth
Maisie Gomm
Marjorie Burn
Maureen Donovan
Nancy Wilmot
Vera Smithers
Viola Emery
Winnie Silksworth (Winifred)

TANSWICK CHALET SCHOOL:
Miss Wilson
Alison Grant
Anne Gordon

Diana Skelton
Eileen Osborne
Hilary Bennett
Janet Overton
Janice Richards
Laila Semple
Marian Tovey
Maureen Grey
Meta Gordon
Pamela Morton
Primrose Trevoase
Ruth Lamont
Sally Winslow
Sarah Lomax
Sylvia Peacock
Ursula Vane

AUDREY'S FORMER SCHOOL:
Miss Dwight
Miss Jones
Miss Spender
Audrey Everett
Celia Everett

RUEY'S FORMER SCHOOL:
Miss Curtis
Miss Harland
Dilys Jones
Ruey Richardson

Girls Gone By Publishers

Girls Gone By Publishers republish some of the most popular children's fiction from the 20th century, concentrating on those titles which are most sought after and difficult to find on the second-hand market. Our aim is to make them available at affordable prices, and to make ownership possible not only for existing collectors but also for new ones, so that the books continue to survive. We also publish some new titles which fit into the genre.

Authors on the GGBP fiction list include Margaret Biggs, Elinor Brent-Dyer, Dorita Fairlie Bruce, Patricia Caldwell, Gwendoline Courtney, Monica Edwards, Josephine Elder, Antonia Forest, Elizabeth Goudge, Lorna Hill, Phyllis Matthewman, Violet Needham and Malcolm Saville.

We also have a range of non-fiction titles, either more general works about the genre or books about particular authors. Our titles/subjects include *The Chalet School Encyclopaedia*, *Heroines on Horseback*, Girl Guiding, and Monica Edwards and her books. The non-fiction books are in a larger format than our fiction, and they are lavishly illustrated in black and white.

For details of availability and when to order, see our website or write for a catalogue to GGBP, The Vicarage, Church Street, Coleford, Radstock, Somerset, BA3 5NG, UK.

www.ggbp.co.uk
www.facebook.com/girlsgonebypublishers

FRIENDS OF THE CHALET SCHOOL
Fostering friendship between Chalet School fans all over the world

Quarterly Magazines over 70 pages long
Sales & Wants Booklets
Ripping Reads (for other books)
A Lending Library of all Elinor Brent-Dyer's books and other titles as well

For more information send an A5 SAE to
Ann Mackie-Hunter or Clarissa Cridland
The Vicarage, Church Street, Coleford, Radstock, Somerset, BA3 5NG, UK
focs@rockterrace.org
www.chaletschool.org.uk
Find us on Facebook: www.facebook.com/friendsofthechaletschool

---

You may also be interested in the New Chalet Club.
For further details send an SAE to Membership Secretary, The New Chalet Club,
5 Pinetree Gardens, Whitley Bay, Tyne & Wear, NE25 8XU